Inter-American Politics Series

SPONSORED BY THE

Center for Inter-American Relations/New York

GENERAL EDITOR: RONALD G. HELLMAN

BRAZIL AND MEXICO

Patterns in Late Development

editors:

Sylvia Ann Hewlett & Richard S. Weinert

ISHI A Publication of the
Institute for the Study of Human Issues
Philadelphia

Manufactured in the United States of America

1 2 3 4 5 6 7 8 9 90 89 88 87 86 85 84 83 82

Library of Congress Cataloging in Publication Data

Main entry under title:

Brazil and Mexico.

    (Inter-American politics series; v. 3)
    Includes bibliographical references and index.
    Contents: Introduction: the characteristics and consequences of late de-
velopment in Brazil and Mexico/Sylvia Ann Hewlett and Richard S. Weinert
—Mexican and Brazilian economic development/Douglas H. Graham—Popu-
lar sector incorporation and political supremacy/Ruth Berins Collier—[etc.]
    1. Brazil—Economic conditions—1945-   —Addresses, essays, lectures.
2. Mexico—Economic conditions—1918-   —Addresses, essays, lectures. I.
Hewlett, Sylvia Ann. II. Weinert, Richard S. III. Series.
HC187.B8657   330.972'082   81-7216
ISBN 0-89727-022-3   AACR2

For information, write:

Director of Publications
ISHI
3401 Science Center
Philadelphia, Pennsylvania 19104
U.S.A.

Preface

The Center for Inter-American Relations has worked, since it began operations in 1967, to build in the United States an understanding of the other nations in the Western hemisphere. Through its Literature, Visual, and Performing Arts programs, the Center promotes a broader awareness in the U.S. of the cultural achievements of the Americas. In numerous meetings scheduled each year by the Center's Public Affairs program, political, social, and economic subjects of inter-American interest are discussed and debated. The Center offers an unofficial platform from which public and private leaders, scholars, and social critics can make their thoughts known to diverse international audiences.

The purpose of this publication is to expand the Center's efforts by reaching those interested in inter-American affairs who are not able to participate personally in the Center's activities. We hope that this work, along with previous and forthcoming volumes sponsored by the Public Affairs program, will contribute significantly to the permanent body of research and commentary.

RONALD G. HELLMAN
CENTER FOR INTER-AMERICAN RELATIONS

Contents

BRAZIL AND MEXICO

Introduction: The Characteristics and Consequences of Late Development in Brazil and Mexico

SYLVIA ANN HEWLETT and RICHARD S. WEINERT

Brazil and Mexico are two of the most important and most successful examples of late development in the contemporary Third World. Since the 1940s these nations have managed to achieve growth rates that have averaged 7 to 8 percent per year. Being a late starter in the industrialization process does have some advantages, and in both countries foreign capital and sophisticated technologies from the advanced world have been successfully bent to the task of rapid development.

However, as is evident from the Brazilian and Mexican experiences, industrial take-off in the mid-twentieth century has had some extremely painful social consequences. Contemporary growth strategies have not produced full employment or broadly rising urban and rural real wages, and massive poverty and increasing inequality remain the dominant fact of life for the majority of the Brazilian and Mexican people. In a similar vein, development has been grounded in considerable degrees of political repression.

The greatest difference between Brazil and Mexico seems to lie in their political systems. Brazil has been subject to broader swings than Mexico—from a political volatility and intensity in the period from 1946 to 1964 that was more extreme than anything seen in Mexico since the 1920s, to a degree of repression and dictatorship following 1964 greater than any Mexico has experienced in this century. In turn, Mexico has sustained a limited degree of bourgeois political freedom and regular elections over five decades, a record matched by few other nations in the developed or developing world. On the other hand, while both nations have evolved an impressive series of institutional mechanisms for containing lower class grievances, Brazil has periodically found it necessary to suppress civil liberties and political freedoms in order to maintain favorable conditions for economic growth. This is true to a much lesser extent in Mexico.

The purpose of this introductory chapter is to examine certain critical structural characteristics of twentieth-century development held in common by Brazil and Mexico, and to begin to demonstrate why these characteristics seriously limit the possibilities for social welfare and political freedom within these nations. We shall further consider the meaning and significance of the differences which our analysis turns up.

Our conviction is that the institutional, technological, and demographic conditions of contemporary take-off are immensely more constraining than those faced by the early developers in Western Europe and North America. Therefore, the social and political costs of growth borne by late-developing countries are heavier and longer lasting than those triggered by the original industrial revolution.

The State

A central fact of late development in both Brazil and Mexico is that the growth strategies have depended on powerful interventionist states. By stimulating and channeling industrial activity (for example, through protecting the domestic market for final consumer goods), by providing huge amounts of taxation revenues for investment purposes, and by becoming active producers in the infrastructural and basic industrial spheres, the Brazilian and Mexican states have become the leading actors in the development process.

Early industrialization in today's developed world took place within an environment of laissez faire, and an entrepreneurial class provided the initiative, the know-how, and the investment capital for the expanding industrial economies. Twentieth-century conditions preclude private national capital from playing these central roles, and instead the state must step in to orchestrate the development effort.

Consider, for example, the investment needs of industrial take-off. During the first industrial revolution in Britain, individual capitalists provided the rather modest amounts of capital investment needed for the small-scale manufacturing of this era.[1] Later industrializers in France and Germany required investment banks for the same purpose since the scale and capital-intensiveness of industry had grown in the intervening years. In even later industrializers of the twentieth century, the still more powerful taxation powers of the state itself are needed to generate the huge amounts of investment capital required for modern industrialization.

In the productive sphere we also find some sectors where the contemporary Brazilian and Mexican states have stepped in because the private sector either can't or won't deal with the problems at hand. In the areas of infrastructural and basic industrial investment, for example, the state has several distinctive traits as a producing unit which make it the "natural" agent for this kind of activity in modern development strategies. First, the state can exert control over national economic resources such as mineral deposits and hydroelectric power potential. Second, through access to government revenues, the state can mobilize the huge amounts of capital necessary to construct an electricity grid, a modern steel mill, or a road network. Third, because of the nature of public as opposed to private accountability, state enterprises do not have to recoup investments within a few years and are able to contemplate much longer time horizons than private firms. Finally, since their objective is to maximize the national product rather than the product of a single firm or sector, they can afford to ignore the indivisibilities and externalities characteristic of much modern infrastructural investment.

Obviously, many of the conditions that encourage the state to assume a prominent role in infrastructural and basic good investment in contemporary development did not exist for early developers (or were much less pronounced). Contemporary industrial take-off has enormous start-up needs because nations that begin large-scale industrialization in the twentieth century have a two-hundred-year technological gap to bridge. Providing the high-quality steel for a car manufacturing plant, or installing an up-to-date and comprehensive telephone system (without which no one can do business efficiently in the modern world), involves the massive capital outlays and long-run time perspectives mentioned earlier. Domestic private firms cannot fill the bill (they have neither the technological nor the financial capability) and foreign private corporations generally will not (they are too profit conscious and do not like the long time horizons involved).

Because of these constraints of late development, the state has little option but to assume an increasingly important role in the development process. The Bennett and Sharpe chapter stresses the fact that state intervention in Brazil and Mexico is often initially somewhat reluctant, since the governing elites in both countries would prefer the private sector to assume more responsibility for industrialization.

There have been some differences between the Brazilian and the Mexican experiences in that Mexico has succeeded in developing the role of private national capital more fully than Brazil, while the Brazilian state has taken more initiative. In both nations, however, the state has conditioned investment in basic areas of production and has self-consciously shaped the overall development strategy. Laissez faire policies and private entrepreneurial initiative no longer provide the best breeding ground for industrial growth.

What are the political effects of massive state economic activity in Brazil and Mexico? First, the state has unavoidably adopted the goals of high growth rates and economic efficiency. There is some variation between our two cases—Mexico has paid slightly more attention to job creation in the public sector, while Brazilian state firms have adopted internal rationales similar to those of any foreign multinational. Still, the economic role of the state precludes it from playing the role that was filled by the state in earlier industrializers—namely, to interrupt established economic relations in order to help redress social inequities. In late industrializers, the state is inevitably one of the primary actors in establishing the relations which create social inequities. The resultant tension between the state as producer and the state as redresser of inequity is new, and is invariably resolved in favor of the former so long as growth rates matter.

Second, in making these choices, the state has inevitably forged a close alliance with the economic elites. This is not different per se from the situation of earlier industrializers, but the alliance is richer since the state and the elites are often literally partners. The closeness of this alliance would appear to circumscribe the limits of potential state activity which runs counter to elite interests. The social results of this are quite predictable. The state in both Mexico and Brazil has been a powerful agent of accumulation, but has not undertaken significant redistributive or welfare state policies. In each case the state has been an active and eager partner in a highly successful and extremely inequitable growth strategy.

Foreign Capital

A second critical fact of late development in Brazil and Mexico is that it has been heavily dependent on direct foreign investment and on capital-intensive technologies. This means that fast rates of growth in the industrial sphere often do not generate a significant increase in employment in the modern sector, and this serves to widen the gap between the privileged few and the impoverished many.

In both countries, the strategy of import-substituting industrialization, initiated in the 1940s, led to an emphasis on sophisticated consumer durables (the goods which had previously been imported). As the technologies and the foreign exchange required to make these sophisticated goods were effectively monopolized by multinational firms, this produced a substantial dependence on direct foreign investment. The production techniques of multinational corporations have evolved in contexts of capital abundance and labor scarcity (remember that 98 percent of all industrial research and development has taken place in the advanced world!).[2] It is therefore not surprising that the industrial processes they bring to countries such as Brazil and Mexico are large-scale and highly mechanized, and as such unlikely to absorb much labor.[3] As the chapters by Graham and Evans and Gereffi point out, Brazil and Mexico differ somewhat in that the former has a larger foreign presence in its industrial sector and has a poorer record in the labor absorption sphere. However, both countries are characterized by highly capital-intensive and skill-intensive industrial structures that produce sophisticated goods for elite groups and employ a small and privileged group of workers. Rapid industrialization in Brazil and Mexico has therefore bypassed the majority of the population, since a large proportion of the potential labor force remains uninvolved in the growth process either as consumers or as producers.

All this contrasts quite markedly with early development in Western Europe and North America. As Felix points out in Chapter 8, the simple technologies of the original industrial revolution were relatively labor intensive and gradually absorbed the bulk of the population into highly productive (and better paying) occupations.[4] This positive trend was helped by the demographic factors discussed in the next section, but the fact that late developers have had to rely on foreign investment to bridge a two-hundred-year technological gap, and have adopted sophisticated capital-intensive industrial techniques, is an important part of the explanation for why so many millions of Brazilian and Mexican workers have failed to find jobs in the rapidly expanding industrial sector.

The important role that foreign capital has played has further strengthened the economic role of the state and helped forge its alliance with local elites. For reasons of national pride and to protect national sovereignty, the state in both Brazil and Mexico adopted various policies to restrict the activities of foreign capital and direct it into chosen areas. In earlier industrializers, the state might have been content with this role, leaving it to domestic private companies to interact with foreign private companies. In late industrializers, however, this relationship would have been so one-sided that the state had to step in more actively, to ally itself with domestic firms.

Demographic Factors

The introduction of capital-intensive industrial technologies into the Third World often coincides with the transfer of another type of technology from developed countries, that of medical know-how. Within a few years, killer diseases are wiped out, death rates fall drastically, and population growth rates assume explosive proportions.

The coincidence of these types of technological transfer has important implications for social welfare in late-developing nations such as Brazil and Mexico. Industrial growth rates are extremely high by any historical standard, but, given an imported capital-intensive technology and an accelerated rate of population increase, the rate of growth of industrial employment is often less than the rate of growth of the population. This means quite simply that the modern work force will be a declining proportion of the potential labor pool. Industrial workers become small, privileged minority, a labor aristocracy that is quite distinct from the mass of the people, who remain in a state of miserable poverty.

In Chapter 2, Graham points to the pronounced inadequacy of modern-sector job creation in Brazil and Mexico, given the rapid rates of population expansion in these countries since the late 1940s. He then describes some contrasts in the Brazilian and Mexican experiences. Mexico has promoted a slightly more labor-intensive industrial structure than Brazil, mainly because small-scale domestic private firms have retained a larger role in the manufacturing sector. However, this difference has been counteracted by the fact that population growth rates have been higher in Mexico than in Brazil in recent years, rising to over 3 percent per year. This makes the labor absorption problem virtually insurmountable within the existing growth strategy.

These demographic circumstances contrast quite dramatically with early industrialization in advanced nations. In Western Europe and North America during the eighteenth and nineteenth centuries there was a much slower and milder demographic transition (provoked by a general rise in standards of living, gradual improvements in public health standards, the spread of literacy, and an increased adoption of birth control measures to complement the new lifestyles). Over the course of a century, first death rates and then birth rates fell, and by the beginning of the twentieth century population growth rates had stabilized in most industrial nations. The whole process was facilitated by large-scale migration from Europe to the Americas, which acted as a population safety valve. During the nineteenth century, thirteen million people emigrated from the British Isles to the New World.[5] Without this mass exodus it would have taken longer for Britain (and many other European nations) to absorb its labor force into higher-productivity, modern-sector occupations. This elimination of the "reserve army of the unemployed" through falling birth rates and mass emigration was a critical factor in enhancing the bargaining power of the working class.

The roots of political authoritarianism in both Brazil and Mexico may be found in this demographic picture. Demographics create a set of social problems that the economic system cannot ameliorate. The clear political imperative becomes that of controlling and suppressing the unavoidable social tension so that economic growth can proceed. Failure to do so would be fatal for development aspirations.

Labor Organizations

A fourth major difference between early and late development is found in the political and social attributes of the working class. An important reason for the gains of the working class in Europe and North America was the fact that labor began to organize, both in trade unions and in political parties. The precondition was obviously an "organizable" lower class, in the sense of a mass of urbanized and substantially literate workers. There are fifteen advanced countries which present a fairly reliable statistical picture of the beginnings of modern economic growth. All except one (Japan) had over 35 percent of the labor force outside agriculture and a greater than 50 percent literacy rate. An extremely different situation prevailed in most underdeveloped nations when they entered their take-off phases. In general, only 10 to 25 percent of workers were outside of agriculture, a similar percentage were literate, and the gap between their output and those of agricultural workers was far greater than was the case in developing nineteenth-century Europe or North America.[6]

Primarily because of the technological and demographic factors described earlier in this chapter, late industrialization in countries such as Brazil and Mexico has confirmed rather than countered these previously existing differences. The industrial work force consequently emerged as a labor aristocracy with more to lose than to gain from sharing the benefits of economic growth with the mass of the people, and the trade union movement grew up as an instrument to control and coopt this elite group. The net result is that "organized labor" in late-developing nations is likely to fight against equalizing measures, whereas in early developing nations it spearheaded them.[7]

In both Brazil and Mexico the industrial working class approximates a labor aristocracy, and labor organizations have been deliberately used by the state to buy off this critical segment of the working classes so as to prevent them from joining with the masses. However, as one might expect, the specific structures and techniques used by the Brazilian and Mexican governments to control and coopt labor are different and reflect the separate national histories of these countries. Erickson and Middlebrook demonstrate that in Brazil the elite-dominated system of corporatist labor controls was intended to prevent autonomous labor organization and mobilization. In Mexico, on the other hand, the labor force was deliberately mobilized and incorporated into the official political party. However, despite a greater ability to negotiate in the national decision-making process than its Brazilian counterpart, Mexican organized labor remains under the firm control of the state and has very little independent control over the economic fate of its membership.

The political implications of these differences in labor management explain much of the divergence between the political systems in Brazil and Mexico. In Brazil in the mid-1960s, the decision to try to prevent an autonomous and mobilized labor movement was inconsistent with any semblance of democratic politics. Democracy could flower only if the labor policy failed. In Mexico, by contrast, a mobilized but wholly coopted labor movement permitted the adoption of some democratic forms. It also facilitated more stable politics, uninterrupted by episodic rumblings and the suppression of a restive labor movement.

Social Structures

A fifth critical difference between early and late development is centered in social structures. Traditional social structures, which rest on ascribed roles rather than achieved functions, are prone to channel the fruits of economic advance to a nonproductive elite. In early industrializers, these traditional social structures had been undermined by violence or had withered away before the advent of industrialization. But in late industrializers, traditional social structures persist, many of them a legacy of a colonial era, and they do much to reinforce the inequitable trends within late development.

Capitalism in most underdeveloped countries has never confronted traditional social structures as it did, for example, in Cromwell's England or late eighteenth-century France. In Europe, the new inequalities of capitalism, to some extent nonhereditary, replaced the relics of feudalism; in today's late-developing nations they often reinforce a still thriving traditional social structure. In concrete terms, the landlord class has often been coopted rather than destroyed and survives into the modern period to impede the evolution of a political system that could direct the benefits of development towards the lower classes.

It is in this sphere of social structures that the differences between Brazil and Mexico seem most pronounced. Brazil approximates a typical late-developing nation in this regard. Several centuries of colonial rule and plantation agriculture generated a highly differentiated social structure with power firmly vested in a landlord class. As Collier describes in Chapter 3, twentieth-century industrialization saw the absorption rather than the destruction of this traditional social structure, which survives to the present day and is responsible for the great extremes of wealth and poverty in the Brazilian countryside.

Mexico deviates quite markedly from this typical pattern of late development. The Mexican revolution did confront the traditional society quite violently, and in subsequent years large estates were broken up so that land could be given to the peasants. Mexico then embarked upon industrialization, having destroyed, at least temporarily, its traditional social structure. Nevertheless, revolution and reform did not prevent the reconstitution of a highly differentiated social structure in Mexico. The inability to provide enough jobs in industry and the continued existence of a surplus labor force has meant that traditional patterns of relationships were reestablished, especially in the countryside.

Social Equity

In Chapters 7 and 8, Felix and Hewlett describe a situation in which a third of all contemporary Mexican and Brazilian families continue to exist in a state of wretched poverty. In the distributional sphere, the top 10 percent of these populations appropriate 50 percent of national income, while the top 1 percent receives the same proportion of national income as the bottom 40 percent put together! All this adds up to a rather grim social welfare picture. There are, however, some differences of detail between the Brazilian and the Mexican experiences. In Mexico, the very richest class (the top 1 percent) has not done so well as its counterpart in Brazil, and there seems to be some difference in the timing of the income concentration process. In Brazil, income inequality became rapidly worse in the mid-1960s, while a similar trend was true of Mexico in the early 1970s. Despite these variations between our case examples, the overall pattern is clear enough. Rapid growth in Brazil and Mexico has, thus far, failed to provoke significant trickle-down of the fruits of development to the lower echelons of society.

The differences noted above are consistent with the political differences discussed at the outset. While Mexico's lower classes have not fared any better than Brazil's in winning a larger slice of the pie, Mexico's upper middle classes have. While it would be hard to credit this directly to Mexico's more stable, somewhat more democratic political system, the two factors seem consistent with one another.

Political Rights

There are two aspects to consider with respect to political rights: democratic procedures and political freedoms. On both counts, Mexico has provided more political rights more consistently than has Brazil.

As we noted at the outset, Brazilian political life prior to 1964 was richer and more volatile than anything in Mexico since the 1920s, but the past 15 years in Brazil have provided little concession to the democratic process. This process seems to be appearing again in Brazil, however, and some degree of democracy may emerge in the 1980s. In Mexico, by contrast, the democratic process has been both ever present and consistently limited. Elections have been held regularly for many offices, with several parties offering candidates. On the other hand, only the PRI candidate ever had any realistic chance of winning, so elections were not truly competitive. Mexico recently has reserved one-third of the legislature for opposition parties and has legalized the communist party. These small moves will increase competitiveness without threatening the political dominance of the PRI.

With regard to political freedom, the differences between the two countries are similar. Brazil sharply restricted political activity in the years following 1964 and engaged in forced exile for opposition leaders, torture of protesters, press censorship, and the like. These practices have abated in recent years, but are periodically being restored. Mexico never resorted to such wholesale abuse of political freedom.

DO THE DIFFERENCES MAKE A DIFFERENCE?

The question that remains is what to make of these differences between Mexico and Brazil. Do they have any significance? There appear to be two answers.

First, these political differences have no impact on social equity. We find striking similarity in indices of social welfare as well as in the need to control and manipulate the labor movement. For the majority of people who share a thin slice of the economic pie, the degree of democracy seems to make no difference to their material well-being. It may of course provide other satisfactions, but that is a matter for social psychologists and is outside the scope of this work.

Second, the very fact that political diversity coexists with such similar patterns of economic development and social equity demonstrates the looseness of fit between politics and socioeconomic structures. Evidently there is much interaction, and we have pointed out numerous ways in which political imperatives were created by the socioeconomic structure. Yet in the end there is no determinism. Political outlines may be indicated, but politics may still develop in directions more or less repressive, more or less democratic, more or less free.

Notes

1. Alexander Gerschenkron, *Economic Backwardness in Historical Perspective* (Cambridge: Harvard University Press, 1966), p. 7. This point is elaborated in the chapter by Douglas Bennett and Kenneth Sharpe.

2. Frances Stewart, "Technology and Employment in LDC's," in Edgar O. Edwards (ed.), *Employment in Developing Nations* (New York: Columbia University Press, 1974), p. 100.

3. This is discussed by Constantino V. Vaitsos in "Employment Problems and Transnational Enterprises in Developing Countries: Distortions and Inequality" (Geneva: International Labor Organization, 1976, mimeo), p. 1. See also Frances Stewart, "Choice of Technique in Developing Countries," *Journal of Development Studies*, vol. 9, no. 1 (October 1972), p. 114; and G. K. Helleiner, "The Role of Multinational Corporations in Less Developed Countries' Trade in Technology," *World Development*, vol. 3, no. 4 (April 1975), pp. 161–90.

4. In Europe, industrial employment "came to represent half, or more than half, of total employment." In contrast, in late industrializing nations, "industrial employment represents one-third of urban employment, and often even less." See discussion in Stephen H. Hellinger and Douglas A. Hellinger, *Unemployment and the Multinationals* (London: Kennikat Press, 1976), p. 24.

5. Between 1815 and 1899, thirteen million people emigrated from the British Isles. See B. R. Mitchell, *European Historical Statistics 1750–1970* (New York: Columbia University Press, 1975), pp. 134–40.

6. These figures are taken from Michael Lipton, *Why People Stay Poor* (Cambridge: Harvard University Press, 1977), pp. 39–41.

7. This point is elaborated by E. J. Hobsbawm, *Laboring Men: Studies in the History of Labor* (Garden City, N.Y.: Doubleday, 1967), p. 272.

2

Mexican and Brazilian Economic Development: Legacies, Patterns, and Performance

DOUGLAS H. GRAHAM

This chapter points out the similarities and contrasts in the growth patterns and development strategies of Mexico and Brazil in recent decades. In doing so, rather than trace out separate narratives of development for each country, I have adopted a comparative perspective throughout. First, the historical legacy is established within which we can place the contemporary contrast between the two countries. Next, contrasts between the countries will be emphasized in the more recent period, for which structural patterns, institutional change, and policy performance will be discussed in detail. This emphasis on contrasts is deliberate, since the similarities between these two countries (as compared to other LDCs) are more commonly known. Third, prospects for the future will be set forth in the light of past development strategies and contemporary world trade conditions.

The similarities in the recent patterns of economic growth of Mexico and Brazil are numerous and bear repeating in this introduction. We are talking about the two countries in Latin America with the largest population bases, the largest domestic markets and gross domestic products, and thus, not surprisingly, among the largest and most developed industrial structures when compared to other LDCs in or outside of Latin America. The two countries have recorded similarly high rates of economic growth in recent decades, in general much higher than those recorded in other Latin American countries. Both countries register comparable levels of rapid population growth, extensive rural poverty, economic dualism, labor surpluses, and income inequality. Since they are large geographical units, both exhibit more pronounced regional disparities than most LDCs. The role of foreign capital and foreign technology is also high in the import-substitution industrialization process of both countries, creating similar patterns of economic dependency on the one hand, and significant structural change on the other. Finally, active and independent political party initiative, as well as interest group and trade union activity, is strictly controlled in both settings. In summary, in many important ways, we are dealing with similar bureaucratic-authoritarian regimes within which populist interests and participatory politics are reduced in scope, distributional concerns ignored or placed in low priority, and the maximization of economic growth and rapid industrialization given a top priority. Despite these similarities, there are important differences in policy initiatives and patterns of growth, as will be seen shortly.

Historical Legacies

Many of the contemporary contrasts between Mexico and Brazil have historical roots, and a comparative review of nineteenth- and early twentieth-century developments makes this clear. The first historical contrast centers on Mexico's constant crises—corrupt governments, civil wars, the loss of national territory, and frequent humiliation at the hands of foreign invaders. Brazil, on the other hand, preserved a stable political legitimacy following independence under the rule of a branch of the Portuguese royal family.[1] Instead of losing territory, Brazil expanded its frontiers through aggressive diplomacy and never experienced significant civil conflicts or humiliation through foreign intervention comparable to those experienced by Mexico. In short, Brazil's sovereignty and national identity were never threatened as blatantly as Mexico's. At the same time, the Portuguese patrimonial heritage was much more effective in promoting a stable accommodation of political and economic interests in the Brazilian setting than was the Spanish colonial legacy in Mexico, where a lack of legitimacy ruled and violent dissent was common.

In a similar fashion, the slave legacy and the pattern of labor exploitation in rural Brazil never created the unrest and peasant uprisings that marked Mexican history. This is particularly clear in the relatively nonviolent changes of regime that took place in Brazil (i.e., the abolition of slavery and the Empire and the creation of a republic in the late nineteenth century), events which provide further examples of the strength and stability of the country's patrimonial tradition.

Not only did this tradition act to accommodate elite competition, it also stabilized the semifeudal class relations in rural society.

The contrast between stable Brazil and unstable Mexico explains why Mexican policies have reflected, in Reynolds' terms, extreme introspection and defensiveness.[2] In Mexico, a succession of ruling elites had to be constantly aware of the possiblity of violent internal revolt which could destroy their institutional base of power. At the same time, these oligarchic governments were hemmed in by the intimidating presence of the United States in the north and by U.S. colonial policy in the Caribbean and Central America to the south.

Brazil, on the other hand, was far more cosmopolitan in its historical role on the South American continent. With no superpower on the country's flank, Brazilian governments in the nineteenth and early twentieth centuries felt far more confident and indeed aggressive in working out their own *grandeza,* or manifest destiny, through wars, as in the triple alliance, or through aggressive diplomatic bargaining, such as that which took place during the first years of the twentieth century. The Brazilian elite circulated widely in international circles, and figures such as Rui Barbosa presumed to play important roles in international tribunals. Even Emperor Dom Pedro Segundo acted as a man in tune with modern scientific trends and enlightenment. In brief, Brazil, free from internecine internal revolts, external aggression, or foreign intervention, displayed within its elite a national psychology that reflected a confident, expansionist, cosmopolitan state in control of its destiny and optimistic about its future role in history.

The political and cultural contrast between Mexico and Brazil carries over to their respective export-led patterns of early economic development. The Mexican pattern under Porfirio Díaz was more dominated by foreign investment, which in time led to a strong antiforeign revolutionary tradition. At the same time, this process of foreign involvement had a strong enclave feature which limited the feedback to domestic development.[3] More important, the land consolidation that also occurred during this period of export expansion increasingly marginalized a substantial majority of the Mexican population, reduced the production of local foodstuffs for rural and urban populations alike, and dramatically increased rural poverty.

The role of foreign capital, though important, was less extensive in the Brazilian setting. Furthermore, the pattern of export expansion, led by coffee exports, induced substantial domestic development.[4] Since the factors of production in the coffee sector were largely locally owned, many of the earned profits were either locally consumed, stimulating output in other sectors, or invested, thereby stimulating local industry. Of equal significance was the demographic revolution introduced into Brazil through the substitution of foreign immigrants for slave labor in the coffee sector.[5]

In retrospect, the Porfirian period of export-led growth in Mexico was more exclusionary, exploitative, and foreign dominated than the Brazilian coffee boom.[6] The latter, though still an example of unequal development, represented a significant improvement over the earlier slave society, and the impact of immigration on Brazilian society was substantial in terms of broadened markets, urban growth, social mobility, and early industrialization. The net result of these contrasting historical paths (from the 1880s to World War I) was that the increased tensions and social pressures of the more closed Mexican system ripped apart the institutional facade in a violent revolution. In contrast, the pressures for change in Brazil led to a series of social and economic accommodations within a slightly broadened patrimonial framework, but still within the old republic.

Evidence on economic growth during this period is hard to assemble in acceptable comparative terms, particularly for the years before 1900. Nevertheless, demographic data can reflect, in an indirect way, the degree of economic progress in a society—and nothing stands out more in the contrast between these two countries than the different paths of population growth from 1800 to 1900, or to 1920. Table 1 shows that Mexico had nearly twice the population of Brazil in 1800 (5.8 to 3.3 million). By 1900, Brazil had grown to 17 million, while Mexico registered only 13.6 million inhabitants. By 1920, Brazil had approximately twice the population of Mexico (27 to roughly 14 million). Of particular interest here is the fact that even if one accounts for international immigration, the annual rate of natural increase in Brazil in the nineteenth century (1.6 to 1.7 percent) was roughly twice

Table 1 / Total Populations of Mexico and Brazil, 1800–2000 (in millions)

	1800	1900	1920	1940	1960	1970	2000[a]
Mexico	5.8	13.6	14.3	20.1	36.0	48.0	128.0
Brazil	3.3	17.0	31.0	41.1	70.0	93.0	202.0
			(27.0)[b]				
Ratio, Mexico to Brazil	1.76	0.80	0.53	0.49	0.51	0.52	0.63

Sources: Thomas W. Merrick and Douglas H. Graham, *Population and Economic Development in Brazil: 1800 to the Present* (Baltimore: Johns Hopkins University Press, 1979); Robert W. Fox, *Urban Population Growth Trends in Latin America* (Washington, D.C.: Inter American Development Bank, 1975).

[a]Projected.

[b]Corrected for overenumeration.

the rate of total population growth in Mexico during this period. This fact alone is sufficient evidence that economic progress must have been more widespread in the Brazilian setting. This significant shift in demographic ranking by the end of the century was to set the base for the predominance of the Brazilian market and enlarge the scope of its industrial development in the twentieth century.

The final significant development in the recent histories of Mexico and Brazil is the revealing contrast in each country's reaction to the Great Depression of the 1930s. This reaction was to carry significance for later development. Both countries experienced a drastic reversal in their terms of trade after 1929, with the drop in export revenue causing a sharp decline in their gross domestic products.[7] In the face of this crisis, Brazil reacted with expansionary fiscal and monetary policies in the early 1930s. The coffee defense program, which purchased and destroyed over 62 million bags of coffee during the 1930s, led to a substantial increase in the monetary base beyond that covered through foreign loans.[8] Budgetary deficits became endemic during this period, and exchange controls and devaluations raised the level of effective protection for domestic industry. Thus the purchasing power released through these expansionary measures fueled one of the most rapid cycles of industrial growth in twentieth-century Brazil. From 1932 to 1939, manufacturing output grew at an annual average of 11 percent per year. In reaction to this rapid growth in domestic manufacturing, Fishlow reports that industrial imports as a percentage of total industrial supply decreased from 50 to 25 percent from 1919 to 1939.[9]

Mexico, in contrast, experienced no significant import-substitution industrialization (ISI) during this period. The ratio of imports to total supply, according to Villarreal, declined only from 57 to 49 percent from 1929 to 1939. In contrast to Brazil, the first half of the decade witnessed a conservative reaction to the impact of the depression, bringing on restrictive monetary and fiscal policies. Only in the last half of the decade did the new Lázaro Cárdenas regime engage in explicit expansionary measures. In this case, however, these measures were directed towards establishing the role of the government in the area of infrastructure and agricultural reform. Indeed, the energies of the Cárdenas regime were directed towards economic, political, and social reforms of major significance. Economic growth and industrial growth in particular were given secondary priority.[10] In the end, Brazil experienced more impressive industrial growth, but Mexico underwent more significant political and institutional reforms. Getulio Vargas' populist but authoritarian regime in the 1930s was "exclusionary" in not directly incorporating the labor and peasant sectors into the government. In contrast, Cárdenas' regime in Mexico was an "inclusionary" populist authoritarian regime for having included these sectors in its reformed political institutions and having undertaken many policy actions to allow them to benefit from these reforms.

This scenario illustrates the contrasting styles with which Mexico and Brazil dealt with the pressures for socioeconomic change. Mexico, with a checkered history of revolts and repression, sacrificed a substantial amount of potential economic growth through long stretches of time and in the process fell victim to a series of social upheavals generally absent in the Brazilian experience. Still, by 1940 the country had finally forged an institutional order that was to guarantee a far more secure sense of legitimacy for her future strategy of economic development than was to be found in Brazil.

Brazil, on the other hand, weathered the strains of social and economic change without the violence and upheavals of Mexico. The Brazilian patrimonial system was sufficiently flexible to absorb the loss of slavery and imperial institutions, the creation of a republic, the impact of immigration, the process of urban-industrial growth, and finally the impact of the Depression and the creation of a new political order in the 1930s without decisively changing the system in any revolutionary fashion. Thus the peculiarly stable domestic social history of Brazil stands out in sharp contrast to the internal violence of Mexico. This has, in turn, given the Brazilian ruling elite greater degrees of freedom for an outward-oriented, cosmopolitan perspective in foreign affairs, a less hostile nationalism in dealing with foreign capital, and a more natural inclination to promote economic growth and ignore important social reforms. As Clark Reynolds has stated, the time of accelerating aspirations has yet to come for Brazil,[11] whereas Mexico, at least in part, had met this challenge by 1940. This contrast was to condition the patterns and strategies for economic development in the two countries in the contemporary period.

The Contemporary Period: Comparative Patterns and Performance

ECONOMIC GROWTH

As mentioned in the early part of this paper, there are many similarities in the contemporary patterns of economic growth between Mexico and Brazil. The high rates of growth between 1940 and 1975 (in excess of 6 percent) and the high rates of industrial import substitution are common to both countries. Table 2 underscores these postwar trends, which cannot be matched by any other major Latin American

*Table 2 / Percentage Rates of Growth of Gross
Domestic Product and Industrial Output in the
Mexican and Brazilian Economies, 1950–1978*

	Mexico		Brazil	
Period	GDP (1)	Industry (2)	GDP (3)	Industry (4)
1950–55	5.6	5.6	6.8	7.8
1955–60	5.7	7.3	6.8	10.0
1960–65	7.1	8.6	4.5	3.7
1965–70	6.9	8.9	7.5	10.8
1970–75	5.5	6.3	9.3	11.8
1975–78	4.0*	4.5*	5.8*	6.7*

Sources: La Economía Méxicana en Cifra (México, D.F.: Nacional
Financiera S.A., 1972); Clark Reynolds, "Why Mexico's 'Sta-
bilizing Development' Was Actually Destabilizing (With
Some Implications for the Future)," *World Development*, vol.
6, nos. 7/8 (1978), pp. 1105–18; Banco de México, *Informe
Anual*, various issues; and *Conjuntura Economica* (Rio de
Janeiro: Fundação Getulio Vargas), various issues.
*Preliminary estimates.

nation. Nevertheless, within this common framework of rapid growth
of GDP and even higher rates of industrial growth, a sharp distinction
emerges between the two countries. Except for the brief downturn at
the end of the Echeverría *sexenio* in the mid-1970s, Mexico's growth
record is remarkably uniform, while Brazil's is clearly more cyclical.
This contrast stands out particularly sharply when one considers the
patterns of industrial growth in columns 2 and 4 of Table 2. While the
standard deviation for the Mexican industrial growth rates is relatively
small throughout the postwar period, that of Brazil, on the other hand,
records sharp cyclical patterns of industrial growth with peaks (1955–
60, 1970–75) and troughs (1960–65, 1975–78). Moreover, if we look at
Brazil during the periods 1962–67 and 1968–73, we note a remarkably
low rate of industrial growth of only 2.9 percent per year for the
earlier period and the remarkably high rate of 14.3 percent per year
for the later period. At no time does the Mexican pattern of industrial
growth ever reflect anything resembling these sharp cyclical swings.
In large part, this Mexican record reflects not only a more balanced
and cautious development strategy but also a more effectively institutionalized political regime. In the end, this has given Mexican authorities greater leverage (i.e., more policy instruments) to control inflation, to contain popular demands on economic resources through
the political system, and to maintain a more consistent economic
discipline.

SECTORAL PATTERNS OF GROWTH

Table 3 offers us insights into the changing patterns of sectoral income and labor force shares, as well as the relative product per worker, in the postwar period. It is quite apparent that both countries have moved substantially into sustained industrial growth, with increasing shares of national product recorded for this sector during the period from 1950 to 1970 (panel A). These percentages of industrial output in total product are close to those recorded in many developed economies. At the same time, there has been a substantial decline in the relative shares of agricultural GDP and a slight rise in the share of the service sector, which Kuznets' classic work has documented as the typical process of economic growth.[12]

Within this process of changing income shares, an interesting difference between the two countries emerges. By 1960, Brazil records a much greater increase in the manufacturing share of its GDP than Mexico and maintains this relative advantage up to 1970. Mexico, on the other hand, increases the relative share of its service sector income substantially more than Brazil does by 1960, although by 1970 this difference has disappeared. Clearly, the decades of the fifties and the sixties reflect a different pace and pattern of industrial growth in the two countries, a point that will be evident throughout this analysis.

The changing labor force shares (panel B) represent equally interesting contrasts between the two countries which suggest some relevant differences in their industrial growth patterns and strategies. First, though both start in 1950 with roughly the same share of labor in the agricultural sector, by 1970 Mexico ends up drawing more people out of the agricultural labor force than Brazil. Second, there is a much more substantial transfer of labor into the service sector in Brazil during the 1950s than there is in Mexico. Finally, the pattern of service sector labor transfers is associated with a substantially smaller share of labor being absorbed into the industrial sector in Brazil. This is the most interesting feature of the contrasting pattern of labor absorption and intersectoral labor shifts within the two countries. In the 1950s, Brazil engaged in a much more capital-intensive pattern of ISI, with the excess labor spilling over to service sector employment. Mexico, on the other hand, experienced a much more labor-absorptive pattern of industrial growth and, relatively speaking, less labor spillover into service sector employment. By 1970, the service sector differentials in the labor force shares narrow, but the contrasting shares in industrial (and manufacturing) labor absorption are maintained. In other words, Mexico has absorbed a much more significant proportion of its total labor force into its industrial sector.

Table 3 / National Product and Labor Force Shares and Relative Product per Worker by Major Sectors for Mexico and Brazil, 1950–1970

Sector	1950		1960		1970	
	Brazil	Mexico	Brazil	Mexico	Brazil	Mexico
A. Percentage Distribution of National Product						
Agriculture	24.9	22.5	19.2	15.9	10.2	11.6
Industry	26.0	30.4	32.6	29.2	36.3	34.3
Manufacturing	(20.2)	(20.4)	(25.1)	(19.2)	(27.4)	(22.6)
Services	49.1	47.1	48.2	54.9	53.5	54.1
Total	100.0	100.0	100.0	100.0	100.0	100.0
B. Percentage Distribution of National Labor Force						
Agriculture	60.0	57.8	53.7	54.2	44.6	39.4
Industry	13.7	15.8	13.1	18.9	18.0	25.1
Manufacturing	(9.4)	(11.6)	(8.9)	(13.7)	(11.1)	(18.6)
Services	26.3	26.4	33.2	26.9	37.4	35.5
Total	100.0	100.0	100.0	100.0	100.0	100.0
C. Relative Product Per Worker (Percentage Product/Percentage Labor Force)						
Agriculture	0.41	0.39	0.36	0.29	0.23	0.29
Industry	1.90	1.92	2.49	1.54	2.01	1.37
Manufacturing	(2.15)	(1.76)	(2.82)	(1.40)	(2.47)	(1.22)
Services	1.86	1.78	1.45	2.04	1.43	1.52
Total	1.00	1.00	1.00	1.00	1.00	1.00

Sources: For Brazil: National product data from Conjuntura Economica, vol. 31, no. 7 (1977); labor force data from population censuses, 1950, 1960, 1970. For Mexico: National product data for 1950 from Clark Reynolds, The Mexican Economy: Twentieth Century Structure and Growth (New Haven: Yale University Press, 1970); for 1960, 1970 from Banco de México, Informe Anual, various issues; labor force data from population censuses, 1950, 1960, 1970.

Table 5 / *Percentage Distribution of Industrial Value Added for Selected Industrial Sectors in Mexico and Brazil, 1949–1950, 1958–1959, 1969–1970*[a]

	1949–50		1958–59		1969–70	
	Mexico	Brazil	Mexico	Brazil	Mexico	Brazil
Traditional sectors	70.9	64.0	66.3	47.3	52.0	40.7
Food, beverages, and tobacco	(36.4)	(26.3)	(39.2)	(20.6)	(29.2)	(17.1)
Textiles	(12.2)	(19.7)	(9.8)	(12.0)	(7.7)	(9.3)
Apparel	(11.3)	(4.3)	(8.7)	(3.6)	(7.5)	(3.3)
Others (furniture, wood and leather products, printing, miscellaneous)	(11.0)	(13.7)	(8.6)	(11.1)	(7.6)	(11.0)
Dynamic sectors A (process industries)	22.7	30.1	25.3	37.7	33.3	38.9
Chemicals	(6.4)	(9.3)	(7.9)	(13.4)	(13.3)	(16.9)
Iron and steel	(6.9)	(9.4)	(9.4)	(11.8)	(10.4)	(11.6)
Others (paper, rubber and nonmetallic minerals)	(9.4)	(11.4)	(8.0)	(12.5)	(9.6)	(10.4)
Dynamic sectors B (equipment and machinery)	6.2	5.9	8.5	15.0	14.6	20.4
Mechanical equipment	(1.4)	(2.1)	(1.8)	(3.4)	(3.0)	(7.0)
Electrical equipment	(2.3)	(1.6)	(3.0)	(4.0)	(5.2)	(5.4)
Transport equipment	(2.5)	(2.2)	(3.7)	(7.6)	(6.4)	(8.0)
Total[b]	99.8	100.0	100.1	100.0	99.9	100.0

Sources: For Mexico: Villarreal, "The Import Substitution Model," p. 282. For Brazil: *Censo Industrial 1950* (Rio de Janeiro: Fundação IBGE, 1957); *Censo Industrial 1960* (Rio de Janeiro: Fundação IBGE, 1967); *Censo Industrial 1970* (Rio de Janeiro: Fundação IBGE, 1974).

[a]Mexican value added percentages derived from constant 1960 pesos. Brazilian value added percentages derived from constant 1970 cruzeiros series.

[b]Totals do not necessarily add up to 100 because percentages have been rounded to the nearest tenth of a percent.

Table 3 / National Product and Labor Force Shares and Relative Product per Worker by Major Sectors for Mexico and Brazil, 1950–1970

Sector	1950 Brazil	1950 Mexico	1960 Brazil	1960 Mexico	1970 Brazil	1970 Mexico
A. Percentage Distribution of National Product						
Agriculture	24.9	22.5	19.2	15.9	10.2	11.6
Industry	26.0	30.4	32.6	29.2	36.3	34.3
Manufacturing	(20.2)	(20.4)	(25.1)	(19.2)	(27.4)	(22.6)
Services	49.1	47.1	48.2	54.9	53.5	54.1
Total	100.0	100.0	100.0	100.0	100.0	100.0
B. Percentage Distribution of National Labor Force						
Agriculture	60.0	57.8	53.7	54.2	44.6	39.4
Industry	13.7	15.8	13.1	18.9	18.0	25.1
Manufacturing	(9.4)	(11.6)	(8.9)	(13.7)	(11.1)	(18.6)
Services	26.3	26.4	33.2	26.9	37.4	35.5
Total	100.0	100.0	100.0	100.0	100.0	100.0
C. Relative Product Per Worker (Percentage Product/Percentage Labor Force)						
Agriculture	0.41	0.39	0.36	0.29	0.23	0.29
Industry	1.90	1.92	2.49	1.54	2.01	1.37
Manufacturing	(2.15)	(1.76)	(2.82)	(1.40)	(2.47)	(1.22)
Services	1.86	1.78	1.45	2.04	1.43	1.52
Total	1.00	1.00	1.00	1.00	1.00	1.00

Sources: For Brazil: National product data from *Conjuntura Economica*, vol. 31, no. 7 (1977); labor force data from population censuses. 1950, 1960, 1970. For Mexico: National product data for 1950 from Clark Reynolds, *The Mexican Economy: Twentieth Century Structure and Growth* (New Haven: Yale University Press, 1970); for 1960, 1970 from Banco de México, *Informe Anual*, various issues; labor force data from population censuses, 1950, 1960, 1970.

Panel C highlights the relative intersectoral inequality of output per worker within each country (i.e., the share of sectoral product divided by the share of the sectoral labor force). As we would expect from our conclusions in the preceding paragraphs, there is consistently a stronger pattern of inequality in relative product (or output) per worker among the major sectors in Brazil than in Mexico. This reflects in particular the more capital-intensive and less labor-absorptive role of industrial growth in Brazil.

Several additional contrasts surface in these results. Most important, the range between the lowest and highest sectoral relatives are considerably higher in Brazil (for example, in 1970 the highest sectoral relative in Brazil is 2.47 for manufacturing and the lowest is 0.23 in agriculture; thus the productivity of the manufacturing sector in terms of output per worker is 10.7 times higher in manufacturing than in agriculture, or 2.47/0.23). Moreover, this range of relative sectoral inequality in Brazil has been growing substantially from 1940 to 1970 (i.e., from a differential of 5.2 to one of 10.7). Mexico, on the other hand, not only registers a considerably lower relative differential between the highest and lowest productivity sectors in 1970 (that is, 1.52/0.29, which generates a differential magnitude of only 5.2) but has also experienced a decline in this range of sectoral inequality from 1960 to 1970. Finally, it is curious to note that the service sector records the highest sectoral relative productivity in Mexico, whereas the manufacturing sector stands out in Brazil. Contrary to most LDCs, Mexico has a relatively more capitalized service sector.

In summary, Mexico has succeeded in allocating its labor force more evenly among her major sectors and, as a result, has recorded a far less severe pattern of sectoral inequalities in product per worker, as well as a decline in these inequalities. Brazil, on the other hand, has followed sectoral growth paths that are far more unequal—and growing more so. As we have seen, the crucial factor in this sectoral growth pattern and performance is the relative lack of labor absorption in Brazil's manufacturing sector.

STRUCTURAL DIVERSIFICATION

When one looks at the pattern of structural diversification within industry, it is apparent that both Brazil and Mexico have created extensive backward linkages into the intermediate and capital goods sectors. Table 4 highlights this process over the last two decades and makes it clear that while both countries started from roughly comparable thresholds of industrialization in 1950 the process of backward linkage industrial growth progressed much more extensively in Brazil

Table 4 / *Manufactured Imports as Percentage of Total Domestic Supply for Selected Manufacturing Sectors in Mexico and Brazil, 1950–1969**

	Intermediate Goods			Capital Goods		
	1950	1960	1969	1950	1960	1969
Mexico	24.5	17.3	10.6	55.1	44.3	29.3
Brazil	25.9	11.7	n.a.	63.7	32.9	23.1

Sources: For Mexico: René Villarreal, "External Disequilibrium and Growth Without Development: The Import Substitution Model, The Mexican Experience (1929–1975)," Ph.D. dissertation, Yale University (1976), p. 275. For Brazil: Joel Bergsman, *Brazil: Industrialization and Trade Policies* (New York: Oxford University Press, 1970), p. 92; Pedro S. Malan and Regis Bonelli, "The Brazilian Economy in the Seventies: Old and New Developments," *World Development*, vol. 5, no. 1/2 (January/February 1977), pp. 19–45.

*Based on manufactured imports as a ratio of gross value of production in both countries.

in the 1950s. This is particularly true in the capital goods area, where Brazil's import coefficient was cut in half, while Mexico's declined only slightly. During the 1960s, Mexico experienced a more substantial decline than was present in the 1950s, but it still recorded a greater import coefficient than did Brazil. In brief, Mexico stretched out its ISI process over a longer period of time and substituted less extensively into the capital goods area—findings that are consistent with both the less cyclical pattern and the more labor-absorptive pattern of industrial growth. Still, despite these differences, Mexico and Brazil have both created a more significant and structurally diversified pattern of industrial growth than most other LDCs.

Table 5 underscores the two countries' contrasting patterns of industrial growth in a more disaggregated sectoral fashion. In it one can clearly see the greater degree of industrial growth in the intermediate and capital goods industries in Brazil. In 1949 and 1950, Brazil enjoyed a slight edge in the intermediate goods or process oriented industries (dynamic sectors A), but actually recorded less value added than Mexico in the capital goods area (dynamic sectors B). By 1958 and 1959, however, this had changed sharply, with Brazil having increased its relative share of intermediate goods sectors (and, in particular, capital goods), while Mexico experienced only a modest relative increase in value added in these sectors. This supports Villarreal's findings that Mexico experienced relatively little "import-substitution" industrial growth in the 1950s.[13] By 1970, Mexico had narrowed the gap, but was still substantially below Brazil in the value added that was registered in both these modern sectors (and consequently was

Table 5 / Percentage Distribution of Industrial Value Added for Selected Industrial Sectors in Mexico and Brazil, 1949–1950, 1958–1959, 1969–1970[a]

	1949–50		1958–59		1969–70	
	Mexico	Brazil	Mexico	Brazil	Mexico	Brazil
Traditional sectors	70.9	64.0	66.3	47.3	52.0	40.7
Food, beverages, and tobacco	(36.4)	(26.3)	(39.2)	(20.6)	(29.2)	(17.1)
Textiles	(12.2)	(19.7)	(9.8)	(12.0)	(7.7)	(9.3)
Apparel	(11.3)	(4.3)	(8.7)	(3.6)	(7.5)	(3.3)
Others (furniture, wood and leather products, printing, miscellaneous)	(11.0)	(13.7)	(8.6)	(11.1)	(7.6)	(11.0)
Dynamic sectors A (process industries)	22.7	30.1	25.3	37.7	33.3	38.9
Chemicals	(6.4)	(9.3)	(7.9)	(13.4)	(13.3)	(16.9)
Iron and steel	(6.9)	(9.4)	(9.4)	(11.8)	(10.4)	(11.6)
Others (paper, rubber and nonmetallic minerals)	(9.4)	(11.4)	(8.0)	(12.5)	(9.6)	(10.4)
Dynamic sectors B (equipment and machinery)	6.2	5.9	8.5	15.0	14.6	20.4
Mechanical equipment	(1.4)	(2.1)	(1.8)	(3.4)	(3.0)	(7.0)
Electrical equipment	(2.3)	(1.6)	(3.0)	(4.0)	(5.2)	(5.4)
Transport equipment	(2.5)	(2.2)	(3.7)	(7.6)	(6.4)	(8.0)
Total[b]	99.8	100.0	100.1	100.0	99.9	100.0

Sources: For Mexico: Villarreal, "The Import Substitution Model," p. 282. For Brazil: Censo Industrial 1950 (Rio de Janeiro: Fundação IBGE, 1957); Censo Industrial 1960 (Rio de Janeiro: Fundação IBGE, 1967); Censo Industrial 1970 (Rio de Janeiro: Fundação IBGE, 1974).

[a]Mexican value added percentages derived from constant 1960 pesos. Brazilian value added percentages derived from constant 1970 cruzeiros series.

[b]Totals do not necessarily add up to 100 because percentages have been rounded to the nearest tenth of a percent.

recording a greater share for value added in traditional industries).

In summary, in the postwar period Brazil and Mexico traced out different sequential paths for industrial diversification into the modern sectors of industry. Brazil promoted this earlier, in the heyday of her import substitution policies of the 1950s, while Mexico largely delayed her thrust into backward linkage industrialization until the 1960s. In the end, Brazil moved more extensively into these sectors than Mexico and in the process developed a more capital-intensive and less labor-absorptive process of industrialization and far greater intersectoral inequalities in the economy.

This development raises interesting questions: Why didn't Mexico move further back into the ISI process more quickly? What does this tell us about the strategy of tariff protection for local industry and the cost in efficiency in the two countries? Work on Mexico by Reynolds, King, Bueno, and Villarreal, and on Brazil by Baer, Bergsman, and Fishlow establishes the patterns and policies of protection in the two countries.[14] In summary, the levels of nominal and, more important, effective protection are considerably lower in Mexico than in Brazil. This would imply that backward linkage industrialization would not extend as far in the Mexican case. However, nontariff quantitative controls on imports have been resorted to much more extensively in the Mexican case in more recent years. Villarreal reports that in the late fifties only 25 percent of Mexican imports were subject to these controls. In contrast, by 1970 almost 70 percent of imports were controlled under these rules.[15]

Despite this, the net result in efficiency would appear to support the conclusion that Mexican industrialization policy, while more nationalistic in controlling foreign investment (as we shall see in the next section), was less nationalistic in terms of forced industrial integration, and thus was more efficient. Villarreal, drawing upon the static efficiency measure used by Bergsman in determining "X-inefficiency" in the Brazilian ISI context, concludes that X-inefficiency and monopoly returns together amounted to little more than 2 percent of GDP. In contrast, Bergsman discovered that this cost in the Brazilian context approached 7 percent.[16] In short, Mexican authorities appear to have been more concerned about efficiency in their ISI strategy than Brazilian authorities. In part, the country's proximity to the United States influenced this strategy since industrial contraband would tend to increase if Mexico followed an extreme protectionist policy.

FOREIGN CAPITAL

An associated feature of the patterns of industrial growth in Brazil and Mexico has been their experience with and treatment of foreign investment. Evans and Gereffi treat this theme in extensive detail in this volume; nevertheless, it is appropriate to review several general features here. First, the historical experience of the two countries during the earlier export-led pattern of economic growth was clearly different. Foreign capital swept into Mexico on a massive scale from 1880 to 1910. Furthermore, most of this activity was enclave in nature, came largely from the United States, and focused on extractive operations and the associated transport facilities. Both the scale of this activity and its sectoral focus on extractive industry created a hostile reaction against foreign capital following the revolution. As a result, the inflow of new capital was cut to a trickle from 1910 to 1950.

Brazil, on the other hand, did not experience the same scale of direct foreign investment (DFI) and that which it did experience came not only from the United States but also (and even more) from European countries. In other words, it was more diversified in geographical origin. Furthermore, the direct foreign investment which did enter the country moved more into the manufacturing sector, which was embryonic at that time. In part, this was due to the lack of readily exploitable mines, such as those that were available in Mexico, but it was also due to the natural attraction of foreign investment to the consumption needs of a growing immigrant-fed, urban-industrial growth pole in São Paulo and neighboring areas. In the end, Brazil's experience with direct foreign investment up to 1930 was less massive, less oriented towards enclave activities, of more diverse origins, less threatening, and, as a consequence, produced a far less negative reaction than did the experience in Mexico.

The first postwar experience (from 1955 to 1970) of both countries with foreign investment occurred within their ISI phase. The growth and contribution of DFI towards overall economic growth in Mexico and Brazil at this time was more substantial in amount and more extensive in vertical linkages than that which occurred in other Latin American or Third World countries. This activity also largely occurred within the manufacturing sector, thereby causing a sectoral convergence of the former historical patterns of enclave investment in Mexico and manufacturing investment in Brazil. However, the contrasting geographical origins were still maintained, with European and Japanese investment creating a more diversified source of capital for Brazil, while American investment predominated in Mexico.

Another contrast during the postwar period lies in the two countries' different treatment of foreign investment. The nationalistic heritage of the Mexican Revolution explains Mexico's more explicit attempts to control the role of direct foreign investment in its economy.[17] Foreign capital has generally been required to take on local partners in many activities, and after 1973 all future investments in all sectors have been required to have majority Mexican participation. This restriction has never held in Brazil. In addition, foreign banks and related financial entities are allowed to operate in Brazil but not in Mexico. Comparable data on the changing role of foreign capital in industry are not easy to arrive at. Still, the ISI growth cycle of the fifties was predominantly generated by foreign investment in both countries; however, the comparative advantages given to foreign investors in Brazil, as well as the greater degree of import substitution seen earlier, strongly suggest a relatively greater foreign role in this process in Brazil. Fishlow estimates that well over 30 percent of total industrial growth in Brazil came from import-substitution activity in which foreign investment played an overwhelming role.[18] Comparable figures for Mexico are unavailable.

From 1965 to 1975, direct foreign investment in both countries adjusted successfully to a strategy which emphasized export diversification and the promotion of manufactured exports. However, this movement progressed more rapidly in Brazil, where the subsidy package inducing DFI exports was more extensive. The result of this is that overall and manufactured exports grew more rapidly in Brazil than in Mexico. In addition, the growing concern over the regulation of foreign investment in the Echeverría administration limited the rate of DFI in Mexico.

Table 6 summarizes the growth of total direct foreign investment and foreign debt outstanding in the two countries from 1967 to 1975. The considerably more important role of both foreign investment and foreign debt stands out clearly in the Brazilian context. From 1967 to 1975, foreign investment grew in Brazil at an unusually high average rate of almost 20 percent per year (panel C), while GDP was growing at a little more than 9 percent per year. Thus in the course of the last decade, foreign direct investment doubled its relative role in the Brazilian economy. In contrast, Weinert reports that foreign investment actually declined from 8.6 to 7.7 percent of GDP in Mexico during the same period.[19] Again, in comparative terms, the amount of direct foreign investment in Mexico in 1967 was only 59 percent of the total direct foreign investment in Brazil for the same year. By 1975, Mexico's total had declined sharply to only 28 percent of the Brazilian figure (panel B).

Turning to foreign debt (panel C), the contrast is less sharp, but again there was a more rapid rate of growth of foreign debt in the Brazilian economy from 1967 to 1975 (a 27 percent annual average) than that recorded within the Mexican economy (a 22 percent per year average). Thus, in comparative terms, the total Mexican foreign debt

Table 6 / Selected Measures of Recent Foreign Investment Activity and Foreign Debt Outstanding in Mexico and Brazil, 1967–1975

A. Direct Investment and Debt Outstanding for 1967 and 1975 (in millions of U.S. dollars)

Period	Total Direct Investment (Cumulative as as of 31 Dec.)		Total Foreign Debt Outstanding (Cumulative as of 31 Dec.)	
	Mexico (1)	Brazil (2)	Mexico (3)	Brazil (4)
1967	2,096	3,539	2,176	3,344
1975	4,219	14,811	10,578	22,171

B. Relative Shares of Direct Investment and Foreign Debt, 1969 and 1975

Period	Total Direct Investment Mexico/Brazil (1)	Total Foreign Debt Mexico/Brazil (2)
1967	0.59	0.65
1975	0.28	0.48

C. Average Annual Rates of Growth Between 1967 and 1975

Period	Total Direct Investment		Total Foreign Debt	
	Mexico (1)	Brazil (2)	Mexico (3)	Brazil (4)
1967–1975	9.1%	19.6%	21.8%	26.7%

D. Foreign Debt as Multiple of Direct Foreign Investment

Period	Mexico	Brazil
1967	1.04	0.95
1975	2.51	1.50

Sources: For Brazil: Cumulative stock of direct foreign investment from Malan and Bonelli, "The Brazilian Economy," p. 34; total foreign debt, *ibid.*, p. 38. For Mexico: Cumulative stock of direct foreign investment and total foreign debt from Richard S. Weinert, "The State and Foreign Capital," in José Luis Reyna and Richard S. Weinert (eds.), *Authoritarianism in Mexico* (Philadelphia: Institute for the Study of Human Issues, 1977), p. 123.

outstanding when considered as a percentage of Brazilian debt declined from 65 to 48 percent from 1967 to 1975 (panel B). A final feature of interest that is implicit in these data is that both countries relied more on debt financing than on equity investment during the last decade. This is not surprising, given the rapid growth in the supply of loanable funds in the Eurodollar market from the late sixties onwards. In 1967, the total foreign direct equity investment was roughly equal to the debt financing in both countries (panel D). By 1975, foreign debt had grown to 1.5 times the level of direct investment in Brazil and more than 2.5 times the level of direct foreign investment in Mexico.

This substantial recourse to foreign debt was necessary so that both countries could maintain their rates of economic growth and, at the same time, finance their growing balance of payments deficits, which were so important in servicing this growth. In the case of Mexico, the growing overvaluation of the peso in the 1970s acted as a drag on export earnings and stimulated imports, thus aggravating the merchandise balance of trade deficit. Internally, the deficits in the Mexican development budgets were also covered in part through foreign borrowing, which further added to the external deficit.[20]

In the case of Brazil, despite the rapid growth of exports and partial minidevaluations of the exchange rate, the unusually rapid rates of overall and industrial growth from 1968 to 1974 became highly import intensive with the large-scale importation of capital and intermediate goods to fuel this economic "miracle" at the height of the growth cycle. Later, of course, the emergence of the post-1974 energy crisis and world recession merely aggravated this deficit as a decline in the growth of exports combined with a continuing rise in import costs. In the final analysis, both countries followed a strategy of industrial and economic growth in the 1970s that required substantial foreign debt financing in order to maintain these high levels of economic activity. Without this financing, Brazil and Mexico would have been forced back into a more extensive use of domestic resources. This would have forced policymakers to accept either a lower target rate of growth or, alternatively, a drastic change in the fiscal, financial, exchange, and trade policies in order to mobilize sufficient domestic resources to have serviced the higher desired rates of growth. Given the obvious political demands and costs of the latter strategy, the lower growth scenario would have been more likely in the absence of a convenient supply of Eurodollar funds. Thus the availability of foreign debt financing permitted both countries to achieve higher rates of short-term cyclical growth than they could have achieved otherwise. However, this came at the price not only of ignoring the need to alter policies and institutions to mobilize domestic resources more effectively, but also of saddling future administrations with burdensome foreign-debt service obligations.

Returning now to the direct foreign investment component, the greater relative role of foreign equity financing in Brazil reflects the historically confident and cosmopolitan attitude towards foreign investment that has characterized Brazil throughout her history (except for the momentary period of nationalistic measures in the early 1960s). This stands in sharp contrast to the Mexican experience and that country's concern about the political danger that uncontrolled foreign investment represented to the nationalistic heritage of the revolution. Since 1975, however, this considerable growth of foreign investment in Brazil has finally given rise to growing concern. The process of denationalization in the post-1964 years is seen in data reported by Malan and Bonelli on the rising share of foreign capital in the total stock of capital in manufacturing.[21] In 1965 this share was 19 percent; by 1970 this had risen to 24 percent, and by 1975 to roughly 30 percent of the total capital stock in manufacturing. With this in mind, it is not surprising that some serious questions are being raised about the implications of the growing role of multinational corporations in the present Brazilian growth strategy. Certain recent ad hoc decisions have controlled or, in the end, frozen out foreign capital (as in the computer field) and thus preserved local options. Still, no generalized and explicit set of regulations, such as Mexico's 1973 Foreign Investment Law, has been created, nor is it likely that this will be done in the near future since Brazil usually likes to deal with the situation pragmatically on a case-by-case basis.[22] The degree to which these ad hoc decisions will gradually converge towards the Mexican position on national control and joint participation with local capital remains to be seen.

In summary, foreign capital has played an important role in the economies of both Brazil and Mexico throughout the twentieth century. In the beginning, there was a divergence between the two countries in terms of the sectoral focus and the geographical source of this foreign investment activity. Through time, however, the sectoral contrast disappears as manufacturing becomes the primary focus of foreign investment in both economies, a focus developed much more extensively than in other Third World nations in or out of Latin America. However, differences still remain between the two countries. Brazil's sources of foreign capital are still far more widespread (from European and Japanese as well as U.S. companies) than those in Mexico, where U.S. capital still predominates. Mexico's revolutionary heritage has been translated into more generalized and formal policies controlling foreign investment than are characteristic of Brazil and, as a result, the scope and magnitude of foreign investment is much larger in Brazil. This in large part explains our earlier findings on the two countries, which highlighted the greater relative degree of capital intensity in the Brazilian ISI drive, the lesser degree of labor absorption, the more extensive movement into backward-linkage investment in the capital goods sectors, and the greater degree of intersectoral inequality in output per worker in the Brazilian economy. All these structural and technological features of change and inequality are characteristic of an economy experiencing a substantial inflow of foreign capital and foreign technology.

THE ROLE OF DOMESTIC CAPITALISTS
AND STATE ENTERPRISES IN THE GROWTH PROCESS

The preceding discussion has emphasized the rapid pace of growth and structural change in the economies of Brazil and Mexico and the role of foreign capital in this process. In both countries, an issue of growing controversy throughout the more recent period has been the relative role of domestic entrepreneurs and the state sector in the contemporary growth process. This point is frequently discussed in terms of the "triple alliance" in which state enterprises play the major role in the intermediate goods, primary metals, and infrastructure sectors, while foreign capital dominates the sophisticated consumer durable field as well as some capital goods sectors, and local capitalists are relegated to a minor role, primarily as producers in the traditional, consumer nondurable goods areas where the capital requirements and technology are less demanding. While this is an acceptable rough generalization in both countries, it should also be recognized that local capitalists have made some inroads into the capital goods and intermediate goods areas. However, I would like to argue that within this format local private capital and local capitalists are relatively stronger in the Mexican than in the Brazilian setting. This is due to four factors: (1) a strong tradition of fiscal conservatism in Mexico limiting the expanding role of public expenditures and public investment (an area that will be discussed later); (2) the absence of high inflation and the growth of local capital markets in Mexico; (3) the role of the Mexican state in controlling foreign capital and forcing joint ventures; and (4) the absence of a strong role for the military in the Mexican scene comparable to the statist-oriented military technocracy in Brazil.

Table 7 offers some insight into the relative role of local capitalists among the top 50, 100, and 200 nonfinancial firms in the two countries

Table 7 / Ownership Distribution of Assets of Largest 50, 100, and 200 Nonfinancial Firms by Foreign, Private, and State Ownership in Mexico and Brazil in 1972

Firm Category and Country	Percentage Distribution			
	Foreign	Private	State	Total
Largest 50 firms				
Mexico	20	38	42	100
Brazil	28	16	56	100
Largest 100 firms				
Mexico	33	37	30	100
Brazil	31	23	46	100
Largest 200 firms				
Mexico	34	45	21	100
Brazil	35	33	32	100

Source: Richard Newfarmer and Willard Mueller, *Multinational Corporations in Brazil and Mexico: Structural Sources of Economic and Noneconomic Power,* Report to the Subcommittee on Multinational Corporations of the Committee on Foreign Relations, United States Senate, August 1975, pp. 53 and 106.

Note: Firms in which foreign ownership was greater than 25 percent were classified as foreign, except where the joint venture partner was the state.

in 1972. Among the top 50 firms, the more predominant role of state and foreign enterprises in Brazil stands out, as does the greater relative strength of local private firms in Mexico. This relative strength for Mexican capitalists and relative weakness for Brazilian entrepreneurs is seen throughout for the top 100 and top 200 firms. In contrast, state enterprises are, in relative terms, much more important in Brazil. At first glance it would appear that, except for the top 50 firms, foreign firms play a roughly equal role in both countries. However, this is misleading since private (i.e., nonstate) firms with as little as 26 percent foreign ownership participation were considered foreign. Joint ventures are much more widespread in Mexico as a result of the "Mexicanization" regulations, whereas in Brazil the wholly owned subsidiary or substantial majority foreign control is more common. Therefore, the data in Table 7 clearly overestimate the relative role of foreign firms (and underestimate the presence of private capitalists) in the Mexican case in comparison to the Brazilian case. The conclusions are clear: foreign and state enterprises predominate in Brazil and private firms, relatively speaking, play a much more striking role in the growth process in Mexico.

Among the various factors tending to promote a greater role for the private sector in Mexico is the relative absence of inflation. Table 8 sets forth the contrasting patterns of inflation in the two countries. From 1950 to 1970, Brazil has recorded substantially higher levels of

Table 8 / Rates of Inflation in Mexico and Brazil,
1950–1977

Mexico		Brazil	
Period	Rate of Inflation	Period	Rate of Inflation
1950–60	6.4	1950–60	18
1960–65	2.0	1960–65	60
1965–70	2.8	1966–70	28
1970–75	11.9	1970–73	18
1976	15.8	1975	29
1977	29.1	1976	45
1978	17.4	1977	39
		1978	41

Sources: For Mexico: Reynolds, "Mexico's 'Stabilizing Development,'"
p. 1006, and Banco de México, *Informe Anual* (1978), for 1976–78 data.
For Brazil: *Conjuntura Economica*, various issues.

inflation than Mexico. Even in the more inflation-prone decade of the
seventies, Mexico's recent experience with double-digit inflation was
still considerably below Brazil's. Furthermore, the decline in Mexico's
inflation in 1978 stands out in contrast to Brazil's inability to lower her
inflation rate below 40 percent per year, with a growing tendency for
this to rise even further in 1979.

Persistent inflation and distortions in the economy invariably
weaken the private sector and strengthen the public sector. Private
savings dry up in an environment of negative real rates of interest,
which invariably emerge in an economy unindexed for price rises.
Individuals hold a minimum of financial assets and shift over into land,
urban real estate, and other inflationary hedges. The relative decline
in private voluntary savings compromises the growth of money and
capital markets and limits the resources for private sector industrial
growth to retained earnings. In the meantime, the public sector can
draw upon fiscal resources or development bank funds, which characteristically favor public investments over private ventures. For example, during the "inflationary" era from the 1950s to the mid-1960s over
80 percent of Brazil's National Development Bank (BNDE) funds
went into public sector projects.[23] The net result of this process is that
public sector investment activity tends to grow at a faster rate than
private sector investment, which is starved for medium- to long-term
funds.

The rapid growth of the public sector in Brazil from the early
1950s through the early 1960s clearly reflects the weakening of the
local capitalist sector in this kind of inflationary scenario. Mexico, on
the other hand, did not experience rising rates of inflation during this

period. As a result, in comparison to Brazil, local Mexican money and capital markets and private savings grew substantially through the emergence of a positive real rate of interest environment in which nominal rates of interest were higher than the rate of inflation.[24] In the end, the private sector in Mexico was less penalized and in a position to progress more satisfactorily than was the private sector in the inflationary financial environment of Brazil.

Another factor promoting the greater relative growth of the private industrial sector in Mexico was the government policy to control foreign investment and, more important, force Mexicanization upon many of these foreign investors. On the one hand, these policies controlled the degree of penetration of foreign capital and, on the other, created profitable outlets for domestic capital through joint ventures. In short, the fruits of foreign capital growth and expansion in the Mexican economy were, at least in part, returned to Mexican hands. In Brazil, the joint venture experience was until very recently neither required nor encouraged. As a consequence, direct foreign investment had much more freedom to compete against and acquire local concerns without being concerned with sectoral prohibitions or required joint participation with domestic entrepreneurs. In the end, local capitalists faced more open and unrestrained competition.

A final factor of importance which did not exist in Mexico that inadvertently cut into the growth and expansion of a domestic capitalist sector in Brazil was the role of the military in promoting and managing a large number of state enterprises. The Brazilian military has played a crucial role in developing the National Steel Company, Petrobrás, the National Electric Supply Company, Electrobrás, and other state enterprises. The doctrine of national security grew to include industrialization in certain key heavy industries as well as certain sensitive infrastructure and natural resource areas. Clearly, from the late 1930s onward the state was better equipped than the private sector to play this role quickly and on a large scale, considering not only the heavy demands on capital and technology that were involved but also the desire to limit the role of foreign investment in some areas, especially oil explorations.[25]

The net result of this effort was that the creation and management of state enterprises in Brazil was not strongly associated with a civilian socialist ideology or political movement. As a consequence, following the post-1964 military coup, which had a strong antisocialist and pro-free-enterprise tone, there was no move to curb the growth of public enterprises in Brazil.[26] This stands out in stark contrast to the behavior of the conservative military regime in Chile which, after 1973, began dismantling many of the state enterprises that had been established during previous administrations within a more civilian socialist-statist political ideology. Indeed, if anything, the period from 1967 to 1974 saw a resurgence of state enterprise activity in Brazil. Many of these enterprises were allowed to raise their prices and become more self-financing in order to cut down on the inflationary impact of covering their deficits through the general government budget. At the same time some entities, such as the Companhia de Vale do Rio Doce mining complex, moved into conglomerate activities that had previously been served by the private sector. The increased autonomy through the leverage of greater self-financing, as well as the need for state activity in the recession of the mid-1960s in order to promote economic recovery, contributed to the continuing growth of state enterprises in Brazil during this period. What is of significance here is that these enterprises have acquired an institutional legitimacy regardless of the nature of the regime in which they operate and an internal dynamic of their own in the growth process in Brazil.[27]

In summary, state or public enterprise growth has been pronounced in both Mexico and Brazil, as one would expect in relatively large nation states undergoing late or delayed capitalist development in the mid-twentieth century. Still, as in the case of their private sector development, some interesting differences emerge. Public firms in Brazil are more independent and autonomous than their counterparts in Mexico. Reflecting this pattern, the goal of economic expansion (or internal capital accumulation) is more explicitly stated and followed. In short, the performance criteria emphasize economic rather than political goals.

The pattern of recruiting is also different. A stronger permanent career pattern is evident in the Brazilian scene, with an internalized managerial ethic and promotion ladder reflecting the profit or capital accumulation goals of many important firms. In Mexico, the existence of a strong institutionalized revolutionary political party cuts into the degree of autonomy that can be enjoyed by public enterprises. Political patronage and substantial personnel turnover occur with each *sexenio* change of administration, thereby creating less of an entrenched managerial bureaucracy within these institutions. At the same time, Mexican state firms are held to a greater degree of political accountability and must offer their services at low or subsidized rates or prices. Moreover, the conflict between ministerial bureaucrats on the one hand and state enterprise managers on the other appears to be much less apparent than it is in the Brazilian context.

Finally, it is curious to note the difference between the two countries in the private sector reaction to the role of the state in the economy in the mid-seventies. In Mexico this was galvanized into an open attack on President Echeverría's administration, which had begun to emphasize greater taxation of the private sector, greater public services for the poor, and a stronger general commitment to redress the inequalities created in the earlier *desarrollo establizador* period. In the end, much of this reform effort was either undermined or watered down and President Echeverría's political power was substantially compromised by the offensive launched by the private sector.[28]

In Brazil the "statization" debate which reemerged in the post-1974 economic slowdown was, in contrast, much more defensive in nature. Private sector organs made much of the unfair advantages that state firms enjoyed vis-à-vis the private sector, and announced the impossibility of creating a strong, healthy, competitive private sector in the Brazilian economy in the face of the overwhelming predominance of the state in the economy.[29] Exaggerations were common on both sides of the debate; nevertheless, the government in the end did alter some tax regulations, changed some capital market and stock market procedures, and revised some State Development Bank loan practices in an attempt to redress a few of the more obvious discriminatory advantages that public firms had enjoyed. However, in no way could either the criticisms or the concessions be compared to the private sector offensive that had been launched in Mexico. The Brazilian private sector critics were weaker, more defensive in their posture, and never went beyond the specifics of their complaints. The Brazilian government, on the other hand, had no problem in creating certain limited concessions which, in any event, did not seriously compromise the role or strength of the public sector enterprises in the economy; they were, in essence, the sort of concessions that general anti-inflationary or balance of payments stabilization strategies would require. In short, the private sector in Mexico is, relatively speaking, a stronger participant in the development process than it is in Brazil, while the state sector (though clearly important in both economies) would appear to be relatively stronger and more autonomous in the Brazilian setting.

THE AGRICULTURAL SECTOR: OUTPUT, PRODUCTIVITY, AND WELFARE

Another sharp contrast between Brazil and Mexico lies in their agricultural sectors. In brief, Mexico suffers from a much smaller agricultural resource base than Brazil. This has been one of Mexico's historical structural weaknesses and, as a result, a constant source of tension and social unrest. There has never been a "frontier escape value" available to Mexico. The country has been forced to face the necessity of land reform at various stages in her modern history, as well as the need for substantial investment in productivity-enhancing initiatives such as the new seed varieties developed at CIMMYT (The International Corn and Wheat Improvement Center). The events leading to the 1910 revolution, the political and institutional reforms of the Cárdenas period, and the more recent social crises during Echeverría's administration are all closely linked to the issue of agricultural reform.

Brazil, on the other hand, has enjoyed the comparative luxury of an expanding agricultural frontier. This proved decisive in allowing the country to engage in a successful agriculturally based export growth cycle at the end of the last century. This frontier facilitated the incorporation of millions of European immigrants who were to generate substantial externalities for later industrial growth. In more recent times, the new frontier in Goías, Paraná, and Mato Grosso has provided the outlet for massive waves of internal migration from rural areas of the impoverished Northeast that otherwise would have overwhelmed the urban settings in the central and southern areas of the country.[30] Finally, substantial foreign exchange earnings from the agricultural frontier have provided the capital for ISI initiatives and, up to the early 1970s, increased output in this sector has supplied foodstuffs for the urban population at a reasonable cost, thus allowing Brazil to avoid the agricultural "stagnationist" trap common to other Latin American countries such as Chile. Furthermore, all this has been accomplished without any meaningful attempts at land reform or, for that matter, any substantial investment in improving either agricultural productivity or the human capital of the rural labor force. In the face of relatively abundant and reasonably fertile land (in comparison to Mexico), Brazil could expand her output at the margin (i.e., moving onto new lands) without being concerned with the problem of achieving higher yields per hectare on older lands or less fertile new lands. Only recently have advances been made in increasing productivity, but these have been associated with increased output per man (mechanization) rather than increased output per hectare through better seed varieties and related "green revolution" innovations.

Several interesting contrasts emerge in the comparative data on agricultural output for the two countries, as set forth in Table 9. First,

Table 9 / Rates of Growth of Agricultural Output for Selected Periods in Mexico and Brazil

Country	1940–50	1950–60	1960–65	1965–70	1970–74
Mexico	8.2	4.3	4.6	2.7	1.7
Brazil	n.a.	4.5	6.2	4.7	6.5

Sources: Reynolds, "Mexico's 'Stabilizing Development,' " p. 1006; *Conjuntura Economica,* various issues.

in the decade of the 1940s Mexico achieved unusually high levels of agricultural output. This followed the reform measures of the thirties and was accompanied by substantial investment in roads and irrigation to promote commercialization in the unreformed or private sector. This pattern of dealing with the issues of reform and modernization in agriculture before or simultaneous with the emphasis on import-substitution industrialization stands out in contrast to the pattern in Brazil, which placed industry first after 1940.

The second feature seen in Table 9 is the steady decline in agricultural output in Mexico from 1950 to the present, which is clear and alarming. At the same time there was a marked leveling off in productivity yields in the 1960s, following the rises in corn and wheat yields in the 1950s. This decline in both output and productivity clearly represents a danger in the Mexican context, especially in the light of a high rate of population growth (3.3 percent). Several consequences have resulted from this turn of events: increased illegal migration to the United States, increased food imports in the 1970s, and increased social unrest in the countryside.

Third, the comparative profile in Table 9 shows that Brazil, in contrast to Mexico, has maintained and even increased its agricultural output up to the mid-1970s. Associated with this performance has been a diversification and increased productivity in several export lines of activity. In brief, the agricultural sector is experiencing a second-generation technological bottleneck in the Mexican setting which will require another investment of both public resources and political commitment for continuing modernization, research, and social reforms. A danger here is a tendency to sit back and let the newly found oil discoveries finance food imports and thus postpone a determined drive to deal with the problems in the agricultural sector. In Brazil, there are greater potential productivity gains available in this sector than for Mexico, and at less cost, since for all practical purposes Brazil still has "easier" productivity paths to follow. This is due to the fact that Brazil has not engaged substantially in many of the first-generation innovations to improve seed and land productivity, as has Mexico. What is needed here is the inducement (or crisis) that will force this determined policy action.

This inducement may be coming sooner than was originally thought likely in that domestic foodcrops in Brazil have suffered output and productivity declines in the 1970s, a fact that is hidden in the otherwise respectable aggregate data on agricultural output.[31] This has in large part grown out of the overwhelming emphasis Brazil has placed on agricultural exports to contribute to the foreign exchange earnings needed to continue her import-intensive industrial capital formation (from 1968 to 1974) and make up for her growing energy deficit through expensive oil imports (from 1974 to the present). The net result of this policy emphasis has been a decline in acreage for domestic crops and a rise in acreage for export crops. At the same time, subsidized credit and other policy initiatives have artificially increased the relative profitability of export over domestic market crops. By the late 1970s, Brazil began importing beans, corn, rice, and other food-stuffs at uncomfortably high levels, and the foodstuff component of the domestic cost of living index has been rising more rapidly than other elements in the market basket index.

A final feature of importance in the rural setting of both Brazil and Mexico is the similar pattern of increasing proletarianization of the rural peasantry in the face of growing agricultural moderniza-tion.[32] In the case of Mexico, this process was arrested during the height of the land reform initiatives in the 1930s. However, in the following decades, the push for rapid commercialization of the "un-reformed" sector with substantial government credit and investment in roads, irrigation, and so forth, combined with a slowdown in fur-ther land redistribution and a striking public sector neglect of the reformed *ejido* areas, created the basis for growing rural poverty. In time, continued redivision of *ejido* family plots under population pres-sure made it impossible for most *ejido* families to maintain an adequate subsistence livelihood. The result was a rise in rural poverty, rapid growth in *ejido* family labor migration as seasonal wage labor to spo-radic employment on commercial farms, land invasions, and a rise in "illegal" migration to the United States.

In Brazil, there was no comparable land reform initiative to tem-porarily improve the welfare of the rural peasantry. Nevertheless, there was an agricultural frontier escape valve that made up for this institutional inertia. Large rural migrations into the frontier areas of Paraná, Goías, and Mato Grosso in the 1940s, 1950s, and 1960s eased the incidence of rural poverty in the East and the Northeast. Various forms of homesteading, tenancy, sharecropping, and squatting in these new areas created subsistence and market outlets for many poorer segments of the rural population that would have been difficult or impossible to achieve in the older areas.

By the late 1960s, however, the balance had begun to shift so that today resident tenant or sharecropping farmers are declining in most areas of the central South (including frontier areas such as Paraná and Goías) and temporary daily wage labor from nonresident workers (i.e., the *"bóia-fria* syndrome") is the most rapidly growing element of the agricultural labor force. The major factors that have contributed to this development include increased emphasis on labor-displacing export crops such as soybeans or import-substituting crops such as wheat, both of which are highly mechanized operations; cheap agricultural credit (i.e., loans with high negative real rates of interest), which promotes mechanization and land consolidation; the relative decline of labor-absorbing crops such as coffee; and the growth of minimum wage and social security legislation for resident rural workers in São Paulo and other southern states. This latter initiative merely induced landowners to push resident tenants off their properties and hire temporary or daily wage laborers who are excluded from these benefits. The net result of this process has been a decline in the living standards of the former tenants, a decline in the production of domestic foodcrops which the former tenants typically grew and marketed, and a worsening of the distribution of income.[33]

In summary, while the performance of the agricultural sector in Brazil has been more promising than that in Mexico, danger signs are apparent and policy actions are required to redress the current decline in foodstuff output. In addition, social equity requires some initiative to arrest the growing use of nonresident rural labor. Both countries face challenging tasks in reforming and modernizing their agricultural sectors and making some progress towards alleviating the incidence of rural poverty in their societies. Brazil clearly has a more promising natural advantage in this area and less volatile rural social pressure than Mexico, which has no frontier outlets except through migration to the United States. Unfortunately, recent policy initiatives in Brazil emphasizing export crops and subsidized credit for larger farms have compromised domestic foodstuff production and small farm growth and have displaced an inordinate number of resident tenants. Greater concern for improving the human capital of the rural labor force, greater possibilities for small-to-medium farm size growth, and greater emphasis on technological packages to increase the productivity of domestic foodcrops on small farms are called for in both countries before their agricultural sectors can contribute substantially to alleviating rural poverty, redressing the process of income concentration, and removing a potential cost bottleneck to future economic growth.

THE FINANCING OF DEVELOPMENT

Another area of contrast between Brazil and Mexico centers around the strategy for financing post-1950 ISI development, which in turn is associated with the two countries' contrasting experiences with inflation (as summarized in Table 8). Whereas Mexico was able to control its inflation throughout most of this period, Brazil clearly did not. Throughout the 1950s, Brazil's rate of inflation averaged three times higher than Mexico's, and the early and mid-sixties saw remarkably high rates of inflation in Brazil when Mexico was enjoying price stability. Even in the early to mid-seventies, under an authoritarian regime, Brazilian inflation remained substantially above the price increases in Mexico.

Political factors and the institutional base for regime legitimacy and regime maintenance are important here. Mexico had sufficiently established its revolutionary institutional legitimacy that it could engage in the process of capital accumulation without resorting to the politically induced "fix" of inflationary injections to cover its development costs. This was accomplished in two ways: (1) limiting the populist political demands for increased public spending activity and, as a result, holding back government expenditures and; (2) creating conditions for a local private capital market to mobilize and channel private and foreign savings for economic expansion. Brazilian institutions were not so favorably structured. The government could not permit increased political participation in the country's embryonic populist politics during the fifties and sixties and, at the same time, extract the surplus from society needed to cover its development costs. The lack of a strong, disciplined, legitimate base to the imperfectly tested democratic institutions of the postwar period meant that Brazil could not limit the political demands for increased spending beyond her tax and borrowing resources.[34] Indeed, the inflationary increase in public spending and credit expansion was deliberately utilized to create this legitimacy in the populist *desenvolvimentista* period from 1950 to 1964. Both regimes engaged in deficit financing, but Mexico covered her deficits through noninflationary borrowing from local and foreign capital markets. Brazil, on the other hand, could not develop a capital market or stimulate domestic voluntary savings in an inflationary setting. Therefore, she resorted to increasing the money supply to cover these deficits through inflationary financing from the Central Bank.

Several interesting consequences emerged from this pattern. First, it was impossible to develop local voluntary private savings or a supportive domestic financial sector in Brazil prior to the mid-1960s. In contrast, in the Mexican setting the private financial sector became a viable institution to channel savings into development. For example, liabilities of the Mexican banking system (private savings and inflows of financial capital from abroad) in the 1960s were growing at a rate of around 18 percent per year, far faster than the GNP, and in the process expanding the capacity for medium- to long-term financing.[35] Second, with no private capital markets most development financing in Brazil was dominated by foreign or government investment. This had a negative impact on credit available to the private sector. From 1953 to 1963, Syvrud reports that credit to the federal government in Brazil increased by a multiple of nine while credit to the private sector increased only 20 percent. Federal government credit (as a percent of GNP) increased from only 2.2 percent in 1953 to 10.5 percent in 1963. Credit to the private sector declined from 25 percent of GNP to 17 percent during this period.[36] This relative decline of private credit was not a feature of the Mexican growth pattern.

Third, the process of capital accumulation fell much more to the public sector in Brazil than in Mexico. It has been estimated that by the early 1960s well over half of the gross fixed capital formation in Brazil was associated with the public sector. Moreover, as can be seen in Table 10, this percentage has been on the increase. In Mexico, on the other hand, public sector gross fixed capital formation, which was as high as 52 percent of the total in the period from 1940 to 1946, had declined to 30 percent in the period from 1963 to 1967. It was this relative decline of public capital formation in Mexico during the 1960s that gave rise to much criticism of the *desarrollo estabilizador* strategy. This criticism emphasized the importance of the public sector and the need to correct the growing social deficit implicit in the existing development process.[37]

These contrasts clearly highlight the more developed role of statization in the Brazilian economy in the 1950s and 1960s and the relatively more important role for the private sector in Mexico. Chronic inflation, deficit financing through inflationary means, and the lack of a strong private sector financial market contributed heavily towards

Table 10 / Public Sector Share in Gross Fixed Capital Formation for Mexico and Brazil, 1940–1969

Mexico		Brazil	
Period	Percentage	Period	Percentage
1940–46	52	1947	16
1954–60	26	1956	28
1963–67	30	1960	50
		1969	60

Sources: Roger D. Hansen, *Mexican Economic Development: The Roots of Rapid Growth* (Washington, D.C.: National Planning Association, 1971), p. 43; Werner Baer, *Industrialization and Economic Development in Brazil* (Homewood, Ill.: Irwin Press, 1965), p. 84; *Conjuntura Economica*, vol. 25, no. 9 (1971).

Table 11 / Government Taxes and Expenditures as a Percentage of Gross Domestic Product in Mexico and Brazil, 1947–1977

	Mexico				Brazil		
Period	Taxes/GDP	Period	Exp/GDP	Period	Taxes/GDP	Period	Exp/GDP
1949–51	10.8	1950	9.4	1947	15.0	1947	17
1959–61	10.6	1960	10.4	1955	17.0	1955	20
1969–71	13.6	1970	12.7	1960	23.0	1960	26
1975–77	16.0	1976	18.7	1963	20.0	1963	27
				1970–73	26.0	1968	25
				1974	28.0		

Sources: For Mexico: Arthur J. Mann, "The Evolution of Mexico's Public Revenue Structure, 1877–1977," *Bulletin for International Fiscal Documentation*, Amsterdam, Holland, vol. 32 (July 1978), pp. 297–300. For Brazil: Bergsman, *Brazil*, p. 57; Inter American Development Bank, *Economic and Social Progress for Latin America: 1976 Report* (Washington, D.C.), p. 68; Fernando A. Rezende da Silva, *Avaliação do sector publico na economia brasileira* (Rio de Janeiro: Relatório de Pesquisa 13, IPEA /INPES, 1972).

Note: Taxes include all levels of government, decentralized agencies (for nontax revenue), and social security contributions. Expenditures include all levels of government, current expenses, and public investment.

this increased role for the state in Brazil, just as the opposite pattern strengthened the private sector in Mexico.

Fiscal policy, as set forth in Table 11, is another area of contrast in the pattern of financing development in Brazil and Mexico. Focusing on the more recent time period, we can see the much higher Tax/GDP and Expenditure/GDP ratios in Brazil, more than double the rates in Mexico for most of this period. This is another illustration of the fiscal conservatism of the Mexican government and the tendency in that country to finance deficits through private financial borrowing. This conservatism, limiting government taxation and public expenditures, was a crucial factor limiting public sector economic expansion to less than that recorded in Brazil and, in the end, promoting the relative growth of private sector activity. Despite the legitimacy and stability of the Mexican regime, it is curious to note that the state is apparently not strong enough to raise its tax base to finance a larger role for government investment. When it attempted this during Echeverría's administration, private sector resistance was strong enough to compromise the effort. The Brazilian state, on the other hand, did not experience any comparable resistance against its successful effort to raise taxes substantially through the sixties and early seventies. In this sense, the more exclusionary military authoritarian regime in post-1964 Brazil has shown itself to have considerably more political power over the private sector than the aging but still more inclusionary revolutionary authoritarian coalition in Mexico.

Mexico, in not raising its tax base, is also restricted in the degree to which it can expand its public expenditures. This exacerbates the social deficit—i.e., makes it more difficult to correct for inequities and poverty. Borrowing from the financial sector is possible but it has its limits, particularly in the inflationary setting of the mid-seventies. Since the Mexican economy, in contrast to Brazil's, is not indexed for inflation, policymakers in normal circumstances would either have to reduce inflation or be forced to more frequent use of the fiscal tool of taxation as private financial savings decline. However, the recent oil bonanza will very likely create sufficient revenue to relax this fiscal constraint. Unfortunately, in acting as a fiscal substitute, oil revenues may postpone any initiative for the vital fiscal reforms that Mexico needs to truly become a modernized nation state.

INCOME DISTRIBUTION AND POPULATION GROWTH

Two final areas of comparative interest that merit discussion are income distribution and the recent patterns of population growth. Table 12 sets forth the comparative data on income distribution for the two

Table 12 / Relative Income Shares for Selected Population Groups for Selected Years in Mexico and Brazil, 1950–1968 (percentage of total income)

Population Group	Mexico[a]			Brazil[b]	
	1950	1963	1968	1960	1970
Richest 5 percent	39.8	28.7	27.9	27.7	34.9
Next richest 5 percent	9.2	12.8	14.2	12.0	12.9
Next richest 10 percent (i.e., the 9th decile)	10.8	17.5	16.2	14.7	14.5
Next richest 10 percent (i.e., the 8th decile)	8.6	11.8	11.3	10.9	9.6
Next richest 10 percent (i.e., the 7th decile)	7.0	8.0	8.3	9.4	7.4
Poorest 30 percent	10.0	6.5	6.5	6.9	6.1

Sources: For Brazil: Carlos Langoni, *Distribuicão da renda e desenvolvimento econômico do Brasil* (Rio de Janeiro: Editora Expressão e Cultura, 1973), p. 64. For Mexico: Hansen, *Mexican Economic Development,* pp. 73–74; *Encuesta sobre ingresos y gastos familiares en México,* 1963, 1968.
[a]Disposable family income reported in household surveys.
[b]Individual income of employed individuals reported in censuses.

countries, both of which are highly unequal societies. Still, several interesting contrasts are apparent. First, at least up until 1968, the richest 5 percent in Mexico have been experiencing a relative decline in their share of total income whereas the opposite has been the case in Brazil. Second, the next richest 5 percent has gained considerably in Mexico whereas this group has experienced no significant change in Brazil. If we combine the seventh, eight and ninth deciles with the second richest 5 percent to approximate a middle-class income spread in both countries in the period from 1968 to 1970, we discover that this group receives 50 percent of total income in Mexico and only 44 percent in Brazil, while the richest 5 percent in both societies have secured 28 and 35 percent respectively. Finally, it is clear that the poorest 30 percent in relative terms are equally poor in both countries, with this process of growing relative deprivation standing out in Mexico from 1950 onwards.

In summary, this set of contrasting profiles of income inequality is not surprising, given what we know about the political economy of growth in both countries in recent decades. It is quite likely that comparable measures would have shown much less inequality in Mexico in 1940, reflecting the impact of the institutional reforms and asset redistribution of the Cárdenas years. However, economic growth since 1940 has clearly been more unequalizing in its design and impact than that in the 1930s. This is in effect the statistical reflection of the "freezing" of the revolution or, if you will, the shift from a working class and peasant focus to a middle class emphasis in the post-1940 thrust of the neocapitalist growth strategy.

Still, the very rich have paid their price in Mexico. In sharp contrast to Brazil, where even a middle class revolution has yet to occur in these terms, the rich in Mexico have lost some of their wealth and income status to the growing deciles of the middle class. In Brazil, the middle class deciles from 1960 to 1970 actually lost in relative terms to the very rich. Up to 1970, there was a much greater tolerance for inequality in Brazil and less pressure for social reforms or policies promoting income redistribution not only for the benefit of the very poor but even for the benefit of most elements comprising the middle class.

Clearly, the unusually high rates of economic growth in Brazil from 1968 to 1974 did much to mitigate some of the more serious negative repercussions of the concentration of wealth and defuse the potential for political tension. This was accomplished through reducing the levels of unemployment, maintaining real levels of absolute income for the middle class (and very likely raising them), and generating substantial occupational and some social mobility through the social pyramid encompassing these income deciles. However, following the downward shift in economic growth since 1974, this partial legitimizing process of growth and mobility was compromised, and the possibilities of economic improvement for many sectors of the population were reduced. Thus, it is not surprising to see the pressures growing for political relaxation in Brazil and a gradual opening up of the system. The degree to which this political opening up translates into an economic opening up to incorporate more income-equalizing policies (or at least fewer income-concentrating measures) remains to be seen. The prognosis is not promising, given the reduced prospects for economic expansion in the 1980s.

A related area of concern in both Brazil and Mexico is the rate of population and labor force growth. Table 13 shows some revealing demographic contrasts between the two countries. The crude birth rate and the total fertility rate are substantially higher in Mexico and growing more so in the recent decade. This fact, combined with the more rapidly declining crude death rate, creates a significantly higher annual rate of natural increase in Mexico as compared to Brazil (3.6 vs. 2.7 percent).

The truly striking statistic is the contrasting behavior in the growth of the labor force in the two countries (panel 6). Preliminary but unofficial findings for Brazil suggest that the rate of growth in the labor force in the early 1970s is around 2.0 percent per year, whereas

Table 13 / Selected Demographic Measures for Mexico and Brazil,
1950–1970

Measure and Country	1950	1960	1970
Annual total fertility rate			
Mexico	n.a.	6.45	6.54
Brazil	n.a.	6.30[a]	5.80[a]
Annual crude birth rate			
Mexico	46.3	44.9	43.0
Brazil	44.4	43.3	37–40
Annual crude death rate			
Mexico	16.2	11.2	10.0
Brazil	20.0	14.2	13.0
Annual rate of natural increase			
Mexico	3.01	3.37	3.3
Brazil	2.34	2.91	2.40–2.70
Annual rate of total population growth			
Mexico	3.1	3.4	3.3 (1970–75)
Brazil	3.0	2.8	2.5 (1970–80)[c]
Annual rate of labor force growth			
Mexico	2.0	2.7	3.7
Brazil	2.9	2.3	2.0[b]

Sources: For Brazil: Merrick and Graham, *Population and Economic Development in Brazil,* chapter 3. For Mexico: U.S. Department of Commerce, Bureau of the Census, *Country Demographic Profiles—Mexico* (Washington, D.C.: Government Printing Office, 1969), pp. 6 and 9.
[a]These are interdecade estimates.
[b]Preliminary estimate.
[c]1970–1980 rate of population growth for Brazil from *Sinopse preliminar do censo demografico, IX, Recenseamento general do Brasil 1980,* vol. 1, tomo 1, no. 1 (Rio de Janeiro: Fundacão IBGE, 1980), p. xxix.

the comparable statistic for Mexico is 3.7 percent per year, almost double Brazil's rate. Moreover, as can be seen in Table 13, Brazil's labor force growth has been declining from the 1950s to the present in response to the decline in both its birth rate and its rate of total population growth. In contrast, Mexico's labor force growth has been rising, reflecting the consistent rise in her rates of natural increase and total population growth throughout the postwar period. Thus, in contrast to Brazil, Mexico's labor force has a large built-in momentum for rapid growth in the future.

What these results show is that the demographic transition of declining fertility following the decline in death rates had only barely begun in Mexico by 1970. In contrast, this process has begun in Brazil in recent years, though the experience has not been as strong as that seen in the developed countries in the past century. The unusual pattern in Mexico has given rise to a growing literature on the effect of economic development on the country's fertility behavior.[38] Contrary to conventional wisdom, the growing "modernization" of the Mexican economy—i.e., the rise in literacy, income, and industrial growth; increased female participation in the nonagricultural sector; urbanization; and so forth—has not been reflected in a change in age at marriage, family size, and fertility patterns, as has been the case in Brazil. The major negative economic consequence of such a demographic pattern in Mexico is the difficulty of absorbing this growing labor supply into the economy. This, in turn, leads to increasing underemployment and poverty, increased illegal migrations into the United States, and a worsening of the profile of relative income distribution for the poorest 30 to 40 percent of the population. Members of this group are both the primary high fertility participants and the primary victims of the economic consequences of un- or underemployment. This problem has alerted Mexican authorities to the dangerous implications of failure to control population growth. As a result, in the 1970s President Echeverría changed Mexico's traditional pronatalist population policy into a neutral stance, and in more recent years the government has assumed a more active position in promoting family planning.

Up to the early 1970s, both Brazil and Mexico had been following a laissez-faire policy in income distribution (i.e., not directly intervening in the economy in any substantial way to alter the unequalizing impact of natural market forces) and in population policy (i.e., not intervening to control population growth). Clearly this double laissez-faire strategy reinforced the dynamics of poverty—the average sizes of families among the poor became larger at the same time that social services and income and employment opportunities declined for this very group. Recognition of the potential danger in these policies is more widespread in both countries now than it was at the beginning of the decade; however, it is clear that in the Mexican case the built-in dynamics of the country's demographic behavior are a critical factor which will limit Mexico's ability to achieve a more modern and equitable society for some time to come.

Future Prospects

Forecasting economic growth scenarios for Mexico and Brazil can be a hazardous exercise. Proof of this can be seen in the two comparative reversals that have occurred in the last fifteen years. Looking back to the early sixties, most observers would have predicted that Mexico had found the right formula for rapid growth, minimal inflation, and social peace. Brazil, on the other hand, was stumbling along with little or no growth, rampant inflation, and political and social unrest. Clearly, Mexico was in the better position.

However, ten years later, in 1973, the roles had reversed. Now Brazil was in the driver's seat, with one of the highest rates of growth in the world (double Mexico's rate), controlled inflation, and apparent social and political stability. Brazil was clearly destined to be a member of the club of developed nations, an emerging world power finally realizing her *grandeza*. On the other hand, Mexico was experiencing a decline in growth and rising inflation, as well as growing external disequilibria and rising social unrest in an uncharacteristically politicized environment. Nevertheless, by 1978, if we have not had another reversal, we have at least clearly eliminated the differential that existed in 1973. The decline in world economic growth and world trade, combined with the new high cost of energy, has severely compromised the earlier Brazilian economic "miracle." Further, the oil discoveries in Mexico have apparently given that country a decided edge over Brazil in exploiting a growth potential in an energy-scarce world.

Politically, it would also appear that Mexico, under López Portillo, has laid to rest the destabilizing elements that characterized the mid-seventies. The political legitimacy of the PRI coalition has been restored, inflation has been substantially lowered, the balance of payments deficit has been brought under control, and economic growth has risen to respectable levels. Brazil, on the other hand, is currently traveling through uncharted political waters with considerable uncertainty about the proper institutional base for political rule in the 1980s. The unattractive economic prospects for expanding Brazilian trade in the late seventies and early eighties, the high and rising rate of inflation, and the continuing dependence on high cost petroleum have produced an uncharacteristically low to modest growth profile that could further destabilize the political environment. Hence the potential exists for another comparative reversal in the early 1980s.

It is useful at this juncture to review the major economic issues that will condition this future growth path in both countries. In the case of Brazil, both economic growth and economic policy space (i.e., room for maneuver) have been reduced considerably in recent years. The economic base for growth from 1968 to 1973 was highly dependent on a continuing rapid rate of growth among the developed economies of the world and the unusually high rates of growth of world trade that emerged from this process. Brazilian manufactured exports, which grew at an average annual rate of over 50 percent per year from 1968 to 1973 (in contrast to Mexico's 37 percent), are highly dependent upon rapidly growing economies elsewhere. These prospects for overseas sales are not as promising in the future. Furthermore, rising protectionist sentiment can and very likely will reduce the growth in exports to developed economies such as the United States. Overall, export earnings have declined from a rate of growth of almost 20 percent per year in the earlier period (1968–73) to little more than five percent per year from 1974 to 1977.

The economic miracle in Brazil was also highly dependent on cheap energy, and there is no comparable low-cost source of energy for the future. In effect, Brazil's capital output ratio is bound to rise, and rise significantly. In addition, the degree of freedom for managing this reduced potential for growth is compromised by the constraint of a heavy foreign debt which through the years has accumulated a repayment obligation that currently takes more than half of Brazil's export earnings. It is this debt burden, among other things, that is making it difficult for Brazil to devalue her currency closer to an appropriate equilibrium rate of exchange to promote her exports since any substantial devaluation would raise the local cruzeiro cost of the external dollar obligations of Brazilian debtors. As a result, much of the export subsidy for manufactured goods has been eroded by the growing overvaluation of the cruzeiro since 1974. At the same time, the need to create large foreign exchange reserves to maintain foreign banker confidence in the economy has added substantially to the local money supply. This in turn has contributed to the inability to contain domestic inflation, weakening the local money and capital markets and compromising the efficiency and equity of the system of indexing for inflation. The earlier mystique of Brazil's brilliant and adept economic policymakers has disappeared with the shrinking of the freedom to use certain economic policy instruments.

Brazil does have two strong suits in its attempts to deal with the future—a reasonably efficient industrial sector and an adaptive and responsive agricultural sector. However, both are compromised by the reduced policy space that prevents any substantial devaluation, and agriculture is subject to the instability of world commodity markets. Currently, more of an ISI strategy has been reintroduced into Brazil's future growth strategy. Unfortunately, this more nationalistic policy maintains high tariff barriers and is less labor absorptive and more income concentrating than an export-oriented drive which favors national producers and reaches further into the labor force through labor-absorptive light industries and agriculture. The net result will probably be a sequence of stop-and-go spurts of growth averaging no more than 5 to 6 percent per year (and relying more on the domestic market), greater ISI emphasis, a decline in economic status, and continued inflation and foreign debt burdens.

Mexico also has important outstanding problems, despite her new oil discoveries. The low tax and low expenditure effort of the Mexican state merely postpones or exacerbates the social deficit of inequities and poverty that is being reinforced by a lopsided distribution of income and a rapid rate of population growth. Relying heavily upon monetary rather than fiscal instruments to finance deficits and development costs creates a built-in acceptance of the current socioeconomic status quo. If the Mexican political environment precludes any substantial asset redistribution, then the only instrument available to deal with social inequalities is the fiscal instrument of increased taxation of the wealthy and increased government expenditures on public goods to benefit the poor. Unfortunately, the halting attempts of the Echeverría administration to increase taxes and spending stimulated a strong and powerful political resistance from the private sector, which in the end aborted the state's attempt to play a larger role in this area.

Another current problem in Mexico concerns the financial markets, which have been that country's perennial strength, particularly in comparison to Brazil. Double-digit inflation in an economy unindexed for inflation can spell trouble for the effective functioning of financial markets; private voluntary savings will dry up if negative real rates of interest surface.[39] As a consequence, the government would have to increase taxes, index the economy, or engage in inflationary financing of the deficit. A final and preferred solution would be to lower the rate of inflation. This issue will continue to challenge the Mexican government in the future, since it is unwise and dangerous for Mexico to maintain a considerably higher rate of inflation than the United States for any great length of time. Given the long common border, this process would disrupt the financial markets and lead to capital flight such as that which occurred in the mid-1970s.

Finally, the decline in output and productivity in the Mexican agricultural sector will have to be faced in the future. Agricultural exports are still important to Mexico, and the growing cost of food imports adds to domestic price rises. With the continuing high rate of population growth, the inability of Mexico to feed herself could lead to another round of social unrest in the countryside, increased migration to the United States, and a worsening distribution of income for the growing rural proletariat.

Two events which have improved Mexico's economic future are the discovery of oil and the long overdue devaluation, which will both add to Mexico's export revenues. The potential rise in oil revenue diminishes what otherwise would have been a serious foreign debt problem. Furthermore, the substantial devaluation in late 1976 created the possibility for reducing tariff barriers and promoting more labor-intensive national manufacturing production for exports rather than continuing to emphasize a more capital-intensive, foreign-investment-dominated ISI strategy, as Brazil has been forced to do. A potential problem here is that following her devaluation Mexico still adheres to a fixed exchange rate rather than adopting the trotting peg common to Brazil. With rising domestic prices, this creates the possibility for a gradually accumulating external disequilibrium through an over-valued exchange rate, as occurred from 1965 to 1975.

The growing Mexican oil revenues are associated with three potential problems. First, the ease of gaining government revenues through oil production and sales may permanently shelve any attempts to reform and expand the tax base to include a more substantial contribution from the wealthier segments of Mexican society. Second, in removing the balance of payments constraint, oil exchange earnings may redirect Mexican foreign trade policy back to the import-intensive pattern of the late sixties in which more labor-intensive manufactured exports are penalized and local ISI efforts with foreign capital, along with all the capital-intensive methods associated with them, are encouraged. Finally, the mere existence of oil revenues does not automatically translate into wide-ranging and comprehensive government programs to deal with the problems of agricultural reform and low productivity, increased employment, and better health care and educational opportunities for the poor.

In conclusion, both Mexico and Brazil face problematic futures, but Mexico is in a much better position than Brazil to exploit its growth potential in an energy-deficient world. The major outstanding question is whether Mexico will have the political wisdom and skill to tackle the problems of poverty and inequality within the currently favorable economic environment. Another issue confronting both countries is their growing adversary relationship with the United States.[40] In Mexico's case, the outstanding issues of illegal immigration, Mexican manufactured exports to the United States, agricultural exports, water control, and oil and natural gas negotiations are real and important. In Brazil's case, growing countervailing duties in the United States, human rights issues, the nuclear controversy, and the growing problem of the foreign debt with United States banks are equally difficult problems. The halcyon days of easy consensus and harmony are over. The direction of United States policy in the 1980s (and the response of Brazil and Mexico to this policy) will also play an important role in conditioning the future growth of these countries.

Notes

1. Charles Cumberland, *Mexico: The Struggle for Modernity* (New York: Oxford University Press, 1968); Rollie E. Poppino, *Brazil: The Land and the People* (New York: Oxford University Press, 1973).
2. Clark Reynolds, "Mexico and Brazil: Models for Leadership in Latin America," in J. W. Wilkie *et al.* (eds.), *Contemporary Mexico,* Papers of the Fourth International Congress of Mexican History (Los Angeles: UCLA Latin American Center, 1976).
3. *Ibid.;* and Roger D. Hansen, *The Politics of Mexican Development* (Baltimore: Johns Hopkins University Press, 1971).
4. Stanley Stein, *The Brazilian Cotton Manufacture: Textile Enterprise in an Underdeveloped Area, 1850–1950* (Cambridge, Harvard University Press, 1957); Albert Fishlow, "Origins and Consequences of Import Substitution in Brazil," in Luis Eugenio di Marco (ed.), *International Economics and Development* (New York: Academic Press, 1972); Warren Dean, *The Industrialization of São Paulo 1880–1945* (Austin: University of Texas Press, 1969); Celso Furtado, *The Economic Growth of Brazil* (Berkeley: University of California Press, 1963).
5. Thomas W. Merrick and Douglas H. Graham, *Population and Economic Development in Brazil: 1800 to the Present* (Baltimore: Johns Hopkins University Press, 1979), chapter 5; Annibal Villela and Wilson Suzigan, *Política do governo e crescimento da economia brasileira 1889–1945* (Rio de Janeiro: IPEA/INPES, Série Monografica 10, 1973).
6. Roger D. Hansen, *Mexican Economic Development: The Roots of Rapid Growth* (Washington, D.C.: National Planning Association, 1971), chapter 2; Clark Reynolds, *The Mexican Economy: Twentieth Century Structure and Growth* (New Haven: Yale University Press, 1970), chapter 1.
7. Villela and Suzigan, *Política,* pp. 46–53; René Villarreal, "External Disequilibrium and Growth Without Development: The Import Substitution Model, The Mexican Experience (1929–1975)," Ph.D. dissertation, Yale University (1976), pp. 11–12.
8. Celso Furtado, *The Economic Growth of Brazil* (Berkeley: University of California Press, 1963); Simão Silber, "Analise da política econômica e do comportamento da economia brasileira durante o período 1929/1939," in Flavio Rabelo Versiani and José Mendonca de Barros (eds.), *Formação econômica do Brasil: a experiência da industrialização* (São Paulo: Edição Saraiva, 1977), pp. 188–202.
9. Villela and Suzigan, *Política,* p. 212; Fishlow, "Import Substitution," p. 335.
10. Villarreal, "The Import Substitution Model," pp. 20–21.
11. Reynolds, "Models for Leadership."
12. Simon Kuznets, *Modern Economic Growth: Rate Structure and Spread* (New Haven: Yale University Press, 1966).
13. Villarreal, "The Import Substitution Model," p. 52.
14. Reynolds, *The Mexican Economy;* Timothy King, *Mexico: Industrialization and Trade Policies Since 1940* (New York: Oxford University Press, 1970); Gerardo Bueno, "The Structure of Protection in Mexico," in Bela Belassa (ed.), *The Structure of Protection in Developing Countries* (Baltimore: Johns Hopkins University Press, 1971); Villarreal, "The Import Substitution Model"; Werner Baer, *Industrialization and Economic Development in Brazil* (Homewood, Ill.: Irwin Press, 1965); Joel Bergsman, *Brazil: Industrialization and Trade Policies*

(New York: Oxford University Press, 1970); Fishlow, "Import Substitution."

15. Villarreal, "The Import Substitution Model," pp. 71–72.

16. *Ibid.*, pp. 90–91; Bergsman, *Brazil*, appendix 4.

17. Richard S. Weinert, "The State and Foreign Capital," in José Luis Reyna and Richard S. Weinert (eds.), *Authoritarianism in Mexico* (Philadelphia: Institute for the Study of Human Issues, 1977).

18. Fishlow, "Import Substitution," pp. 345–46.

19. Weinert, "The State and Foreign Capital," p. 112.

20. Villarreal, "The Import Substitution Model," chapter 8; Reynolds, "Mexico's 'Stabilizing Development,' " pp. 1006–11.

21. Pedro S. Malan and Regis Bonelli, "The Brazilian Economy in the Seventies: Old and New Developments," *World Development*, vol. 5, no. 1/2, p. 34.

22. Stefan Robock, "Controlling Multinational Enterprises: The Brazilian Experience," *Journal of Contemporary Business*, Autumn 1977, pp. 53–71; Keith S. Rosenn, "Treatment of the Foreign Investor: The Brazilian Style," in William H. Overholt (ed.), *The Future of Brazil* (Boulder: Westview Press, 1978).

23. Werner Baer and Annibal V. Villela, "The Changing Nature of Development Banking in Brazil," paper presented at the Eighth National Meeting of the Latin American Studies Association, Pittsburgh, Pennsylvania, April 5–7, 1979.

24. Dwight Brothers and Leopoldo Solis, *Mexican Financial Development* (Austin: University of Texas Press, 1966).

25. Baer and Villela, "Development Banking in Brazil."

26. José Roberto Mendonça de Barros and Douglas H. Graham, "The Brazilian Economic Miracle Revisited: Private and Public Sector Initiative in a Market Economy," *Latin American Research Review*, vol. 13, no. 2 (1978), pp. 5–38.

27. Werner Baer, Isaac Kestenetsky, and Annibal V. Villela, "The Changing Role of the State in the Brazilian Economy," *World Development*, vol. 1, no. 11 (November 1973); Mendonça de Barros and Graham, "The Brazilian Economic Miracle Revisited"; Thomas J. Trebat, "An Evaluation of the Economic Performance of Large Public Enterprise in Brazil 1965–1975," paper presented at the Eighth National Meeting of the Latin American Studies Association, Pittsburgh, Pennsylvania, April 5–7, 1979.

28. John F. Purcell and Susan Kaufman Purcell, "Mexican Business and Public Policy," in James Malloy (ed.), *Authoritarianism and Corporatism in Latin America* (Pittsburgh: University of Pittsburgh Press, 1977); Reynolds, "Mexico's 'Stabilizing Development' "; Laurence Whitehead, "The Economic Policy of the Echeverría Sexenio: What Went Wrong and Why?" paper presented to the Eighth National Meeting of the Latin American Studies Association, Pittsburgh, Pennsylvania, April 5–7, 1979.

29. Mendonça de Barros and Graham, "The Brazilian Economic Miracle Revisited."

30. Merrick and Graham, *Population and Economic Development in Brazil*, chapter 6.

31. José Roberto Mendonça de Barros and Douglas Graham, "A agricultura brasileira e a problema da producção de alimentoves," *Pesquisa e Planejamento Economico*, vol. 8, no. 3 (1978), pp. 695–726.

32. David Goodman and Michael Redclift, "The 'Boias-Frias': Rural Proletarianization and Urban Marginality in Brazil," *International Journal of*

Urban and Regional Research, vol. 1, no. 2 (1977), pp. 348–64; Teresa Rendón, "Utilización de mano de obra en la agricultura mexicana 1940–1973," *Demografía e Economía,* vol. 10, no. 3 (1976), pp. 352–85; Jorge Balan, "Agrarian Structures and Internal Migration in a Historical Perspective: Latin American Case Studies" (Buenos Aires: CEDES, mimeo, 1979).

33. Goodman and Redclift, "The 'Boias-Frias' "; Balan, "Agrarian Structures."

34. Riordan Roett, *Brazil: Politics in a Patrimonial Society,* rev. ed. (New York: Praeger, 1978); Thomas E. Skidmore, *Politics in Brazil 1930–1964* (New York: Oxford University Press, 1967).

35. Roger D. Hansen, *Mexican Economic Development,* p. 52.

36. Donald Syvrud, *Foundations of Brazilian Economic Growth* (Stanford: Hoover Institution Press, 1974).

37. Reynolds, "Mexico's 'Stabilizing Development' "; Whitehead, "Echeverría Sexenio"; Purcell and Purcell, "Mexican Business."

38. W. Whitney Hicks, "Economic Development and Fertility Change in Mexico 1950–1970," *Demography,* vol. 11, no. 3 (1974), pp. 407–21; W. Whitney Hicks, "Reply to Comment by Daniel Seiver," *Demography,* vol. 13, no. 1 (1976), pp. 153–55; Daniel A. Seiver, "Recent Fertility in Mexico: Measurement and Interpretation," *Population Studies,* vol. 29, no. 3 (1975), pp. 341–54; Daniel A. Seiver, "Comment on W. Whitney Hicks' 'Economic Development and Fertility Change in Mexico 1950–1970,' " *Demography,* vol. 13, no. 1 (1976), pp. 149–52.

39. Reynolds, "Mexico's 'Stabilizing Development,' " p. 1013.

40. Richard R. Fagen, "The Realities of U.S.-Mexican Relations," *Foreign Affairs,* vol. 55, no. 4 (July 1977), pp. 685–700; Riordan Roett, "The Political Future of Brazil," in Overholt (ed.), *The Future of Brazil.*

3

Popular Sector Incorporation and Political Supremacy: Regime Evolution in Brazil and Mexico

RUTH BERINS COLLIER

The Brazil-Mexico comparison has a particularly interesting role in the current political science literature. Brazil—the first and longest-lived example of the kind of repressive military regime that is currently prevalent in the Southern Cone of South America—has been the "paradigmatic" case in the development of a bureaucratic-authoritarian model of political change, most systematically elaborated by Guillermo O'Donnell.[1] The treatment of Mexico in the literature has been divided. Traditionally, there has been a tendency to treat Mexico as a unique case—a case of revolution, of one-party dominance, and of institutionalized civilian rule. More recently, scholars have stressed important commonalities between Mexico and the bureaucratic-authoritarian systems of Brazil and other South American countries.[2] Those who emphasize the similarities between Mexico and Brazil and those who emphasize the contrasts seem to do so from distinct analytic perspectives, stressing the importance of different variables.

The institutional/political process perspective is more apt to highlight the differences between the two countries. This is not the older, legal/constitutional approach, but one which is nevertheless more institutionally oriented. It is concerned with such issues as stability, military intervention and civil-military relations, competitiveness, and party systems—in short, with the political regime. From this perspective, Mexico and Brazil, both in the contemporary period and over the longer historical run, look quite different indeed. Brazil has displayed a high incidence of regime change characteristic of

Chalmer's "politicized state,"[3] whereas Mexico, since the dust settled following the upheavals of the Mexican Revolution, has had great regime continuity. In Brazil in the post-1930 period, regime changes occurred in 1934, 1937, 1945, and 1964; and during the longest interval between these, 1945–64, the regime was so poorly institutionalized that there was a crisis at virtually every presidential succession point. In the post-1930 period, Brazil has had authoritarian-civilian, multiparty competitive, and military regimes. In contrast to this, Mexico since 1917 has had regime continuity based on a single constitution and a single legitimating myth. During most of this period, Mexico has had a one-party-dominant regime—a type not included among the variety found in Brazil. The party has, of course, undergone some change, as has the locus of decision-making, and the state has grown, but these are changes within a well-institutionalized system. Finally, in the past decade and a half, Brazil, like many Latin American countries, has gone through a period of harshly repressive military rule characterized by widespread violations of human rights. Mexico, by contrast, has been able to come through the challenges of the 1960s and 1970s without a major, convulsive regime change, and though the past decade has seen episodes of sharp repression, political liberties have been preserved to a greater degree than in Brazil and other South American countries, and the political system has remained more pluralistic.[4]

The second perspective for comparing Brazil and Mexico is that of political economy, and it is one from which the two countries look much more similar. In fact, not only are they similar, but in many ways they are distinct in comparison with the other Latin American countries. Within the context of a dependent capitalist development strategy in which foreign capital and foreign technology play a crucial role, these two countries have achieved relatively high levels of industrialization. However, unlike other relatively industrialized countries in the region (i.e., those in the Southern Cone), the large industrial cores in Brazil and Mexico exist alongside an extensive underdeveloped hinterland which provides a large reserve of cheap labor. Also, these two countries are the most populous in Latin America and, unlike the Southern Cone, have potentially large internal markets. In the last several decades, they have developed strong, industrialized economies which have experienced, at least in certain periods, rapid and sustained growth, and they are the two Latin American countries to which the term "economic miracle" has been applied. At the same time, this record of aggregate economic success has proceeded without any dramatic improvement in the standard of living of the bulk of the population—and perhaps even at the cost of greater inequalities in the distribution of income and, at times, of greater absolute impoverishment at the lower income levels. More recently, unlike many other Latin American economies, Brazil and Mexico have continued to attract large quantities of direct foreign investment in manufacturing. They have also emphasized the development of an export sector in manufacturing to a far greater degree than countries in the Southern Cone. Finally, again in contrast to the more market-oriented policies of the Southern Cone, there has in recent years been little movement towards a diminishing economic role for the state.[5] Thus, though differences do of course exist,[6] Mexico and Brazil have been pursuing similar models of dependent capitalist development which have met with substantial success in their own terms. These models have in many ways involved similar patterns of benefits to different class groups and, at the most general level, similar types of political and economic domination.

Are Brazil and Mexico basically similar or basically different? Clearly some of each. What is needed in comparing the two cases is a perspective which can deal conceptually with both the similarities and the differences. One useful attempt to develop such a conceptualization has been presented by Fernando Henrique Cardoso.[7] He has suggested that it is important to distinguish between the "state" and the "regime." By the state he means the pact of class domination, in other words, the class relationships, the distribution of economic and political resources, and the broad policy outlines and priorities that flow from the overall type of economy. By regime he means the mode or particular institutions of domination, the form of the state, and he argues that similar states can coexist with and be maintained by different types of regimes. It may be noted that this distinction corresponds to that between the political economy perspective and the institutional/political process perspective. The question which follows from Cardoso's distinction is: how do different regimes come to coexist with similar states and how effective are different regimes in supporting those states?

In this chapter, after briefly elaborating Cardoso's distinction, I shall suggest some factors which account for the different evolution of the regimes in Brazil and Mexico. I will argue that the way in which the political incorporation of lower class groups occurred in each country earlier in this century had important consequences for the subsequent emergence of different party systems and class alliances, which then affected the capacity of the regime to provide legitimacy for the state. This in turn affected the stability of the regime itself.

State and Regime

Since this chapter devotes central attention to the characteristics of the regimes of Brazil and Mexico, it is appropriate to indicate what I mean by regime and what the relationship is between regime and state. As a first approximation, I find it helpful to refer to the state as the public sector. As such, however, it is more than the aggregate of specific institutions—it is an analytic abstraction.[8] It is the public mechanisms and institutions of collective goal attainment or of the authoritative allocation of values. Since the state pursues goals and allocates values for the collectivity, and since a given pattern of allocations favors certain interests at the expense of others, the state is, as Weber no less than Marx put it, "a relation of men dominating men" or "organized domination." Since the state makes binding decisions for the whole collectivity, it requires compliance. It makes decisions and extracts compliance through its various components: public administration, legal order, coercive apparatus, and political institutions.

We can therefore think of the state in terms of two distinct analytic categories: the structures and mechanisms of decision-making and the structures and mechanisms of "decision-compliance." The latter can be separated into coercive mechanisms and legitimating mechanisms. As analysts from Marx, Gramsci, and Althusser to Weber and Lasswell and Kaplan have asserted, the preferred and more secure basis of compliance is acceptance of the decisions by the people. Acceptance is based on the attribution of legitimacy to both the decisions and the decision-making process. To the extent that there is no legitimacy, compliance is dependent upon coercion.

This brings us to the definition of regime. Discounting for the moment the coercive arm of the state, we can think of the two analytic categories of the state as the decision-making structures and the legitimating structures. Following Lasswell and Kaplan, we may say that the regime is the authority structure, or the structure of formal, legitimate power.[9] In this sense, the regime may be thought of as the legitimating structure of the state.[10] It should be stressed that this conception of regime distinguishes it analytically from the decision-making structure. This corresponds to the distinction that Lasswell and Kaplan have referred to as the pattern of effective power versus the pattern of formal power. The word formal is used to refer to the fact that the regime is the pattern or structure that is the part of the political myth which describes the legitimate structure of power. The word formal is thus used to convey two ideas: the idea of authority or legitimacy and the idea of symbolic status. In other words, the regime may be fictive.[11]

For instance, the political myth may, as is common in the modern world, assert that legitimate decisions should stem from the people. The political formula in turn may call for voting in elections. Voting, however, is a formal practice that "may or may not actually constitute the making of a decision."[12] And so it is with the other components of regime. It is perfectly clear that the Mexican legislature does not play the role formally assigned to it. The regime as the authority structure may coincide with the decision-making structure or it may not. However, even if it does not the regime may play an important role which affects legitimacy, coercion, and governmental capacity.

In these terms, then, the state is the set of public institutions concerned with making and enforcing decisions for the collectivity. The regime is a part of the state, the legitimating apparatus. It is the structure of formal legitimate authority—which in addition may or may not constitute the decision-making apparatus. States can differ with respect to the class which controls them and the consequent pattern of collective goals pursued, as well as with respect to the structure of the regime, the fictiveness of the regime (or the extent to which it coincides with the decision-making structure), and the degree of legitimacy generated by the regime.

Cardoso's point is that similar patterns of collective goals or allocations do not necessarily require similar regimes. The classical Marxist argument is that patterns of allocation are determined by the productive forces and the relations of production. While we may view the state on this general and abstract level as being at least in part the superstructural expression of the economic base, the economic base does not take us so far in providing an explanation for the regime. This is not to say that the range of regime possibilities is not severely constrained by economic and class considerations, nor is it to deny that regime change has often been prompted quite directly by these considerations. Rather, we may adopt Althusser's position that though the base may be determinant "in the last instance," each level (base and superstructure) has its own substantially autonomous history.[13] Thus, we must also look at political factors if we are to explain regime.

Popular Sector Incorporation

The starting point in this analysis for explaining differences in regime evolution and in the capacity of the regime to provide legitimacy for the state is the way in which the political incorporation of the popular sector occurred earlier in this century. This "initial" experience established the parameters for subsequent patterns of state-popular sector relationships. This is obviously not the only explanation of the regime differences, but within the framework of a larger literature on national political change in Latin America that has placed heavy emphasis on socioeconomic explanations, there is clearly a need for more analyses that focus on political explanations. One goal of this chapter is to address this need. Though it does so at the cost of a fuller explanation, which would necessarily have to delimit and elaborate those economic and social factors, it is my contention that the effects of these socioeconomic factors are mediated through (and themselves often affected by) the political sphere.

The entry of the lower classes into participation in national political life has been a major concern of analysts of social change. For Bendix, it was a central aspect of nation-building; for Marshall, it was a political requirement for capitalist industrialization; and for the Committee on Political Development of the Social Science Research Council, it was one of the major "crises" of political development.[14] However, despite the fact that the political incorporation of the masses has received wide attention in political science literature as a major transition in the process of political change, an adequate understanding of the different ways in which this transition has occurred has only begun to emerge. Distinctions have been made between "autonomous" and "mobilized" participation,[15] as well as between a kind of pluralist model, in which the lower classes successfully demand participation in politics, and a preemptive model, in which the elite extends participation before it is demanded, in a way that coopts the new participants. However, more subtle distinctions need to be made.

In this chapter, I will argue that two rather different types of political incorporation have occurred in Brazil and Mexico. I will focus initially on the first major period of political incorporation, a period which involves the extension to the popular sectors of many of the civil, political, and social rights analyzed by Marshall, as well as the formation of political coalitions which include the newly participant groups or the presence of governments which champion their political goals. These are the periods which are often called populist. The analysis will then turn to the nature of the regime that emerged out of this initial period. Attention will focus particularly on the type of party system that was established and the class alliances and ongoing patterns of popular sector incorporation embodied in the party system.

Initial Incorporation in Mexico and Brazil

To understand the initial major periods of incorporation, we must go back to the collapse of the traditional, oligarchic state and examine the nature of the intra-elite factionalism that accompanied it. The collapse of the "ancien régime" involved the end of the political dominance of the export oligarchy. This occurred at a time of social and economic change—new urban and industrial economic elites had emerged as rivals to the oligarchy, the middle sectors were growing and exerting a new influence, and an incipient and often radical working class was developing. In general terms, this was a period of transition from an export economic model to one of import-substituting industrialization, and one which saw the emergence of an urban industrial sector with interests different from those of the export sector. One important starting point for the contrasting patterns followed by Mexico and Brazil is found in the differences in the relationship between these sectors—in differences in the nature of the conflict between the two elite groups and in the way in which the popular sectors, particularly the emerging working class, were incorporated into the political system.

The ancien régime in Brazil ended with the Revolution of 1930. This was not, of course, a popular revolution but rather one that primarily expressed an intra-elite cleavage. However, this cleavage was not extremely intense, and there was no real sectoral clash between the agricultural and industrial sectors to the degree that has been found elsewhere. Though the relative power of the industrial sector was increased, the revolution did not represent a frontal attack on the agricultural export sector, most importantly the coffee growers, who in fact tended to support the revolution and whose interests were well-served by Getúlio Vargas, whom the revolution brought to power. With this political realignment of coffee and industrial interests, Vargas was not dependent upon popular or sectoral support, except for the army. Nevertheless, many groups and economic sectors prospered under Vargas and joined the political movement which he began to put together in the last two years of his rule. In this way Vargas managed to weld together a broad coalition, and, according to Skidmore, the opposition was a surprisingly small group, consisting primarily of the UDN (União Democrática Nacional) as well as the Communists.[16] The revolution, then, added new groups to the social bases of politics, but did not end the political power of the old oligarchy, forcing them rather to share it within the framework of a widely noted accommodationist style of elite interaction. Instead of a sectoral clash, there was a process of accumulation or sedimentation of elite groups in the power arena, resulting in what Anderson has called a "living museum" in which the old groups were never really supplanted.[17]

The point should not be overstated: there were clearly differences of interest—and to some extent of political alignment—among different sectors of the elite. The political movement that Vargas finally set into motion was split into two separate parties, the PSD (Partido Social Democrático) and the PTB (Partido Trabalhista Brasileiro). Cerqueira's description of these parties suggests that they in fact corresponded rather closely to the sides in the classical situation of sectoral cleavage.[18] According to him, the PSD was a classical conservative party of landed property and of rural *coronelismo* which espoused economic and financial policies favoring the export of primary products and industrialization through foreign investment. The PTB represented more of a classical populist coalition of the national part of the industrial bourgeoisie, urban labor, and the big cattle ranchers. The ranchers, like the industrial bourgeoisie, were interested in an expanded domestic market which could be created with a land reform that did not affect pasture land and also with an increase in urban wages, although in this last the ranchers differed with the industrial bourgeoisie. Thus the classical sectoral rivalry was present and manifested in the formation of two, rather than one, Vargas movements. Nevertheless, the point is that the two shared power; neither was able to supplant the other. Out of stalemate arose a modus vivendi.

This situation is quite different from that of Mexico, where the ancien régime fell with the overthrow of Porfirio Díaz in 1911. In this case, the export elite did not fare so well, and the political museum effect was reduced. The Mexican Revolution has often been seen as a kind of sectoral clash or bourgeois revolution, terminating the dominance of the export model of economic growth and facilitating a transition to an import-substituting model of industrial growth. As Womack suggests:

> On the big difference the Revolution made, the great majority of historians and economists sing in harmony. Over the long run the meaning of the Mexican Revolution lies in its repudiation of foreign checks on the country and its destruction of an internally blocked system, which allowed the subsequent reorganization of land, capital, and labor into a dynamic system. On this interpretation the Revolution amounted to the historic overthrow of an internationally dependent, semifeudal, semi-

comprador oligarchy, its replacement by an authentic bourgeoisie, and the shift from a neocolonial dictatorship to the rule of a nationalist party that evoked broad popular consent.[19]

It has been suggested that this sectoral clash between an emerging national industrial bourgeoisie and the entrenched ruling coalition of foreign interests and agro-mining export elites is reflected in the fact that important leaders of the 1910 movement came from a segment of the entrepreneurial class centered in northern Mexico. These included the leader of the movement, Francisco Madero, who was installed as president upon its success, as well as Venustiano Carranza,[20] who would subsequently lead the fight against both a political restoration and, when civil war broke out, the threat of a genuine social revolution.

This interpretation of the Mexican Revolution as a sectoral clash must be treated with some caution. The Porfirian elite included powerful members of the industrial bourgeoisie, and, as Womack has pointed out, revisionist interpretations are beginning to see much greater continuity between the pre- and postrevolutionary situations.[21] It is not necessary here to go into the details of the historiography of the Mexican Revolution. What seems important for present purposes is that in several important ways the Mexican Revolution differed significantly from the Brazilian "Revolution" of 1930. First, it represented a major escalation of intrafactional elite conflict that changed the rules of the conflict and introduced the mobilization of the popular sectors as a tactic in this rivalry. This pattern contrasted with the more accommodationist pattern of intra elite relations that followed the events of 1930 in Brazil, in which the popular sectors played no significant role. Second, the Mexican events of 1910 to 1917 resulted in the economic and political displacement of the old landowning class.[22] Though it may be too simplistic to see the sides in the elite cleavage in terms of a rural-urban sectoral clash, the new constitution of 1917 defined an interventionist state empowered to expropriate private land and property. It laid the basis for an altered concept of private property and for a radical agrarian reform which represented a fundamental assault on the landed elite. As Hamilton has stated, the function of the state "was no less than the elimination of previously dominant institutions and structures."[23] In fact, the implementation of land redistribution has, of course, been limited and discretionary, and large holdings remain or have been reconsolidated. Nevertheless, the Mexican Revolution led to a very different constellation of political power among elite factions and the adoption (despite the limited implementation) of agrarian policies that would have been inconceivable in Brazil.

Out of these differences in intra-elite patterns in Brazil and Mexico came different elite-mass patterns. In Brazil, where there was a greater balance among factions, there was a need to pursue policies which did not antagonize the various elements of the elite. Politics was accommodationist. The result of the stalemate among the divided elites was a policy towards the popular sectors that was based on a fairly high degree of elite consensus and was rooted in two fundamental points.

The first was that urban labor would have to be deradicalized and tamed. There would have to be a major effort on the part of the state to resolve what was viewed as the "social question"—the radicalization or potential radicalization of the working class, stemming from its intolerable exploitation. The solution to the problem of the "dangerous classes" and the answer to the "social question" involved the introduction of an elaborate corporative system of state-labor relations, which was gradually elaborated in the course of the Vargas period. This was based on both an extensive set of inducements for organized labor that helped to create a legalized labor movement that was dependent on the state and also an extensive set of constraints on labor organizations and labor leaders that severely restricted their activities.[24] The goal of these provisions was to establish a coopted, controlled labor movement that would no longer pose any threat to the elite. In contrast to many other cases of "populism," there was throughout most of the Vargas period virtually no effort to mobilize labor as an active support group within the dominant coalition. The preponderant emphasis was on coopting labor and controlling its functional associations. The second point of elite consensus in Brazil was that a similar solution would not be imposed in the countryside. There would be no land reform, no legalization of rural unions, and the preexisting pattern of social relations would remain untouched.[25]

In Mexico, a different pattern of intra-elite relationships led to very different patterns of elite-mass relationships. In the context of the revolution, elite relations were hardly accommodationist. Open conflict resulted in a pattern of mobilization of the popular sectors by an elite faction as part of an opposition strategy, in contrast to the tacit agreement not to expand the arena of conflict which was a product of the uneasy truce and stalemate among the Brazilian elite factions. With regard to organized labor, the goal of this mobilization in Mexico was not primarily to defuse or deradicalize the labor movement, as in Brazil, but to use it as a counterweight to the power of other elite sectors or factions. Mobilization of labor support became a feature of the Mexican Revolution when Carranza made a pact with the Casa del Obrero, which organized the Red Battalions to fight and propagandize on behalf of the Constitutionalists.

This pattern of mobilization of labor support in intra-elite rivalry continued after the revolution in Alvaro Obregón's pact with CROM (Confederación Regional Obrera Mexicana). In return for his support of this labor confederation, CROM established the Labor Party to help Obregón oust Carranza. Plutarcho Elías Calles subsequently made use of this alliance as a counterweight in his effort to control the local military opposition. (Later, Cárdenas' support for the founding of a new labor confederation, the CTM (Confederación de Trabajadores de México), as part of his effort to gain dominance over the Calles faction was a continuation of this same pattern.) Under the presidency of Calles (1924–28), CROM rose to "an unrivalled position of political strength." This was a period in which central control in Mexico was still not well established following the upheavals of the revolution, and power relationships were fluid. In this setting, the creation of new political resources, in the form of an organized popular sector, proved decisive. "The only permanent national organisations, centralised and highly disciplined, were CROM and the Labour Party, which alone proved capable of mobilising significant sections of the population across the Republic."[26]

The result was not a powerful, autonomous labor movement that succeeded in extracting a host of tangible benefits for the working class. Rather, there emerged a coopted union movement under an increasingly corrupt leadership. Nevertheless, because of the political resource labor represented, a major effort was made to include organized labor within the support coalition of the government, and under these conditions the power situation of organized labor was quite unlike anything seen at a comparable period in Brazil. At the height of CROM's influence, its leader, Luis Morones, was Minister of Industry, Commerce, and Labor and was second in influence only to President Calles himself.[27] CROM also had significant strength in the Chamber of Deputies. "In the capital CROM dominated the City Council and those of the main suburbs as well as, at one time, the governorship of the Federal District. Further, its strength among journalists and printing workers gave it considerable influence over the news media. All added up to a position of political strength unique in the history of Mexico and unequalled at the time elsewhere in Latin America."[28]

With regard to the rural popular sectors there was no intra-elite agreement to perpetuate existing social relations in the countryside. The Mexican Revolution had set a precedent both for peasant rebellion and for the use by elites of peasant support in intra-elite struggles, as occurred in the Madero-Zapata alliance in 1910. Given this prior mobilization and the widespread destruction of rural social and economic organization that occurred during the revolution and ensuing civil war, the agrarian popular sector remained fair game for mobilization by elite factions. Because of this strategic position, agrarian interests were particularly strong during the presidency of Obregón, when the Agrarian Party controlled the National Agrarian Commission and oversaw a significant extension of peasant organizations. Agrarian leagues were formed in many states, and in 1923 the First National Agrarian Congress was held under the auspices of the Agrarian Party and was subsidized by the government.[29] Thus, agrarian as well as labor sectors played important roles in the balance of power among different elite factions in Mexico throughout the 1920s.[30] In contrast to Brazil, both urban and rural popular sectors figured in early Mexican incorporation.

The initial period of the political inclusion of the popular sectors culminated in Mexico in the Cárdenas presidency from 1934 to 1940, and in Brazil in the Estado Novo, the dates of which for present purposes we may put at 1937 to 1943. (Though the Estado Novo is usually said to be coterminous with Vargas' presidency, which lasted until 1945, his style of rule and the nature of political coalitions changed rather decidedly during his last two years in office. Therefore, we will say that the Estado Novo as a distinct political period ended in 1943.)[31]

Lázaro Cárdenas assumed the Mexican presidency while struggling for autonomy from the political control of Calles. The linchpin of his strategy was the political mobilization of urban labor and *campesinos,* to establish a power base independent of Calles. The result was a period of "radical populism," which Erickson has defined as one which not only promises improvements in status and material well-being but also raises the possibility of the actual transfer of power to the popular sectors.[32] Though a reformer dedicated to working within the capitalist system rather than a radical bent on its overthrow, Cárdenas believed that the state should intervene to equalize the relative weight of labor and capital. Given this predilection and the political situation in which he found himself, Cárdenas championed the cause of urban and rural workers—he strengthened organizations which were to defend their interests, he encouraged strikes and committed the state to intervene on behalf of workers in industrial disputes, he greatly increased the distribution of land to *campesinos,* he favored collective ownership in the countryside and the "socialization" of the means of production in industry, he changed the curriculum of schools to include socialist education, and he employed the rhetoric of class struggle and Marxism.

Organized labor held a strategic position in Cárdenas' effort to mobilize support against Calles. Again, this had important implications for the power position of organized labor and the newly formed labor confederation, the CTM. In return for its political support, "the CTM was favored by government subsidies and consistently pro-labor decisions in the nation's arbitration boards and courts. CTM leaders obtained seats in both houses of the federal congress and frequently played an important role in the nomination and election of state governors, municipal presidents, and other state and local officials."[33]

Armed with this opposition strategy, Cárdenas won his battle against Calles. A further result was the deep polarization of Mexican politics along class lines. Cárdenas' alliance with the popular sectors entailed a confrontation with capital which "suggested that while the state continued to perform the functions of accumulation in the interests of the dominant class, it had abdicated its social control function and was in fact participating in the class struggle on behalf of the subordinate class."[34] The industrialists, who were opposed to working class mobilization from the beginning, were further frightened by the nationalizations and economic deterioration towards the end of Cárdenas' term. Their economic response was the flight of capital abroad; the formation of an opposition party, the PAN (Partido de Acción Nacional), was in part the political expression of these fears. The middle classes also became increasingly hostile as they sought to defend their position against the rise of the proletariat.[35] In fact, opposition to Cárdenas' policies was expressed from all sides—a military revolt occurred, opposition emerged within the government, and Mexico's nationalized petroleum was boycotted abroad.[36] Fascist movements appeared, including a rival mass movement in the form of the *sinarquistas* (literally, "without anarchy"), and the contemporary example of Spain made the threat of civil war in Mexico seem all the more real.

In Brazil, the Estado Novo presented a very different picture. On an ideological level it preached class harmony; in the countryside, it oversaw the continuation of clientelistic relations; and with respect to the urban working class, its inclusionary politics took the cooptive form that Erickson has labeled paternalistic-administrative,[37] the principal aim of which was to deradicalize the working class and preemptively organize workers into a politically docile and controlled labor movement. In contrast to the political mobilization in Mexico, the "Estado Nôvo was . . . not dependent on articulate popular support in Brazilian society."[38] Rather, the emphasis was on the depoliticization of the lower classes. This strategy rested on an elaboration of a system of corporatist interest groups which channeled the activities of organized labor into highly controlled structures. The right to strike and to pursue economic and political goals was severely limited, and unions became primarily agencies for the dispensing of social services which were paternalistically and preemptively extended by the state.[39] Whereas the form of inclusionary politics under Cárdenas alienated the Mexican industrialists, Brazilian industrialists supported both the Estado Novo generally and its social legislation in particular.[40] While some opposition—which later coalesced into the politically and economically liberal UDN—did not favor the Estado Novo, this opposition was relatively ineffective during that period,[41] and thus there was comparatively little polarization during the Estado Novo. In this period, the major elite interests fared well, at the same time that social welfare benefits were provided for urban labor.

A concomitant of the distinct Mexican and Brazilian patterns of initial inclusionary politics involves the contrast between what may be called party/movement incorporation and state incorporation. In Mexico, where populism as an opposition strategy led to the political mobilization of the popular sectors, the political incorporation of those sectors took place mainly through a political movement that was later institutionalized in a political party. In Brazil, where inclusionary politics was part of an accommodationist strategy, the attempt was rather to insulate the working class from political activities and to incorporate it into the state apparatus rather than into a political movement or political party.

In Mexico, the organization of popular sectors into political parties was important in the game of intra-elite factionalism. This began with Alvaro Obregón, who relied on the support of both the Agrarian Party and Morones' Labor Party. The latter was subsequently an important basis of support for Calles as well. The next step was the founding of the PNR (Partido Nacional Revolucionario) by Calles in 1929. Though the Labor Party did not join the PNR, the reasons for this seem to be largely circumstantial,[42] and other labor and *campesino* groups were incorporated into it as part of Calles' effort to establish a power base from which he could control the presidency.[43] Much more extensive and more radical partisan mobilization of the urban and rural popular sectors subsequently took place as part of the political strategy surrounding the nomination and election of Cárdenas.[44]

The most important event in the party incorporation of the popular sectors in Mexico was, of course, the reorganization in 1938 of the official party to form the PRM (Partido de la Revolución Mexicana), which from that time formally included the political and functional arms of the urban and rural working classes. There are two plausible interpretations of the way in which this happened. In the first, it is seen as part of the ongoing political mobilization of the popular sectors which was part of an effort to increase the power base of one elite faction in its struggle against other factions. The political mobilization of the popular sectors continued, even accelerated, after Cárdenas assumed the presidency. As Cárdenas struggled to develop a power base from which he could gain autonomy from Calles, the popular sectors achieved significant power. Cárdenas distributed arms to *campesinos* and urban workers on a fairly large scale, and urban labor took the initiative to a significant degree in the final expulsion of Calles. Cárdenas was clearly dependent upon their support and upon an increase in their power. In the years that immediately followed Calles' expulsion (from 1936 to early 1938), either by conviction or by political necessity—or probably both—Cárdenas continued his reform program of land distribution, nationalizations, prolabor industrial settlements, and support for the growth of peasant and labor organizations.[45] In this context, the reorganization of the official party into the PRM can be seen as an attempt by Cárdenas to consolidate his power base into a kind of "popular front" of progressive forces or a coalition party to unite political and functional groups on the left.[46] This interpretation is consistent with the fact that Cárdenas first spoke of reorganizing the party in 1935, at a time when he was unquestionably interested in continued mobilization, and with the fact that the reorganization of the party came at a time when Cárdenas was increasing the power resources of popular groups on other fronts, as in the formation of workers' militias.[47] Finally, at about the same time as the founding of the PRM, economic problems became increasingly severe, and opposition to Cárdenas and his reform program mounted, while European fascism gained influence within Mexico and *sinarquismo* grew as a rival mass movement. In this context, then, the reorganization of the PRM can be seen as an (ultimately unsuccessful) attempt by Cárdenas to further mobilize and strengthen the progressive forces against increasing opposition from the right and thus to safeguard his program of reforms.

In the second interpretation, the reorganization of the party is seen not as a part of the mobilization of the popular sectors but as precisely the opposite—as an about-face on the part of Cárdenas which signaled the end of mobilization and an effort to exert a new control over the mobilized groups. It can be argued that political mobilization as an elite strategy is viable only during economically favorable times and that more basically there is a contradiction in pursuing a radical reform program within the context of a capitalist state. By 1937, when

Cárdenas announced his intention to reorganize the party, the facts of economic life, in part a result of the reform program, had begun to turn against the mobilization strategy. After 1938, with the reaction to the oil expropriation, the economic situation was alarmingly bleak. In this situation, Cárdenas' relations with the popular sectors deteriorated. Concerned with the economy, Cárdenas called for industrial peace, struck notes of class harmony, and sent in the army to put down strikes, at the same time that the rate of land distribution declined. The reorganization of the party in this context can be seen as an effort to eliminate the political autonomy of the popular sectors, to channel their activities into politically controllable organizations, and thus to deactivate them.

I find it difficult to make a conclusive case for one interpretation over the other. The fact that the party since 1940 has come to be used as an agent of political control does not allow one to argue ex post facto that control and demobilization were necessarily the motivation for the reorganization.[48] Other evidence can be garnered to support both interpretations. This specific question aside, the general interpretation of the period being advanced here is that Cárdenas was not a social revolutionary, but a reformer and, perhaps most importantly, a political entrepreneur. In order to mobilize the popular sectors as a political resource, he had to champion their cause and encourage a genuine increase in their political power. At the same time, Cárdenas wanted to be able to channel that political resource and was careful not to allow too much autonomous power to accrue to the popular sectors. Whether he was trying to call off political mobilization through the creation of a corporative party or strengthen the progressive forces through the formation of a coalition party, either interpretation is consistent with the idea that radical populism involves a mobilization of the popular sectors into a political movement or party as part of an elite opposition strategy which necessitates both augmenting the real power of the popular sectors and controlling and channeling that mobilization.

In Brazil, there was no comparable party role in the initial inclusionary period (prior to 1943). In fact, a major principle of trade union policy under Vargas was "the rigorous separation of labor unions from political parties."[49] This was part of Vargas' effort to depoliticize workers, and it explains his decision not to form an official party.[50] During the Estado Novo, then, the structure that was to incorporate those popular sectors which were part of the politics of inclusion (i.e., urban but not rural workers) was the state rather than the party. Though unions were not officially a part of the state structure—as they were in the Italian fascist state, which provided the model for the

Estado Novo labor law—the system in effect "defined labor leaders as semi-governmental officials and unions as quasi-governmental institutions."[51]

Thus, by the end of the initial incorporating periods—that is, by about 1940—there were very different situations in Mexico and Brazil. In both, a legalized labor movement had been established and had grown considerably. In Brazil, the new labor movement was regulated by the greatest proliferation of corporative provisions in any country in Latin America.[52] New unions were created, and a coopted leadership was installed and tied to the state. Politically, Vargas was not dependent upon active popular support, but was more concerned with depoliticizing labor. Accordingly, urban labor was not incorporated into any political party or movement and remained politically unmobilized. In the countryside, the *campesinos* did not figure into the politics of inclusion at all. Social relations remained untouched as the power of the rural oligarchy was preserved in an accommodationist pattern of elite relationships.

In contrast to the pattern of state incorporation of urban labor in Brazil, political or party incorporation of both labor and peasants was well advanced in Mexico. This party incorporation was a part of the political mobilization of both the urban and rural popular sectors in a pattern of intra-elite rivalry. In this situation, the power of the popular sectors was increased, culminating in a period of radical populism which polarized Mexican politics and perhaps even threatened civil war.

The Party Heritage of Initial Incorporation

The different experiences in the period of initial incorporation in Brazil and Mexico set into motion distinct political dynamics that had implications for the kinds of party systems that subsequently emerged in each country, for the subsequent patterns of ongoing popular sector incorporation, and for the degree to which the party system was an effective source of legitimacy for the state.

In Mexico, in the face of growing political polarization that resulted from radical populism and mounting conservative opposition to it, Cárdenas was instrumental in bringing the two sides together. The progressive coalition which had been ascendant was weakened by increasing demoralization; by inflation; by the contradictions implicit in the role of workers in nationalized, worker-managed enterprises; and by corruption in government agencies.[53] Decisive, concerted action by the progressive forces was also made difficult by the fact that

Cárdenas had structured his basis of support so that the different support groups served as counterweights to one another. The popular support of the labor sector was countered by that of the agrarian sector (which Cárdenas had deliberately kept organizationally separate), and the popular militia formed within both had a counterweight in the coercive resources of the military. Out of this alignment of forces came a presidential successor, legitimated if not actually chosen by Cárdenas,[54] who adopted a program which was not threatening to the middle class and bourgeoisie and who was able to retain the support of the popular sectors. In this way, the party was kept intact and a broad coalition was eventually put together under its banner. The result in subsequent years was the institutionalization of the official one-party system (under the renamed PRI—Partido Revolucionario Institucional), which incorporated the popular sectors under the hegemony of conservative interests (though these were not formally represented in the party). During the presidencies of Manuel Ávila Camacho (1940–46) and Miguel Alemán (1946–52), government policy turned against workers and *campesinos*. Under the former labor suffered a dramatic loss of real wages, while under the latter coercive methods were used to establish tight organizational control over the union movement and to install a state-dependent, coopted union leadership. Parallel developments occurred in the agrarian sector, where the distribution of land and agricultural credit to *campesinos* fell off and *campesino* organizations became firmly subordinated to and controlled by the PRI. Thus, the ultimate heritage of the Cárdenas period was a party which embodied a progressive ideology, which held the partisan loyalties of the popular sectors, and which bound the functional organizations of the popular sectors to a conservative state. The one-party system became an important conflict-limiting mechanism which avoided or minimized future polarization.

In Brazil, political parties had no important role during the initial incorporating period. When party politics subsequently reemerged, a multiparty system was established which exhibited no parallel conflict-limiting mechanisms and in which the major centrist parties continued to do only a very partial job of popular sector incorporation. The first period of incorporation had proceeded without political mobilization and party incorporation. In 1943, when it became clear that the authoritarian Estado Novo would fall and that Vargas' future political career would depend on electoral support, he began to make the necessary preparations by sponsoring a political movement—or movements—that would support him. But even then his mobilization of labor and popular groups was vacillating and partial. The PTB, which was Vargas' potential vehicle for mobilizing mass support, was geared more to bureaucrats in the vast Labor Ministry and Social Security Institutes and to the coopted union leadership than it was to the working masses.[55] Though he evoked some populist themes, he was also careful to avoid both polarizing political life and limiting his own options by seeking a major support base in a more traditional, conservative party, the PSD, as well as in the more classically populist PTB. Again, no direct appeal was made to rural workers. In the years that followed, Vargas never completely overcame his initial orientation toward depoliticizing the popular sector—or at least he remained ambivalent about this. In his campaign to regain the presidency in 1950, he ran as a PTB candidate, engaged in populist rhetoric, and made a direct appeal to the working class. Even then, however, he was inconsistent in his rhetoric and campaign messages and drew his support from other parties at least as much as the PTB.[56] During his new presidency (1951–54), this ambivalence continued to be manifest, as he vacillated between appeals to the popular sectors and to groups on the right, never really using the PTB to mobilize popular support.[57] Thus the Brazilian popular sectors were not as thoroughly incorporated into the major political parties as they were in Mexico. As a result, though working class functional organizations were tightly controlled, severely constrained, and dependent on the state, the working class remained *politically* more autonomous and was thus in a better position to join or organize more radical, class-based political movements or parties in the context of a relatively open multiparty system.

These then were the two different political and coalitional patterns which emerged from the period of incorporation. In Mexico, there was a one-party-dominant system in which the popular sectors were politically incorporated into the party. In Brazil, there was a multiparty system in which the popular sectors were not clearly incorporated into any of the centrist parties.

To what extent did the regimes based on these party systems contribute to the legitimacy of the state? In answering this question, it is useful to draw on Gramsci's analysis of hegemony and the role of the party in establishing hegemony. For Gramsci, there are two types of supremacy.[58] The first, called dictatorship or domination, is based on coercion. The second, called hegemony or leadership, is based on socialization, or the widespread acceptance throughout society of the values of the dominant class. The first consists of control of the state only. The second consists of control not only of the state but of civil society as well. The question of the legitimacy generated by the regime is thus the question of supremacy.

In the first part of the twentieth century, with the collapse of the oligarchic state the traditional agricultural/export elite lost its hegemony and even its supremacy. The initial incorporation of the popular sectors, which has been examined above, was an important factor in shaping the way in which a new supremacy was established and the "dictatorship/leadership" or "domination/hegemony" mix on which it was based. The state/party incorporation distinction made above is parallel to Gramsci's distinction between types of supremacy. It also has parallels to Althusser's distinction between the two types of state apparatuses: the repressive state apparatuses (including the government, the bureaucracy, the legal system, and the armed forces and police) and the ideological state apparatuses (including the party system and the political system more generally, as well as the trade unions, among many others).[59] In the case of state incorporation in Brazil, supremacy over the working class was achieved through the control of its interest associations by the legal system and by its cooptation through other state institutions such as the labor ministry and the social security institutes. In the absence of political mobilization and incorporation, supremacy thus rested on control of the state only, and thus suggests domination, rather than hegemony. In the case of Mexico, supremacy was achieved mainly under the aegis of the party, which Gramsci has singled out as the most important hegemonic agent of modern times. From this perspective, we may consider three aspects of a potential hegemonic role of the major party or parties in Mexico and Brazil: the ideological role of socializer or propagandist, the role of maintaining control over organizations in civil society, and the role of mobilizing electoral support.

First, then, the official Mexican party has played the role of socializer or propagandist for the regime. As Cockcroft has suggested, the role of ideology has been a crucial element in the regime's establishment and maintenance of supremacy or, more specifically, of hegemony.[60] The Mexican PRI has clearly played this hegemonic role. It has monopolized the symbols of the revolution and has thus embodied a set of social and moral values and a normative "world view" of social life that has had widespread acceptance throughout Mexican society and has served to legitimate the actions of the state. The PRI has not, of course, articulated a sophisticated, coherent ideology, but it has claimed a pantheon of heroes and a collection of myths and symbols, and these play an important role in attracting and binding mass allegiance.[61] In this sense, it is the genius of Mexican politics that the social revolution, which was defeated during the civil war, nonetheless became the most important national myth and source of legitimacy of every subsequent Mexican government, and Emiliano Zapata and Pancho Villa, the leaders of the defeated opposition, became national heroes while their constituencies became the backbone of support of the Mexican regime. It is no small testimony to the ideological success of the Mexican political elite that they have also sold the myth of the revolution to professional political observers of the country, so that even those who are critical talk of the "betrayal" of the revolution or question the future of the "continuing" revolution. To assert that Mexico even experienced a successful popular revolution is, as Schattsneider said when describing a comparable legitimacy myth in the United States, a "humorous inversion of the truth, an invention of persuasive politicians who told the fable to the historians."[62]

In addition to the Gramscian role of pedagogue, the PRI has played another important role for the establishment of hegemony and control over civil society. The PRI has been the agent of the political incorporation of the functional associations in civil society. The functional organization of the PRI and its institutional incorporation of interest groups, such as labor and peasant unions, are too familiar to repeat here. It is perhaps necessary only to remember that the PRI has become so efficient and all-encompassing in its incorporation of interest groups that it embraces not only those unions which support it politically but even those which do not. In fact, the ability of the party to coopt and incorporate (and perhaps even sponsor) dissident groups has been one of the pillars on which hegemony is based.[63]

Finally, the PRI plays an important legitimating function in its active mobilization of electoral support. The importance of electoral support as a legitimating symbol is seen not only in the mobilizational efforts undertaken by the PRI, but also in the perceived need to give the appearance of near unanimity, which is reflected in the stuffing of ballot boxes, the rigging of elections, and the strict limitation on the number of opposition candidates who are "permitted" to win in the face of these tactics, even when an overall PRI majority is not in doubt. For instance, in presidential elections since 1940, the PRI has never failed to claim in the official returns less than roughly 75 percent of the popular vote, and often this figure is closer to 90 percent. It is important to the legitimacy of the regime and to the notion of popular government not only that the PRI win the presidency overwhelmingly but also, increasingly, that voting be widespread and that opposition parties be allowed: hence the recent anxiety over high levels of abstentions and the political reforms of López Portillo.

In Mexico, then, there has been a multiclass, integrative, hegemonic, one-party dominant system. In the electoral arena, in the interest group arena, and in the symbolic arena, the PRI has been able to bind and integrate popular sector groups to the state.

Brazil presents an entirely different picture. From 1946 to 1964,

Brazil had a factionalized, multiparty system which became increasingly class based. Some analysts have viewed this period as being dominated by the two Vargas parties, the PSD and the PTB, which, for most of the period, formed a coalition that in many ways was similar to a multiclass integrative single-party system.[64] This characterization gives a misleading picture that deemphasizes the contrasts with Mexico. The "coalition" between the PSD and PTB was much more problematic than this indicates; together the two parties did not attract levels of popular support that were at all comparable to that of the PRI; they did not enunciate a comparable ideology or national myth on which to base a hegemonic position; and they did not politically incorporate groups in civil society in a comparable way.

The first point to note, then, is the fluid, shifting nature of coalitions during the period from 1946 to 1964 rather than the formation of a governing coalition between the PSD and the PTB. Politics after the fall of the Estado Novo has often been described in terms of the political opposition of the "ins" (under Vargas) and the "outs."[65] Surely this characterization points to a major line of cleavage: two of the three major parties (the PSD and the PTB) were originally founded with Vargas' support at the end of the Estado Novo period and represented the social forces he had attracted, while the third (the UDN, actually the second largest during most of the period from 1946 to 1964) was publicly and often stridently anti-Vargas. Yet the situation was more complex and less stable than this suggests.

In 1946, Eurico Dutra assumed the presidency as the PSD candidate of the "ins," yet Vargas, then a PSD senator, soon broke with him openly. Furthermore, the period was characterized by hostile relationships between the state and organized labor,[66] which was presumably the main constituency of the supposedly "in" PTB. On the other hand, there was during this period a kind of national pact that included the UDN and that at the same time excluded the PTB.[67]

The complexity of coalitional patterns further increased in 1950 when Vargas was elected president. He was unable to gain the nomination of the PSD, though he did win substantial PSD support, and ran instead as head of a coalition of the PTB and the PSP (Partido Social Progressista). The latter provided an important part of his urban support as well as his vice-presidential candidate. The complex nature of coalitional politics during this period is suggested by the fact that Vargas' alliance "rested on Adhemar's PSP . . . , the PTB, and the PSD where its loyalty was negotiable. In one state . . . Vargas . . . was forced to ally with the UDN, the party whose *raison d'être* was opposition to *getulismo.* "[68] Once installed in the presidency, Vargas gave four ministries to the PSD and one each to the PTB, the PSP, and the

UDN, a distribution reflecting the relative importance to Vargas of the various parties and one which hardly suggests a dominant PSD-PTB coalition. In Congress, the PSD was the largest party, but it had only about a third of the seats. Vargas clearly needed coalition partners. It is interesting to note that he first made overtures to the UDN, the second largest party, at the expense of alienating some members of the PTB.[69] When this failed, he made a dramatic move to attract support from the PTB, thereby incurring the ever more strident wrath of the UDN and the alarm of large sectors of the military.

These events point to two general observations about politics in the 1946-64 period. First, the UDN must not be viewed simply as the major opposition party but as a potential coalition partner which all presidents explored—sometimes successfully.[70] The second and related point is that rather than government by a stable PSD-PTB coalition with the UDN in opposition, the 1946-64 republic was characterized by much more complex, fluid, and constantly shifting relationships and coalitions among all four major parties. Vargas' inability to find a stable coalition on which to base policy decisions and govern and his vacillation in the search to forge a political alliance first with the right and then with the left, thereby alienating each in turn, became a characteristic pattern of the 1946–64 period. Vargas, Quadros, and Goulart were all unable to find a stable basis of support for governing, and as a result none finished his term of office.

The one partial exception to this general picture occurred under the presidency of Juscelino Kubitschek (1955–60). Kubitschek and João Goulart, who was his vice-president, were PSD-PTB coalition candidates; and in congress the two parties tended to form a parliamentary coalition, voting together in 80 percent of the roll calls that have been analyzed by Santos.[71] Once again, however, this image conveys a false sense of a politically stable and dominant coalition. In the 1956 election, Kubitschek, the coalition candidate, won as a minority president, beating his two major opponents with slightly more than a third of the vote (which was divided 36 percent to 30 percent to 26 percent).[72] Furthermore, as Santos has suggested, unless there was nearly perfect party discipline (which there was not), the two parties together did not have sufficient strength to form a congressional majority.[73] Hence, other alliances had to be made. The years of relative political stability under Kubitschek are explained not in terms of the strength and stability of the coalition of the PSD and the PTB but rather in terms of other (temporary and to the present analysis extraneous) factors which made this a period of unusual consensus among all four major parties. In nearly half the roll calls analyzed by Santos, all four parties voted together and in another 47 percent, three of the parties voted together. Thus, in about 90 percent of the roll calls analyzed there was a multiparty coalition; the coalition of the PTB and the PSD alone accounted for only 5 percent.[74]

Not only was the PSD-PTB coalition under Kubitschek less than a majority coalition, but the effect of the coalition "was to preclude any remaining chance, however slight, that the PTB might develop into a leftist party. Instead it became increasingly . . . manipulable."[75] In light of this, it is perhaps no accident that though this was a period of relative political stability in the governing process, at another level there occurred the rapid development of increasingly powerful and popular leftist and populist movements. In the electoral sphere, radical populists such as Leonel Brizola emerged as strong forces on the left within the PTB. In the union movement, there was widespread ferment as new groups and new alignments arose, calling for more radical, structural economic and social changes and championing independent unionism. In the countryside, this period saw a great upsurge in the mobilization and organization of rural workers. These developments will be detailed below, but for present purposes what is important is the result that in the 1960 presidential elections, the last before the 1964 coup, the coalition candidate lost.

Compared to Mexico, then, the Brazilian PSD and the PTB were unable, either separately or together, to dominate the political spectrum as the Mexican PRI has done, to attract anywhere near comparable levels of popular support, or to provide the basis for the emergence of any stable policy orientation. The two parties formed neither a stable governing nor even an electoral alliance. In terms of a governing alliance, it is clear that parliamentary coalitions were not fixed along stable lines but were fluid and constantly shifting. In terms of an electoral alliance, there was no consistent pattern at the local level, and in fact the two parties were often in competition with each other. During the 1946-64 republic, electoral alliances became increasingly important, and by 1962, 41 percent of the vote for congressional elections was cast for coalition candidates, as opposed to only 15.6 percent for the PSD, the largest vote-getter on its own.[76] Interestingly, in this context of increasing importance of electoral alliances, there was no tendency for the PSD and the PTB to combine forces. In fact, in the 1960 and 1962 elections, state governors and federal deputies were elected on alliances in which both the PSD and the PTB participated in only two and three states respectively.[77] Even as an electoral alliance at the national level, the coalition was only minimally effective. In 1945, Dutra won 55 percent of the vote, and that percentage declined steadily in every subsequent election. Vargas (whom the PSD formally opposed) won only 49 percent of the vote in 1950, followed by Kubitschek in 1955 with just 36 percent.[78] The nadir of support for the two parties was reached in the election of 1960, when the coalition candidate lost. The election of Jânio Quadros in 1960 was not merely due to the appeal of a particularly charismatic leader; it was also part of a long-run trend of increasing disaffection from the PSD-PTB coalition candidates during a period of growing political polarization. The election of Goulart to the vice-presidency in 1960 (presidential and vice-presidential elections were separate) as a coalition candidate should not be interpreted as a major exception to the decline of this electoral coalition. First, it must be noted that he won with fewer votes than Quadros. More important, however, Goulart had been identified with the populist, prolabor wing of the PTB. His victory, alongside that of Quadros, represented the victory of a realigned populist coalition and thus something quite different from the PSD-PTB coalition, which was clearly based on the supremacy of the PSD and the subordinate role of the PTB. In fact, to the extent that there was any recurring political pattern during the 1946–64 republic which broke down by the 1960s, it was not a PSD-PTB coalition but a party system defined in terms of the dominance of the PSD and its ability to form any one of several coalitions on an ad hoc basis, in which the PTB was merely one potential partner. Over the years, the position of the PSD declined, and it was increasingly unable to play a dominant role in a governing coalition. In 1960, it lost both the presidency and the vice-presidency. Compared to Mexico, then, the two Vargas parties, either separately or together, were unable to dominate the political spectrum as the PRI has done, to attract anywhere near comparable levels of popular support, or to provide the basis for the emergence of any stable policy orientation.

Given this picture, it is not surprising that the role of ideology also differs in Brazil and Mexico. In the case of Mexico, the dominant ideology is formally embodied in the 1917 Constitution, which defines a number of ideological symbols as readily available to Mexican political leaders. Though, or perhaps because, these symbols may be fictive, their formal statement gives political leaders greater latitude for using rhetoric which would appeal to the popular classes without posing a genuine threat to the political right. Furthermore, the legitimacy of these symbols mitigates political conflict. For instance, the profit-sharing decision was strongly opposed by Mexican business interests; yet, since the Constitution legitimated such a measure, the business community could not oppose the principle of profit-sharing but had to concentrate on neutralizing its effects by influencing the form it would take.[79]

The Brazilian regime had no similar integrative ideological resource. The very fluid, transient nature of electoral alliances and even of party identification reinforced the personalistic, nonideological basis of electoral and party politics. To the extent that ideological themes, such as *trabalhismo* or *getulismo,* were employed in national politics, they were a source of polarization rather than integration in the context of a fluid, factionalized multiparty system.

Finally, Brazil presents a very different picture in terms of the relationship between the major parties and the popular sector functional groups in civil society. In Mexico, the party has had a very important role in the organization, cooptation, and control of popular sector interest associations. Even in a context of a divided labor movement which cannot unify in a single confederation, most labor groups have joined the PRI. Again, in the case of Brazil, this hegemonic function was largely missing, and primary reliance was placed on the state rather than the party for control of interest associations through elaborate legal constraints as well as through cooptation. Unlike countries such as Mexico where "party membership, loyalty, and discipline act as powerful organizers of associational activity . . . this sort of dependency [of interest associations on parties] is not at all common in Brazil."[80] In his survey of union leaders, Schmitter found that two-thirds were not members of a party and about the same number did not think it would be advantageous for a union to be allied to a party.[81] Trade union policy, as initiated under Vargas, was very concerned with separating labor unions from political parties, and Schmitter maintains that this separation continued after the fall of the Estado Novo.[82] Because some leaders may have been reluctant to admit party ties, this finding might be exaggerated. Nevertheless, from the very beginning, the PTB failed to become the dominant political force within organized labor, despite the role of the coopted PTB union leadership. The founding of the PTB coincided with the (temporary) legalization of the Communist Party, which had substantial strength within organized labor, and also with the founding of the PSP, which went on to achieve substantial success among the working class in the industrial core of São Paulo. Furthermore, during the second half of the 1940s the PTB was not closely tied to Dutra's government. As a result, the state did not have a political base in the labor movement, and the Labor Ministry competed directly for control of organized labor with the Communist Party and the PTB, which grew increasingly hostile to the Ministry and the repressive policies it was adopting.[83] The PTB was backed by only a minority of organized labor,[84] and as the labor movement became more politicized, especially from the mid-fifties on, many political groups, including not only the Communists but also Marxist groups to their left, competed for influence.

With the lack of party incorporation, the centrist parties were not in a position to be used as mechanisms of political control or for the hegemonic leadership of unions as the PRI was in Mexico. In fact, in many places the PTB was so weak that it had to depend on the (again illegal) Communist Party to carry out rank-and-file organization and mobilization on its behalf. In light of this and of the general radicalization of the period, there developed within the PTB an independent left wing which served more as a vehicle for opposition than for political control from the center.

In sum, the dominant single-party system, which emerged out of the period of radical populism and which has continued to characterize the Mexican regime, has simultaneously served the interests of the dominant class alliance and incorporated the popular sectors in a way that has undermined attempts to organize an effective opposition. This incorporation has been secured through the cooptation of popular sector interest groups, a vague but appealing ideology, and the mystification which accompanies the mobilization of overwhelming—even if controlled and manipulated—electoral support.[85] If the Mexican party system has been multiclass, integrative, and hegemonic, the Brazilian system has been just the opposite. Following state incorporation of the working class, which explicitly avoided its politicization and incorporation into a political movement or party, political space was left vacant and the centrist establishment parties which emerged had very little advantage over radical opposition parties in the competition both for workers' loyalty and for influence within the organized labor movement. This situation, combined with the division of the pro-Vargas forces into two separate parties and the larger multiparty system which was established, meant that the popular sectors remained politically more autonomous (though highly regulated and constrained functionally and economically) and had somewhat more room for political maneuver, regrouping, and protest. Whereas the Mexican system was a conflict limiting, integrating mechanism, the Brazilian party system provided a vehicle through which increasingly class-based antagonism could be carried out.

Economic Crisis and Political Opposition in the 1950s and 1960s

By about 1950, then, Mexico was characterized by a hegemonic one-party system into which the popular sectors were politically and functionally incorporated as a support group, while Brazil was characterized by an increasingly fluid multiparty system that neither incorporated the popular sectors in a similar way nor permitted the emergence of any stable hegemonic coalition or policy orientation. From these different positions the dominant groups in the two countries had different political resources with which to face the political and economic developments of the 1950s and 1960s. Likewise, the popular sectors had different resources, opportunities, and constraints in their political struggle. The difference in the balance of forces and in the hegemonic position of the state can be illustrated with respect to two developments, one economic and one political. Economically, the period was characterized by postwar inflationary pressure; politically, it was characterized by increasing radicalization, which derived from a variety of factors, including the abandonment of the Communist wartime tactic of popular front collaboration, the influence of the Cuban Revolution, and a number of internal conditions. The emergence of radical and independent political movements in the postwar period can be seen in three areas: political parties, labor organizations, and peasant organizations.

INFLATION

Following World War II, the pent-up demand in Latin American markets led to a major increase in imports. This resulted in the depletion of accumulated foreign exchange, in trade and balance of payments deficits, and in high rates of inflation.[86] It soon became apparent to economic policymakers in both Brazil and Mexico that the state would have to intervene and pursue a stabilization program to offset these trends.

In 1949 and again in 1954, Mexico devalued the peso. The immediate effect was to give a further impetus to the rise of domestic prices. In 1954, the rate of inflation reached a record 25.9 percent. This inflation was translated into a fall of real wage rates, provoking demands for commensurate wage increases. These demands were backed by a strike threat and, in addition, a more impressive threat by Fidel Velázquez, leader of the CTM, to return to "revolutionary unionism" and to take the CTM out of the PRI. In this way, the CTM was able to demand a modified interpretation of government wage policy in which increases that were equal to cost-of-living increments were allowed, thus defending the level of real wages. Congress voted a 24 percent increase in wages, and in subsequent wage negotiations with employers, labor—and particularly the CTM unions—won such increases.[87] Thus, given the political importance of the CTM as a support group within the governing coalition, an accord was reached which protected the workers' purchasing power and at the same time did not compromise the stablization program. There followed a period of prolonged price stability in Mexico.

In the 1970s, when once again prices were pushed upwards, the government was able to undertake another stabilization program with the support of much of the organized labor movement, despite the ensuing fall in real wages. In this case, the government extended a series of inducements to the labor movement to secure its cooperation. These included such distributive measures as control over a workers' housing fund, the establishment of a new bank to provide loans to workers, and new provisions for job-safety training. Underlining the typical and important role of ideology and symbolism in the Mexican system, another inducement offered to labor (provoking opposition on the right despite the absence of any substantive content) was the redefinition of the PRI as a "workers' party."[88]

In contrast to the experience of Mexico, the pre-1964 history of Brazil reveals a record of nearly constant unsuccessful attempts to implement stabilization programs under every president since Dutra. These occurred in 1953–54, 1955–56, 1958–59, 1961, and 1962–63. In the short run, stabilization policies adversely affect the economic interests of many groups in society and may be the object of widespread opposition. However, probably most important in preventing implementation was the opposition of labor and the more independent position from which it attempted to defend its class interests under the regime in Brazil.[89] In the context of a lack of party incorporation and of the unravelling of state control (see below), the various governments had little leverage over the labor movement for controlling its demands and were unable to secure its cooperation. On the contrary, labor was able to exert political pressure on the government to prevent the implementation of a policy clearly detrimental to its interests. In a regime characterized by shifting coalitions and competitive party politics, the political costs of working-class opposition were unacceptable. The labor movement was not strong enough, however, to win the adoption of an alternate policy to meet the economic problems. In each case, the stabilization effort was abandoned, and the government was immobilized, unable to act effectively in this policy area.

POLITICAL PARTIES

We may begin the discussion of the contrasts in the role of leftist parties in Brazil and Mexico by noting that the Brazilian Communist Party (PCB) has historically been one of the strongest Communist parties in Latin America. It was the only one to attempt violent revolution (in 1935), and though it has been banned almost continually since that time, it remained a strong political force in the period from 1946–1964. The PCB was legalized in 1945, the same year in which the PTB was founded, so there was only a limited sense in which the PTB would have preempted the left-leaning part of the political spectrum. As a result, during the short period from 1945 to 1947 when the PCB was not banned it quickly developed a level of electoral support comparable to that of the PTB.[90] The threat that this success seemed to represent led to the hasty suppression of the PCB. However, even during the ensuing period of illegality, the party remained a force to be reckoned with, given the kind of coalition-building that characterized the period. From 1950 on, though illegal, the PCB was allowed to operate quite openly and to run candidates on other party tickets, and the fortunes of other parties, such as the PSP and the PTB, were sometimes dependent on the support of the PCB.

In addition to the Communist Party, there was during the course of the 1946–64 period a proliferation of other opposition parties and groups on the left which had substantial support and strategic power. In addition to the minor parties, some of which had representation in the legislature, independent left-wing factions developed in all three major parties and became particularly important in the post-Kubitschek period. The most important of these factions was in the PTB. This wing of the party defied attempts by PTB President Goulart to control it. In fact, rather than become a reliable support group for Goulart, this faction joined forces with the other left-wing factions and formed the FPN (Frente Parlamentar Nacionalista) a parliamentary group which coordinated their activities and continually pressured Goulart from the left. This group was opposed on the right by another parliamentary group, Ação Democrática Parlamentar. It is clear then that although legalized class-based parties never played a dominant role in Brazilian politics, the factionalization of the major parties and the regrouping of these factions reflected increasing polarization and led to a pattern of increasingly class-based politics. This polarization of political alignments in parliament was mirrored in other groups among students, workers, peasants, businessmen, and the military. In this situation, the politics of compromise became more difficult as the political game became more zero-sum. The result was immobilism in presidential leadership and periodic about-faces, particularly by Goulart, in an attempt to seek alternative support coalitions.

No comparable factionalization of the party or polarization of politics occurred in Mexico. Though parties have formed on both the right and the left of the PRI, these have not been able to mount a major challenge to the dominance of the PRI. The Communist Party, the

PCM, has a long history of collaboration with the government. According to Alexander, the PCM was subsidized by Calles and by subsequent presidents for most of the next thirty years.[91] It fared well in the thirties under Cárdenas, increasing its strength substantially. However, following the Comintern's Popular Front policy, the PCM failed to use its position to become a source of leftist pressure on the government. Rather, even before comparable action was taken by the major labor confederation (the CTM), the PCM fell enthusiastically in line behind the presidential candidacy of Avila Camacho, and later announced its willingness to act as "the shock brigade of avilacamachismo."[92] Though Communists have subsequently been important in independent labor and peasant organizations and political movements on the left of the PRI, the "decidedly middle class and frankly bourgeois"[93] PCM has not constituted a serious challenge to the government. In 1979, as a registered party for the first time, it failed to win a single directly elected seat in the congressional elections, though it was allocated eighteen under the terms of the new electoral reform.

Nevertheless, the PCM fared better in the 1979 elections than the PPS (Partido Popular Socialista), the other "major" party to the left of the PRI. The PPS, founded in the late 1940s by Vincente Lombardo Toledano (leader of the CTM under Cárdenas), represented a diverse group on the left. Soon, however, the various components broke away —some were attracted back into the PRI, others objected that the PPS was too moderate. The party was further weakened by the uneasy relationship between the Communists, who wanted to dominate the party, and Lombardo, who rejected their leadership, preferring to retain control himself. By 1954, the party was so weak that Lombardo attempted to bring it back into the fold of the PRI. In 1958, in the context of a break with the orthodox Communists, the PPS supported PRI candidate Adolfo López Mateos for president, though it ran its own congressional candidates, only one of whom was successful.

Following the Cuban Revolution, there was renewed political activity on the Mexican left. In 1961, the MLN (Movimiento de Liberación Nacional) was formed as a left unity movement. However, Lombardo and the PPS (and the POCM, Partido Obrero Campesino Mexicano, along with it) broke with this movement, leaving the MLN and the party which it formed seriously weakened. In 1964, following the first (and more limited) electoral reform allocating seats in the Chamber of Deputies to parties able to capture at least 2.5 percent of the national vote, the PPS won ten seats amid hints of a deal with the government.[94] The presence of the PPS, which is only nominally independent from the PRI, does not constitute a challenge from the left but rather enhances the legitimacy of the Mexican regime through the appearance of multipartyism and of greater leftist representation. It is clearly the intention of the Mexican political elite that the new participation of the PCM and the smaller parties that have participated in the political reform will function in the same way.[95]

LABOR ORGANIZATIONS

In both Mexico and Brazil, the end of the 1940s was a period of repression and deactivation of the labor movement. In Mexico, this followed the Cárdenas presidency and reached its height under Miguel Alemán, who repressed the left, intervened in the unions, and purged the CTM of Communists and leftists in 1947. The result was a coopted, controlled labor movement which agreed to a pact of industrial peace. In Brazil, this period of repression and deactivation occurred on the heels of the political opening following the fall of the Estado Novo, when political freedoms had been restored and the Communist Party had been legalized. The success of the PCB both in the elections and in the unions, combined with an increase in the militancy and independence of the unions, led to the banning of the PCB and to government intervention in the unions.

By the late 1940s, then, the labor movements of both Brazil and Mexico had come under the control of the coopted leadership of the *pelegos* in the one case and the *charros* in the other, who were divorced from the grass roots of the labor movement. During the 1950s, both countries experienced independent movements within organized labor in reaction to this "kept unionism" and the repression and decline in real incomes that accompanied it. In Mexico, the reaction first appeared with the opposition of Vincente Lombardo Toledano, in the late 1940s. Lombardo tried at various times to create an independent labor movement, at one point attempting to take the CTM out of the PRI and at others attempting to form an independent labor confederation which would rival the CTM. He met with very limited success in these efforts. Through a combination of suppression and responsiveness the government was able to retain or regain the loyalty of the leading confederations and unions.[96] In the early 1950s, the remaining dissident unions formed two new confederations, the CROC (Confederación Revolucionaria de Obreros y Campesinos) and the CRT (Confederación Revolucionaria de Trabajadores). Characteristically, these stayed independent from the CTM, but joined the PRI.

In the 1950s, two other important instances of labor revolt occurred. The first, the 1954 threat of Fidel Velázquez to take the CTM out of the PRI, was discussed above. The second was the wave of strikes that occurred in 1958 and 1959, this time primarily among unions which were not members of the CTM. In addition to bread-and-butter issues, a major element in these strikes was the rebellion against the coopted leadership and the attempt to supplant it with a democratically elected independent leadership. The pattern of official response to these strike movements was one of flexibility. The government played a sophisticated game involving many concessions, but would not allow independent unionism to go so far as to threaten the PRI-labor alliance upon which the legitimacy of the state is, in part, based. Repression of the independent movements was resorted to only after leaders refused the terms of cooptation, which exchanged concessions for cooperation with the PRI.[97] Even after the government reasserted its control, the wage demands of the dissident unions were often met.[98] In Mexico, then, unions were under strong pressure to join the PRI and contribute to the legitimacy of the state. The economic weakness of most Mexican unions and their need to find allies in their collective bargaining makes them particularly vulnerable to this kind of pressure.[99] However, the government has also been very flexible and willing to tolerate substantial independence within the framework of sustaining the overall PRI-labor alliance.[100] The result has been a coopted and yet pluralistic labor movement which has tended to contribute to rather than oppose the legitimacy of the capitalist state.

The 1950s in Brazil was also a period in which the labor movement rebelled against the coopted leadership. Whereas the movement was contained within the single-party, cooptive system in Mexico, it became increasingly independent of the mainstream within the major parties in Brazil. This development, of course, paralleled the radicalization of the left and the general political polarization. The PTB was a weak cooptive instrument and proved "inept at mobilizing union rank and file."[101] This weakness, combined with Communist Party strength in the unions and a competitive regime based on ad hoc alliances, meant that the appeal for union support was made on a different basis than it was in Mexico.

In 1950, as part of his appeal to urban labor for support in his bid for the presidency, Vargas held out the promise of more freedom and fewer restrictions within the labor movement. He allowed union elections, which had been suspended under Dutra, and cancelled the ideological oath which had been the basis for disqualifying Communists and leftists from union leadership. As a result, the younger, more independent PTB leaders and the Communists tended to win control of the unions, regaining the position they had lost in 1947.[102] Yet, despite these concessions, Vargas tried to attract labor loyalty with a minimum of mobilization and gave "surprisingly little importance to either the party or the [Labor] Ministry during the 1951–1952 period."[103] With greater freedom accompanied by little political mobilization, independent and radical movements within labor grew, and the rise of labor militancy, reflected in the major strike movement of 1953, frightened the right. In the course of the ensuing polarization, Vargas vacillated, finally granting a wage increase that signaled his decision to seek working-class support at the expense of the support of other sectors and his concomitant abandonment of his stabilization program. However, given his failure to mobilize the working class and strengthen its political organizations, he was unable, with this single move, to secure the support he needed as a counterweight to the gathering opposition.[104]

Under Kubitschek, the independent movement within organized labor became more vigorous. In 1956, new Marxist groups, some of which had split from the increasingly collaborationist PCB, began to operate within the labor movement. The MRS (Movimento Renovador Socialista), which promoted union autonomy and a reorganization of the union structure to increase worker participation, arose partly from the ranks of these groups. At the same time, horizontal inter-union groupings began to emerge, which, although not legal, were tolerated in the political context of competitive bidding for popular support. In 1958, strikes increased substantially at the same time that the congressional election returns reflected increasing radicalization and disaffection from the populism of the PTB among workers in the major industrial cities.[105] Increasingly independent, labor tended to become a free-floating political resource not tied to the Vargas coalition. Although divided, many labor groups, including the MRS, backed Quadros against the PSD-PTB coalition candidate in the 1960 presidential elections. Even the *pelegos* in the federations and confederations declined to support actively the coalition ticket after breaking with Goulart at the Third National Union Congress. Although Goulart won the vice-presidency, he lost in those areas with the greatest concentrations of labor and the most class-conscious workers, evidence that the PTB had declined as a vigorous force in labor, especially in the most industrialized areas.[106]

After Goulart regained the presidency, the political strength and independence of the labor movement grew. In 1962, the CGT (Comando Geral dos Trabalhadores) was founded by left-wing militants and quickly became the most important labor confederation. Under this radical leadership, labor tried to increase its leverage over Goulart to use him as a vehicle for promoting its program of basic reforms. Labor's tactic was what Erickson has described as "dissensus" politics, through which labor tried to break up the broad, diverse coalition that Goulart, like other presidents before him, tried desperately to hold together.[107] In an effort to gain concessions and to influence overall national policy, labor leaders threatened to withdraw their support, a serious threat given Goulart's dependence on labor backing. At the same time, they took positions likely to lead other coalition members to withdraw their support. (In this they were supported by the parallel developments, mentioned above, in the sphere of party politics. In fact, their activities were coordinated in the FMP [Popular Mobilization Front], which included the CGT, the FPN, and other radical groups.) All in all, they pursued a policy of polarization in an attempt to limit Goulart's options so that he would have no choice but to rely on labor and adopt its program. In the end, of course, labor did not have the cohesiveness and strength to pursue this strategy, which in the event helped to precipitate the 1964 coup.

PEASANT ORGANIZATIONS

Finally, there have been independent movements among the peasantry in both Mexico and Brazil. In Mexico, the major groups were the UGOCM (Unión General de Obreros y Campesinos Mexicanos), founded in the late 1940s, and the CCI (Central Campesina Independiente), founded in 1963. The PRI responded to these movements flexibly and cooptively in its characteristic fashion. "The government managed to weaken the UGOCM by using its usual means of control: land petitions, applications for credit, requests for water-use preference, and so forth, were resolved favorably only if they had the backing of the CNC [the official peasant confederation]."[108] As a result, while the UGOCM maintained its agrarian militancy, it supported the candidacy of Gustavo Díaz Ordaz and found it helpful to cooperate with rather than oppose the PRI.[109] Similarly, pressure was put on the CCI, which split into two factions: one favored closer ties to the CNC and the PRI; the other, which resisted cooptation, was dealt with through a combination of repression (its leaders were jailed) and responsiveness to its demands.[110]

In Brazil, when militant peasant organizations appeared in the second half of the 1950s, the government had no loyal organization which it could use as an instrument for cooptation of the new, independent groups. Rather, these groups appeared in a vacuum, posing a threat both to the major political leaders, who had no control over them, and to the landowning elite, whose power rested on their political control of the rural areas in a country which had never had an agrarian reform.

Organizing activity among the peasants accelerated in the 1960s. In his attempt to win support and gain control of this movement,

Goulart put into effect in 1963 a rural labor law which offered protection to rural unions and facilitated their formation.[111] By 1964, the Communist Party, by now quite moderate and cooperating with the government, was beginning to consolidate its control over the rural labor-union structure, with the help and support of Goulart. Nevertheless, given the extreme weakness of Goulart's political position and the nature of the political situation at the time, this development did not constitute a reliable vehicle for cooptation. In the end (a month before the coup), a desperate and beleaguered president decreed an agrarian reform as part of a more decisive turn to the left. Yet the decree was attacked by both right and left. The militancy of the rural unions grew and armed conflict broke out in the countryside, but Goulart was unable either to control or to capitalize on these developments.[112] The cooptation of independent movements among the peasantry in Brazil was thus less effective than in Mexico.

The preceding discussion has focused on the relative power (or political) resources of the state and popular sector groups in the policy arena of inflation and on their ability to inhibit or succeed in, respectively, the formation of autonomous political movements within the functional organizations of the popular sectors and the party system. These issues are interrelated. The stabilization policies typically adopted to deal with inflation impose heavy costs on the popular sector and thereby stimulate polarization and the development of leftist movements. The more politically autonomous position of these movements in the competitive party context in Brazil enabled them to defend their interests at least to the extent of preventing the implementation of such policies. Their position was not strong enough, however, to lead to the adoption of an alternate approach. As a result, the government was immobilized in this important area of policy. On the other hand, in Mexico the incorporated position of labor meant that labor was not able to prevent the adoption or implementation of such policies, and indeed the official labor sector played a crucial intermediary role between the state and the working class, a role which both neutralized the political impact of opposition groups and facilitated the implementation of (antiworker) stabilization policies. (However, the political incorporation of labor, and its contribution to the legitimacy of the state as a component of the official coalition, also meant that there was some limit beyond which the state could not go in undermining the basic interests of labor.) In this sense, these factors were cumulative: the resolution of one contributed to the resolution of the other, and the inability to deal with one accelerated the other.

In Mexico, the early pattern of mobilization and incorporation weakened the popular sector political organizations by binding them to the dominant political party and gave the state more ideological, symbolic, and cooptive flexibility in maintaining political domination. With these resources, the Mexican state has had a greater capacity to pursue anti-popular sector policies on a short-term basis and to contain and coopt radical and independent political movements. It is important to stress that the initial period of incorporation did not tie the popular sectors to the state "once and for all"—there have been regular attempts since that period to establish autonomous political movements and functional organizations. The point is that the heritage of the initial period formed the parameters of the on-going struggle, giving the state important resources with which to coopt such movements on a continuing basis and making opposition movements more difficult to mount.

Though repression is used in Mexico, the first line of attack constitutes an attempt to coopt the wayward movement by offering concessions in exchange for the adoption of a supportive role. A common feature of this process in Mexico has been the creation of ever higher levels of organization to include and incorporate the independent movements. This has occurred in the party arena and in the arena of urban and rural unions. In the field of labor unions, for instance, many of those unions which wanted to remain independent of the CTM were incorporated in the BUO (Bloque de Unidad Obrera), an inter-confederation grouping which allowed the component parts organizational autonomy but united them for the purpose of supporting the PRI politically. When some groups declined to affiliate with the BUO and formed the rival CNT (Confederación Nacional de Trabajadores), once again an overarching organization, the Congreso de Trabajo, was formed both to accommodate and to incorporate the dissident unions. Encompassing all of these, of course, is the PRI, with which virtually all unions are affiliated. A similar pattern has occurred among peasant organizations. One part of the response to the independent UGOCM and CCI was the formation of the Permanent Agrarian Congress (CONPA) which simultaneously granted some concessions, became a new umbrella organization embracing the CNC as well as the UGOCM and the CCI (or one faction of it), and tried to bring the activities of the dissident peasant organizations back within a legal framework. This development was followed by the Pacto de Ocampo, in which the organizations decided to unite around the CNC.[113] Finally, in the sphere of party politics, this process of incorporation has a parallel in the reforms which grant (minor) opposition parties more legislative seats than they are able to win electorally. In each of these arenas—party politics, labor unions, and peasant organizations—independent groups get concessions and organizational benefits in exchange for playing according to the rules of the game and supporting the system. This organizational cooptation has of course been accompanied by an extraordinarily extensive system of leadership cooptation.[114] In the process, Mexico has developed a system which tolerates a fair degree of pluralism in its political and functional organizational life. This limited pluralism has contributed to the integration of the parts and the stability of the system as a whole.[115] Thus, Mexico has avoided the kind of harsh, repressive military regime that has come to power in Brazil and other relatively industrialized countries of Latin America and has instead dealt with this period of crisis and challenge within the framework of the existing civilian political system, which has continued to serve the dominant class alliance well.

In Brazil, the initial elite compromise did not allow mobilization and did not provide a basis for policies and ideologies which permitted a comparable appeal to the popular sectors. The Brazilian state entered the 1950s without the hegemonic and cooptive resources available to the Mexican state. The PTB, the potential populist party which would embrace both the popular sectors and the elites in control of the state, did only a very partial job of popular sector mobilization and competed with other, often class-based, parties. Furthermore, the inclusion of the PTB in the governing coalition was often problematic. The division of the initial Vargas coalition into two distinct parties, and the clear, though decreasing, dominance of the PSD during most of the 1946–64 period, when coalitions were fluid, meant that even leaving aside the question of mobilization, the PTB did not serve the elites as the instrument of cooptive control of the popular sectors as the PRI did in Mexico. As a result, the popular sectors had some room to begin to develop autonomous political movements.

In this context of increasing popular sector demands and autonomy, with at best only a weak instrument of cooptive control and with competition for popular sector loyalty from other parties and movements, the Brazilian elite could rely only on further state control—i.e., on control through the legal-regulative system, through the repression of independent groups, and through cooptation into the Labor Ministry and social security institutes. However, all three of these elements of state control began to break down under the competitive bidding for popular sector electoral support which accelerated during the course of the 1946–64 republic. Key provisions of the Estado Novo labor law were not enforced and others were under strong attack by organized labor. Repression became increasingly unfeasible in a competitive, electoral context, and independent movements assumed important roles in the labor movement. In the end, even much of the patronage of the social security institutes, the main source of state cooptation of labor, was given over to independent leaders in an unsuccessful bid for their support.[116]

At the same time that the system of control of organized labor broke down, two other systems of control also began to erode. The first was the system of peasant control, which relied on the continuing clientelist control by landlords and the continued absence of politicization and mobilization of the peasantry. The increase in peasant leagues and peasant mobilization in the early 1960s constituted a potential threat to the system of political domination in the countryside. The second was the electoral system—and ultimately the regime itself. Throughout the 1946–64 period, the initially dominant PSD fared less and less well. Its representation in the federal chamber went from 53 percent of the seats (compared to only 8 percent for the PTB) in 1948 to 30 percent in 1962, a position of near parity with the PTB (which was then at 27 percent). The UDN representation remained nearly constant during this period at about a quarter of the seats.[117] In the executive, of course, the PSD suffered outright defeat. Furthermore, the electoral system brought to power both in Congress and in the governorships independent leaders of the left who represented credible challenges. Finally, the regime produced in Congress and in political life in general increasingly class-based political groups, which made the political game increasingly zero-sum, precluding the formation of any hegemonic position and immobilizing policy. The repeated unsuccessful attempts to adopt a stabilization program are an example of this stalemate among the country's political forces. More broadly, Santos' analysis shows the paralysis of the state—the decreased capacity to make decisions on major issues—that occurred by the end of the 1946–64 republic in the context of increased radicalization, polarization, and political fragmentation.[118]

The strength of the left by 1964 should not be overstated.[119] Clearly it was not powerful enough to prevent the coup or to determine the course of events before or after it. However, the important point is that with the breakdown of the system of control, the left was *perceived* as strong by both right and left, and this perception led to further polarization. It led the left itself to take positions and make demands it did not have the power to back up, and it led the right to view the left as an unacceptable threat. In this context, there emerged a substantial coalition favoring a military coup aimed at installing a new regime capable of breaking the political deadlock and establishing domination by the political right through coercion.

In summary, the differences between Brazil and Mexico that have been discussed in the previous section help to account for their contrasting experiences in the 1950s and 1960s. The first is the different bases of legitimacy of the two regimes. In Mexico, the incorporation and cooptation of the popular sectors is consistent with the revolutionary myth. The one-party dominant system derives its legitimacy from the perception of the party as embodying the "goals of revolution" and the alliance between the state and the popular sectors. This myth requires that the PRI occupy the political space on the left and is consistent with its practice of absorbing and perhaps even sponsoring dissident groups on the left. In Mexico, then, party incorporation continues to be legitimated by the revolutionary myth. In Brazil, on the other hand, the initial pattern of popular sector incorporation became illegitimate with the fall of the Estado Novo. In 1950, when Vargas tried to attract labor support, he could point to the welfare benefits he had provided during the Estado Nôvo but at the same time had to renounce the "paternalistic" state-labor relations of that period and promise greater independence for the labor movement.[120] This change was forthcoming, and the system of state incorporation began to crumble.

The second related difference between Mexico and Brazil is that as Mexico entered the 1950s, "political space" and "syndical space" were largely filled with coopted unions and an encompassing party, whereas in Brazil this space was not filled in the same way. This difference meant that the economic crises and opposition movements of the 1950s and 1960s posed different challenges to the dominant elites. In Mexico, the state had to coopt dissident factions as they broke away from the party or the major confederations, whereas in Brazil the ongoing task was to win, rather than maintain, the support of the greater part of the increasingly autonomous popular sectors. From the point of view of the popular sectors, the Mexican state presented the much more formidable arsenal of organizational, cooptive, and ideological resources of a one-party dominant, hegemonic regime. The Brazilian popular sectors, by contrast, faced a severely constrained industrial relations system but were gaining room for political maneuver within a nonhegemonic, multiparty regime.

Finally, a major difference between Mexico and Brazil during this period was that Brazil had a competitive regime which to a greater extent coincided with the decision-making apparatus of the state, whereas Mexico had a one-party dominant regime, largely separate from the decision-making apparatus. The competitive bidding for popular sector support in Brazil worked to the advantage of the popular sectors, which were thus in a better position to exert pressure in the arena where policy decisions took place. In Mexico, by contrast, the regime has served to perform the legitimating task and the constituency work of the state and at the same time has insulated the decision-making arena from popular pressures. These differences in regime and pattern of popular sector incorporation are crucial to understanding why Brazil experienced a harshly repressive, exclusionary military coup, whereas the dominant elites of Mexico have been able to rely on somewhat blander forms of political control.

Conclusion

The similarities and differences between Mexico and Brazil can perhaps be summarized by saying that the two countries have broadly similar patterns of collective goals and consequently of allocations throughout society but have quite different regimes. The questions addressed in this chapter are: how did the two countries come to have such different patterns of regime evolution and how well did the different regimes perform what may be viewed as their primary function—legitimating and supporting the pattern of collective goals and allocations, specifically, of course, the pattern of accumulation under similar models of capitalist development. The basic argument of this chapter is that to understand the differences in patterns of regime evolution and regime legitimacy one must go back to the way in which the initial political incorporation of lower class groups occurred in each country earlier in this century. This set the context for the subsequent emergence of different party systems and class alliances, which in turn affected the political resources of both the state and the popular sectors and thus formed the parameters of the ongoing political struggle of the dominant elite and the state to secure supremacy on the one hand and of the popular sectors to establish their political autonomy and defend their economic and material interests on the other. In Mexico, the organized popular sectors became a crucial part of the support coalition for the Mexican state—one that could be alienated only at high cost to the legitimacy and stability of the system. This position has given them a minimal—or potential—political resource. However, given the enormous political resource the state has derived from official unionism and from the cooptive, hegemonic role of the party, the popular sectors have been able to reap the advantage only very sporadically and partially. In Brazil, where the popular sectors did not initially form a support group for the state, and what I have called state rather than party/movement incorporation occurred, the urban popular sectors remained politically more autonomous and hence in a somewhat better position, in the face of a competitive, nonhegemonic regime based on shifting alliances, to pressure the government and ultimately to mount a more sizable autonomous movement, unlike any that has occurred in Mexico.

The difference in the pattern of initial incorporation of the popular sectors in Mexico and Brazil has implications for our theoretical understanding of populism. Many authors have argued that this initial incorporating period in Latin America comes about when the newly emerging industrial bourgeoisie forms a coalition with the newly emerging working class, thus creating a multiclass alliance within the industrial sector aimed at ending the hegemony of the landed export elite. Within this alliance or populist coalition, the bourgeois elite is seen as dominating and controlling the mobilized popular sectors, channeling their mobilization in nonthreatening ways supportive of capitalist industrialization. The two cases which are the subject of this book suggest that this characterization is a composite description of at least two distinct types of historical experiences and as such is an accurate description of neither. Some elements fit one type, some another, but they should not be combined.

In the first type of inclusionary period, characteristic of Mexico, the above-mentioned sectoral clash may be an important feature; however, the intrasectoral alliance across classes is weaker than has often been asserted. To the extent that such a bourgeoisie-working class alliance within the industrial sector exists at all, it quickly ruptures as the inherent contradictions of such a coalition come to the fore. When the industrial working class is politically mobilized for the purposes of intra-elite conflict, that mobilization often does not consist in as unequal a pattern of power distribution or as great a degree of domination as has sometimes been assumed. The power of the elite group may be dependent on the augmentation of real power of the popular sector groups. The leaders of these groups often act with the knowledge that they are a valuable power resource to the elite, and they extract real concessions from the alliance. The result of this mobilization is a "radical populism" which produces political polarization along class lines. The national industrial bourgeoisie, if ever in the dominant coalition, at this point leaves it. Hence, in these cases, the widely posited labor-industrialist coalition does not exist. Rather, class conflict within the urban-industrial sector is a prominent feature. Though the populist leader may be pro-industrialization, his pro-worker stance, necessary to attract the support needed to gain power in the first place, serves to alienate industrialists. In this case, greater real benefits tend to accrue to the popular sectors. The eventual outcome of this kind of inclusionary politics may leave the popular sectors weak, penetrated, and dominated, but this must be seen as a *reaction* that follows populism rather than as a part of it.

This type of inclusionary politics is what I have called party/movement incorporation. It is characterized by a more or less extensive mobilization of the popular sectors—usually both urban and rural —which is part of an opposition strategy of a political elite that seeks to gain or consolidate power. As part of the mobilization and the attempt to channel that mobilization, the popular classes are politically incorporated in the sense that the populist elites create a political party home for the newly mobilized groups. This is not the place to elaborate the details of other cases which fit or approximate the party incorporation category. Suffice it to say that the cases of Perón's Argentina, López's Colombia, and the *trienio* in Venezuela, for instance, demonstrate substantial "fit" with the party/movement incorporation "model."[121]

In the second type of inclusionary politics, sectoral clash is much more subdued, since there is a stalemate among the different elite factions, which reach a kind of accommodationist modus vivendi. This includes an understanding that they will not politicize and mobilize the popular sectors. In this situation, the incorporation of popular sector groups is a product of elite consensus rather than a tactic in their rivalry. The result is a paternalistic incorporation intended to weaken, depoliticize, and dominate the popular sectors.

This second type of inclusionary politics I have called state incorporation. It derives less from the political strategies of contending elite factions and more from elite agreement on the potential threat posed by the "dangerous" classes (that is, the working class) and the need to do something about the "social question." Inclusion then takes the form of cooptive legalization of the labor movement. There is a fairly extensive elaboration of labor law which structures the system of trade union representation and explicitly controls unions with respect to the demands they can make, their internal governance, and their leadership selection. However, nothing is done to legalize unions among rural workers. The rural elite typically strikes a bargain that they will go along with the legalization of urban trade unions in exchange for noninterference in the structure of class relations in the countryside. There is little or no political mobilization of either the urban or rural popular sectors. Consequently, little or no polarization occurs. Furthermore, with the emphasis on depoliticization of the popular sectors, little or nothing is done to incorporate them into a populist political party. Again, just in passing, it may be noted that Chile during the Alessandri/Ibáñez period had much in common with the state incorporation pattern.[122]

Brazil and Mexico thus represent two quite distinct types of initial inclusionary periods. These differ with regard to the goals of the particular elites who initiate them, the composition of the coalition which supports these elites, the strategic political location of the popular sectors, the degree to which they are politically mobilized, and the degree of class polarization that results. Furthermore, as the labels indicate, the two types imply different relationships between the popular sectors and the major political parties. The process of political mobilization that occurs in the first type of inclusionary politics involves the incorporation of those sectors into a populist party. In contrast, the demobilization that is part of the state incorporation pattern precludes the establishment of a populist party during this period.

This distinction between the two different types of inclusionary periods raises a series of questions. In the case of party incorporation, or radical populism, how was the political polarization resolved and what was the consequence for the continued participation of the popular sectors in the dominant coalition? In some cases, it was resolved under the aegis of the populist leader, as in Mexico, whereas in others it was not worked out until later, if at all. In no case, however, were the popular sector groups, which always occupied subordinate positions in the populist coalition, able to triumph. Rather, the alienated bourgeoisie was brought back into the dominant coalition at the expense of the popular sectors. In the case of state incorporation, the key question is, do the popular sectors remain politically quiescent, or do other parties develop or move in to fill the void? In general, then, what was the party heritage of the way in which the popular sectors were initially incorporated?

Somewhat paradoxically, perhaps, it is out of the cases of greater initial polarization, of more radical populism and party incorporation, that multiclass integrative party systems emerged, whereas greater polarization was the ultimate outcome of state incorporation. Party incorporation attracted the political loyalties of the popular sectors, whereas state incorporation left this political "space" relatively unoccupied, to be filled by more class-based parties or party factions.

In the case of party incorporation, the situation was unacceptable to the alienated economic elite, and radical populism and polarization had, in their view, to be terminated. This was accomplished either under the aegis of the populist leader, as under Cárdenas, or more typically through a counterrevolution effected by a military coup. In either case, the clearly unacceptable status of radical populism in the eyes of the economic elite led the populist leaders to develop conflict-limiting mechanisms which would preclude a repetition of these earlier confrontations. In Mexico, this took the form of the further institutionalization of the one-party system. Elsewhere, where a major goal of political leaders was the restoration of civilian rule, it typically took the form of the party pact, which included an agreement on a moderate program and usually, in addition, on some form of co-participation of the parties involved. The "success" of these arrangements in the various countries and the ability of the resulting regimes to provide legitimacy have depended on their capacity to incorporate the popular sectors on an on-going basis in the face of this fossilization of politics around conservative interests, and thus to prevent the polarization that would result from their alienation and subsequent attraction to radical parties. In this respect, Mexico has remained relatively successful, as has Venezuela. Colombia, and especially Uruguay, have proved less so. Argentina has also been unsuccessful, given the strength of the anti-Peronist counterrevolution which formally excluded Peronism for nearly two decades.

If the establishment of conflict-limiting mechanisms was an aspect of the party heritage of radical populism, in the cases of state incorporation such as Brazil and Chile comparable mechanisms for limiting party conflict were not developed. During the initial incorporating period, political parties had no important role. When party politics subsequently reemerged, a multiparty system was established which had no parallel conflict-limiting mechanisms and in which the centrist parties continued to do relatively little to incorporate the popular sectors. State incorporation has the purpose of demobilization, of preventing the emergence of autonomously organized lower class groups, of establishing a dependent labor movement controlled by the state. Yet, the lack of party incorporation of the popular sectors means that in certain contexts, and particularly in the context of a competitive party regime, the popular sectors may have more room for maneuver and greater potential for the development of more autonomous class-based parties. In contrast to a single party or party pact, which at least to some degree incorporated the popular sectors and tied them to the state, there emerged instead multiparty or factional coalition politics which became increasingly class based.

These two types of regimes had very different resources and thus very different degrees of success as legitimating mechanisms for the state. The comparison of Mexico and Brazil seems to suggest that in order to provide legitimacy for a capitalist state pursuing accumulation policies which severely limit the benefits that are allowed to flow to the popular sectors, the regime must contain conflict-limiting mechanisms and incorporate the popular sector as a coopted junior partner. This occurred in Mexico; it did not in Brazil.

In Mexico, the popular sectors have been electorally, ideologically, and functionally incorporated into the single party, which has helped to mediate the relationship between the state and the popular sectors. The party has had vast cooptive resources and thus has been a major instrument of control of popular sector leadership, and through them of the grass roots. Though coercion and repression have certainly been used, the level of cooptation exercised by the party suggests that its control has been largely political. The Mexican system of control has aptly been described as "two carrots then a stick."[123] In Althusser's terms, primary reliance has been placed on the "ideological state apparatus" rather than on the "repressive state apparatus."

In Brazil, a comparable system of political control did not emerge. The initial elite consensus on popular sector control continued to define the parameters of popular sector mobilization. Though there was bidding for popular sector support, no president was willing to commit himself to a period of radical populism as Cárdenas had done in Mexico. Such a policy has the potential for politically incorporating the popular sectors, but it has the consistent effect of alienating the political right and would clearly upset the fragile modus vivendi among the elite. Thus party incorporation never occurred in Brazil, and in the context of a competitive regime, state control broke down. Independent and leftist movements based on popular sector support were able to develop enough strength to veto policy and polarize politics. Thus, not only did the regime fail to secure the hegemonic leadership of the ruling-class alliance, but in the end it seemed to fail in securing the control of this alliance over the state to the point that the capitalist parameters of society appeared to be threatened. The result was the military intervention of 1964, which reasserted control through undisguised reliance on the coercive power of the state, abandoning in fact (and virtually abandoning even in appearance) the use of "ideological" or potentially hegemonic structures.

In stressing the contrast between Brazil and Mexico, I do not intend to take the stability and continuity of the Mexican regime for granted. Quite the contrary: the postincorporation history of Mexico is one of frequent attempts by popular sector groups, both industrial workers and *campesinos,* to free themselves and their functional organizations from control by the party. In the face of these attempts, the Mexican state has had to respond with continual exchanges and concessions central to the ongoing process of cooptation. In the 1970s, Mexico's hegemonic resources seemed to be eroding in response to the most recent of these attempts. The revolutionary ideology has seemed increasingly empty as unemployment has grown to crisis proportions, as real wages have deteriorated, and as agrarian reform, a hitherto unassailable component of the official revolutionary ideology, is explicitly abandoned. Furthermore, increasing electoral apathy reflects the party's weakening ability to mobilize the population. In fact, it has been suggested that the winner of the 1979 congressional elections was not the PRI but "the party of abstention."[124] This context has provided an opening in which more autonomous organizations—both parties and functional organizations—have been able to articulate and attempt to defend the class interests of the popular sectors. It has been reported that since the last elections and the allocations of seats to the Communist Party, the federal chamber has become an arena of real debate on policy, with some members of the PRI taking stands in opposition to the government. The impact of the political reform has also put pressure on the official CTM and the PRI.[125] In addition, new labor organizations have emerged which are striving to supplant *charro* unionism with independent unions better able to defend working class interests. On the other side, the resources of the state include policy flexibility and the continued cooptation of popular sector leadership. The first has served the Mexican state well in the past and may continue to do so, though it has been noted that this flexibility is ultimately constrained by the complex nature of the elite coalition that controls the state and by the delicate political balancing that is required to keep that coalition intact.[126] With regard to the second, the breadth and depth of leadership cooptation in Mexico is extraordinary. Again, this capacity for cooptation may continue to be a decisive resource for the state. Nevertheless, in view of the trends mentioned above, increasing alienation of the rank-and-file from the coopted leadership and from the system in general may prove to be a vulnerable point which provides an opportunity for the popular sectors.

The Mexican system has in the past come through many periods of instability and "disintegration."[127] The fact that it presently seems vulnerable should not be overemphasized. The state, after all, has been effectively pursuing yet another stabilization program, a policy goal which has eluded the vast majority of civilian governments in Latin America. Thus, in a sense, we may be as impressed with the present strength of the Mexican system as with its weaknesses. Furthermore, the most intense phase of the recent protest movements, such as the *tendencia democrática* within the labor movement, may have already passed. Writing in 1980 and commenting on analyses of Mexico that emphasized its potential instability, Cleaves suggests that the picture now seems to have changed: "It is less fashionable today than in the mid-1970s to assert that the Mexican political system is in crisis."[128] Nevertheless, vulnerable areas can be identified. The question for progressive forces in Mexico, as well as for those in Brazil, as that country attempts to move haltingly towards more open, civilian rule, is how to take advantage of this vulnerability without stimulating a counterrevolutionary coup such as the one which occurred in Brazil in 1964 and those that have occurred in the 1970s in the Southern Cone.

Acknowledgments

This article was written with support from the Social Science Research Council and the National Science Foundation, Grant No. SOC 75–19990 and SES 80–17728. I am grateful for helpful comments from several people who read an earlier draft of the manuscript: David Collier, Guillermo O'Donnell, Robert Kaufman, Edson Nunes, Susan Kaufman Purcell, Wanderley Guilherme dos Santos, Kenneth Sharpe, Thomas Skidmore, Evelyn Stevens, and Judith Tendler. I would also like to acknowledge the research assistance of Richard Miller. The Institute of International Studies at Berkeley provided institutional support and skilled typists.

Notes

1. Guillermo A. O'Donnell, *Modernization and Bureaucratic-Authoritarianism: Studies in South American Politics* (Berkeley: Institute of International Studies, University of California, 1973); and "Reflexiones sobre las tendencias generales de cambio en el estado burocrático-autoritario," Documento CEDES/G. E. CLASCO/no. 1 (1975).

2. O'Donnell, "Reflexiones"; Robert R. Kaufman, "Industrial Change and Authoritarian Rule in Latin America: A Concrete Review of the Bureaucratic-Authoritarian Model," in David Collier (ed.), *The New Authoritarianism in Latin America* (Princeton: Princeton University Press, 1979).

3. Douglas A. Chalmers, "The Politicized State in Latin America," in James M. Malloy (ed.), *Authoritarianism and Corporatism in Latin America* (Pittsburgh: University of Pittsburgh Press, 1977).

4. Evelyn P. Stevens, "Protest Movements in an Authoritarian Regime: The Mexican Case," *Comparative Politics*, vol. 7, no. 3 (April 1975), pp. 361–82; Alejandro Portes, "Legislatures Under Authoritarian Regimes: The Case of Mexico," *Journal of Political and Military Sociology*, vol. 5, no. 2 (Fall 1977), pp. 185–201.

5. *Latin America Economic Report*, vol. 5, no. 50 (December 1977), p. 23.

6. See the chapter in this volume by Douglas Graham. For a comparative discussion of Mexico and Brazil as well as other "semiperipheral," "middle-income," or "semi-industrialized" countries, see Peter Evans, *Dependent Development* (Princeton: Princeton University Press, 1979), chapter 6; and Joel Bergsman, "Growth and Equity in Semi-Industrialized Countries," World Bank Staff Working Paper No. 351, 1979.

7. Fernando Henrique Cardoso, "On the Characterization of Authoritarian Regimes in Latin America," in Collier (ed.), *The New Authoritarianism*, pp. 38–40.

8. Murray Edelman, *The Symbolic Uses of Politics* (Urbana: University of Illinois Press, 1967), p. 1; Guillermo A. O'Donnell, "Tensions in the Bureaucratic-Authoritarian State and the Question of Democracy," in Collier (ed.), *The New Authoritarianism*, pp. 286–87.

9. Harold D. Lasswell and Abraham Kaplan, *Power and Society: A Framework for Political Inquiry* (New Haven: Yale University Press, 1950), pp. 130–32.

10. The regime, of course, is not the only source of legitimacy, nor is it a necessary one. Rather, the regime is one possible source of legitimacy—it is the institutional apparatus through which the state may attempt to establish legitimacy. This apparatus may be minimal or relatively elaborate; furthermore, it may be relatively successful in actually establishing legitimacy, or it may not be. Thus, a state could lack an effective institutional legitimacy apparatus and yet be regarded as legitimate by those who approve its particular policies, respond to a charismatic leader, and so forth. In such a situation, a state could also lack legitimacy, relying almost exclusively on coercion.

11. Lasswell and Kaplan, *Power and Society*, p. 132.

12. *Ibid.*, p. 130.

13. Louis Althusser, *Lenin and Philosophy and Other Essays* (New York: Monthly Review Press, 1971), p. 135; and *For Marx* (London: Allen Lane/The Penguin Press, 1969), p. 111. See also Norman Geras, "Althusser's Marxism: An Assessment," in *Western Marxism: A Critical Reader*, edited by *New Left Review* (London: Verso, 1978), p. 253.

14. Reinhard Bendix, *Nation-Building and Citizenship* (New York: John Wiley and Sons, 1964); T. H. Marshall, *Class, Citizenship, and Social Development* (Garden City, N.Y.: Anchor Books, 1965); Leonard Binder *et al.*, *Crises and Sequences in Political Development* (Princeton: Princeton University Press, 1971), and Raymond Grew (ed.), *Crises of Political Development in Europe and the United States* (Princeton: Princeton University Press, 1978).

15. Samuel P. Huntington and Joan M. Nelson, *No Easy Choice: Political Participation in Developing Countries* (Cambridge: Harvard University Press, 1976).

16. Thomas E. Skidmore, *Politics in Brazil, 1930–1964* (New York: Oxford University Press, 1967), pp. 11, 31–32, 46–47, 55–56.

17. Charles W. Anderson, *Politics and Economic Change in Latin America* (Princeton: Van Nostrand, 1967), pp. 104–10; Philippe C. Schmitter, *Interest Conflict and Political Change in Brazil* (Stanford: Stanford University Press, 1971), pp. 70–71; Kenneth P. Erickson, *The Brazilian Corporative State and Working Class Politics* (Berkeley: University of California Press, 1977), p. 185; Riordan Roett, *Brazil: Politics in a Patrimonial Society*, rev. ed. (New York: Praeger, 1978), p. 27; Luciano Martins, "Aspectos políticos de la Revolución Brasileña," *Revista Latinoamericana de Sociología*, vol. 1 (November 1965); Ronald M. Schneider, *The Political System of Brazil* (New York: Columbia University Press, 1971), p. 34.

18. Silas Cerqueira, "Brazil," in Richard Gott (ed.), *Guide to the Political Parties of South America* (Middlesex, England: Penguin, 1973), p. 661.

19. John Womack, Jr., "The Mexican Economy During the Revolution, 1910–1920: Historiography and Analysis," *Marxist Perspectives*, vol. 1 (Winter 1978), p. 96.

20. Dale Story, "Industrialization and Political Change: The Political Role of Industrial Entrepreneurs in Five Latin American Countries," Ph.D. dissertation, Indiana University, 1978, pp. 38–39.

21. Womack, "The Mexican Economy."

22. Arnaldo Córdova, *La formación del poder político en México* (México, D. F.: Ediciones Era, 1977), p. 15.

23. Nora Louise Hamilton, "Mexico: The Limits of State Autonomy," Ph.D. dissertation, University of Wisconsin, Madison, 1978, p. 42.

24. Ruth Berins Collier and David Collier, "Inducements Versus Constraints: Disaggregating 'Corporatism,' " *American Political Science Review*, vol. 73 (January 1979), pp. 967–86.

25. Roett, *Brazil,* p. 134; Schneider, *The Political System of Brazil,* p. 34; Erickson, *The Brazilian Corporative State,* p. 86.

26. Barry Carr, "Organised Labour and the Mexican Revolution, 1915–1928," Latin American Centre Occasional Papers No. II, St. Antony's College, Oxford University, 1972, pp. 13 (first quote) and 15 (second quote).

27. *Ibid.,* p. 13.

28. *Ibid.,* p. 13. See also Marjorie Ruth Clark, *Organized Labor in Mexico* (Chapel Hill: University of North Carolina Press, 1934); and Richard U. Miller, "The Role of Labor Organizations in a Developing Country: The Case of Mexico," Ph.D. dissertation, Cornell University, 1966, p. 29.

29. Gerrit Huizer, "Peasant Organization and Agrarian Reform in Mexico," in Irving Louis Horowitz (ed.), *Masses in Latin America* (New York: Oxford University Press, 1970), p. 451.

30. Robert E. Scott, *Mexican Government in Transition* (Urbana: University of Illinois Press, 1964), pp. 119–21.

31. Skidmore, *Politics in Brazil,* pp. 31, 39–41.

32. Kenneth P. Erickson, "Populism and Political Control of the Working Class in Brazil," *Proceedings of the Pacific Coast Council of Latin American Studies,* vol. 4 (1975), p. 132. See also Erickson, *The Brazilian Corporative State,* pp. 50–51.

33. Wayne A. Cornelius, "Nation Building, Participation, and Distribution: The Politics of Social Reform under Cárdenas," in Gabriel Almond *et al.* (eds.), *Crisis, Choice, and Change: Historical Studies of Political Development* (Boston: Little, Brown, 1973), p. 457.

34. Hamilton, "Mexico," p. 570.

35. Albert L. Michaels, "Mexican Politics and Nationalism from Calles to Cárdenas," Ph.D. dissertation, University of Pennsylvania, 1966, p. 71.

36. Hamilton, "Mexico," p. 570.

37. Erickson, *The Brazilian Corporative State,* pp. 50–52.

38. Skidmore, *Politics in Brazil,* p. 32.

39. Erickson, *The Brazilian Corporative State,* pp. 36–39.

40. Warren Dean, *The Industrialization of São Paulo, 1880–1945* (Austin: University of Texas Press, 1969), pp. 207–13, 224–27; Dale Story, "Industrialization and Political Change," pp. 228–29; Schmitter, *Interest Conflict,* p. 182.

41. Skidmore, *Politics in Brazil,* p. 57.

42. Scott, *Mexican Government in Transition,* p. 122.

43. *Ibid.,* p. 121–22.

44. Lyle C. Brown, "General Lázaro Cárdenas and Mexican Presidential Politics, 1933–1940: A Study in the Acquisition and Manipulation of Political Power," Ph.D. dissertation, University of Texas, 1964, chapter 1.

45. Cornelius, "Nation Building," pp. 445–62.

46. Brown, "Lázaro Cárdenas," pp. 281–90; Cornelius, "Nation Building," pp. 462–63.

47. Cornelius, "Nation Building," p. 463.

48. See also Liisa North and David Raby, "The Dynamic of Revolution and

Counterrevolution: Mexico under Cárdenas, 1934–1940," *Latin American Research Unit Studies*, vol. 2, no. 1 (October 1977), p. 26.

49. Erickson, *The Brazilian Corporative State*, p. 28.

50. *Ibid.*, pp. 19, 23.

51. Timothy Harding, "The Political History of Organized Labor in Brazil," Ph.D. dissertation, Stanford University, 1973, p. 160; Erickson, *The Brazilian Corporative State*, p. 35.

52. Collier and Collier, "Inducements Versus Constraints," pp. 972–76.

53. North and Raby, "The Dynamic of Revolution and Counterrevolution," p. 45.

54. *Ibid.*, p. 47.

55. Schmitter, *Interest Conflict*, pp. 273–75.

56. Skidmore, *Politics in Brazil*, pp. 79–80.

57. *Ibid.*, chapter 3, see especially pp. 83, 102, 108, 112–13, 130–34, 137; and John D. Wirth, *The Politics of Brazilian Development, 1930–1954* (Stanford: Stanford University Press, 1970), pp. 222–23.

58. Antonio Gramsci, *Selections from the Prison Notebooks* (New York: International Publishers, 1971), pp. 12, 56.

59. Althusser, *Lenin and Philosophy*, p. 143.

60. James D. Cockcroft, "Coercion and Ideology in Mexican Politics," in James D. Cockcroft, Andre Gunder Frank, and Dale L. Johnson (eds.), *Dependence and Underdevelopment: Latin America's Political Economy* (New York: Anchor Books, 1972), pp. 258–62.

61. See Alistair Davidson, "Gramsci: On The Party," *Australian Left Review* (October/November 1968), p. 57. That the ideology of the PRI has succeeded in attracting political support has been suggested by Charles L. Davis, "The Mobilization of Public Support for an Authoritarian Regime: The Case of the Lower Class in Mexico City," *American Journal of Political Science*, vol. 20, no. 4 (November 1976), and "The Persistence and Erosion of a Legitimating Revolutionary Ideology Among the Lower Class in Mexico City," *Journal of Political and Military Sociology*, vol. 7 (Spring 1979).

62. E. E. Schattschneider, *Party Government* (New York: Holt, Reinhart and Winston, 1942), p. 48.

63. Bo Anderson and James D. Cockcroft, "Control and Co-optation in Mexican Politics," in James D. Cockcroft *et al.* (eds.), *Dependence and Underdevelopment* (see also Cockcroft, "Coercion and Ideology," pp. 252–58); and Portes, "Legislatures Under Authoritarian Regimes," p. 191.

64. See especially Schmitter, *Interest Conflict*, p. 382. As Santos says, one of the most universally accepted assertions about Brazilian politics between 1946 and 1964 is that "a strong, if tense, coalition through the period between the rural-based Social Democratic Party and urban-based Brazilian Labor Party lent stability to Brazil's limited constitutional regime." Wanderley Guilherme dos Santos, "The Calculus of Conflict: Impasse in Brazilian Politics and the Crisis of 1964," Ph.D. dissertation, Stanford University, 1979, p. 128.

65. Skidmore, *Politics in Brazil*, pp. 55, 146, 189, 214.

66. Harding, "Organized Labor in Brazil," chapter 5.

67. Santos, "The Calculus of Conflict," p. 135; Phyllis J. Peterson, "Brazilian Political Parties: Formation, Organization, and Leadership, 1945–1959," Ph.D. dissertation, University of Michigan, 1962, p. 74; and Harding, "Organized Labor in Brazil," p. 172.

68. Skidmore, *Politics in Brazil*, p. 78.

69. *Ibid.*, p. 102.
70. Santos, "The Calculus of Conflict," pp. 145–46.
71. *Ibid.*, p. 142.
72. *Brazil: Election Factbook*, No. 2, September 1965 (Washington, D.C.: Institute for the Comparative Study of Political Systems), p. 56.
73. Santos, "The Calculus of Conflict," p. 134–38.
74. *Ibid*, p. 142.
75. Skidmore, *Politics in Brazil*, p. 158.
76. *Brazil: Election Factbook*, p. 60.
77. *Ibid.*, pp. 59, 63.
78. *Ibid.*, p. 53.
79. Susan Kaufman Purcell, *The Mexican Profit-Sharing Decision: Politics in an Authoritarian Regime* (Berkeley and Los Angeles: University of California Press, 1975).
80. Schmitter, *Interest Conflict*, p. 272.
81. *Ibid.*, p. 273–74.
82. *Ibid.*, p. 273.
83. Harding, "Organized Labor in Brazil," p. 200.
84. Roett, *Brazil*, p. 76.
85. Guy Hermet, "State-Controlled Elections: A Framework," in Guy Hermet, Richard Rose, and Alain Rouquié (eds.), *Elections Without Choice* (New York: John Wiley, 1978), pp. 14–15.
86. Thomas E. Skidmore, "The Politics of Economic Stabilization in Postwar Latin America," in James J. Malloy (ed.), *Authoritarianism and Corporatism in Latin America*, p. 153.
87. Michael D. Everett, "The Role of Mexican Trade Unions, 1950–1963," Ph.D. dissertation, Washington University, 1967, pp. 126–30.
88. *Latin American Political Report*, vol. 12, no. 32 (18 August 1978), p. 255.
89. Skidmore, "The Politics of Economic Stabilization," p. 179; Harding, "Organized Labor in Brazil," pp. 390–98.
90. Harding, "Organized Labor in Brazil," pp. 174–78.
91. Robert Alexander, *Communism in Latin America* (New Brunswick, N.J.: Rutgers University Press, 1957), p. 323.
92. North and Raby, "The Dynamic of Revolution and Counterrevolution," p. 51.
93. Kenneth F. Johnson, *Mexican Democracy: A Critical View* (Boston: Allyn and Bacon, 1971), p. 114.
94. L. Vincent Padgett, *The Mexican Political System* (Boston: Houghton Mifflin, 1966), p. 78.
95. "Mexico: Class Struggle and 'Political Reform,' " *Contemporary Marxism*, no. 1 (Spring 1980), pp. 73–79, written by collaborators of *Punto Crítico* (Mexico).
96. Everett, "Mexican Trade Unions," pp. 53–56.
97. *Ibid.*, pp. 130–37; Howard Handelman, "The Politics of Labor Protest in Mexico: Two Case Studies," *Journal of Interamerican Studies and World Affairs*, vol. 18 (August 1976), pp. 271–79; and Evelyn P. Stevens, *Protest and Response in Mexico* (Cambridge: MIT Press, 1974), chapter 4.
98. Miller, "Labor Organizations," p. 297.
99. Everett, "Mexican Trade Unions," p. 165.
100. Handelman, "The Politics of Labor Protest in Mexico," p. 289.
101. Harding, "Organized Labor in Brazil," p. 209.

102. *Ibid.*, p. 244–45.

103. *Ibid.*, p. 250.

104. Skidmore, *Politics of Brazil*, pp. 136–37.

105. Harding, "Organized Labor in Brazil," p. 353.

106. *Ibid.*, pp. 450–51.

107. Erickson, *The Brazilian Corporative State*, p. 122 and part III.

108. Rosa Elena Montes de Oca, "The State and the Peasants," in José Luis Reyna and Richard S. Weinert (eds.), *Authoritarianism in Mexico* (Philadelphia: Institute for the Study of Human Issues, 1977), p. 55.

109. Anderson and Cockcroft, "Control and Co-optation in Mexican Politics," p. 383.

110. *Ibid.*, p. 386.

111. Harding, "Organized Labor in Brazil," p. 573.

112. Skidmore, *Politics of Brazil*, p. 291.

113. Montes de Oca, "The State and the Peasants," pp. 60–61.

114. Johnson, *Mexican Democracy*, chapter 3; Susan Kaufman Purcell, "Clientelism and Development in Mexico," paper presented at a conference on Political Clientelism, Patronage, and Development, Bellagio, Italy, August 1978, pp. 9–10.

115. Portes, "Legislatures Under Authoritarian Regimes," p. 191.

116. Erickson, *The Brazilian Corporative State*, pp. 62–63.

117. Roett, *Brazil*, p. 77.

118. Santos, "The Calculus of Conflict."

119. The weakness of the radical labor leaders has been analyzed by Erickson, *The Brazilian Corporative State*, p. 97; and Hewitt has emphasized the coopted position of the Pernambucan peasant movement by 1964 in Cynthia N. Hewitt, "Brazil: The Peasant Movement of Pernambuco, 1961–1964," in Henry Landsberger (ed.), *Latin American Peasant Movements* (Ithaca: Cornell University Press, 1969), p. 395.

120. Harding, "Organized Labor in Brazil," p. 235.

121. David Collier and Ruth Berins Collier, "Labor, Party, and Regime in Latin America," paper presented at the Eleventh World Congress of the International Political Science Association, 1979.

122. Collier and Collier, "Labor, Party, and Regime," pp. 8–15.

123. Cited in Peter H. Smith, *Labyrinths of Power: Political Recruitment in Twentieth Century Mexico* (Princeton: Princeton University Press, 1978), p. 57.

124. *Latin America Political Report*, vol. 13, no. 27 (13 July 1979), p. 212.

125. *Punto Crítico*, vol. 6, no. 69 (31 January 1977), pp. 20–22; Arnaldo Córdova, "Catastrófica, retrasar más las reformas económicas," *Proceso*, no. 171 (11 February 1980), pp. 27–28; Alan Riding, "Mexico's Congress Wins New Attention," *New York Times*, 10 January 1980, p. 6.

126. Susan Kaufman Purcell and John F. H. Purcell, "State and Society in Mexico: Must a Stable Polity Be Institutionalized?" *World Politics*, vol. 32 (January 1980).

127. Purcell, "Clientelism and Development in Mexico," p. 2.

128. Peter S. Cleaves, "Mexican Politics: An End to the Crisis?" *Latin American Research Review*, vol. 16, no. 2 (1981).

4

Foreign Investment and Dependent Development: Comparing Brazil and Mexico

PETER EVANS and GARY GEREFFI

Brazil and Mexico occupy a distinctive position in the structure of the capitalist world economy. They bear little resemblance to the classic model of a "peripheral" country. They are too industrialized, and contain too many of the modern industries typically found only at the center of the world economy; they supply themselves with too large a share of the finished goods consumed domestically; their exports are too diversified and include too many manufactured goods; and so on. But at the same time neither Brazil nor Mexico possesses the characteristics commonly associated with "developed" or "core" nations. Their gross national product per capita is far below that of the United States, Japan, or most of the countries of Western Europe; their distribution of income is extremely skewed compared to that of any of the developed countries, they are the recipient rather than the source countries of foreign investment; they are debtor rather than creditor nations; and they tend to be on the receiving rather than the originating end of product innovation and new production techniques.

This paper has been published in Spanish under the following title: Peter Evans and Gary Gereffi, "Inversión extranjera y desarrollo dependiente: una comparación entre Brasil y México," *Revista Mexicana de Sociología*, vol. 42, no 1 (January–March 1980), pp. 9–70. In addition, the data used in this paper form the basis of a much shorter version published under the following title: Gary Gereffi and Peter Evans, "Transnational Corporations, Dependent Development, and State Policy in the Semiperiphery: A Comparison of Brazil and Mexico," *Latin American Research Review*, vol. 16, no. 3 (Fall 1981), pp. 31–64.

Mexico and Brazil should not be taken as simply "intermediary," lying midway along a developmental path that leads from the poor periphery to the rich core. Structurally they play a special role in the international division of labor, serving as a profitable outlet for capital flows and a market for capital and intermediate goods. Their potential role in the international division of political labor is distinctive as well. Immanuel Wallerstein has argued that "semiperipheral areas" are a "major political means" by which crises and disintegrating struggles, which might otherwise be provoked by the inequities of reward in the world capitalist system, are avoided. While our focus here is on the economic aspects of semiperipheral status, it is worth remembering that there is also a political side to the semiperiphery.[1]

Just as Brazil and Mexico are characterized by a particular structural position in the international division of labor, so they are also characterized by a particular process of development, one which has been labeled "dependent development": "development" because it is characterized by the sort of accumulation of capital and increasingly complex differentiation of the internal productive structure that was integral to the evolution of current "core" countries, and "dependent" because it is indelibly marked by the effects of continued dependence on capital housed in these countries.[2] In terms of the traditional Marxist theorizing of Paul Baran (1957) and Andre Gunder Frank (1967) on the relationship between imperialism and economic growth, dependent development is a highly contradictory phenomenon. For Baran and Frank, dependency was not only associated with underdevelopment; it was part of its very definition. Imperialism was assumed to have an interest in a form of extractive exploitation that perpetuated stagnation, not in the industrialization of the periphery. Increasingly, the idea is taking hold that for certain countries dependency may be compatible with development as long as development is defined strictly in terms of capitalist accumulation and not in more welfare-oriented terms that involve the "quality of life."[3]

The process of dependent development has been tied to massive infusions of foreign capital which, in the post-World War II period, have mainly taken the form of investments by transnational corporations in the manufacturing sectors of those countries that now make up the semiperiphery. To at least some extent, the interests of these foreign corporations have become harnessed to rapid accumulation of capital in key sectors of the semiperipheral economy, and to the prosperity of the growing urban middle and upper classes who buy the consumer goods these companies produce.

For the mass of the population, the costs of this development path are high because the negative equity effects of capitalist development are exacerbated. Dependent development is based on a regressive profile of income distribution and emphasizes luxury consumer durables as opposed to basic necessities. It also contributes to social marginality and the underutilization and exploitation of manpower resources.[4] The frequent reliance of foreign firms on capital-intensive technologies increases rather than solves unemployment problems. Politically, the preconditions for industrial growth "from above and outside" tend to have been created by repressive regimes which, in order to provide the stability required for large-scale foreign involvement, have reduced or eliminated altogether the instruments of pressure and defense available to the popular classes (e.g., the right to strike, autonomous trade unions, wage demands, and so forth). Regimes which are oriented towards external development have typically been established by a coup carried through by the military.

Our concern here is only partly with the present character of dependent development. We are also interested in the long-run issue of whether dependent development holds out the eventual possibility of "nondependent development" or, to put the question even more strongly, whether dependent development is a strategy that might eventually allow these countries to transform their structural position from "semiperiphery" to "core."

Any answers to these questions must rely on speculative extrapolations, but Brazil and Mexico are certainly the ideal cases on which to base such speculation. Among those countries that are considered part of the Third World, these two are the most industrialized (with the possible exception of Argentina); they have developed strong states with sophisticated administrative apparatuses capable of promoting and protecting local interests; they are both rich in resources; and they have sufficiently large domestic markets to make possible some scale economies. At the same time, they are also among the most dependent countries in the world economy. Of all the Third World nations, Brazil and Mexico are the most deeply in debt. Furthermore, their manufacturing sectors, especially the most dynamic industries, continue to be thoroughly penetrated by foreign capital. It is that penetration which is the focus of this chapter.

An analysis of foreign investment must be at the heart of any analysis of dependent development. The transnational corporation (TNC), the main institutional form of foreign investment in the contemporary period, exemplifies the contradictory character of economic growth in semiperipheral countries. TNCs are both the instruments of local capital accumulation and the instruments of the consolidation of dependence. In both Brazil and Mexico, TNCs have a predominant role in shaping the future mix of consumer products, the introduction of changes in techniques of production, and the allocation of capital in the most dynamic sectors of the industrial establishment. To the degree that they contribute to industrial growth, especially that of leading sectors of the economy, they also have the power to determine the direction of that growth.

Direct foreign investment (DFI)[5] is a topic particularly suited to comparative analysis, since much of the data are collected by investing countries on a comparable basis for all host countries. In the case of Brazil and Mexico this is particularly true, since as major recipients of investment they are almost always considered individually. Yet despite the existence of a number of recent studies which include rich reservoirs of data on Brazil and Mexico, we find that our endeavor fills a surprising gap. With a few notable exceptions[6] there has been relatively little comparison of even the descriptive outlines of foreign investment in the two countries, to say nothing of attempts to explain the similarities and differences between Brazil and Mexico.

Our own view is that despite widely differing historical, political, and ideological contexts there has been an overall convergence between Brazil and Mexico in terms of the way in which foreign capital has been integrated into the two economies. This convergence is most evident in trends in the sectoral distribution of DFI in the two countries. There are also important commonalities between Mexico and Brazil with respect to the relationship between TNCs and local private capital, as well as signs of convergence in state policy toward DFI.

Although we emphasize the similarities between Brazil and Mexico, important differences between the two countries remain. Mexico's long common border with the United States has resulted in a particularly heavy flow of American capital into Mexico. At the same time, it has also stimulated Mexico's tourist sector, its agricultural export sector, and a large assembly industry just south of the Texas border. Brazil has maintained a diversified relationship with a half dozen countries in terms of both investment and trade patterns. The argument in the literature has been that such diversity should favor the host country by strengthening its bargaining position with the TNCs.[7] Another difference is the existence, since 1964, of a military regime in Brazil, whereas Mexico has maintained its tradition of civilian rule throughout the century. Finally, Mexico has emphasized restrictions on foreign ownership, whereas Brazilian policy has used behavioral more than ownership controls in its regulation of foreign firms. In our view, the existence of these differences makes the convergence of these two countries around a common model of dependent development all the more interesting.

The bulk of our empirical analysis will be built around quantitative data collected in the late sixties and early seventies, complemented by examples from case studies of individual industries. In order to provide greater historical depth, we precede this analysis with a brief characterization of the four phases through which the role of DFI has evolved over the past hundred years. But, before trying to situate our analysis historically, we want to be as clear as possible on what we mean by dependence, and how we see it related to DFI and development.

Dependence, Development, and DFI: A Framework for Analysis

When development is used in a teleological way to imply movement toward some known and desired future state, it is a highly problematic concept. Using development in the restricted sense of local capital accumulation accompanied by increased differentiation of the internal productive apparatus makes it more manageable.

Dependence is more difficult to handle. We can begin with Dos Santos' definition of a dependent country as one whose development is "conditioned by the development and expansion of another economy,"[8] but the forms and sources of that conditioning are complex. They do not change in the same ways. A central indicator of dependence in one period may be only a trivial feature in another. Forms of production or economic policy that seem to be the solution to dependence in one period may seem its causes in another. In order to avoid a simplistic assessment of the role of DFI, some exploration of these complexities is required.

Even though dependence must be defined in relation to core economies and the world economy generally, the internal side of dependence is as critical as the external. The dominant classes in every society define a "standard of living" which in turn defines a range of required goods. When the range of goods that can be produced internally is narrow relative to the socially defined range of required goods, then reliance on external sources of those goods becomes a central part of maintaining the "standard of living." The more extensive this external reliance, the more dependent the country is, at least along this particular dimension of dependence.

A narrow, undifferentiated internal productive apparatus also creates vulnerability to external markets and economies on the other side of the exchange—that is, on the export side. If the range of a country's potential exports consists only of those natural resources that can be extracted and exported, its vulnerability to fluctuations in the world market and changes in its own market position is extreme.

A differentiated internal economy is likely to imply a diverse set of potential exports and flexibility in adapting exports to market conditions. Diversification and flexibility should mean more power and less vulnerability internationally—which is to say, less dependence.

Along with questions of flexibility, diversification, and market power, the composition of internal production also has implications for productivity, profits, and the generation of surplus. Certain roles within the international division of labor are placed in the category of "hewers of wood and drawers of water"—in other words, relatively low return activities. Engaging in these activities or, more precisely, being able to engage only in these activities, is both part of the definition of underdevelopment and a source of increased vulnerability in the international market. It must be remembered, of course, that the definition of what constitutes a "hewer of wood" changes from one period to the next. Building radios may be a high return activity in one epoch and a low return activity in another. The same is true of producing textiles, steel, or even oil. It is because the definition shifts that having an internal productive apparatus capable of diversification and flexibility is important.

DFI plays a role in all of these aspects of dependence. To begin with, TNCs are a factor in the definition of the standard of living itself. DFI produces needs as surely as it produces goods, both by creating demand for new kinds of consumer goods and consequently by expanding the required range of capital and intermediate goods. At the same time, of course, DFI is presumably contributing to the further differentiation of the local productive apparatus, but the balance between these two roles should not be taken for granted.

Reliance on external flows of capital is even more central to dependence than reliance on external flows of goods. To begin with, capital flows are in general much more asymmetrical. Loans, portfolio investment, and most especially DFI flow from the core to the periphery. Unlike commodities, flows of capital, again especially flows of DFI, bring with them external control over the internal productive apparatus.

Direct investment gives external owners of capital, in theory at least, the prerogative to decide how production will be structured, what products will be produced, and what will happen to the surplus that is generated. Since most DFI is carried out by TNCs, it entails the incorporation of local productive facilities into a centrally controlled, global administrative apparatus. Insofar as DFI implies the displacement of local capitalists, it has an effect on the structure of the local dominant class as well as on decision-making within individual firms.

Since external control of the internal productive apparatus is the aspect of dependence most intimately connected to DFI, it is important to point out that the amount of control implied by external ownership depends on the context. If the economies of dependent countries were perfectly competitive, the market, not the owners, would be in control, and the owners' external origins would be less important. Even in the highly concentrated markets in which most TNCs operate within dependent countries, oligopolistic competition may limit to some degree the ability of firms to depart from competitive norms. Much more important, however, are the political constraints imposed on foreign owners by local dominant classes through the state apparatus. It is at this juncture that local or national interests are represented in their most tangible form.

The alliance between the entrepreneurial side of the state apparatus, elite local capital groups, and the multinationals, which is characteristic of dependent development, complicates the relationship between ownership and control. However, despite these complications, foreign ownership is still a good "first cut" indicator of external control of the internal productive apparatus. This is especially true when this ownership occurs in highly concentrated industries which are also the leading sectors of the economy and where ownership is reinforced by other sources of power such as control over technology or control over markets.

In sum, dependence implies vulnerability to the external economy and important limitations on local control of even the internal productive apparatus. An overall assessment of dependence requires, then, evaluating a number of different factors, all of which are related but which cannot be counted on to vary in the same direction from country to country or from period to period.

Our conception of dependence can be further clarified by looking at the opposing construct of "nondependence" that it implies. "Nondependence" means diminished external determination of the course of a country's development. It means having an internal productive apparatus which is capable of producing a broad range of goods—broad relative to the goods that are required by the socially defined standard of living and broad in the sense of providing flexibility and market power in the international economy. It also means having an internal productive apparatus which is locally owned and controlled—or, at least, one in which leading sectors and sectors which are not disciplined by market forces are dominated by local capital.

The possibility of nondependence is conditioned in part by geographic size and resource endowment. Belgium will never have an internal productive apparatus commensurate with the range of products it consumes and will always be dependent in this sense. At the same time, nondependence is not synonymous with autarky; the necessity of relying on imports and exports is only one facet of dependence. Despite high levels of imports and exports, Japan and Germany are not vulnerable to the international market in the same way that Mauritania, Chile, or even Venezuela is. The diversification and flexibility of the German and Japanese economies give them the possibility of focusing on high return goods and of exercising market power in the international economy. The strength of their international market position makes them much closer to nondependence than other countries that rely less on trade.

Patterns of past domination also affect levels of dependence or nondependence, especially as far as external ownership of the internal means of production are concerned. Canadians enjoy the material comforts of life to much the same degree that British or American citizens do, but Canada's development has not eradicated the control of British and American capital over Canada's industrial establishment.

Dependence and nondependence are relative concepts which must be interpreted in the context of a country's overall position in the structure of the capitalist world economy. Without a set of "core" nations disproportionately housing capital which in turn controls production in other countries, external ownership would not carry the same implication of dependence. The core also defines the range of goods against which the productive capacity of peripheral countries is considered narrow. Without the market power of core capital, the idea of the "vulnerability" of peripheral states to the international market would have no meaning.

It is important to keep in mind the fact that changes in dependence or in degree of development are linked to changes in structural position within the world economy. The process of dependent development has enabled Brazil and Mexico to move out of the periphery and into the semiperiphery and to consolidate their status as members of the semiperiphery. Our main task is the analysis of this process and the role which DFI has played in it.

We assume that endogenous political and economic forces are at least as important in the process of dependent development as external ones. The contemporary character and role of DFI has arisen from the interaction of TNC strategies with the political and economic strategies of local classes and the host country states. TNC strategies are conditioned both by the world economic environment, especially as it impinges on their home states, and by the forces of oligopolistic competition. The strategies of local groups vis-à-vis DFI are primarily expressed through the policies and actions of the state apparatus. These are conditioned not only by the international political and economic context but also by an historically given configuration of class structure, ideology, and local productive base. The local class structure and local productive base are, of course, in turn the outcome of previous interaction between foreign capital and local classes.

In examining the current character and role of DFI and the interaction of local and external forces that produced it, we will not be able to speak to all the issues that are raised by our definitions of dependence and nondependence and our views of their relation to structural position within the world economy. We do hope, however, to address at least four questions that come out of this general framework:

1. Does the evidence with regard to DFI in the two countries support the idea that both Brazil and Mexico have converged around a single model of dependent development and that both have consolidated a semiperipheral position within the world capitalist economy?
2. To what extent has the level of external control over the internal productive apparatus that accompanies the growth of DFI been exacerbated by the displacement of the local bourgeoisie? To what extent has it been diminshed by shared control of subsidiaries and effective state regulation of their behavior?
3. What has been the role of TNCs in reducing the vulnerability of Brazil and Mexico to external sources of needed inputs? Have they increased the diversity and flexibility of export offerings while narrowing the range of required imports?
4. Overall, has the evolution of DFI resulted in a decline of effects which increased dependence relative to effects which diminish dependence, or the reverse?

Our discussion of the evidence will begin with an historical-structural summary of the phases of DFI in Brazil and Mexico in which we hope to provide some sense of the political and economic chronology that has accompanied changes in the role and character of DFI itself. We will then try to provide a more quantitative and analytical discussion, focusing primarily on the last two phases.

Four Phases of DFI in Brazil and Mexico

Both Brazil and Mexico began the century as classic peripheral countries—exporters of primary products. In both countries, the primary product export phase was superseded by an emphasis on "horizontal" import-substituting industrialization (ISI) during the Great Depression, a phase which focused on local production of consumer nondurables and the local assembly of consumer durables. By the mid-fifties, horizontal ISI was superseded by a phase of "vertical ISI" in which the emphasis was on internalizing all phases in the manufacture of consumer goods and integrating backwards in the direction of intermediate products and capital goods. In the seventies, this was replaced by a phase with a dual emphasis: the expanded local production of capital goods on the one hand and diversified export promotion on the other.

There is a rough correspondence between movement from one phase to another, changes in structural position within the world economy, and the emergence and consolidation of the process of dependent development. The transition from periphery to semiperiphery began with the horizontal ISI phase and was accomplished during the vertical ISI phase. Dependent development also began with the movement from horizontal to vertical ISI. The current capital goods/diversified exports phase represents an attempt to consolidate semiperipheral status and lay the foundation for moving beyond it to nondependent development or even to core status.

DFI has been important in each phase, but most crucial in the latter two phases, which is why we have chosen to focus on them. The role of DFI in the two countries has also converged significantly over the course of the four phases, which is one of the reasons for reviewing all four rather than restricting discussion to the more recent period.

THE PRIMARY PRODUCT EXPORT ECONOMY (1880–1930)

The primary product phase had quite a different character in Brazil than it did in Mexico. In Mexico, mineral exports were the most important sources of export earnings, and until the Revolution mining was thoroughly dominated by foreign capital. Minerals were not particularly important in turn-of-the-century Brazil and had not been since the eighteenth-century gold boom in Minas Gerais. Coffee was king, and the coffee plantations were run by Brazilians.

Brazil was nonetheless extremely dependent during the primary export phase.[9] Its internal division of labor was narrow,[10] and it was forced to rely on British imports to provide almost all its need for manufactured goods. Its fortunes were determined to a frightening degree by fluctuations in the New York coffee market. But there was not the same degree of direct foreign control over internal production in the export sector in Brazil that there was in Mexico.

DFI also played a different role in the transition from this first phase to the horizontal ISI phase. Between the Mexican Revolution and the beginning of the Depression, there was almost a complete halt in the growth of DFI in Mexico. From the 1870s to 1912, Mexico had attracted more direct investment from the United States than any other country in the world.[11] After 1912, the only substantial growth of American DFI was in the petroleum sector.[12] Even after 1929, when stability had been restored, the growth of DFI was slow. In fact, American investment fell absolutely during the Depression and did not regain the 1914 level until 1950 (see Tables 1 and 2).

HORIZONTAL IMPORT-SUBSTITUTING INDUSTRIALIZATION (1930–55)

Horizontal ISI had its beginnings in both Brazil and Mexico during the phase of primary exports. In Brazil, local textile manufacturers had begun to replace British imports as early as the turn of the century. In Mexico as well, manufacturing ventures sprang up during the mineral export phase of development.[13] It was not, however, until the Great Depression made export-oriented growth untenable that horizontal ISI—which is to say, the development of local manufacturing of light consumer goods—became the dominant aspect of development in the two countries.

The shock was particularly great for Brazil. Coffee prices collapsed, and the massive public debt which the country had built up in the process of trying to improve its urban infrastructure became an overwhelming burden as public debt service soared to 43 percent of export earnings in the period from 1932 to 1933.[14] The collapse of export earnings was complemented by other effects of the Great Depression to help push both Brazil and Mexico out of the nest of the "classic dependence" of the primary export phase.[15] Sharp devaluations made local production more profitable, but foreign capital, particularly British capital, was not in a position to respond aggressively to the shift in the situation.

Overall, the period of horizontal ISI appears to be one of diminished dependence, a relative weakening of the importance of DFI, and a relative flowering of local industrial bourgeoisies. In Brazil, major multinationals had been marginally involved in domestic manufacturing since the World War I, but local capital played a strong role in the consumer goods that were the focus of horizontal ISI.[16] During the Depression there was even some "renationalization" of local manufacturing operations as, for example, when the Votorantim rayon mill was bought from the British by the Ermírio de Moraes group in Brazil. The opening for local capital was further reinforced by the World War II and the inability of core countries to export either manufactured goods or capital in amounts that would satisfy the increasingly industrial economies of Brazil and Mexico.

State strategies reinforced the impact of the external environment. This was particularly true in Mexico, where Lázaro Cárdenas' nationalization of the petroleum industry in 1938 eliminated the possibility that petroleum would become the basis of a return to the foreign-dominated primary product export model of Porfirio Díaz. Getúlio Vargas in Brazil made no moves which were quite so dramatic, but he did take important initiatives in terms of state involvement in basic industries: first in the steel industry with the establishment of Volta Redonda as Latin America's first fully integrated coke-based mill in the 1940s, and then later in the petroleum industry with the creation of Petrobrás in 1953. The willingness of the state to provide tariff barriers behind which local manufacturing could be profitable was also an essential element of horizontal ISI.

By the end of World War II, an optimistic nationalist in Brazil or Mexico might easily have predicted that dependence had essentially been overcome and that nondependent development was a possibility. This was particularly true for Mexico, looking back at the extreme foreign domination of the Porfiriato. A local manufacturing sector of substantial power had been established. The combination of foreign exchange savings accumulated during World War II and the buoyant postwar market for exports made it appear that the positions of Brazil and Mexico in the international economy had substantially improved as well. The Korean War, which generated further increases in export prices, helped reinforce the impression of diminished vulnerability.

VERTICAL IMPORT-SUBSTITUTING INDUSTRIALIZATION (1955–70)

The year 1955 marked a key turning point, both in these optimistic perceptions and in the development process of the two countries. The Korean War boom was over, and demand for Mexican and Brazilian exports had fallen. Mexico had experienced a severe recession after the Korean War, and by 1954 balance of payments pressures forced a 50 percent devaluation of the peso. Brazil confronted a fall of coffee prices in 1955 that left the country 30 percent below its Korean War peaks, while imports of machinery and equipment were up 60 percent over the late forties.[17] The clear message from the external sector was that a shift in development strategy was necessary.

The horizontal ISI had to be "deepened," replaced by a vertical ISI which would broaden the range of local production to include consumer durables, especially the automobile, and build up local manufacture of the capital and intermediate goods that were causing the big drain on the balance of payments. The investments required were more technologically sophisticated and capital-intensive than those required by horizontal ISI, thus making TNCs rather than local capital the most likely instrument. And the TNCs were conveniently ready to respond. The growth of investment in the core, especially in the United States, no longer demanded all the resources at their command.

Political shifts within Brazil and Mexico helped open the way for new kinds of participation by TNCs. The shift was most dramatic in Brazil, where the nationalist thrust of Vargas' second administration (1951–54) was brought to an abrupt end by his suicide. In Mexico, President Adolfo Ruiz Cortines (1952–58) shifted gears in mid-administration and moved to attract foreign capital rather than keep it at arm's length, as had been the case before. In both countries, imports of machinery and equipment were subsidized in order to encourage manufacturing investment. In Brazil, SUMOC (Superintendência da Moeda e do Crédito, Brazilian Monetary Authority) Instruction No. 113 allowed foreign manufacturers exceptional exchange advantages in importing equipment and machinery.[18] In Mexico, Rule 14 of the General Tariff granted a 65 percent subsidy towards machinery and equipment duties, while the Law for New and Necessary Industries (1955) allowed partial or total exemption from several taxes (including up to 40 percent off on income tax).[19] In both countries these incentives were combined with quantitative controls on imports of manufactured goods which essentially "closed the border" once local manufacture had been undertaken.

Local elites interested in development had found some common ground with TNCs interested in global expansion. Local manufacture rose, imports as a percentage of total consumption fell, DFI burgeoned, and local manufacturing became increasingly foreign-owned. It is this initial period of the vertical ISI phase that has been characterized as "the internalization of imperialism"[20] or the "internationalization of the internal market."[21] Vertical ISI created the foundations for the "triple alliance" of the state, the multinational corporation, and local capital. The vertical ISI stage marks the full blossoming of the process of dependent development and the final stages of transition from the periphery to the semiperiphery.

Despite the striking parallelism of the emergence of the vertical ISI stage in both countries, there were also some important differences in state policy that in turn affected the immediate results. From the beginning, Brazil focused almost exclusively on eliciting specific behavior from TNCs while Mexico divided its attention between ownership and behavioral controls of transnationals. In the auto industry, for example, Brazil pushed the TNCs harder than Mexico in terms of the levels of local content required. Brazil began implementing its local integration program in 1956; Mexico did not start until 1962. By 1962, Brazil already required that 99 percent of the weight of passenger cars be local content (i.e., manufactured domestically). Mexico required only 60 percent and gave the companies much more leeway by measuring the 60 percent in terms of proportion of direct cost rather than weight.[22] On the other hand, Mexico managed to preserve some local ownership in the industry, whereas in Brazil local and state capital played a marginal, mainly portfolio role in the terminal industry.

In other areas the differences were in the same direction. By 1960, imports of capital goods in Brazil had been reduced from their 1955 level of 43 percent of total consumption to 23 percent, whereas in Mexico the level had hardly diminished at all. A similar pattern could be observed in intermediate and consumer goods.[23] Yet Mexico had been more aggressive in trying to open some space in the vertical ISI process for the local bourgeoisie. Making "Mexicanization"—that is, local equity participation and preferably majority control by locals— a condition of foreign entry was a consistent informal policy of Mexican regimes in the late 1950s and 1960s, whereas in Brazil there never appeared to be a similar commitment to "Brazilianization" as such.

In both Brazil and Mexico there were nationalist reactions to the denationalization that accompanied vertical ISI. But the character of the reactions and their impact on DFI were quite different. In Mexico, nationalist periods continued to alternate with periods of conciliatory policies towards capital in general and foreign capital in particular. Adolfo López Mateos (1958–64), like Ruiz Cortines, moved first in a more nationalist direction and then in a more conciliatory one. Whether the fluctuations were within *sexenios* or between them, they were always "within the Constitution"—which is to say, under the control of the powerful PRI political apparatus.

When nationalism reached full flower in Brazil during the brief regime of João Goulart (1962–64), it was much less under control and therefore much more threatening to capital, both local and foreign. "Jango" Goulart, like Getúlio Vargas but unlike any of his Mexican counterparts, was thrown out of office before completing his term. The inability of the Brazilian bourgeoisie to "keep the lid on" while exploring nationalist alternatives opened the way for the Brazilian military (with the appropriate cooperation of foreign capital) to embark on the "internationalist" antithesis under General Humberto Castello Branco (1964–67). Thus, vertical ISI came to fruition in Brazil under political conditions quite different from those that prevailed in Mexico. The military regime in Brazil was closer to the Porfiriato in political tone than anything that had appeared in the interim in either country and its attractiveness to foreign investors was similar.

The political contrasts resulted in differences in the rate, distribution, and to a lesser extent national origins of DFI, but the common outcome was in the end more important than the differences. Both countries ended up with substantial manufacturing capacity, the leading sectors of which were substantially owned by foreign capital.[24] In short, by the end of the vertical ISI phase, dependent development had become thoroughly established as the dominant mode of economic growth in both countries.

DIVERSIFIED EXPORT PROMOTION (1970 TO THE PRESENT)

Diversified export promotion (1970 to the present)[25] has emerged as the most recent phase in the evolution of dependent development for much the same reasons that vertical ISI succeeded horizontal ISI. In both Brazil and Mexico, vertical ISI was not resolving the problem of imbalanced economic relations with the outside world. Chronic balance of payments deficits were growing larger in both countries. Something new was needed. At the same time, reduced levels of profits in the core and increased confidence in the profitability of manufacturing in the semiperiphery made it possible to gain the cooperation of the TNCs in the promotion of manufactured exports.

It is important, of course, to remember that even more than in the case of horizontal and vertical ISI, "export promotion" is a shorthand for a complex of characteristics. To being with, diversification of exports, not merely their expansion, is its key feature. Moreover, the further consolidation of ISI in the capital goods sector is a crucial part of the overall strategies of both Brazil and Mexico. When Mexican petroleum and Brazilian iron ore and soybeans are also brought into the picture, it is clear that the current strategy even contains elements of the primary export economy. Nonetheless, it is the promotion of diversified exports that is the focus of the new role played by TNCs in the current phase.

While it does not entail the same dramatic implantation of new industries that accompanied vertical ISI, the export promotion phase does involve a significant transformation of the place of the semiperiphery in world-wide TNC strategy. Brazil and Mexico are no longer to be seen as simply profitable domestic markets—rather, they are treated as part of an overall strategy of "worldwide sourcing." Semiperipheral subsidiaries play a role more like that of facilities in the core, and yet at the same time their fate becomes more thoroughly determined by the plans of the parent. The markets in which they sell are now less under the potential political control of Brazil and Mexico and more under the administrative control of the TNC.

Brazil entered the current phase with certain advantages in its relation to TNCs. Having apparently exorcised left-leaning nationalism, Brazilian military regimes had created the best possible investment climate. In Mexico, Luis Echeverría, while hardly a radical, was continuing to push the interests of the local bourgeoisie by expanding the scope of Mexicanization and taking a generally nationalist stance in relation to DFI. The contrast was manifest. As the seventies drew to a close, however, the tendency towards convergence had reasserted itself. By the time López Portillo entered the Mexican presidency, the costs of trying to pursue a more nationalist course were evident, and movement toward a more conciliatory stance began. In Brazil, local capital (not to mention the potentially explosive discontent of the working class) was putting more pressure on the military and the technocrats to attend to the needs of the country by taking a more nationalist line towards TNCs.

The extent of contemporary convergence is nicely illustrated by two recent policy decisions. Ownership became the critical variable in Brazil in allocating a massive contract for telecommunications equipment. Telebrás announced that none of the three competing TNCs could win the contract unless they presented immediate plans for "Brazilianization," that is, evidence that 51 percent of their equity would be locally owned. In Mexico at about the same time a broad set of Brazilian-type incentives was established for firms that would undertake local production of capital goods and balance imports by exports. Most important, in what *Business Latin America* called "an encouraging sign of flexibility," reductions in import duties were available to foreign-owned firms as long as they balanced their imports with exports. It would seem, in short, that the mix of policy emphasis on ownership and behavior is becoming more and more similar in the two countries.[26]

Predicting when the current phase will exhaust itself or what the dominant strategy in the next one will be would go beyond our powers of deduction. But the common process of change in previous transitions cannot be ignored. In each case, pressure on the balance of payments caused in part by shifts in the international market was an important impetus for change. The direction of this change was determined by the interaction of TNC strategies and local state policies, but in most cases there was a strong correspondence between what the state wanted from the TNCs and the TNCs' own global strategies.

Reviewing the four phases, the transformation in the nature of dependence is clear, but it is much harder to say whether there has been a change in the overall level of dependence. For Mexico, with its much higher level of dependence in the Porfiriato and its greater nationalist thrust in subsequent periods, the movement may have been in the direction of less dependence. For Brazil, the direction of change is less clear and depends more on the relative importance assigned to dependence as generated by vulnerability to the external market and dependence as generated by external control over the internal productive apparatus. In both countries, a more precise assessment would involve a more detailed analysis of the data on DFI. The data are thin for the earlier phases, but, fortunately, rich sources of data allow a more detailed assessment for the late sixties and early seventies, and this will be our objective in the next section of the chapter.

DFI in Brazil and Mexico: An Empirical Analysis

CONTRASTS AND CONVERGENCE IN THE EVOLUTION OF DFI

If DFI in Brazil and Mexico has followed a similar evolution in the post-World War II period, it is not because the two countries have always had similar relationships with international capital. They began the century with very different distributions, both in terms of the national origins of foreign investment and the sectors in which it was concentrated within their economies. Table 1 provides a starting point by showing the distribution of DFI in each country at the time of World War I, according to the national origin of the investment.

It is clear from the table that from the beginning investment in Brazil came from a more diverse set of national origins than did investment in Mexico. The dramatic decline of British investment in the period between the two world wars exacerbated this difference,[27] since Britain was the most important competitor of the United States in Mexico, whereas other European investors were important forces in Brazil.

Figures on the sectoral distribution of DFI in the two countries at this early period are more difficult to come by. What evidence there is[28] indicates that foreign capital in both countries was invested first of all in railways and government bonds. The major divergence appears to have been a relatively greater concentration on extractive enterprises in Mexico and a greater concentration on investments in public utilities in Brazil. This divergence is evident in the earliest available Department of Commerce figures comparing the two countries, and it appears consistent with data on the sectoral distribution of European investment.

Table 1 / Direct Foreign Investment at the End of 1914 by Country of Origin

A. Absolute Amounts (in millions of U.S. dollars)

	Host Country		
Investor	Brazil	Mexico	Total for Latin America
U.K.	609	635	3,585
U.S.	50	542	1,394
France	391	—	711
Germany	n.a.*	—	320
Others	146	—	1,559
Total	1,196	1,177	7,569

B. Percentage Distributions

	Host Country			
Investor	Brazil	Mexico	Rest of Latin America	Total for Latin America

1. Brazil and Mexico as Percentages of Total Direct Foreign Investment in Latin America

U.K.	17.0	17.7	65.3	
U.S.	3.6	45.6	50.8	
France	55.0	—	45.0	
Others	9.4	—	90.6	
Total	15.8	15.6	68.6	

2. Percentage Distributions by Investor

U.K.	50.9	54.0	45.1	47.4
U.S.	4.2	46.1	15.4	18.4
France	32.7	—	6.2	9.4
Germany	n.a.	—	6.2	4.2
Others	12.2	—	30.0	20.6
Total	100	100	100	100

Source: Economic Commission for Latin America, *External Financing in Latin America* (New York: United Nations, 1965), p. 17.

*n.a. = not available

One final difference which should be noted about foreign investment in Brazil and Mexico prior to World War I refers to its composition. It appears that Brazil's reliance on external public debt (i.e., indirect foreign investment) greatly exceeded Mexico's. In 1914, Brazil had over $700 million in foreign loans (mostly from Britain) to complement its $1,200 million in DFI; in 1911, Mexico had acquired just $250 million of external public debt, compared with $1,450 in DFI. By 1930, the volume of external public debt held by Brazil had continued to grow until it was nearly equal to the level of total DFI—$1.3 and $1.4 billion, respectively.[29]

Turning to long-run data on DFI in Brazil and Mexico, the best source is provided by the United States Department of Commerce—with the major drawback that it is limited to U.S. direct investments only. Table 2 summarizes the trends in U.S. DFI in Brazil, Mexico, and Latin America from 1929 through 1976. Focusing first on the earlier period (1929–50), we can discern a number of interesting trends.

First, there is the dramatic difference in the growth of U.S. investment in the two countries. While investment in Mexico fell absolutely from 1929 to the end of World War II, U.S. DFI in Brazil was increasing during the same period at an extremely rapid rate. If the data in Table 1 for U.S. investment in 1914 are accurate, the level of U.S. DFI present in Mexico at the end of the Porfiriato was not regained and held until the middle of the 1950s. Brazil, on the other hand, with less than a third the amount of U.S. DFI as Mexico in 1929, surpassed Mexico in this regard by 1946. Brazil was much less affected than the rest of Latin America by the retraction of U.S. investment during the Depression. During the 1930s and 1940s, U.S. investors moved into Brazil, replacing the retreating British investors. By the 1950s, the United States held the lion's share of total DFI in Brazil, at a level more than twice that of the next largest investing country.[30] Thus, while Mexico's share of total U.S. investment was cut in half, Brazil's more than doubled, transforming Brazil from a relatively minor locus for U.S. investment into a much more important arena for the expansion of U.S. transnational corporations.

The disparate trends in U.S. investments in Brazil and Mexico between the two world wars reflect in part the different political contexts in the two countries, as discussed earlier. The nationalism of Cárdenas in Mexico was directly threatening to foreign investors, while the more strictly corporatist nationalism of Vargas in Brazil was something they could tolerate without great difficulty. There is, however, an additional factor involved. The trends in overall levels of U.S. DFI in the two countries also reflect in part the initial sectoral distribution of that investment. Three-fourths of U.S. direct investment in Mexico in 1929 was in petroleum and the extractive industries (mining and agriculture). Extractive DFI declined dramatically throughout Latin America. In 1938, petroleum investment was wiped out by Cárdenas' nationalization of the Mexican oil industry. In Brazil, on the other hand, petroleum and the extractive industries represented an

Table 2 / U.S. Direct Investment in Brazil, Mexico, and Latin America, 1929–1976

		1929	1940	1946	1950	1957	1963	1967	1973	1976
		A. Absolute Amounts (in millions of U.S. dollars)								
Extractive[a]	Brazil	[b]	[b]	[b]	7	10	30	68	81	140
	Mexico	289	178	115	124	149	116	100	85	88
	Latin America	1,524	866	913	1,148	1,673	1,093	1,277	1,194	1,163
Petroleum	Brazil	23	31	45	112	130	60	79	198	336
	Mexico	206	42	7	13	31	66	44	10	17
	Latin America	589	516	697	1,233	2,702	3,094	2,903	2,162	1,653
Manufacturing	Brazil	46	70	126	284	378	663	893	2,033	3,667
	Mexico	6	10	66	133	335	503	890	1,798	2,223
	Latin America	231	210	399	780	1,270	2,103	3,305	5,992	8,642
Public utilities[c]	Brazil	97	112	125	138	182	190	32	16	26
	Mexico	164	116	112	107	134	25	27	31	47
	Latin America	886	960	880	927	1,001	710	621	377	250
Other[d]	Brazil	28	27	27	110	128	185	256	544	609
	Mexico	18	12	16	38	90	197	281	454	949
	Latin America	233	154	116	357	1,208	1,657	2,159	3,802	5,404
Total	Brazil	194	240	323	644	835	1,128	1,327	2,885	5,403
	Mexico	683	358	316	415	739	907	1,343	2,379	2,984
	Latin America	3,462	2,705	3,005	4,445	7,434	8,657	10,265	13,527	17,116

B. Relative Proportions

Brazilian investment as a proportion of total Latin American investment	0.06	0.09	0.11	0.14	0.11	0.13	0.13	0.21	0.32
Mexican investment as a proportion of total Latin American investment	0.20	0.13	0.11	0.09	0.10	0.10	0.13	0.18	0.17
Brazilian investment as a proportion of Mexican investment	0.28	0.67	1.02	1.55	1.13	1.24	0.99	1.21	1.81
Manufacturing investment as a proportion of total investment in Latin America	0.07	0.08	0.13	0.18	0.17	0.24	0.32	0.44	0.50
Manufacturing investment as a proportion of total investment in:									
Brazil	0.24	0.29	0.39	0.44	0.45	0.59	0.67	0.70	0.68
Mexico	0.01	0.03	0.21	0.32	0.45	0.55	0.66	0.76	0.74

Source: United States Department of Commerce, *Survey of Current Business*, various years.
[a]Mining and agriculture.
[b]Included in Other.
[c]Includes transportation.
[d]Includes trade, finance and insurance, and other sectors.

insignificant part of total U.S. DFI prior to 1950, with U.S. investment in manufacturing and public utilities accounting for the great bulk of the total.

The pattern of dependent development, as we have outlined it earlier, is one in which DFI in manufacturing predominates, followed by service sector investments. Mexico approximated this pattern only after U.S. holdings in petroleum and the extractive sector were practically wiped out—DFI was reconstructed with an overwhelming emphasis on manufacturing after 1940. Brazil, on the other hand, began with a surprisingly "modern" distribution of investments. While manufacturing accounted for less than 1 percent of all U.S. investments in Mexico in 1929, it already represented almost one-quarter of the total U.S. investments in Brazil.

By the end of the World War II, the sectoral distribution of DFI was already beginning to converge around a common model of dependent development. The proportion of DFI in manufacturing in Mexico was still only half that of Brazil, but manufacturing investment in Mexico was rising at a rapid rate. By 1957, U.S. DFI in Mexico's manufacturing sector for the first time equaled the proportion held by U.S. investment in Brazilian manufacturing (45 percent of total DFI). And by 1967, Mexico had fully closed the gap with Brazil in terms of the absolute level of total U.S. DFI in each country, as well as the proportion of this total in the manufacturing sector (two-thirds) and in the "Other" (largely service) sector (one-fifth).[31]

Two trends become evident as we follow these data on U.S. DFI in Brazil and Mexico into the 1970s. One is related to manufacturing investment as a proportion of total U.S. investment in the two countries. Mexico in 1973 and 1976 for the first time showed shares of total DFI in manufacturing that were higher than those in Brazil. In 1976, 74 percent of total U.S. DFI in Mexico was in manufacturing, while in Brazil this proportion was 68 percent. The second trend to be noted is the fact that while U.S. DFI more than doubled its volume in Mexico between 1967 and 1976, it *quadrupled* its level in Brazil during the same period. Thus, by the latter year Brazil had almost twice as much U.S. DFI as Mexico. How should these trends be explained?

Three factors need to be highlighted: (1) In absolute terms, the rate of growth of U.S. direct investment in manufacturing was about 50 percent higher in Brazil than it was in Mexico. (2) In part, the increase in the proportion of U.S. DFI in manufacturing in Mexico, and especially in Latin America, reflects significant *dis*investment in the petroleum and extractive sectors of these economies. (3) Brazil, in sharp contrast to the disinvestment elsewhere, received a major increase of U.S. DFI in petroleum and the extractive sector. In the Latin American context, therefore, Brazil is a major exception while Mexico follows the rule in this most recent period.

Why is Brazil such an exception, and in particular why should Brazil's U.S. DFI have increased twice as fast as Mexico's from 1967 to 1976? The reasons are largely political. Brazil's military government, which gained office through a military coup in 1964, worked hard to attract foreign sources of financing for its economic programs. By 1967, foreign investors were reasonably sure that the military would provide a stable and lucrative "investment climate" for DFI, and therefore were eager to avail themselves of Brazil's natural resources and large internal market.

Mexico, although it also showed a considerable increase in U.S. DFI during this period, was not as attractive as Brazil politically. A stream of nationalizations and Mexicanization requirements during the late 1950s and 1960s had been a constant source of irritation and uncertainty for foreign investors. For example, in 1958 Mexico reserved the production of "basic" petrochemical products to the state, and in 1959 set the maximum level of foreign participation in the manufacture of "secondary" petrochemicals at 40 percent; in 1960, the government nationalized the two large foreign companies remaining in the electrical power industry; in 1961, legislation was passed requiring Mexicanization of the mining industry so that 66 percent of the ownership related to any new mining concessions had to be in Mexican hands; and in 1967, the large and profitable foreign-dominated sulphur industry was nationalized.

In the 1970s, with the extirpation of nationalist, or at least left nationalist, elements from the Brazilian political scene, Mexican nationalism stood out more than it had in the early sixties. While the Brazilian military was revising the mining code to allow more foreign participation and circumscribing the Petrobrás monopoly, Echeverría's strident brand of economic nationalism was an increasing source of concern to foreign investors, which finally led to a substantial flight of capital from Mexico in 1975 and 1976. In summary, one could argue that the growth of U.S. DFI in Mexico was restrained (even though it doubled from 1967 to 1976) by two related factors: (1) from the point of view of DFI, greater *caution* in investing in Mexico (as compared to Brazil, for example) was called for because of Mexico's heightened degree of economic nationalism; and (2) from the point of view of Mexico, greater *selectivity* was exercised (again as compared with Brazil) in terms of the conditions under which DFI would be allowed to establish itself or expand in the country.

Tables A-2 through A-4, found at the end of this chapter, provide 1967 data on total (not just U.S.) DFI in Brazil and Mexico. This information supports the differences we have noted between the two countries with respect to the national origins of investing countries as well as the main commonalities regarding the sectoral distribution of DFI.

Turning first to the question of sectoral distribution, Table A-2 makes it clear that the pattern of dependent development we have used to characterize DFI in Brazil and Mexico is hardly appropriate in talking about developing countries in general or Latin America in particular. Petroleum, mining, and agriculture absorb one-half of the developing world's DFI, yet, as we have already noted, these sectors are relatively unimportant as loci for DFI in Brazil and Mexico. Manufacturing, on the other hand, accounts for less than one-third of all developing-country DFI, yet in Brazil and Mexico over two-thirds of total DFI goes into this sector. The data therefore confirm our initial assumption that Brazil and Mexico are undergoing a common process of development which distinguishes them from the majority of Third World countries.

A closer look at the trends suggests some interesting refinements. First of all, it appears in Table 2 that there may be a peak in the proportion of DFI going into manufacturing at somewhere between 70 and 80 percent of the total, and that both Brazil and Mexico have now passed this peak. This hypothesis is also supported by the decline in the proportion of manufacturing investment from all investing countries, at least in Brazil, for the period from 1971 to 1976, as shown in Table 3. The possibility that future DFI in the semiperiphery might move gradually away from manufacturing in the direction of an increased focus on service sector investment is intriguing, and certainly suggests the importance of increased attention to the service sector in future studies of DFI in the more advanced Third World countries.

The apparently large proportion of DFI in public utilities in Brazil is a very different sort of phenomenon. It is a holdover from the past that was rectified in 1978 when the nationalization of Brascan's Brazilian electric utility subsidiary, Light-Serviços de Eletricidade, was announced. Brascan, a Canadian TNC, accounted for 95 percent of the $607 million of DFI in public utilities in Brazil, a state of affairs that had continued for some time (see Table A-4). As a foreign-owned public utility, Brascan was an anomaly in the 1970s. Mexico had na-

Table 3 / Changes in Direct Foreign Investment in Brazil and Mexico in the Seventies

	1971		1976	1975
	Brazil	Mexico	Brazil	Mexico
A. Percentage Changes in National Origins of DFI				
U.S.	37.7	80.9	32.2	68.7
Germany	11.4	2.8	12.4	2.3
Japan	4.3	0.7	11.2	1.3
U.K.	9.4	3.0	4.7	5.6
France	4.5	1.7	3.6	1.0
Canada	10.1	1.7	5.3	2.3
Switzerland	6.6	2.8	10.9	3.0
Other	16.2	6.6	19.7	15.8
Total	100.2	100.2	100.0	100.0
(Amount in millions of U.S.$)	(2,911)	(2,297)	(9,005)	(4,736)
B. Percentage Changes in Sectoral Distribution of DFI				
Extractive (agriculture, mining, and smelting)	0.9	5.9	2.5	4.1
Manufacturing	81.8	75.2	76.5	77.5
Service	14.9	16.4	18.6	18.1
Other	1.4	2.5	2.0	0.2
Total	99.0	100.0	99.6	99.9
(Amount in millions of U.S.$)	(2,911)	(2,297)	(9,005)	(4,736)

Source: United Nations, Center on Transnational Corporations, *Transnational Corporations in World Development: A Re-Examination* (New York: United Nations, 1978), panel A, p. 256; panel B, p. 259.

tionalized its electric power industry in 1960, and the rest of the electric power sector in Brazil was also state-owned.[32] Even the management of Brascan agreed that running an electrical utility was no longer an appropriate role for foreign capital. They complained in their 1977 annual report about their "inability to generate internally a reasonable proportion of the funds required for capital expansion." When the nationalization occurred, Brascan was reported to feel that Light-Serviços "bulked too large in its portfolio of investments in Brazil" and to be quite happy with the $380 million in cash from the sale that it could put to other uses.[33]

The lack of negative reaction by Brascan with respect to the nationalization of Light-Serviços shows the extent to which foreign capital has accepted a division of labor in which it is excluded from ownership of public utilities. Nationalization of the electric power industry in Brazil and Mexico followed behind the earlier wave of nationalizations in both countries which brought railways under state control.[34] In each country, developmentalist interests within the state apparatus saw the possibility of breaking through bottlenecks by increasing state investments in infrastructure, like electric power and railroads. The TNCs involved in the leading sectors in manufacturing who would benefit from the increased availability of infrastructural services had no reason to disagree.

Convergence is overwhelming in the sectoral distribution of DFI, but the differences in the sources of DFI have remained strongly in force right up to the present. The United States remains the dominant investor in Mexico, while the dispersed national origins of Brazil's DFI noted in 1914 continue to characterize it today (see Table A-3). Table 3 suggests, however, that the U.S. share of total DFI in Brazil and Mexico may be on the decline, as it dropped from 81 to 69 percent in Mexico between 1971 and 1975, and from 38 to 32 percent in Brazil between 1971 and 1976. It does not appear likely, however, that the relative strength of U.S. DFI in either Mexico or Brazil will change substantially in the coming years.

U.S. TNCs seem to feel far more comfortable investing just across their border in Mexico than they do in going to Brazil. Various reasons could explain why this is so. Undoubtedly the U.S. TNC presence in Mexico is bolstered by the magnitude of traditional commercial ties between the two countries (the U.S. accounts for roughly 65 percent of Mexico's imports and exports). Furthermore, despite Mexico's economic nationalism, it has been characterized by a greater degree of economic and political stability than that found in Brazil.[35] Finally, European and Japanese TNCs have been cautious in their decisions to invest in Mexico because of the long-established U.S. presence there.

As Table A-3 indicates, it is the position of Brazil that is unusual within the Latin American context rather than the position of Mexico. With the exception of a few small former European colonies, the majority of DFI in every country in Latin America except Brazil originates in the United States. In Brazil, German investment developed from ground zero in the beginning of the 1950s to a position second only to the United States in the 1970s (see Table 3). The Japanese did not begin to develop their Brazilian interests fully until the late 1960s and early 1970s, but as Table 3 indicates their growth in the 1970s has been spectacular. The absolute amount of Japanese investments in Brazil increased eightfold between 1971 and 1976, putting them in third place behind the U.S. and Germany.

The importance of Brazil to Germany and Japan (as well as to Canada, for reasons noted above) comes out clearly in Table A-3, panel B. As early as 1967, DFI in Brazil represented over 40 percent of German investments *in all developing countries,* and 30 percent of all Japanese investments in developing countries. Relatively speaking, Brazil is much more important to Germany and Japan than it is to the United States, even though the absolute amount of North American DFI in Brazil remains much larger. This same table shows us that Brazil and Mexico each represented less than 8 percent of U.S. direct investments in all developing countries, thus making the U.S. far less committed to Brazil and Mexico combined than either Germany or Japan is to Brazil alone.

Table A-4 reveals one final bit of information which is important in understanding the significance of the national origins of DFI in these two countries. The Europeans and the Japanese have concentrated a far greater percentage of their total DFI in manufacturing than have the North Americans. This means that the rising and non-hegemonic core powers have played a crucial role in the consolidation of dependent development in Brazil and Mexico, with the U.S. being relatively more involved in both extractive and service sector investments.[36]

In terms of any bargaining model which emphasizes the importance of core competition for increasing the leverage of Third World states, Brazil's position appears quite different from that of Mexico. Brazil has several deeply committed core powers to play off against each other. Mexico remains in a position where most of its bargaining is likely to be in a bilateral context with the U.S.

The high proportion of DFI in manufacturing sets Mexico and Brazil apart from the overall pattern of DFI in Latin America, but what about the distributions of investments within manufacturing? That is, do distributions of DFI within manufacturing show shared patterns for Brazil and Mexico which distinguish them from the rest of Latin America? Although it is difficult to get sufficiently detailed data across a range of countries, Table 4 presents information on the distribution of U.S. and non-U.S. TNCs in Brazil and Mexico across a sampling of industries.

DFI, especially as represented by TNCs, has almost always been a "leading sector" phenomenon in developing countries, which is to say that it tends to concentrate in industries which become growth poles of the host economy. In the post-World War II period, the leading industries in Brazil and Mexico were those connected to the im-

Table 4 / Percentages of Assets of Largest 300 Manufacturing Firms in Brazil and Mexico Held by U.S. and Other Foreign TNCs for Selected Industries, 1972

Industry	U.S. TNC Share		Other Foreign TNC Share		Total Foreign Share	
	Brazil	Mexico	Brazil	Mexico	Brazil	Mexico
Food	2	20	30	6	32	26
Textiles	6	0	38	5	44	5
Metal fabrication*	4	48	21	8	25	56
Nonmetallic ores	11	—	11	—	22	—
Chemicals	34	54	35	14	69	68
Rubber	100	100	0	0	100	100
Nonelectrical machinery	34	36	40	58	74	95
Electrical machinery	22	35	56	25	78	60
Transportation equipment	37	70	47	9	84	79
Total manufacturing	16	36	34	16	50	52

Source: Richard S. Newfarmer and Willard Mueller, Multinational Corporations in Brazil and Mexico: Structural Sources of Economic and Non-Economic Power, a report to the Sub-Committee on Multinational Corporations, Committee on Foreign Relations, U.S. Senate (Washington, D.C.: Government Printing Office, 1975), pp. 55, 108.

*"Metal fabrication" does not include "primary metals" in Mexico. Percentages for "primary metals" in Mexico are as follows: U.S. TNCs, 31 percent; other foreign TNCs, 10 percent; total foreign share, 41 percent.

port-substitution process: chemicals, transportation equipment, electrical and nonelectrical machinery, and, to a lesser extent, food processing. Newfarmer and Mueller found that these industries accounted for two-thirds of all U.S. DFI in the industrial sector in Mexico in 1972; in Brazil in the same year, U.S. manufacturing investments were even more highly concentrated, with three-quarters to be found in the chemicals, transportation, and machinery industries alone.[37] Thus, U.S. DFI does show common characteristics in its location within the manufacturing sector in Brazil and Mexico.

Table 4 allows us to determine whether the addition of non-U.S. TNCs changes the picture. The data in this table clearly support our earlier arguments in this section. In Mexico, U.S. TNCs represent over two-thirds of this foreign share, and in Brazil non-U.S. TNCs have over two-thirds of the foreign holdings. In both Brazil and Mexico, however, U.S. and non-U.S. TNCs combined hold about one-half of the assets of the largest 300 manufacturing firms, giving them exceptionally strong leverage in these economies. Furthermore, within the manufacturing sector, the industries showing the highest levels of foreign penetration are those central to the "vertical" import-substituting phase of industrialization: transportation equipment (and closely related to this, rubber), electrical and nonelectrical machinery, and chemicals. In sum, TNCs are not only concentrated in the leading industries in Brazil and Mexico, but within these industries they are also predominant among the leading firms.

DEPENDENT DEVELOPMENT AND DENATIONALIZATION

Foreign ownership of local industry is a classic measure of dependence. In order to assess whether dependent development has been associated with diminished local ownership shares and therefore with increased dependence according to this dimension, we need to look at DFI in Brazil and Mexico not in terms of its distribution by sector nor in terms of its relation to total U.S., European, and Japanese foreign investments, but in terms of the importance of TNCs[38] relative to local capital.

Unfortunately, good longitudinal data on denationalization for both countries are hard to come by. There are data available for Mexico, however, on the TNC share of industry sales for the years 1962 and 1970. The figures show that significant denationalization of Mexican industry has occurred during this period. If we look at only those firms with ten or more employees, the TNC share rises from 38 percent in 1962 to 45 percent in 1970.[39] While they cover a shorter period

(1966–70), the findings of the U.S. Bureau of Economic Analysis Survey also support the hypothesis of increasing denationalization.[40]

It should be made clear at this point that the fact of increasing denationalization in Mexico or Brazil does not imply that the share of the respective local private sectors is growing smaller in absolute terms. Given the rapid growth of the Mexican and Brazilian economies since the 1940s, the value of production which can be attributed to local capital has in fact increased quite markedly in recent years. What the denationalization argument states is that the value of TNC output has grown even faster than that of local private firms. TNCs are gaining *relative* to local capital, and hence their relative power within the domestic economies of Brazil and Mexico is also increasing.

Evidence of a growing TNC share of local industries is still difficult to interpret. If TNC growth can be attributed to pioneering entrepreneurship in new industrial sectors that local capital was incapable of entering, then denationalization might be seen as a price for broadening the internal division of labor and in this sense diminishing dependence. If, on the other hand, TNCs were concentrated in industries in which local firms had previously been operating, then the effects of denationalization must be seen as more negative.

To address this issue, we turn to data on the mode of entry of TNCs into Brazil and Mexico. Other things being equal, entry by acquisition is an indication of direct displacement of local capital, whereas a newly formed subsidiary is more likely to represent an expansion of the internal division of labor. Of course, no aggregate analysis is conclusive. A TNC might enter Brazil or Mexico by acquiring a local firm in the textile industry and still be providing an innovative new contribution to the local economy that no national firm could have offered. Still, the mode of entry provides some basis for the interpretation of denationalization.

Table 5 presents data on acquisition as a mode of entry into Brazil and Mexico by U.S. TNCs. The table shows that in both countries there has been a linear increase in the percentage of new manufacturing affiliates that have been established by acquisition as opposed to formation or reorganization. In Brazil, the percentage goes from less than 10 percent prior to 1950 to just over 60 percent in the early 1970s. Mexico also had fewer than 10 percent of new U.S. TNC manufacturing affiliates established by means of acquisition before 1950; by the early 1970s, however, fully three-quarters of the entering affiliates were acquired rather than newly formed.

In recent years, Mexico shows a higher level of acquisitions, as well as in its overall rate, than Brazil. In order to understand the

Table 5 / Acquisition as a Mode of Entry into Brazil and Mexico: Percentage of New U.S. Manufacturing Affiliates Established by Acquisition (Rather than Formation or Reorganization)

Date of Formation	Brazil		Mexico	
	Percentage of New Affiliates Established by Acquisition	Total Number of Newly Established Affiliates	Percentage of New Affiliates Established by Acquisition	Total Number of Newly Established Affiliates
Prior to 1945	0	28	9	35
1946–1950	9	11	6	18
1951–1955	22	22	11	18
1956–1960	33	36	39	54
1961–1965	38	16	43	60
1966–1970	52	46	64	77
1971–1973*	61	18	75	32
Total, all periods	33	177	43	294

Source: Newfarmer and Mueller, Multinational Corporations, pp. 122 and 69.
*The terminal date for Mexico is 1972.

impact of denationalization on the local bourgeoisie as a class in Brazil and Mexico, however, one needs to know something about the nature of the local firms acquired by TNCs in each country. Table 6 provides information on the number and size (in terms of assets) of locally owned companies acquired by U.S. TNCs in Brazil and Mexico between 1960 and 1972.

The first finding one can draw from this table is that in Brazil large firms (i.e., those with assets greater than $5 million) accounted for 85 percent of the total value of the acquired firms, whereas in Mexico large firms were closer to one-half the value of all acquired companies. Acquisitions by U.S. TNCs, even though less frequent in Brazil, have thus been more damaging to large local firms. In Mexico, the small firms have borne a heavier share of the burden than in Brazil. If we restrict our analysis to just the large firms in Table 6, we find that the average value of the large Brazilian company acquired by U.S. TNCs ($16.5 million) is about 25 percent higher than the average value of the large Mexican company obtained by acquisition ($13.1 million), thus reinforcing the above conclusion.

Strictly parallel data do not exist on the acquisitions of non-U.S. TNCs, but it is important to note that in Brazil non-U.S. TNCs account for about one-half of all acquisitions by foreign companies, as compared to only about 15 percent in Mexico.[41] This implies that consideration of non-U.S. TNCs would increase the value of Brazilian acquisitions more than the value of Mexican acquisitions. Looking at the relative size of U.S. and non-U.S. subsidiaries in Brazil and Mexico further strengthens this prediction. Table 7 shows that the average sales per affiliate for both U.S. and non-U.S. TNCs is higher in Brazil than it is in Mexico, but the gap between average sales in Brazil and average sales in Mexico is much greater for the European and Japanese TNCs (their average affiliate in Brazil sells nearly two-and-a-half times

Table 6 / Number and Size of Locally Owned Firms Acquired in Brazil and Mexico by U.S. TNCs, 1960–1972

	Brazil		Mexico	
	Number of Firms	Value of Assets[a]	Number of Firms	Value of Assets[a]
Large firms[b]	15 (30%)	$248.0 (85%)	13 (10%)	$170.5 (57%)
Small firms	35 (70%)	43.8 (15%)	115 (90%)	127.0 (43%)
Total	50	$291.8	128	$297.5

Source: Newfarmer and Mueller, *Multinational Corporations,* pp. 124 and 71.
[a]Millions of U.S. dollars.
[b]Large firms are those with assets greater than $5.0 million.

Table 7 / Average Size of TNC Manufacturing Affiliates in Mexico and Brazil

	Mexico	Brazil	Entire World
U.S. TNCs (1968)			
Percentage of affiliates that operate in:	6.8	4.2	100
Percentage of sales generated in:	4.1	3.4	100
Average sales per affiliate in Mexico and Brazil as a percentage of the world average	60.0	80.0	100
Non-U.S. TNCs (1970)*			
Percentage of affiliates that operate in:	1.7	3.3	100
Percentage of sales generated in:	0.8	3.7	100
Average sales per affiliate in Mexico and Brazil as a percentage of the world average	47.0	112.0	100

Source: Fernando Fajnzylber and Trinidad Martínez Tarragó, *Las empresas transnacionales: expansión a nivel mundial y proyección en la industria mexicana* (México, D.F.: Fondo de Cultura Económica, 1976), p. 206.
*Primarily European and Japanese.

more than the average affiliate in Mexico) than it is for the U.S. TNC (Brazilian sales per affiliate average one-third higher than those in Mexico). The large differential between Brazilian and Mexican sales for the average non-U.S. TNC affiliate implies that the bias of U.S. TNCs toward more large-firm acquisitions in Brazil than in Mexico would be even more accentuated if non-U.S. TNCs were also considered. Our overall conclusion, therefore, is that denationalization via acquisition is probably more detrimental to the local bourgeoisie as a class in Brazil than in Mexico, primarily because large firms are more likely to be acquired in Brazil.

The apparently greater ability of large Mexican firms to resist acquisition by TNCs brings us back again to the role of "Mexicanization." Mexico's commitment to participation by local capital in foreign subsidiaries had its statutory beginnings with Avila Camacho's emergency decree of 1944 which, motivated by governmental and private concern over the growing influx of foreign capital into Mexico during World War II, required that majority ownership in Mexican companies be held by Mexican nationals and that a majority of their directors be Mexicans. The law was never generally enforced after the end of the war, although technically it was still in effect. "Mexicanization" requirements were instead selectively applied to a number of strategic industries in Mexico in the later 1950s and 1960s. These included secondary petrochemicals and automobile parts (where foreign participation was limited to 40 percent) and mining (the 1961 mining legislation prohibited TNC participation in new concessions from exceeding 34 percent).

In 1973, under the Echeverría administration, the Law to Promote Mexican Investment and Regulate Foreign Investment required a minimum of 51 percent Mexican ownership and Mexican management control for enterprises in all industries not previously regulated by more specific laws regarding ownership.[42] From our analysis above, it would appear that Mexicanization was less effective in protecting *small* Mexican firms from acquisition by foreigners than it was in protecting *large* Mexican enterprises. This conclusion supports Bennett and Sharpe's argument that the main effect of the Mexicanization laws has been to provide entree for the largest and most sophisticated Mexican economic groups, allowing them to strengthen both their own position and their ties with the TNCs.[43]

Further evidence of Mexico's commitment to ownership controls which benefit the local private sector is presented in Table 8. We can see from this table that the TNC share of locally established subsidiaries is considerably lower in Mexico than it is in Brazil. For example, one-quarter of all TNC subsidiaries in Mexico are joint ventures with a majority of local capital; in Brazil, only one in eight TNC subsidiaries are majority-owned by local capital. At the other extreme of wholly owned TNC subsidiaries (i.e., 95 percent or more of the equity held by the foreign parent), in Mexico one-half of all TNC affiliates are wholly owned by the foreign parent, while in Brazil the proportion of wholly owned TNC subsidiaries stands at more than 60 percent of the total.

The notion that the local bourgeoisie rather than some abstract "national interest" is the main beneficiary of Mexico's ownership controls is given strong support by panel B of Table 8, which focuses exclusively on the nature of the other owner in TNC joint ventures in Brazil and Mexico. The data show that when ownership of a TNC subsidiary is shared in Mexico, in over one-half of the cases the partner is local private capital in concentrated form. In another 35 percent of the cases, the Mexican share is accounted for by dispersed stock holdings, whose owners are likely to be in the private sector. Thus, in over 85 percent of all joint ventures with TNCs in Mexico, local private capital has been involved. In Brazil, on the other hand, two-fifths of all joint ventures by TNCs are with *other foreign partners*. In only one-third of the cases is concentrated local private capital involved. Thus, even before the 1973 Mexicanization law, local capital in Mexico had a much greater likelihood of participating in the

Table 8 / Local Ownership Participation in TNC Subsidiaries in Brazil and Mexico, 1968 and 1971

A. Percentage of Equity Held by Foreign Parent

Parent	Country	95% or more	51–94%	Exactly 50%	25–49%	6–24%	Total	Number of Subsidiaries
U.S.-based (1968)	Brazil	75	14	5	7	0	100	151
	Mexico	55	17	8	18	2	100	249
Non-U.S. (1971)	Brazil	49	30	4	13	4	100	164
	Mexico	38	20	4	29	9	100	90
Total	Brazil	61	22	5	10	2	100	315
	Mexico	50	18	7	21	4	100	339

B. Nature of Other Owner in Cases of Partial Ownership by Parent (percentage)

Parent	Country	Local Private	Local State	Foreign Private	Stock Widely Dispersed	Total	Number of Subsidiaries
U.S.-based (1968)	Brazil	41	0	29	29	99	34
	Mexico	44	0	9	48	101	80
Non-U.S. (1971)	Brazil	30	13	46	11	100	46
	Mexico	72	3	22	3	100	32
Total	Brazil	35	7	39	19	100	80
	Mexico	52	1	12	35	100	112

Source: James W. Vaupel and Joan P. Curhan, *The World's Multinational Enterprises* (Boston: Division of Research, Harvard Graduate School of Business Administration, Harvard University, 1973), panel A, pp. 269 and 272; panel B, pp. 313 and 316.

profitability of the TNCs' operations than their Brazilian counterparts did.

While the evidence supports the commonly held view that Mexican state policy has been more supportive of the local bourgeoisie, the
reasons for this difference between Mexico and Brazil are harder to
specify. The most plausible explanation would seem to be that private
local capital in Mexico has been better connected to the political apparatus than its Brazilian counterpart.[44] This in turn could be related to
the antiforeign aspects of the "revolutionary tradition," which goes
back to 1911. Perhaps the best argument for a political explanation of
this difference between Mexico and Brazil is the apparent convergence
between the two countries around the issue of ownership in the most
recent period. As we noted in our earlier discussion of the export
promotion phase, and as Domínguez[45] and others have noted as well,
Brazilian and Mexican policies on this issue appeared to be moving
toward a common pattern in the late seventies. It can hardly be fortui-
tous that this convergence coincides with the first real movement in
15 years towards an increased political opening to the local bourgeoisie
in Brazil.

STATE POLICY AND TNC BEHAVIOR IN THE SEVENTIES

Classically dependent countries (i.e., export enclave economies) have
to worry about external trade only when their particular export products experience a crisis of oversupply. Otherwise, the primary sector
is the main engine of both growth and exports, so exports should grow
faster than overall demand and these countries should show balance
of payments surpluses. For countries experiencing dependent development the equation is different. The inputs necessary to create local
industry are mainly imported capital goods and intermediate products, while the output of that industry is consumer goods for the local
market. Growth and balance of trade problems go together for countries attempting dependent development.

For classically dependent countries, balance of payments problems appear as the result of "impersonal market forces"; for countries
undergoing dependent development, external imbalances are intimately related to the behavior of foreign investors. TNCs are likely to
be major importers of capital and intermediate goods and thereby
agents in the creation of trade imbalances. Their decisions with regard
to exporting profits and importing investment capital either mitigate
the problem or exacerbate it.

For both Brazil and Mexico, dependent development has meant
chronic trade imbalances of a magnitude that would have choked off

economic growth had it not been possible to arrange for compensating capital flows. It was the conjuncture of these continuing external imbalances, along with a slowing of growth from vertical ISI as it began to exhaust certain areas of local demand, that motivated first Brazil (around 1968) and then Mexico (a few years later) to begin to embark on a new growth strategy of diversified export promotion, with vertical ISI efforts concentrating on capital goods industries. Thus in Brazil, for example, manufactured exports as a percentage of total exports increased from just over 10 percent in the period from 1966 to 1970 to 20 percent during 1971 and 1972, with the 1972 dollar volume of manufactured exports being four times greater than the annual average from 1966 to 1970. Another notable trend is a shift away from the more protected Latin American Free Trade Association (LAFTA) market to non-LAFTA areas (the former accounted for 56 percent of 1968–69 exports but only 48 percent of 1970–71 exports).[46]

Table 9 presents data on the role of U.S. TNCs in manufactured exports from Brazil and Mexico between 1960 and 1972. It can be seen that U.S. TNC exports in both countries, particularly between 1966 and 1972, have increased substantially.

As indicated in the last column of Table 9, most TNC exports in 1960, 1966, and 1972 are accounted for by sales to affiliates. Furthermore, the percentage of exports which are intracompany sales has generally been increasing over time. By 1972, nearly three-quarters of all manufactured exports from Brazil by U.S. TNCs were sold to an affiliated company; in Mexico, over 80 percent of the manufactured exports were intracompany sales.

In both Brazil and Mexico in 1972, 85 percent of all manufactured exports were concentrated in just four industries: transportation equipment, electrical and nonelectrical machinery, and chemicals.[47] These, of course, were key industries during the vertical ISI phase of TNC-led growth, and in the context of the trend towards nontraditional industrial export promotion these same industries are the leaders. The proportion of intracompany sales as a percentage of total exports of these products from Brazil and Mexico is very high (with the exception of chemicals, for which intracompany sales are 55 to 65 percent of total exports; the other industries sell about 80 percent or more of total exports to affiliates). TNC-led export promotion in key industries is thus largely dependent on the willingness of the TNC parent to buy or allocate production from its Brazilian or Mexican subsidiary. This source of revenues becomes quite vulnerable in the event of a general slowdown in demand or an oversupply.

Table 9 / Exports in Comparison to Sales in the Manufacturing Sector for U.S. TNCs in Brazil and Mexico, 1960, 1966, 1972

Year	Country	Local Sales (1)	Total Exports (2)	Exports to Affiliated Companies (3)	Exports as Percentage of Local Sales (2)/(1)	Percentage of Exports that are Intracompany Sales (3)/(2)
		(in millions of U.S. dollars)				
1960	Brazil	453	1.6	1.1	0.4	69
	Mexico	413	5.4	3.0	1.3	56
1966	Brazil	854	12.0	7.4	1.4	62
	Mexico	1,164	22.2	16.6	1.9	75
1972	Brazil	2,850	98.9	72.6	3.5	73
	Mexico	2,689	137.1	112.7	5.1	82

Source: Newfarmer and Mueller, Multinational Corporations, pp. 181–86.

Both Brazil and Mexico are building substantial manufacturing capacity that could not be used (profitably) to satisfy domestic demand. In many cases, the products being exported are not homogeneous commodities that can be sold on the basis of price competition in hard times. The high proportions of intracompany sales are an indicator of the specific marketing channels that are required. Since there is really only one customer for Pinto engines, the country that exports Pinto engines is in at least this sense more vulnerable than the one that exports coffee or silver.

It should be noted in Table 9 that Brazil's exports substantially caught up with Mexico's during the sixties. Largely because of its proximity to the United States, Mexico began with a larger amount of export production, as well as a much larger import burden relative to sales.[48] Brazil was able to boost its U.S. TNC exports from less than one-third of Mexico's in 1960 to more than 70 percent of Mexico's by 1972.

The results achieved in the auto industry provide the most dramatic example of Brazil's success. Traditionally the Brazilian auto industry has been a great success as import substitution,[49] but a drain on foreign exchange. In 1972, the BEFIEX (Export Fiscal Benefits) Program was created to stimulate exports. Its effect on auto exports was gratifying. By 1977, auto companies were exporting at a yearly rate of almost $700 million, creating a yearly trade surplus of over $300 million, remarkably different from the almost $100 million trade deficit they had generated only three years earlier.[50] This was remarkably different also from the performance of the Mexican auto industry, which generated a net trade deficit of $400 million in 1977, down from 1976's $600 million deficit to be sure, but still discouraging. Exports from the Mexican auto industry ran in 1977 about one-tenth those from Brazil.[51] Brazil had clearly taken the lead in shifting the behavior of TNCs in this key industry.

One might take the position that the success of the BEFIEX program is a prime example of the new bargaining power which sophisticated Third World states such as Brazil have acquired. Closer consideration leads to a more agnostic position. To begin with, there is more than one side to every bargain. In this particular bargain, the TNCs were hardly the losers. For the TNCs, shifting production from Detroit to Brazil is shifting it from an area of lower profits to an area of higher profits, so even if one were to assume a complete displacement of home country production by Brazilian exports, the TNCs would have higher rather than lower profits once the costs of adjustment had been taken care of.

Quite apart from the general profitability of TNC operations in

Brazil, the BEFIEX program provided some very generous subsidies. Among other benefits, the companies were allowed a credit for exports on the taxes that they would normally have paid on their domestic production (state sales tax and industrial products tax). Together these two credits amount to 30 percent of value-added exports.[52] Using the proportions indicated by Newfarmer and Mueller's 1972 financial data for U.S. auto affiliates in Brazil, it is possible to estimate the effects of this credit on profitability. It would appear that for each 10 percent of sales an auto company shifted from the domestic market to exports, the company's return on equity would increase about 20 percent. In short, increasing exports was hardly painful for the companies. On the other hand, each dollar of increased return to the companies represents a dollar of lost tax revenues to Brazil. Put crudely, the Brazilian government was paying the companies 15 to 20 cents for every dollar's worth of improvement in the country's balance of payments. It is hard to evaluate this bargain as indicative of Brazil's tremendous power vis-à-vis the TNCs.

The final irony of Brazil's immense export subsidy program is that in 1977, after the BEFIEX program had been in effect for five years, the TNCs were still voraciously gobbling up imports and exporting much less than they imported. According to CACEX, the foreign trade department of the Bank of Brazil, adding together the deficits of only 19 TNC subsidiaries in 1977 was sufficient to generate a trade gap of $661 million, a gap roughly four times as large as the one calculated by the BEA (Bureau of Economic Analysis) for all U.S. TNCs in 1970. Dependent development remains import intensive, despite all attempts to broaden the internal division of labor and shift a country's position in the international division of labor. For exactly this reason, capital inflows continue to be a central requirement for development in both Brazil and Mexico.

Since both countries have allowed investors high rates of return —generally about 50 percent higher than manufacturers in the U.S. can expect—one might think that capital inflows would be no problem. Surprisingly, however, Mexico suffered in the seventies from severe outflows of DFI. The investors who were there took out more than they left in, and the flow of new DFI was too small to close the gap. For some reason, Mexico between 1973 and 1976 was increasingly defined as a "bad investment climate." In part, the negative image stemmed directly from the state's support of the interests of the local bourgeoisie as evidenced by the Mexicanization laws. A year after the laws had been introduced, *Business Latin America* was still reporting that "many foreign investors hesitate to commit themselves until they get a better feel of how the provisions of the new foreign investment law will be applied."[53] In addition, foreign companies found the Echeverría regime insufficiently tough on labor. *Business Latin America* complained that "Labor is one area where companies are fighting a losing battle to keep costs down."

Taxation was a third area in which the behavior of the Echeverría regime left something to be desired. In his first year in office, Echeverría hit the companies with reduced depreciation allowances, a new limit on their ability to deduct advertising expenses, higher taxes on technical fees, and an increase in the gross mercantile revenue tax. While taxes amounted to 46 percent of pretax earnings in Mexico in 1972, they amounted to only 21 percent in Brazil. Bureau of Economic Analysis figures for 1970 also show higher tax rates in Mexico.[54]

Some of the things that Echeverría was doing wrong can be inferred by the policies that his successor, López Portillo, embarked on to "restore investor confidence" in 1977 and 1978. The government's 1977 policy was "decidedly recessionist." Its success in bringing inflation down was "paid for primarily by the growing number of unemployed and by the drop in the standard of living of those lucky enough to find work," but the IMF was pleased. The correspondence between those policies and the ones embarked upon in Brazil is hard to ignore. The sharp drop in the standard of living of the average Brazilian between 1964 and 1969 is well known, but it is important to keep in mind that this was not only a feature of the anti-inflationary "readjustment period." Between 1969 and 1977, productivity in Brazil increased by 70 percent while the real value of the minimum wage dropped by 20 percent. The positive impact on profits is obvious, but in all likelihood the general "good intentions" implied by such policies are just as important in ensuring that a country is defined as a "good investment climate."[55]

The implications of this analysis for the countries of the semiperiphery are somewhat grim. Mexico, one of the richest and best-behaved nations in the Third World, had only to stray slightly from the path of sound business practice to end up shifting the impact of TNC capital and profit flows from a positive $179 million in the 1960 to 1969 period to a negative $349 million in the period from 1970 to 1976. Since one can hardly accuse Echeverría of being a radical, it would appear that the band of acceptable policy is exceedingly narrow and that the penalties for straying outside it are strict and swift.

Given the necessity of capital flows to compensate for trade imbalances and Mexico's difficulties with the capital flows associated

Table 10 / Comparison of Direct Foreign Investment and Foreign Debt in Brazil and Mexico, 1965–1975 (cumulative total in millions of U.S. dollars)

Year	Brazil			Mexico		
	Direct Foreign Investment	Foreign Debt Outstanding	Foreign Debt as Percentage of DFI	Direct Foreign Investment	Foreign Debt Outstanding	Foreign Dept as Percentage of DFI
1965	2,861	—	—	1,745	1,771	101
1966	3,325	—	—	1,938	1,974	102
1967	3,539	3,344	94	2,096	2,176	104
1968	3,957	3,820	97	2,316	2,483	107
1969	4,374	4,403	101	2,576	2,915	113
1970	4,925	5,296	108	2,822	3,260	116
1971	5,480	6,622	121	3,018	3,711	123
1972	6,698	9,521	142	3,208	4,257	133
1973	8,531	12,572	147	3,495	5,627	161
1974	11,199	17,166	153	3,857	7,627	198
1975	14,811	22,171	150	4,219	10,578	251

Sources: For Brazil: Cumulative stock of DFI, 1965–1975, Pedro S. Malan and Regis Bonelli, "The Brazilian Economy in the Seventies: Old and New Developments," *World Development*, vol. 5, nos. 1/2 (January/February 1977), p. 34; total foreign debt, 1967–1975: *ibid.*, p. 38. For Mexico: Cumulative stock of DFI and total foreign debt, 1965–1975: Richard S. Weinert, "The State and Foreign Capital," in José Luis Reyna and Richard S. Weinert (eds.), *Authoritarianism in Mexico* (Philadelphia: Institute for the Study of Human Issues, 1977), p. 123.

with direct investment, it is not surprising that loan capital became increasingly important to Mexico during the seventies. What is surprising is that loan capital also became increasingly important to Brazil (see Table 10). What are the implications of the more rapid growth of debt relative to DFI in both countries? Given that the TNCs were apparently increasing their share of the ownership of the leading sectors of manufacturing during this period, the increases of loan capital must be seen as an addition to dependence on top of the effects of DFI. The discovery that while DFI was growing rapidly dependence on external loan capital was growing even more rapidly reinforces the impression that the forms of dependence may have been changing, but the overall level of dependence was remaining constant or increasing.

Conclusions

The role played by DFI in dependent development in Brazil and Mexico has followed a strikingly similar path despite the variations introduced by political climate, geographic locations, and endowment, as well as the historically distinct patterns of relation to core countries. The similarities—and the gross contrast with the rest of Latin America taken as a whole—justify using Brazil and Mexico as cases in which the process of dependent development led to a consolidation of "semi-peripheral" status and which therefore confront a set of problems and opportunities quite different from those which are confronted by the periphery.

The similar role of DFI in Brazil and Mexico is all the more impressive because it appears to have increased over time. The process of dependent development in the two countries has resulted first of all in a convergence of the sectoral distribution of DFI. More recently, the mix of state policies toward DFI in the two countries seems to be converging. Brazil is paying more attention to ownership and the protection of the interests of local capital and thereby becoming more like Mexico, while Mexico has maintained flexibility on the issue of ownership and at the same time is becoming more effective in the implementation of behavioral controls, which have previously been a Brazilian specialty.

Brazil and Mexico illustrate both the victories and the limitations which can be expected from dependent development. They show the substantial changes in the nature of dependence that can be achieved, but also the persistence of both vulnerability and external control.

Without reiterating the analysis that has already been done, some points deserve to be highlighted.

If there was ever any thought that relatively rich and rapidly growing semiperipheral countries like Brazil and Mexico might be exempted from the generally tight connection between capital flows and political climate, it should be given up. Whenever regimes became defined as excessively nationalist in either Brazil or Mexico, the inflow of direct investment dropped, capital flight accelerated, and the consequent economic pressure was intense. If the "nationalism" involved gave off hints of being anticapitalist as well, the response was more severe. Strains of anticapitalism combined with evidence that the local bourgeoisie might not be able to retain control of the situation produced the most extreme response of all.

What this means is that dependent-developing countries, however successful they may be at emulating or even surpassing the rates of industrial growth that are found in the capitalist core, do not have the same possibility of exploring the welfare side of capitalist development. While the attachment of TNCs to the geographic area of their origins may be waning, it is still of a different order of magnitude from their attachment to the newly profitable semiperipheral areas. They are more than willing to "pause" in their contribution to accumulation in these latter areas at the first sign of policies that might be threatening to their long-run interests. In part, the reason for this is probably economic, resulting from the greater importance of the functions performed by the TNCs' facilities in the core. In part, it may be political, reflecting the greater confidence of TNC owners and executives in their connections with the bourgeoisies of core countries and greater confidence in the ability of these bourgeoisies to retain control over the political machinery. In part, it may reflect simply the TNCs' estimate that the long-run prospects of semiperipheral capitalism are more precarious than those of the core. Whatever the reason, the result is the same; dependence on direct foreign investment is one more reason why there can be no Swedens in the semiperiphery.

What our analysis suggests is that the centrality of DFI to dependent development must be taken into account in analyzing the association between vertical ISI and the "bureaucratic-authoritarianism" that has been laid out by O'Donnell[56] and others. There are a number of reasons why dependent capitalist development may require more repressive policies than capitalist accumulation in the core, but one of them is certainly the negative response of foreign capital to any hints of left-nationalist tendencies. Brazil and Mexico may have diminished foreign political control over internal decisions, but they have not escaped the political constraints imposed by dependence.

Even if we leave questions of welfare and political constraints aside, judgments regarding either trends in the overall level of dependence or the future limits of dependent development are hard to make. Looking back over the four phases of economic growth that were outlined earlier, it is clear that certain aspects of dependence have diminished. There is a broader internal division of labor, and DFI has contributed to the process of its expansion. The range of required imports is being narrowed, though at a much slower rate than the internal division of labor is being expanded since the definition of the total range of required goods is expanding rapidly. Vulnerability to external markets for export products has been diminished, especially in the recent period, by the push toward the diversification of exports.

Even local control over the internal productive apparatus has increased in some respects. Certain areas which were controlled by foreign capital at the turn of the century—most notably public utilities—are now controlled by the state. In the case of Mexico, though much less so in the case of Brazil, the same movement can be observed in export-oriented extractive industries. In addition, a number of newly created industries, primarily basic ones like steel and petrochemicals, have been introduced under the control of the state apparatus. It is unquestionable that in the most recent period the "triple alliance"—of multinationals, the state, and local capital—has come to be a dominant mode of control in a number of industries.

It can be argued that local control—in the sense of regulation of large foreign firms—has also increased in the recent period. Either by bargaining over conditions of initial entry or by a "carrot-and stick" combination of incentives and threats of incentives to its competitors, the state apparatus has been able to affect the strategies of TNCs. This has been most notable in areas relating to balance of payments, but it can also be seen in other areas of behavior—for example, in the implantation of local research and development facilities.

Unfortunately, for most arguments which lead to a conclusion of diminished dependence there are also equally powerful arguments on the other side. The broadened internal division of labor that has been fostered at least in part by the TNCs has meant greatly increased requirements for externally produced capital goods. In addition, the "demand creation" that has been accomplished by TNCs has led to consumption patterns following tightly in the wake of the development of consumption patterns in the core. This, of course, increases the relative advantage of firms which have a hand in creating demand in the core, i.e., the TNCs. On the export side, diversifying exports within the marketing channels established by the TNCs has led to an increased reliance on access to markets in core countries, not to mention an increased dependence on the intracompany channels that run between the semiperiphery and the core inside each TNC.

The interpretation of trends in ownership is also ambiguous. In the phase of horizontal ISI, it appeared that ownership of the leading sectors, the most dynamic from the point of view of capital accumulation, might be passing into local hands, but vertical ISI and export promotion have both been characterized by externally controlled leading sectors. What longitudinal evidence there is suggests that this control was on the increase during the late sixties.

It can easily be argued that the TNCs have abdicated control of industries which are no longer good sources of profit, turning these over to the state so that they can benefit from subsidized inputs based on low-profit state production of basic and intermediate goods and infrastructure services. While there is no a priori reason why the state should subsidize TNC profits by charging low prices for these products, the state is certainly more likely to have a vested interest in the accumulation-enhancing benefits of such a strategy than a private producer would.

Whether the triple alliance of multinational, state, and local capital reduces dependence is also a question of interpretation. By creating a local stake in the profitability of certain of their vulnerable subsidiaries, the TNCs may have fostered a new kind of "neo-*compradore*" bourgeoisie. Insofar as this bourgeoisie can be tied to external markets rather than the local domestic market, the TNC has acquired a powerful but quite captive set of allies within the local dominant class.

Finally, the apparent success of bargaining and regulation is very questionable. Many bargaining successes consist of providing TNCs with substantially subsidized profits for engaging in strategies that do not injure their global profits at all. Insofar as these subsidies draw on state revenues that could otherwise be used either for direct expansion of local control or for welfare-oriented purposes, the growth of control through incentives may be considered another example of the extra policy constraints under which semiperipheral countries operate.

An overall assessment of DFI and dependent development is still hard to make. The evidence necessary to accept either a solidly negative hypothesis or a solidly positive one is still lacking. There is no firm evidence that Brazil and Mexico are on the verge of a future in which dependence will choke off development. On the other hand, one can hardly accept the hypothesis that the development that has occurred in Brazil and Mexico has definitively reduced dependence in an overall sense. The old forms and specific content of dependence have changed radically in both countries, but the new situations of dependence that have emerged out of them contain sources of vulnerability and external control that are just as problematic. It is the combination of transformation and continuity that is in the end most striking.

An Appendix of Tables begins on page 158. Notes begin on page 164.

Appendix of Tables

Table A-1 / Annual Flow and Cumulative Stock of Direct Foreign Investment in
Brazil and Mexico, 1940–1975 (in millions of U.S. dollars)

Year	Brazil		Mexico	
	Annual Flow of DFI[a]	Cumulative Stock of DFI	Annual Flow of DFI[a]	Cumulative Stock of DFI
1940			9	449
1941			16	453
1942			34	477
1943			9	491
1944			40	532
1945			46	569
1946			12	575
1947	36		37	619
1948	25		33	609
1949	5		30	519
1950	3		72	566
1951	−4		121	675
1952	9		68	729
1953	22		42	790
1954	11		93	834
1955	43		105	953
1956	90		126	1,091
1957	144		132	1,165
1958	110		100	1,170
1959	124		81	1,245
1960	98		78[b]	1,081
1961	108		119	1,130

Year				
1962	9		126	1,286
1963	30		118	1,417
1964	28		162	1,552
1965	70	2,861	214	1,745
1966	74	3,325	109[c]	1,938
1967	76	3,539	89[c,d,e]	2,096
1968	71	3,957	115[e]	2,316
1969		4,374		2,576
1970		4,925		2,822
1971		5,480		3,018
1972		6,698		3,208
1973		8,531		3,495
1974		11,199		3,857
1975		14,811		4,219

Sources: For Brazil: Annual flow of DFI, 1947–1964, Joel Bergsman, *Brazil: Industrialization and Trade Policies* (New York: Oxford University Press, 1970), p. 76; annual flow of DFI, 1962, 1965–1968: Werner Baer and Isaac Kerstenetzky, "The Brazilian Economy," in Riordan Roett (ed.), *Brazil in the Sixties* (Nashville: Vanderbilt University Press, 1972), p. 127; cumulative stock of DFI, 1965–1975: Malan and Bonelli, "The Brazilian Economy in the Seventies," p. 34. For Mexico: Annual flow of DFI, 1940–1968, Harry K. Wright, *Foreign Enterprise in Mexico: Laws and Policies* (Chapel Hill: University of North Carolina Press, 1971), p. 74; cumulative stock of DFI, 1940–1964, *ibid.*, p. 75; cumulative stock of DFI, 1965–1975, Richard S. Weinert, "The State and Foreign Capital," p. 123.

[a]Includes net new investment plus reinvested earnings and intercompany items.

[b]Does not reflect disinvestment of $116.5 million (U.S.) resulting from government's purchase of equity interests in foreign-owned electric power companies.

[c]Does not include reinvested earnings.

[d]Does not reflect disinvestment of $54.4 million (U.S.) for purchases of foreign-owned sulphur companies.

[e]Preliminary estimates.

Table A-2 / Sectoral Distribution of Direct Foreign Investment by Development Assistance Committee (DAC) Countries,[a] 1967 (percentage)

Sector	All Developing Countries	Central and South America	Brazil[b]	Mexico[b]
1. Petroleum	32.1	24.3	2.4 ($89)	2.4 ($43)
Production	18.1	14.2	—	2.4 (43)
Marketing	7.3	2.3	2.4 (89)	—
Refining	3.3	5.6	—	—
Transport	3.4	2.2	—	—
2. Mining and smelting	10.4	10.9	2.0 (76)	7.4 (132)
3. Agriculture	5.8	3.3	0.3 (10)	0.8 (15)
4. Manufacturing	30.8	36.1	67.8 (2,526)	72.1 (1,287)
5. Trade	7.9	9.0	7.2 (269)	11.1 (198)
6. Public utilities	4.5	7.4	16.3 (607)	1.5 (27)
7. Transport	1.9	2.0	0.1 (4)	1.3 (23)
8. Banking	1.7	1.6	2.2 (82)	1.1 (19)
9. Tourism	1.5	1.4	0.5 (20)	1.4 (25)
10. Other	3.2	4.0	1.2 (45)	1.0 (17)
Total	99.8	100.0	100.0 (3,728)	100.1 (1,786)
Total value of DFI (in millions of U.S.$)	35,128	18,449	3,728	1,786

Source: Organization for Economic Cooperation and Development (OECD), Stock of Private Investments by DAC Countries in Developing Countries, End 1967 (Paris: OECD, 1972), pp. 13, 66, 77, 82, 85.
[a]The fifteen DAC countries are: Austria, Belgium, Canada, Denmark, France, the Federal Republic of Germany, Italy, Japan, Netherlands, Norway, Portugal, Sweden, Switzerland, the United Kingdom, and the United States.
[b]Millions of U.S. dollars are given in parentheses.

Table A-3 / Distribution of Origin of Direct Foreign Investment in Developing Countries, 1967

A. Percentage of DFI in Each Area Originating with a Given Investor

Investor	All Developing Countries	Central and South America	Brazil*	Mexico*
United States	49.7	63.8	35.6 ($1,328)	76.4 ($1,364)
Canada	4.2	7.3	16.8 (625)	2.0 (35)
United Kingdom	19.4	9.2	4.8 (179)	6.5 (116)
France	8.5	2.5	7.1 (263)	1.1 (20)
Germany	3.4	4.3	13.9 (517)	2.7 (49)
Japan	2.0	2.2	5.7 (212)	4.3 (76)
Switzerland	2.0	2.3	3.8 (140)	4.5 (80)
Other	10.9	8.4	12.5 (464)	2.6 (46)
Total	100.1	100.0	100.2 (3,728)	100.1 (1,786)
Total value of DFI (in millions of U.S. $)	35,128	18,449	3,728	1,786

B. Percentage of a Given Investor's Investments in All Developing Countries Going to a Given Area

Area of Investment	United States	Canada	United Kingdom	France	Germany	Japan	Switzerland	Other
Central and South America	67.5	90.9	24.9	15.7	65.8	57.7	61.5	40.5
Brazil	7.6	42.3	2.6	8.8	43.1	30.2	20.1	12.2
Mexico	7.8	2.4	1.7	0.7	4.1	10.8	11.5	1.2

Source: Same as Table A-2.

*Millions of U.S. dollars are given in parentheses.

Table A-4 / *Crosstabulation of Sectoral and Origin Distributions for Direct Foreign Investment in Brazil and Mexico, 1967* (absolute amounts in millions of U.S. dollars)

Sector	Host Country	Investor								Total DFI
		United States	Canada	United Kingdom	France	Germany	Japan	Switzerland	Other	
Extractive (mining)	Brazil	68	—	2	4	2	—	—	—	76
	Mexico	122	10	—	—	—	—	—	—	132
Manufacturing	Brazil	893	46	125	246	496	189	95	436[a]	2,526
	Mexico	920	22	111	18	44	58	70	44	1,287
Services[b]	Brazil	277	579[c]	33	11	16	23	15	28	982
	Mexico	254	3	5	2	3	18	5	2	292
Other[d]	Brazil	90	0	19	2	3	0	30	0	144
	Mexico	68	0	0	0	2	0	5	0	75
Total	Brazil	1,328	625	179	263	517	212	140	464	3,728
	Mexico	1,364	35	116	20	49	76	80	46	1,786

Source: Same as Table A-2, pp. 77, 85.

[a] The breakdown of this category is as follows: Netherlands, 152; Italy, 134; Belgium, 103; Sweden, 35; and Other, 12.

[b] Sectoral categories 5–9 from Table A-2 have been combined under Services.

[c] Public utilities account for $575 million of this total, and all of this public-utilities investment is controlled by one company, Brazilian Traction, Light, and Power (the name has since been changed to Brascan).

[d] Petroleum and Agriculture have been added to Other.

Table A-5 / Comparison of Brazil (1968) and Mexico (1970): Distribution of the Largest Industrial Enterprises in Each Country by Percentage of Ownership of Their Capital Stock

Industry	TNCs		Private National Firms		State-Owned Firms		Number of Firms	
	Brazil	Mexico	Brazil	Mexico	Brazil	Mexico	Brazil	Mexico
Food	40	44	60	55	0	1	62	35
Textiles	44	8	56	75	0	17	56	18
Primary metals	24	24	24	52	52	24	48	28
Nonmetallic ores	24	16	76	84	0	0	31	31
Chemicals	66	57	31	18	3	25	55	46
Rubber	93	80	7	0	0	20	6	5
Nonelectrical machinery	56	87	44	13	0	0	21	15
Electrical machinery	68	83	32	17	0	0	21	18
Transportation equipment	92	70	8	7	0	23	19	19
Paper	5	35	95	45	0	16	12	13
Wood	0	32	100	45	0	21	4	4
Total*	46	45	42	42	12	13	376	290

Source: Fajnzylber and Tarragó, Las empresas transacionales, pp. 389–90.
*Also includes petroleum derivatives, printing, and diverse manufacturing.

*Table A-6 / Overall Return on U.S.
Direct Investments in Brazil and
Mexico, 1960–1976 (earnings as a
percentage of book value)*

Year	Brazil	Mexico
1960–65 (average)	9.0	8.8
1966	10.5	9.0
1967	9.0	9.3
1968	11.4	9.4
1969	10.3	9.0
1970	12.0	8.2
1971	11.2	6.8
1972	13.7	10.0
1973	15.9	12.3
1974	12.4	13.4
1975	15.8	14.9
1976	14.7	2.4

Source: U.S. Department of Commerce, *Survey of Current Business,* various issues.

Notes

1. The term "semiperiphery" was introduced by Immanuel Wallerstein. See "Dependence in an Interdependent World: The Limited Possibilities of Transformation Within the Capitalist World Economy," *African Studies Review,* vol. 17, no. 1 (April 1974), pp. 1–26; *The Modern World System: Capitalist Agriculture and the Origins of the European World Economy in the Sixteenth Century* (New York: Academic Press, 1974); "The Rise and Future Demise of the World Capitalist System: Concepts for Comparative Analysis," *Comparative Studies in Society and History,* vol. 16, no. 4 (September 1974), pp. 387–415; and "Semiperipheral Countries and the Contemporary World Crisis," *Theory and Society,* vol. 3, no. 4 (1976), pp. 461–84. Our focus here is really on a subset of semiperipheral countries, those that were formerly part of the periphery. Other richer, more industrialized Third World countries like Argentina, Venezuela, South Korea, Taiwan, and Nigeria are also potential members of this subset, but Brazil and Mexico are the best examples.

2. Peter Evans, *Dependent Development: The Alliance of Multinational, State, and Local Capital in Brazil* (Princeton: Princeton University Press, 1979).

3. See Bill Warren, "Imperialism and Capitalist Industrialization," *New Left Review,* no. 81 (September/October 1973), pp. 3–44, and Fernando Henrique Cardoso, "Associated-Dependent Development: Theoretical and Practical Implications," in Alfred Stepan (ed.), *Authoritarian Brazil: Origins, Policies, and Future* (New Haven: Yale University Press, 1973), pp. 142–76.

4. Cardoso, "Associated-Dependent Development," p. 149.

5. Foreign investment is of two main types: direct and indirect. "Direct" foreign investment refers to the acquisition or control of productive facilities outside the home country. Control is generally thought to mean at least a

25-percent participation in the share capital of the foreign enterprise, although the published U.S. Department of Commerce data are based on equity holdings as low as 10 percent. There are two kinds of "indirect" foreign investment: (a) international portfolio investment, which refers to the purchase of securities issued by foreign institutions without any associated control over or management participation in them; and (b) public loans to foreign countries. Portfolio investments typically take the form of bonds, whereas direct foreign investment entails holding equity. Although both direct and indirect foreign investment in Brazil and Mexico will be discussed in this paper, our primary concern is with the former and in particular with its most important institutional source in recent years, the transnational corporation.

6. See Richard S. Newfarmer and Willard Mueller, *Multinational Corporations in Brazil and Mexico: Structural Sources of Economic and Non-Economic Power*, a report to the Subcommittee on Multinational Corporations, Committee on Foreign Relations, U.S. Senate (Washington, D.C.: Government Printing Office, 1975).

7. Theodore H. Moran, "Multinational Corporations and Dependency: A Dialogue for Dependentistas and Non-Dependentistas," *International Organization*, vol. 32, no. 1 (Winter 1978), pp. 79–100.

8. Theotonio Dos Santos, "The Structure of Dependence," *American Economic Review*, vol. 60, no. 2 (May 1970), p. 236.

9. Peter Evans, "Continuities and Contradictions in the Evolution of Brazilian Dependence," *Latin American Perspectives*, vol. 3, no. 2 (Spring 1976), pp. 30–54.

10. See Richard Graham, *Britain and Modernization in Brazil: 1850–1914* (Cambridge: Cambridge University Press, 1968), *passim;* and Warren Dean, *The Industrialization of São Paulo, 1880–1945* (Austin: University of Texas Press, 1969), *passim.*

11. Mira Wilkins, *The Emergence of Multinational Enterprise: American Business Abroad From the Colonial Era to 1914* (Cambridge: Harvard University Press, 1970), p. 113.

12. From 1911 to 1929, American investment in petroleum jumped from $20 million to $206 million, while the overall stock of U.S. DFI in Mexico rose very little—from $616 to $683 million. See Harry K. Wright, *Foreign Enterprise in Mexico: Laws and Policies* (Chapel Hill: University of North Carolina Press, 1971), pp. 54, 77.

13. Raymond Vernon, *The Dilemma of Mexico's Development* (Cambridge: Harvard University Press, 1963).

14. Eric N. Baklanoff, "External Factors in the Economic Development of Brazil's Heartland: The Center-South, 1850–1930," in Eric N. Baklanoff (ed.), *The Shaping of Modern Brazil* (Baton Rouge: Louisiana State University Press, 1969), p. 26; Eric N. Baklanoff, "Brazilian Development and the International Economy," in John Saunders (ed.), *Modern Brazil: New Patterns and Development* (Gainesville: University of Florida Press, 1971), p. 195.

15. Evans, "Continuities and Contradictions," p. 79.

16. The existence of locally controlled capital in the primary export sector gave Brazil an advantage in the development of horizontal ISI. Liquid capital from coffee found its way into new import-competing industrial enterprises, and government subsidies to the coffee sector further increased the supply of capital. The result was that industrial production fell off less than 10 percent in the early years of the Depression and by 1933 had regained its 1929 levels.

See Werner Baer, *Industrialization and Economic Development in Brazil* (Homewood, Ill.: Richard D. Irwin, 1965), pp. 22–24.

17. Nathaniel H. Leff, *Economic Policy-Making and Development in Brazil, 1947–1964* (New York: John Wiley, 1968), p. 60; Joel Bergsman, *Brazil: Industrialization and Trade Policies* (New York: Oxford University Press, 1970), p. 30.

18. Bergsman, *Brazil,* p. 74.

19. René Villarreal, "The Policy of Import-Substituting Industrialization, 1929–1975," in José Luis Reyna and Richard S. Weinert (eds.), *Authoritarianism in Mexico* (Philadelphia: Institute for the Study of Human Issues, 1977), pp. 73–74.

20. Evans, "Continuities and Contradictions."

21. Fernando Henrique Cardoso and Enzo Faletto, *Dependence and Development in Latin America* (Berkeley: University of California Press, 1979).

22. Rhys Owen Jenkins, *Dependent Industrialization in Latin America: The Automotive Industry in Argentina, Chile, and Mexico* (New York: Praeger, 1977), p. 53; Douglas Bennett, Morris J. Blachman, and Kenneth Sharpe, "Mexico and Multinational Corporations: An Explanation of State Action," in Joseph Grunwald (ed.), *Latin America and World Economy: A Changing International Order* (Beverly Hills, Calif.: Sage Publications, 1978), p. 275.

23. Werner Baer and Isaac Kerstenetzky, "The Brazilian Economy," in Riordan Roett (ed.), *Brazil in the Sixties* (Nashville: Vanderbilt University Press, 1972), p. 133; Villarreal, "Import-Substituting Industrialization," p. 73.

24. It is worth pointing out that in absolute terms the value of foreign investment as a proportion of total investment was relatively small. In Mexico and Brazil, net foreign capital inflows of all types in the period from 1950 to 1965 amounted to only 8 to 12 percent of the total gross investment in each economy, with this proportion being somewhat higher for the manufacturing sector alone. The importance of DFI lies not in its quantity *per se,* but in the fact that it involves control over the largest firms in leading sectors. See Leff, *Economic Policy-Making,* p. 75; Wright, *Foreign Enterprise in Mexico,* pp. 78, 93; and Vernon, *The Dilemma of Mexico's Development,* p. 113.

25. In Brazil this phase actually began a bit earlier, around 1968.

26. *Business Latin America,* 1979, pp. 61, 64.

27. J. Fred Rippy, *British Investments in Latin America: 1824–1949* (Minneapolis: University of Minnesota Press, 1959).

28. *Ibid.;* Paulo Singer, "O Brasíl no contexto do capitalismo mundial 1889–1930," in Boris Fausto (ed.), *Brasíl republicano: estrutura de poder e economia,* tomo 3, vol. 1, *História geral da civilização brasileira* (São Paulo: Difusão Europeia do Livro); Vernon, *The Dilemma of Mexico's Development;* Cleona Lewis, *America's Stake in International Investments* (Washington, D.C.: The Brookings Institution, 1938).

29. For Brazil, see Baklanoff, "Brazil's Heartland," p. 26; for Mexico, see Wright, *Foreign Enterprise,* p. 54.

30. Eric N. Baklanoff, "Foreign Private Investment and Industrialization," in Eric N. Baklanoff (ed.), *New Perspectives on Brazil* (Nashville: Vanderbilt University Press, 1966), p. 109.

31. OECD data, presented in Tables A-2 through A-4 and to be discussed below, will give us a picture of total, not just U.S., DFI in Mexico and Brazil in 1967. They do not, however, contradict the pattern of dependent development as it is outlined here on the basis of U.S. data alone.

32. For a detailed analysis of the nationalization of Mexico's electric power

industry, see Miguel S. Wionczek, *El nacionalismo mexicano y la inversión extranjera* (México, D.F.: Siglo Veintuino Editores, 1967), pp. 31–168. For an analysis of the role of the state in electric power generation in Brazil, see Judith Tendler, *Electric Power in Brazil: Entrepreneurship in the Public Sector* (Cambridge: Harvard University Press, 1968).

33. *Business Latin America,* 1979, p. 11.

34. See Werner Baer, Isaac Kerstenetzky, and Annibal V. Villela, "The Changing Role of the State in the Brazilian Economy," *World Development,* vol. 1, no. 11 (November 1973), pp. 23–24; Wilkins, *Multinational Enterprise,* pp. 114–15; and Wright, *Foreign Enterprise,* pp. 60, 67–68.

35. See Susan Eckstein and Peter Evans, "The Revolution as Cataclysm and Coup: Political Transformation and Economic Development in Brazil and Mexico," in Richard Tomasson (ed.), *Comparative Studies in Sociology* (Greenwich, Conn.: JAI Press, 1978).

36. It is interesting to speculate whether this exceptional degree of diversification of U.S. DFI, both across sectors in Brazil and Mexico as well as across the range of developing countries, confers specific structural and bargaining advantages to the U.S. vis-à-vis the other core powers as well as vis-à-vis Brazil and Mexico.

37. Newfarmer and Mueller, *Multinational Corporations,* pp. 175, 178.

38. A multinational, or transnational, corporation (for our purposes, the two terms are equivalent) may be defined as any business enterprise engaging in direct foreign investment in production facilities spanning several national jurisdictions. The parent firm of the TNC and its network of affiliates are bound together by common ties of ownership, they draw on a common pool of human and financial resources, and they respond to some sort of common strategy. One can get an idea of how large the TNCs that operate in Brazil and Mexico are from a survey of 179 of the biggest U.S. manufacturers located in these two countries that was conducted in 1972 for the U.S. Senate Subcommittee on Multinational Corporations. The profile of the average manufacturing TNC in the survey was as follows: $1.2 billion in worldwide assets; $1.5 billion in total sales; 43,000 employed workers; and 34 subsidiaries in over 15 countries, with 7 of these affiliates located in Latin America. The overseas operations of these TNCs were very profitable, with after-tax earnings of foreign affiliates amounting to 16.1 percent of direct investments in equity and long-term debt, and broad earnings (after-tax earnings plus royalties, payments for management services, and other intangibles) amounting to 20 percent. Consolidated net (after-tax) earnings of these TNCs for their domestic and foreign operations together was only 12.7 percent. See Newfarmer and Mueller, *Multinational Corporations,* pp. 40–41. The sales of the TNC manufacturing affiliates in Mexico average 1.1 percent of the total sales of the parent firm, indicating the small proportion of total resources committed to a single venture for the TNC as compared to the national firm, which often is risking its total assets in competing with the TNC. See Fernando Fajnzylber and Trinidad Martínez Tarragó, *Las empresas transnacionales: expansión a nivel mundial y proyección en la industria mexicana* (México, D.F.: Fondo de Cultura Económica, 1976), p. 205. Also see Table 7 in the text.

39. See Newfarmer and Mueller, *Multinational Corporations,* p. 57. Denationalization has been heaviest in the fields of food products and drugs. For a discussion of denationalization in the pharmaceutical industry in Mexico, see Gary Gereffi, "Drug Firms and Dependency in Mexico: The Case of the

Steroid Hormone Industry," *International Organization,* vol. 32, no. 1 (Winter 1978), pp. 237–86.

40. U.S. Tariff Commission, *Implications of Multinational Firms for World Trade and Investment and for U.S. Trade and Labor,* Report to the Committee on Finance, U.S. Senate (Washington, D.C.: Government Printing Office, 1973).

41. James W. Vaupel and Joan P. Curhan, *The World's Multinational Enterprises* (Boston: Division of Research, Harvard Graduate School of Business Administration, Harvard University, 1973), pp. 331, 334.

42. It should be noted that our data do not cover the post-1972 period in Mexico, for which there is evidence of a sharp drop in the number of TNC acquisitions as a result of the 1973 law. See Newfarmer and Mueller, *Multinational Corporations,* p. 68.

43. Douglas C. Bennett and Kenneth E. Sharpe, "El control de las multinacionales: las contradicciones de la mexicanización," *Foro Internacional,* vol. 21, no. 4 (April–June 1981).

44. Robert R. Kaufman, "Mexico and Latin American Authoritarianism," in José Luis Reyna and Richard S. Weinert (eds.), *Authoritarianism in Mexico* (Philadelphia: Institute for the Study of Human Issues, 1977), pp. 218–20; Jorge I. Domínguez, "National and Multinational Business and the State in Latin America," mimeo, 1979; Guillermo A. O'Donnell, "Reflections on the Patterns of Change in the Bureaucratic-Authoritarian State," *Latin American Research Review,* vol. 13, no. 1 (1978), pp. 20–23.

45. Domínguez, "National and Multinational Business."

46. John M. Connor, *The Market Power of Multinationals: A Quantitative Analysis of U.S. Corporations in Brazil and Mexico* (New York: Praeger, 1977), p. 54.

47. Newfarmer and Mueller, *Multinational Corporations,* pp. 181–84.

48. U.S. Tariff Commission, *Implications of Multinational Firms,* pp. 256–57, 260–61.

49. Kenneth S. Mericle, "The Political Economy of the Brazilian Motor Vehicle Industry," mimeo, 1978.

50. Ronald E. Müller and David H. Moore, "Case One: Brazilian Bargaining Power Success in BEFIEX Export Promotion Program with the Transnational Automotive Industry," paper prepared for the United Nations Centre on Transnational Corporations, New York, 1978.

51. *Latin American Economic Report,* 1978, p. 212.

52. Mericle, "Political Economy."

53. *Business Latin America,* 1973, p. 398.

54. *Business Latin America,* 1970, p. 10; Newfarmer and Mueller, *Multinational Corporations,* pp. 175, 178; U.S. Tariff Commission, *Implications of Multinational Firms,* pp. 451, 452.

55. *Latin American Economic Report,* 1978, pp. 85, 144.

56. Guillermo O'Donnell, *Modernization and Bureaucratic-Authoritarianism: Studies in South American Politics* (Berkeley: Institute of International Studies, University of California, 1973); Guillermo O'Donnell, "Corporatism and the Question of the State," in James M. Malloy (ed.), *Authoritarianism in Latin America* (Pittsburgh: University of Pittsburgh Press, 1977), pp. 47–87; O'Donnell, "Reflections."

5

The State as Banker and Entrepreneur: The Last Resort Character of the Mexican State's Economic Intervention, 1917-1970

DOUGLAS BENNETT and KENNETH SHARPE

There is a growing body of evidence to demonstrate that the Mexican state that was consolidated in the wake of the Revolution deliberately created and has continued to nurture a national bourgeoisie that has been a major force in the spectacular economic growth (the "Mexican miracle") of the past four decades, growth that has had little or no benefit for—indeed some argue that it was built on the backs of—the Mexican lower classes.[1] And yet, paradoxically, the capitalists that have received such benefits rarely view the activities of the Mexican state with more than skepticism, and often portray it as their principal enemy. Then again, perhaps this is not so surprising. The Mexican state—hardly limiting itself to mere infrastructure investments or the provision of investment incentives—has itself emerged as the major banker and entrepreneur in the economy. Its own enterprises have preempted private sector savings to finance public investment; they have closed off opportunities for private investment; and they enjoy special advantages in sectors where public and private firms compete. Even in comparison with other major Latin American countries, the Mexican state has been atypically and forcefully interventionist in its national economy.[2]

These two seemingly opposed views of the Mexican state are both factually accurate and can be reconciled under the following thesis: after the Revolution, the Mexican state took on the role of making

169

capitalism work for Mexico, and since Mexico was a dependent, late-starting industrializer, this task required, for any degree of success, both major restrictions on the demands of the lower classes and the forceful entry of the state into areas of the economy where the private sector was unwilling or unable to enter, or had entered and failed. The central question of this chapter addresses part of this thesis: why has the state emerged as the major banker and entrepreneur in Mexico's economy?[3]

Gerschenkron: The State and the Requisites of Late Industrialization

Alexander Gerschenkron's historical researches provide the most insightful starting point for an explanation of state involvement in an industrializing economy. Diverging from the thesis that developing countries travel the same road towards industrialization as more developed ones, only trailing them by some decades, Gerschenkron argues that the industrialization process in the more backward countries requires (among other things) "the application of institutional instruments for which there was little or no counterpart in an established, industrial country."[4] Thus, where capital formation was accomplished in Great Britain through the exertions of individual capitalists, later industrializers (such as France and Germany) required investment banks for the same purpose, and those embarking still later (such as Russia) needed the still more powerful institutional means of the state itself—its taxation powers—to generate the needed investment capital.[5]

Gerschenkron focused his attention on industrialization in Europe, but in the dependent context of Latin American countries such as Mexico, Argentina, Brazil, and Chile, the dynamics of "late, late" industrialization have been somewhat different. In these countries, industrialization initially focused not on producer goods but rather on consumer goods that had formerly been imported. This took place through a process of import substitution which was originally forced on these countries by depressions and wars in the developed capitalist world.[6] Even more than for the late industrializers of Europe, this late, late industrialization has posed certain problems for these Latin American countries which their private sectors have been unable or unwilling to meet and solve. These problems are greater in scope and character than those of late industrializers for a number of reasons. Products and processes are more sophisticated, and the necessary technology not only expensive (if the owners—often transnational corporations—are willing to sell), but also almost impossible to develop domestically with available talent. The problem of being competitive with production methods utilized elsewhere in the world is not simply a concern for export production, but also for the domestic market because of the penetration of these countries by capital from the more industrialized countries. Labor in these late, late industrializers is often better organized to make good its demands for a sizeable share of the profits than was the case with the first industrializers. These problems (and, of course, there are others) were exacerbated in Mexico by the devastation of the Revolution which extended through much of the second decade of this century. Mexico emerged from the Revolution without an entrepreneurial class capable of leading industrialization; consequently, a "need" arose for special institutional arrangements to confront and solve the problems of late, late industrialization. As Gerschenkron found in Europe, we find in Mexico (and to a certain extent in other Latin American countries) that state institutions have come to meet these problems.

Our basic contention regarding the role of the state in the political economy of Mexico (although only limited evidence can be provided in this chapter) can be stated as follows: (a) the Mexican state has taken on the task of making capitalism work by (b) placing primary reliance on the private sector, promoting and strengthening it to lead the way in rapid economic growth, but at the same time (c) the state has stood ready to intervene in the economy as an institution of last resort, though sometimes an impatient one, acting as banker and as entrepreneur to deal with those problems that the private sector has been unwilling or unable to handle.

Gerschenkron's argument about the role of the state in industrialization in situations of relative backwardness can thus be extended to cover the case of Mexico—and it will prove revealing. But before proceeding we should briefly take note of the fact that his account is incomplete when considered as a *description*, and that it contains an even more serious flaw when considered as an *explanation*.

Gerschenkron's account is limited as a description because its central terms must be filled in historically. The conceptions of "problem," "last resort," and "inability" (or "unwillingness") have objective and subjective moments. The trajectory of growth—the mode of production in its fullest sense—throws up concrete difficulties at particular points in time. But the manner in which these difficulties are defined as problems, the way in which the state's responsibility for solving them comes to be conceived, the recognition of the unwillingness or inability of the private sector to act, the judgment that no other solution can be found except by resort (last resort) to the instrumentality of the state, all must be understood in light of the conceptualizing orientations of state institutions and leaders. And these orientations, in turn, change as problems are defined and confronted, as learning takes place, as generations and regimes change.

The flaws in Gerschenkron's account as an explanation may be noted simply by recognizing its functionalist or teleological character. Adducing that the inability of private sector actors to solve the problems of late, late industrialization creates "needs" for action by the state does not explain why (still less how) the state acts to fulfill these needs. Such a functionalist explanation fails to account for the *will* (or lack of will) of the state to undertake to meet these needs and also fails to account for the state's *power* successfully (or unsuccessfully) to cope with these needs.

In the discussion that follows, we will focus particularly on some of the more dramatic interventions of the state into the Mexican economy, as banker and as entrepreneur, over the period from 1917 to 1970, attending briefly to the manner in which the state's orientations have been formed and reformed, and to the bases of the state's power to carry through its will. At the end, we will present some general if rather speculative and tentative conclusions.

The Period from 1917 to 1940

The political stability that was the masterful achievement of Porfirio Díaz made possible Mexico's first period of substantial and sustained economic growth. During the years of his tutelage (1876–1911), railroads were constructed, mining was modernized and expanded, commercial agriculture was developed, and exports were diversified. A number of characteristics of that growth—particularly the foreign domination of certain leading sectors and the unequal distribution of benefits—served as the tinder that ignited the Revolution. Diverse factions of landless peasants, workers, small landholders, and disgruntled politicians joined to topple Díaz in 1911 and then separated to contest the settlement.

After several years of on-and-off fighting, the Mexican economy was a shambles:

> Security, confidence and public credit vanished. The currency was destroyed and the banking system almost completely wiped out. Railway facilities were destroyed and communications demoralized. The livestock population was seriously depleted and agricultural output gravely declined. Mining output was heavily reduced. . . .[7]

And this disruption came on top of the structural problems that had been caused by the pre-Revolutionary pattern of dependent growth— the underdevelopment of the internal market; the foreign domination of mining, banking, railways, and other sectors; and the substantial inequality of benefits.

Such were the problems facing the country's leaders, those who gradually consolidated power in their own hands after the Revolution, who institutionalized that power through the instrumentality of a single dominant political party (now the PRI), and who first guided the post-Revolutionary state's intervention into the economy as banker and as entrepreneur. When we look at these leaders, two questions deserve our attention—the question of power and the question of intention or orientation. It is the latter—why the state chose to intervene in the economy for the purposes and in the manner that it did —that principally concerns us here, but we need to consider briefly the question of power because the successful intervention of the state into the economy presupposed a strong and unified governmental apparatus. Given the political disorganization brought on by the Revolution, how did the state acquire the power necessary for such intervention?[8]

Building strong political institutions was a prolonged and difficult process. The armed power of peasant groups in various regions, the local and autonomous power of regional *caudillos,* the intraclass as well as interclass conflicts, the religious cleavages which culminated in the Cristero revolt, and the tensions between federalism and centralism all made difficult the task of creating a new, stable political order. The task was accomplished, often painfully, by Presidents Carranza, Obregón, and Calles in the dozen or so years following the Constitutional Convention of 1917. They used their military power to crush armed opposition, built a strong bureaucracy relying heavily on *técnicos* (economists and engineers) in the key ministries of Treasury and Public Works, and were able to coopt and control many dissident elements, an effort which culminated in the skillful construction of the PNR (the predecessor to the PRI). This increasingly strong central party institutionalized and monopolized access to political power by absorbing (or destroying) local *caudillos.*[9] Paralleling this strong party organization was the creation and molding of certain key state institutions: strong ministries (particularly the Treasury); a unified, loyal, and increasingly apolitical military; and so forth.

It should be noted as well, to explain the state's resurgent capability to intervene in the economy, that there were no social classes sufficiently powerful and well organized to be capable of opposing such intervention. The *hacendados* that had been an important foundation of the Porfirian regime were either destroyed or severely weakened by the Revolution. The debt peonage system upon which much of their economic power had rested had been destroyed, and they were preoccupied with efforts to defend what lands remained in their hands against demands for land reform from armed peasant groups. On the other hand, the peasant groups that had fought in the Revolution were regionally organized with local rather than national goals, and the cooptation of some leaders and the assassination of others had severely weakened their capacity to influence the course of events. Labor had always been weak under Díaz because union activity had been forbidden. Despite its acquaintance with anarchosyndicalist ideas and its increasing capability to strike in key industries (railroads, textiles, mining, tobacco), the bloody repression of the army and the *rurales* had kept labor in a weakened position.[10] After the Revolution, labor remained crippled by the control of the CROM, a labor confederation that was not only corrupt (to the point of selling out to business) but also highly dependent on governmental recognition for its rights to strike. Finally, in the early 1930s, both labor and peasantry were incorporated into and finally controlled by the central party. And finally what of business interests? A strong Mexican industrial bourgeoisie had failed to emerge during the Porfiriato. A few import-substituting industries—textiles was the most important—had begun to grow, but they were still small and often at least partially controlled by foreign interests.[11] The Revolution only further weakened this small and disorganized class—except for the relatively strong industrial group in the northern city of Monterrey, whose position in industries such as beer, glass, cement, and even steel remained intact. However, this group was isolated and small, and did not pose a serious threat to the economic activities of the state. In fact, some of those activities (railroads and road construction, for example) were positively to the benefit of these Monterrey industrialists.

Thus, given increasingly strong political institutions, the Mexican state would face relatively little organized opposition to the kinds of economic intervention it would undertake. The only strong national institutions were political institutions; no class could dominate or successfully oppose the state's actions. Indeed, the very kinds of economic problems the nation faced were symptomatic of the weakness of the private sector groups that might have been expected to handle them.

Increasingly, the state had the power to intervene. But would it? And for what purposes? The potential power of the state does not explain its particular orientations. What did it define as problematic, and what did it define as legitimate action to solve its problems? How did it come to take on these orientations?

In the contest for power that followed the assassination of Madero in 1913, those who finally prevailed were neither the agrarian radicals, who saw the Revolution as a social movement to bring massive land reform, nor those drawn from the more advanced segments of the labor and intellectual groups, which nurtured socialist and anarchosyndicalist ideas. Instead, they were predominantly men of the middle class—many from the north (from Sonora in particular); some, like Carranza and Obregón, from landowning families (though not the largest of these); a few, like Calles, small businessmen. It was the vision of these men, and of the lawyers and engineers—technical and professional men—who surrounded them, that prevailed and gave first shape to the consolidating post-Revolutionary Mexican state. Their vision was not, of course, a unified or coherent one. Carranza saw himself as heir to the Liberal-Constitutional ideals of Juárez and Madero. His primary concerns were the re-establishment of lawful order and the electoral mechanism, though he understood, as Madero had not, how difficult it would be to dismantle the Porfirian autocracy. For his part, Obregón saw beyond these measures to the necessity of certain social reforms. He "favored nationalist legislation and agrarian and labor reform which would at one and the same time curtail United States encroachment, break the power of the great landed families, and widen opportunities in the market for both labor and his kind of middle class."[12]

President Carranza acquiesced in the addition of progressive social provisions concerning land reform, public education, labor guarantees, and the Church to his draft for a new Constitution, but neither he nor Obregón nor Calles did much about implementing those provisions of the 1917 Constitution. Their attention was preoccupied by the need to consolidate state power in the hands of the central government.

What was the importance of the northern origins of the "Sonora gang" that dominated Mexican politics until Cárdenas assumed the Presidency in 1934? Cline surely misleads us in tracing their orientation to a surviving Spanish Bourbon tradition in the north.[13] Far more important in shaping their thinking was the proximity of the United States. Nowhere was the domination of foreign capital stronger than in the north. "By 1902 U.S. firms held more than a million hectares in Sonora; in Sinaloa they owned 50 percent of the productive deltaic plain and 75 percent of all irrigable land, where sugar, cotton and fresh vegetables were raised for the market,"[14] often the U.S. market. And foreign (mostly American) domination of mining and manufacturing, often abetted by the protection of Díaz and the *científicos,* closed Mexicans out of other potentially productive endeavors. That foreign domination wove a strongly nationalist threat through the thinking of the Sonoran political leaders.[15] Their nationalist orientation took on concrete form in Article 27 of the Constitution, and later in measures prohibiting foreigners from owning land, forbidding their participation in banking and insurance companies, nationalizing the petroleum and light and power industries, and limiting or excluding their equity participation in a growing number of manufacturing sectors.[16]

If the proximity of Mexico to the United States had allowed a foreign domination which rankled, it also put before the eyes of these Sonorans the image of a modern, rapidly developing country. Beyond political consolidation, their primary concern was with economic growth, and the model to be copied (the only one seriously available to Mexico in 1920, it should be remembered) was the capitalist system to the north with its dramatic successes in industrialization and in the commercialization of agriculture. If the United States was to be a model for development, this was much more in the sense of showing the shape and extent of what could be achieved than in the sense of showing a precise route to be followed. It was recognized that the peculiar conditions of Mexico and its later start might require slightly different means—a more forceful role for the state, for example. But the U.S. model also showed that a central requisite for such development was the creation of a strong national bourgeoisie, both a "yeoman" agricultural class to promote agricultural modernization and a private entrepreneurial class to lead industrialization. In the early 1920s, these orientations came to be firmly embedded in the Ministry of the Treasury (Hacienda) and this ministry rapidly became the most powerful in the state apparatus, a position that has only recently been challenged.

The power of the Treasury inside the state apparatus has stemmed from its control over the sources of revenue (taxation, foreign loans, and so forth) and from its control over the budgetary allocation of these funds. If those allocations required Presidential consultation and approval it should be borne in mind that the Treasury and the umbrella of financial institutions around it (the Bank of Mexico, Nacional Financiera, and so forth) have been nearly (again, until recently) the sole source of well-trained economists in Mexico. In-house Treasury training programs molded the orientations of those who passed through them.

Of course, the orientation of the Treasury has changed over time, partly in response to regime changes in Mexico, partly in response to shifting currents of economic thought outside Mexico. The concerns of Albert Pani and the economists around him who shaped the character of the Treasury in the 1920s have been characterized as "orthodox" and neoclassical in orientation: "They sought to re-establish the nation's foreign trade position, restore confidence in the monetary system, and get channels of domestic trade and commerce operating once more."[17] When Cárdenas came to power, those who staffed the key positions in the Treasury and in the Bank of Mexico came to be more oriented towards Keynesian principles. Growth in GNP, aggregate investment, and employment became major economic indicators.

However, beneath these changes in orientation ran a deep continuity. The Revolution had brought to the surface a series of radical demands or goals: for land redistribution, for recovery of national patrimony from foreigners, and for substantial improvement in the living conditions of the urban and rural lower classes. Such radical goals did not coalesce into a coherent ideology, still less into a strategy for development. While these goals continued to be articulated by the Revolutionary family, the strategy of economic development that came to be adopted, with its guiding intelligence in the Treasury, was one that saw them being pursued only as a by-product of a certain kind of economic growth in which primary reliance would be placed on the private sector.

The common outlook among the middle- and high-level *técnicos* in the institutional complex demarcated by the Treasury, the Bank of Mexico, and Nacional Financiera can be traced, to a large extent, to an in-house training program developed in the Bank of Mexico by Gonzalo Robles and Daniel Cosío Villegas and administered for a number of years by Robles. As a young man, Robles had been a member of Carranza's retinue; he had studied engineering in the United States; and he had been centrally involved in the reorganization of the banking system. For a time, under Cárdenas, he was Director General of the Bank of Mexico, moving later to become director of a new office in the bank, the Department of Industrial Studies, from which he coordinated the training program. Promising young people were brought into the bank for a few years, sent off to foreign countries (often the United States) for graduate study, and then returned for final shaping under Robles' careful attention. The orientation they received was the one we have already discussed: economic independence from the colossus to the north, industrialization, the importance of a middle class, primary reliance on the private sector, and the need for vigorous action by the state to create the conditions for private sector investment and to do what the private sector would not or could not.

Placing such primary reliance on the private sector created immediate difficulties. The national bourgeoisie was small and weak, and often disinclined to make long-term capital investments, preferring instead to invest their funds in real estate speculation, commercial credit, jewelry, and the like. The only alternative, particularly if foreign investment was not to be encouraged (and in the wake of the Revolution it would have needed substantial encouragement), was state activity to foster the growth of a national bourgeoisie and to promote the kinds of conditions under which it would be inclined to invest. Such state intervention was hardly lacking in historical precedents (in the Spanish colonial system and in the Porfiriato), and further legitimation came from the rapid acceptance of Keynesian principles. From an early date, then, the post-Revolutionary Mexican state took upon itself the task of nurturing a national bourgeoisie that would pace economic growth, and of doing what that nascent national bourgeoisie would not or could not do. Major infrastructure investments in road building and in irrigation began in the mid-1920s, but nowhere was the early orientation of the state so clearly seen as in its actions to create a strong financial sector. The consequences of its action in this sphere defined the terms of much of what would happen later.

Mexico faced nearly total financial collapse following the Revolution. Paper currency was worthless, most of the private banks were in ruins, and the country's standing in international financial circles had fallen so low that further credits were unobtainable. Calles and his Treasury Minister saw the reorganization and resuscitation of a private banking system as a critical first step towards generating domestic savings and investments and attracting foreign loans. Unlike the situation in the Porfiriato, the banks were to be kept under close government supervision. In announcing the new legislation that would govern the banking system, the Minister of Finance said that it would now be

> the intent of the state to channel the capital invested in the credit industry toward accomplishing specific objectives. Under the new system, it is not enough that the liabilities issued by credit institutions are well secured; it is necessary that the capital obtained through issues of such liabilities goes to enrich sources of public wealth and this capital may not be used as an instrument in creating monopolies for certain industries or individuals.[18]

Foreign banks (and foreign ownership of domestic banks) were forbidden. To exercise supervision over the banking system, and to perform central bank functions, the Bank of Mexico was created in 1925. A complex scheme of reserve requirements came to be used as a mechanism by which the Bank of Mexico could channel private investment into high priority sectors and could also extract savings for public sector investment.

A private banking system capable of channeling sufficient savings into investment could not be resurrected overnight, and the predilections of the private sector for short-term and speculative investments meant that some sectors that were deemed particularly important for development would be underfinanced unless the state itself provided what the private sector could not or would not. Agriculture was one such critical sector. In 1926, Calles created the Agrarian Credit Bank, a public sector development bank, to finance agricultural development. While this bank did finance large private landholdings (often owned by former Revolutionary leaders who amassed large tracts) it did not meet the needs of peasant *ejidatarios,* a large—and in some areas armed—segment of the rural population. Because of the inalienability of their lands, they could not offer the guarantees necessary to meet conventional bank requirements. The lack of credit available to *ejidatarios* was not seen as problematic until the Cárdenas regime (1934–40). In his struggle to break state and party dependence on Calles and other older Revolutionary elites, Cárdenas' strategy required mobilizing the support of popular sectors—labor and peasantry. And if the peasantry were to be depended upon as a social foundation of the regime, their needs would have to be met. If neither the private sector banks nor the Agrarian Credit Bank would provide ejidal credit, another state financial institution would be necessary. Therefore, in 1935, Cárdenas created the Ejidal Bank.[19]

The state's initial entry into agrarian credit was soon followed by the creation of a number of other public sector development banks— the Worker's and Industrial Development Bank, the Foreign Commerce Bank, the Small Merchant's Bank, and so on. If the general need for such banks was defined by the inability or unwillingness of private sector banks to provide the financing necessary for economic growth, the particular need for each public sector bank was defined by more specific historical factors—the sectors earmarked to lead that growth, as well as the needs and demands of the groups and classes that constituted the social foundations of the post-Revolutionary Mexican state.[20]

Slowly, responding to the ministrations of the state, the private banking system began to grow as well, both in terms of assets and in terms of institutional strength and sophistication. One key measure in the state's nurturance, important in reorienting lending towards longer-term funding for industry and away from more speculative investments, was the authorization in 1932 and subsequent encouragement of the *financiera,* a kind of investment bank.[21] With the lack of an effective bond or stock market, the national bourgeoisie that has developed in Mexico has largely crystallized around the private banking system. It has come to be characterized by a series of groups—a dozen or so major ones and many smaller ones—each of which has a bank or bank complex at its center. The savings from these banks are utilized for investments in affiliated manufacturing, mining, and/or commercial enterprises.[22]

This national bourgeoisie is of comparatively recent origin, as Sanford Mosk's emphasis on the "New Group" in his pioneering study of industrialization in Mexico serves to underscore.[23] But where have they come from? Surely some, such as the Monterrey group (or groups), have their origin in the first surge of industrialization of the Porfiriato. Hansen argues that some were "friends and relatives of successful revolutionary politicians" who capitalized on political ties to secure lucrative government contracts and concessions and that others were sons of dispossessed *hacendados* who had to turn their energies to other fields after the Revolution.[24] Derossi's study of *The Mexican Entrepreneur* confirms this latter contention, but her study shows a surprisingly high number of Mexican entrepreneurs of foreign (especially Spanish) origin.[25]

However, to return to the main argument, the development of a national bourgeoisie capable of carrying forward the project of economic growth was made possible by the successful reconstruction of the banking system. And the general pattern set down in the financial sector in the 1920s and 1930s was one that would be repeated elsewhere. Primary reliance was placed on the private sector, but the state stood prepared to do what the private sector was unable or unwilling to do:

> Mexico's economists conceived of a total network of economic institutions and processes necessary to complete the structure they were creating, and if the private sector could not supply these, it seemed the obligation of the state to do so, in the interests of the private sector itself.[26]

The Period from 1940 to 1970

Calles had set about creating an authoritarian state that was dominated by a strong, unified executive power and stood above, autonomous from, class interests. Cárdenas largely shared this general conception of the state. If Cárdenas took more dramatic action in reasserting national soveignty vis-à-vis foreign interests, that is more to be explained by the different circumstances the two men faced than by any difference of ideology between them. In the face of strong pressure from the U.S. government and Mexico's need to re-establish its international financial bona fides, Calles was forced to moderate his insistence that U.S. mining companies recognize ultimate Mexican ownership over mineral resources. On the other hand, Cárdenas' forceful action to limit or exclude foreign investment in railroads and in the light and power industry was to an important degree prompted by serious bottlenecks that were being created by the inaction of foreign companies. The foreign investors could not be induced to undertake the necessary new investments in these critical basic industries, and because of the high initial investments and long-time horizons on profits private Mexican investors could not be expected to enter either. Only state action could prevent these industries from slowing the pace of growth. In railroads, the foreign investors appear to have been anxious to sell. In light and power, the creation of the Comisión Federal de Electricidad (CFE) did not at that time threaten the right of foreign investors to continue their activities. The case of petroleum is rather more complicated, but even here it is to be borne in mind that the intransigence of the oil companies challenged the sovereignty of the Mexican state and forced Cárdenas' hand.[27]

There were differences between Calles' and Cárdenas' understandings of the proper role of the state, but they principally concerned the state's attitude towards class conflict. Where Calles saw the state's role as one of conciliation, "in which class antagonisms are overcome in the higher interest of the nation," Cárdenas advocated "the exercise of power on behalf of the weaker class."[28] This shift in attitude explains a great deal about state action towards workers and peasants, but it should not be allowed to obscure the strong continuity that is seen in the state's role in the economy. Under Cárdenas, as under Calles before him and Avila Camacho after him, primary reliance was placed on the private sector, with the state complementing but not supplanting the role of private capital—the pattern that was also to be seen in the banking system. The most important explanation for this is the continuity of personnel in key financial positions. For example, Luis Montes de Oca, President of the Bank of Mexico under Cárdenas, had served as General Comptroller and Finance Minister in the cabinets of Calles' *Maximato,* and Cárdenas' Secretary of the Treasury, Eduardo Suarez, retained the same position in the subsequent administration of Avila Camacho,[29] as did Antonio Espinosa de los Monteros, Director General of NAFIN.

Cárdenas had mobilized peasants and labor in his struggle with Calles, and he had used the power of the state on behalf of those lower classes. In 1938, he reconstructed the official party, incorporating the largest labor confederation and the major peasant organization directly into its structure as two of its four quasi-corporatist sectors (the third sector was for "popular organizations"—principally state employees—and the fourth, which quickly disappeared, was for the military). The National Revolutionary Party had become the Party of the Mexican Revolution (PRM), a more effective mechanism of political control for the administrations that followed.

The decades of the 1920s and 1930s had been ones of political and economic reconstruction in Mexico. In those years, the foundations were laid for the surge of industrialization that began in the 1940s and was to be sustained into the 1970s. The Great Depression, in decreasing the volume of world trade, had provided some stimulation for domestic production of consumer goods in Mexico. World War II added to the insulation of the domestic market from imports the possibility of exports to the United States. It was only in 1947, however, that the government implemented a scheme of tariffs and quotas to sustain the import-substitution industrialization into which circumstances had already maneuvered Mexico.

The emerging national bourgeoisie responded quickly to this stimulus (though so too, it should be added, did transnational corporations). The assistance of the government to the private sector took an array of forms: financing for new businesses through its development banks, basic infrastructure facilities and services, and beneficial tax policies. Public sector purchases of goods and services provided important markets for some young firms. The state maintained a considerable measure of control over the labor force through cooptation of its leaders and occasional coercion. And in 1954 the state took steps to damp down inflation; the policy of *desarrollo estabilizador* (stabilized development) had emerged.

However, the state's role went beyond even these measures, since the context of late dependent development created problems that the private sector was unable or unwilling to meet. Public sector investments in a range of basic industries were necessary to sustain the pace of industrialization—investments that, because of their magnitude or because of the long-term character of their expected returns, would not have been made if the state had not stepped in. The instrumentality that was created to make these investments was a state investment bank, Nacional Financiera (NAFIN).[30]

Founded in 1934 to perform a complex variety of functions—including the development of a stock exchange and a capital market for public bonds—NAFIN was reorganized in December 1940 to make the promotion of industrial development its principal focus. NAFIN

rapidly became the major institutional arm of the state's entrepreneurial activities, the instrumentality by which the state's potential
power, in relation to a still maturing national bourgeoisie, became
actualized.

From the beginning, the bank has operated with a considerable
degree of autonomy. This stems in part, no doubt, from the sophistication and success of its activities. NAFIN has achieved a steady record
of earnings (which it has tended to capitalize), and it has increased its
available resources through foreign borrowing and through the sale of
certificates of participation in the bank's equity investments. The relative autonomy of NAFIN from the tricky currents of Mexican politics
is enhanced as well by the close coordination of its activities with the
powerful Treasury Ministry and the Bank of Mexico. Representatives
from both institutions sit on NAFIN's Board of Directors, and there
is a strong tendency for technical personnel to move among the three
institutions, imbuing them with a common outlook. Moreover, there
tends to be more continuity in the terms of top officials within these
institutions than in other ministries and state agencies.

NAFIN plunged directly into a number of industrial ventures
early in World War II, but the bulk of its loans and investments have
gone to public sector infrastructure projects in railroads, irrigation,
electric power, telecommunications, and the like. If we pass over these
to concentrate on NAFIN's industrial promotions it is only because
such infrastructure investments are a more common and less conten-
tious sort of intervention by the state into the economy of a developing
country. On the other hand, NAFIN's financing of industry has been
considerable, steadily accounting since 1950 for between one-third and
one-half of the banking system's total financing of industry.[11] By 1945,
NAFIN held stock in 35 corporations and was majority owner of 5,
and by 1961,

> it was a creditor, investor or guarantor for 533 business enterprises of all
> kinds; it held stocks in 60 industrial firms; and it was majority stockholder
> in 13 firms producing steel, textiles, motion pictures, plywood, paper,
> fertilizers, electrical energy, sugar, lumber and refrigerated meats.[32]

From the beginning, NAFIN's activities were legally circumscribed to keep it from emerging as a direct threat to the private sector.
The legislation by which NAFIN was reorganized in 1940 stipulated
that NAFIN was not to compete with existing banks but rather to
dedicate itself to those activities whose credit needs were not being
adequately serviced by commercial banks and *financieras.*[33] In practice,
particularly in its equity investments, NAFIN has tended to confine

its entrepreneurial activities to cases in which the private sector was unable or unwilling to make investments in areas seen as crucial for industrialization.[34]

NAFIN's involvement in the steel industry is both dramatic and instructive. The Mexican steel industry had begun with the founding of Latin America's first integrated steel plant in 1893, the Compañía Fundidora de Fierro y Acero de Monterrey. Although Fundidora principally produced products for the country's railways, it remained nearly the sole domestic producer of steel. By the late 1930s, Mexico was importing two-thirds of the steel needed for domestic consumption,[35] but the onset of World War II meant that imported steel would no longer be available. A group of private bankers and investors had drawn up a plan for a new steel mill that would produce cold-rolled steel and tinplate from imported hot-rolled strip, but this plan would have left Mexico dependent on imports, imports of uncertain availability, and so planning turned to consideration of an integrated steel mill using Mexican coal and iron ore. Such a project was well beyond the financial and technical resources of the original private investors, so NAFIN intervened and borrowed $6 million from the Export-Import Bank to help finance the project. At first, NAFIN tried to avoid majority ownership of Altos Hornos, as the new firm came to be called, buying the whole of the venture's first bond issue and a majority of the preferred stock, but only a quarter of the common stock. However, the firm took longer to move into production than anticipated, and further financing—which the private interests would not commit—was needed. By 1947, NAFIN was majority owner of the firm.[36] As Raymond Vernon concludes:

> This was a case of a sort which would be repeated several times in later years—a case in which private investors developed the initial concept of the operation and then, frightened off by the size of the commitment and the technical uncertainties that they faced, welcomed government participation as a form of risk insurance.[37]

Altos Hornos was only the beginning of NAFIN's—and the government's—involvement in the steel industry. In 1961, NAFIN extended credit to allow Altos Hornos to acquire the La Consolidada steel works, lest that firm should fail. And as Fundidora has felt the need to modernize its equipment, and as private investors have been hesitant to supply the necessary financing to the aging firm, NAFIN has increasingly filled the gap. By 1975 it had come to hold a third of the equity in that corporation. Similar circumstances have led NAFIN to take on a minority equity holding in Tubos de Acero, another privately initiated firm. And with the Mexican demand for steel far outstripping the capacity of these existing firms, NAFIN has become involved in the development of a new steel mill, the Siderúrgica Lázaro Cárdenas–Las Truchas (SICARTSA), a venture of such size and sophistication as to be well beyond the capability of the private sector.

As in the case of steel, wartime shortages and the failure of the private sector to meet the resultant need led to NAFIN's initial investments in paper and cement. In the paper industry, the Compañía Industrial de Atenquique was formed in 1941 by a group of entrepreneurs headed by sugar magnate Aarón Sáenz. When the capital needs of the project strained the resources of this private group, NAFIN stepped in with financing, first in the form of bonds and preferred stock, but later involving a majority equity position. Through the course of the World War II NAFIN helped promote and finance a substantial expansion of the cement industry from 8 to 19 firms between 1940 and 1948. At the end of that period, NAFIN held securities in 10 of these firms, but a majority holding in only one.[38]

The hesitation of the private sector to make some important investments stemmed from considerations of political risk rather than simply from financial or technical drawbacks. After the Alemán administration came into office, feasibility studies done by U.S. consultants and the Bank of Mexico (Gonzalo Robles' Department of Industrial Investigations) showed the construction of railway freight cars, then imported used from the United States, to be a prime industry candidate for import substitution. Where other such proposed projects found willing private investors, this one did not. The market volume was certain enough, but there would be only one buyer, a state-owned enterprise. Furthermore, the railways had been operating at a loss and were slow to pay bills. Forcing collection from a state enterprise would undoubtedly be difficult. With funding provided through NAFIN, the state itself undertook the creation of Constructora Nacional de Carros de Ferrocarril in 1952.[39]

In Mexico, as elsewhere, unprofitable and inefficient state enterprises have frequently drawn criticism from the private sector, but NAFIN's very success and profitability have made it a target as well —its critics believe that NAFIN has intruded into areas that should be left to the private sector.[40] However, it is difficult to sustain this charge. On the whole, NAFIN's entrepreneurial activities have greatly benefited the private sector (the construction of infrastructure, the provision of supplementary financing, the obtaining of foreign credits and technical assistance), and its own equity investments have been centered in those fields and in those projects demanding effort "well beyond the capacity of the private entrepreneurs and investors of a still newly developing economy," who could not cope with

> the larger capital outlays required, the more complex operations which rendered new ventures technically more difficult to launch, and the higher risks deriving from uncertainties of costs and production flows as well as from the greater market imponderables (i.e., greater than those encountered in industrialization to substitute for consumer goods imports.[41]

The last-resort character of the interventions of the state into the Mexican economy can be seen in the efforts of NAFIN (and other state institutions) to promote and finance projects of critical importance to national industrialization which were beyond the capabilities of the private sector. But this last-resort character can be seen as well in the Mexican state's willingness to bail out private sector firms which were on the brink of failure. Although such failures often involve incompetence, they must be seen against the background of the difficulties faced by national entrepreneurs in meeting the demands of import-substitution industrialization. The cases of Diesel Nacional (DINA) and the Sociedad Mexicana de Crédito Industrial (SOMEX), an industrial firm and a banking firm, are two of the major instances out of a number that could be considered here.

The initiative for DINA came originally from two private sector promotors, Bruno Pagliai and Luis Montes de Oca. Pagliai was an immigrant entrepreneur who had already founded Tubos de Acero, a firm manufacturing steel piping, as a joint venture with Italian steel interests. He would go on to become the central figure in an industrial group with extensive holdings in mining and metal-fabricating firms.[42] Luis Montes de Oca, after heading the Bank of Mexico, had founded his own private bank, Banco Internacional. Together, and on the basis of studies done by themselves, Fiat, and NAFIN, they proposed to manufacture diesel trucks in Mexico using Fiat technology. When these private investors were unable to raise the capital necessary for the venture, they sought public sector assistance. NAFIN subscribed to 59.5 million pesos of stock; the private investors put in 10.5 million; and Fiat was allotted 6 million as payment for its cooperation and technology.[43] The venture, which started operations in 1954, fared poorly: the Fiat truck was ill-adapted to Mexican roads and cargos; the firm was induced to buy expensive and unnecessary machinery from Fiat; and complex problems of distribution were never adequately solved. Efforts to improve sales and profits by domestically assembling automobiles then popular in Mexico (Fiat 1100s and 1400s) proved insufficient. Even without these problems, it is difficult to see how the firm could have succeeded without protection from imported vehicles. By 1958, DINA was nearly bankrupt, and the private investors were eager to withdraw. The Mexican state, acting principally through NAFIN, bought out their shares and recapitalized the venture—it became sole proprietor of a major firm in the rapidly developing Mexican automobile industry.[44]

Founded in 1941 by Dr. Antonio Sacristán, a Spanish immigrant, SOMEX rapidly became one of the most important *financieras* in Mexico. It promoted and financed industrial enterprises in such disparate fields as automobile assembly and parts manufacture, household appliances, and the canning and fishing industries. Sacristán aggressively led SOMEX into areas where few other private entrepreneurs dared to venture, thinking in part that he could lay off losses from the more risky endeavors onto the substantial profits of some of the others, such as the development of Mexico City's Pedgregál (an ancient lava bed) into an exclusive residential district. By 1962, SOMEX owned or participated in more than 40 enterprises, but the company was on the point of bankruptcy, beset by problems of internal administration and an over-long portfolio of unprofitable firms.[45] The Mexican government could not allow the failure of such a major private bank: a number of the enterprises it owned were in sectors that had been marked as priorities for industrial growth; the resultant unemployment would have caused considerable hardship and would have generated substantial pressures for curative government action; and the failure would have shattered public confidence in the banking system, savings from which were crucial for both public and private sector investments. The viability of the entire growth strategy would have been threatened. In taking over SOMEX, the state acquired not only a second major industrial development bank but also holdings in over 40 firms (with a majority position in many).[46]

The Mexican state's acquisition of unprofitable private sugar mills at an accelerating rate during the 1960s and 1970s would seem to present another example of state sector intervention and expansion resulting from private sector failure, but this case is more complicated. The policy of *desarrollo estabilizador* which was adopted after 1954 required a low rate of inflation to encourage the bank savings needed for sustained public and private sector investment. One requisite for containing inflation was that prices of basic commodities be controlled if market forces proved insufficient. In 1958, such price controls were placed on sugar. However, labor costs in the sugar industry were not so strictly controlled, and during the next ten years labor costs rose 75 percent.[47] The expansion of land under cane cultivation and the adoption of more efficient agricultural methods were somewhat limited by the ejidal character of neighboring lands which the government was committed (at least to some degree) to protect.[48] Faced with rising costs but unable to expand production or to raise prices, the private mills began to go bankrupt. The state's first response was to create a special state banking institution, the Financiera Nacional Azucarera, to channel investment capital to the industry. When that proved insufficient and the mills continued to lose money, the state, now often the major creditor, stepped in and took them over. A series of efforts to restructure the industry during the 1970s proved unsuccessful. By 1969, 18 mills (accounting for 30.7 percent of national production) were under government control; by 1975, that number had increased to 31 (50.5 percent of national production).[49]

The failures of the private sector firms were the immediate cause of the state acquisitions in the sugar industry, but those failures were themselves induced by government policies aimed at solving other problems of the industrialization strategy, particularly the problem of inflation. Sugar operations became so unattractive that existing owners would not make needed new investments and no buyers could be found for struggling firms. The state stepped in not merely to recover the loans it had made, but also to maintain a major source of rural employment and to boost sugar production, which was needed so that domestic demand could be met without upward pressure on prices and so that there would once again be export sales.

There are also cases in which private sector investment was available and successful but in which the state intervened nevertheless; they are cases in which the private investment was foreign. Private foreign investment raises special considerations, but not ones that completely deviate from the last-resort character of the interventions of the Mexican state. Earlier we considered a number of state actions towards foreign investors during the Cárdenas regime, arguing that these interventions tended to be triggered by problems (bottlenecks and so forth) that were unlikely to be solved so long as the firms involved remained in foreign hands. After World War II, however, nationalization became a very uncommon response of the Mexican government to foreign investment; "Mexicanization" became the preferred strategy. In order to regulate and control the activities of transnational corporations and to protect and promote the growth of a Mexican national bourgeoisie, foreign investors were first encouraged and then required to share majority ownership (equity) with Mexican partners.[50] For a variety of reasons, it has often proved difficult to locate willing and able Mexican private investors: the high initial expense of the 51 percent equity, the weak capital market, differences between the foreign investors and potential Mexican investors with regard to the reinvestment of earnings, and so forth. For a time, the government helped subsidize Mexicanization through tax incentives and other concessions, but more recently, finding these measures to be too costly in terms of tax revenues forgone, it has promoted Mexicanization by itself acting as an investor of last resort, providing that portion of the Mexican investment which private Mexican capital has been reluctant to put forward. Thus, for example, when Anaconda's giant Cananea mine was Mexicanized in 1971, NAFIN helped put together the consortium of Mexican investors who purchased the 51 percent. Ten percent of the stock went to Banco Nacional de México (a major private banking group), a smaller holding was reserved for workers and employees of the mine, a number of other private investors took small holdings, and NAFIN put in the rest (some through Cobre de México, a subsidiary of NAFIN). NAFIN also made loans to make possible the purchases of some of the other investors.[51] In roughly similar fashion, NAFIN participated as well in the Mexicanization of two other large mining concerns, Azufrera Panamericana and Compañía Minera Autlán.

In the agricultural machinery industry—one in which there had been considerable pressure to Mexicanize—some of the firms had put 51 percent of their shares in trust while they searched for suitable Mexican partners. After several years, when no private Mexican investors showed interest in John Deere, NAFIN purchased the shares itself.[52]

It is worth noting that the "need" for state intervention in these cases arose not strictly from the financial and technical requisites of the industrialization strategy, but was in part defined politically by the Mexicanization project. It should also be added that the entry of the Mexican state into some previously foreign-controlled sectors may have been governed by considerations other than those of last resort. There are indications that some state agencies are coming to see minority ownership as a valuable instrument of industry regulation, providing ready access to information and to decision centers. This pattern seems particularly clear in the mining sector, where the Comisión de Fomento Minero (the Mining Development Commission) has come to be a shareholder in an increasing number of mining concerns (15 in 1970, 38 in 1975).[53] We need to consider this point more carefully, examining particularly both the power and the orientations that parastatal enterprises acquire once the state has first intervened in a sector.

Acting as an institution of last resort, the Mexican state has founded banks, promoted and financed firms in new and critical areas, bailed out bankrupt ventures, and participated in the Mexicanization of foreign-owned corporations. The total extent of these interventions of the state into the Mexican economy is considerable—in 1976, the Secretary of National Properties' directory of state enterprises listed 470 firms.[54] In 1974, these state sector enterprises accounted for about 10 percent of Mexico's Gross Domestic Product.

Considerations of last resort may have guided the state's acquisitions of the large majority of these firms, but on what principles have they been operated? These state enterprises have their own activities, providing certain goods or services; they have substantial resources at their disposal; and they face particular economic problems in the context in which they operate. Many of these firms operate more or less as they would if they were private sector firms; a very few have been operated as deliberate instruments of government regulation in particular industries; and some have been used as political bases by their politically appointed directors. For reasons stemming from these considerations as well as others, some state enterprises have intervened further—acquiring other enterprises or branching out into new areas —in ways that have not strictly followed the lines of last resort. We will touch on only a few examples.

Shortly after it first began production, Altos Hornos, one of NAFIN's first major projects, began to move towards more fully integrated operations—much in the manner of other major steel companies, public and private, elsewhere in the world. It added a plant producing coke and coal tar chemicals (Compañía Mexicana de Coque y Derivados, S.A. de C.V.) and an ammonium nitrate fertilizer plant using by-product coke-oven gases (Fertilizantes de Monclova, S.A.), and then acquired three existing firms in the steel industry, "thereby diversifying its product line and expanding its assured market for steel."[55] The private sector felt threatened by these moves, finding no way they could be interpreted as "last-resort" state actions. When Altos Hornos tried to use its position as a major supplier of steel plate to force a Monterrey steel pipe manufacturer to sell out, the private sector resorted to exerting pressure through the President's office to stop the takeover. Altos Hornos contented itself with acquiring a minority share in the firm.[56] Starting as a single plant in Monclova, Coahuila, Altos Hornos today stands at the center of a complex of 38 firms—wholly owned subsidiaries and companies in which Altos Hornos owns a substantial percentage of the stock—a dramatic example of the changing character and dynamism of some of the major state firms.[57]

A similar pattern is to be seen with DINA. After its takeover and reorganization by NAFIN during the López Mateos administration, it quickly recovered organizational strength—and a measure of independence. Some of its expansions have followed last resort lines. When FANASA, the Mexican-owned manufacturer of the ill-fated Borgward automobile, went bankrupt, DINA stepped in to utilize the firm's plant and equipment. For the assembly plant, DINA organized a subsidiary called Maquiladora Automotriz Nacional (MAN), which contracted first with International Harvester and then with General Motors to assemble their pick-up trucks under license. For the engine machining plant, DINA (30 percent) entered into a joint venture with NAFIN (30 percent) and North American Rockwell (40 percent), the resultant firm being called DINA-Rockwell, to manufacture heavy-duty truck and bus axles.[58] In other cases, however, DINA's expansion has been governed by considerations that go well beyond those of last resort. Until the late 1960s, Fabricas Auto-Mex, a manufacturer of Chrysler corporation automobiles, was majority Mexican owned. Auto-Mex, in turn, was majority owner of Motores Perkins, a diesel engine manufacturing concern. By law in Mexico, all automobile parts manufacturers (but not automobile manufacturers themselves) must be 60 percent Mexican owned. When Chrysler bought majority interest in Fabricas Auto-Mex, Motores Perkins became, contrary to the law, foreign-owned. The Mexican state (particularly through NAFIN) has had, we have seen, a concern to facilitate Mexicanization when private Mexican investors have been hard to find, but rather than search for Mexican private investors to buy up Chrysler's share in Perkins, DINA (with the backing of NAFIN) immediately bought the firm. Concern by state officials to maintain proper control over this crucial sector, given the importance to Mexico's development of efficient, low-cost trucking, may have been an important consideration. However, DINA was already the other major producer of automotive diesel engines, and so the company had a clear economic interest in acquiring its competitor. In acting as it did, DINA acted as any private sector firm might have if faced with the same opportunity and stepped beyond strictly defined last-resort considerations.

Consider in this regard the case of SOMEX. Before its acquisition by the government to forestall a major collapse, SOMEX's activities were hardly governed by last-resort considerations; it was an aggressive, private-sector investment bank. After several years of retrenchment, consolidation, and reorganization, SOMEX has once again taken on an active promotional and investment posture. To some extent, this has happened because SOMEX retained, after the government takeover, many of the same managers in the firms that SOMEX owned; and these managers have continued to suggest acquisitions and expansions, both vertical and horizontal, that would strengthen their firms' positions just as they would if the firms were still privately held. Since 1970, the aggressive attitude of these managers has been reinforced by the orientation of the top staff at SOMEX, many of whom have been drawn from the Treasury–Bank of Mexico–NAFIN complex. Thus, for example, Manufacturera Mexicana de Partes de Automoviles (Mex-Par) has recently moved beyond its original product lines into a joint venture with the Blackstone Corporation (forming Mex-Par–Blackstone) to produce automobile radiators, principally for export. Since 1970, Aceros Esmaltados, S.A., has moved to create a filial manufacturing firm, Estufas y Refrigeradores Nacionales, S.A., and a firm to coordinate the distribution and sale of the products of these two firms, Aceros, S.A. These moves were taken "to complement the production" of Aceros Esmaltados and to "maintain the position which has been attained in the national market and in Central America."[59]

Perhaps the most dramatic example of a recent, more expanded role for the state, in character as well as in size, has occurred in the mining sector. The initiative here comes principally through the Comisión de Fomento Minero (CFM), an agency attached to the Ministry of National Patrimony. The orientations of this Ministry have changed markedly since its creation in 1958. It has always been strongly nationalist, but its initial concerns were with the Mexicanization of mining through private-sector investment in the foreign-owned companies which dominated the industry.[60] It generally promoted public investment only in those cases where the private sector had tried to act but had failed. As a last resort, the state stepped in to save failing mines (often ones that had been abandoned by the private sector) as a means to ensure important sources of local (and rural) employment. This was the case, for example, in the Real del Monte y Pachuca, Santa Rosalía, Macocozac, and Angangueo mines.[61]

Although this Ministry has not displaced private Mexican capital from its position in any mining enterprises, its recent, more aggressive, actions indicate that it has become more "impatient" in its definition of last resort. Instead of simply pressuring foreign companies to sell majority ownership to Mexicans and promoting Mexican private investment (through tax subsidies, for example), it has increasingly taken the initiative itself, generally through the Comisión de Fomento Minero. Since 1970, for example, major mining investments with strong state participation have included a large multinational (i.e., intergovernmental) aluminum complex involving Jamaica and Mexico, a firm developing phosphoric rock resources in Baja, California, the Cedros-Las Torres silver mine, the Real de Angeles (silver, zinc, lead) project, and the La Caridad-Santa Rosa copper exploration project. Through these and other ventures, the state's share in mining investments has risen from 17.8 percent in 1970 to 35 percent in 1975.[62]

In part, this shift towards a larger role for the state in the mining sector has occurred because of the very size and technological complexity of the investments involved and the hesitancy of the Mexican private sector to take full responsibility. But the shift was also shaped by the growing confidence of the technical staff in the Ministry of National Patrimony, the more statist slant of these *técnicos* (particularly those brought into the government by the Echeverría regime), and the enhanced power of the ministry within the government.

If, in recent years, the state has been inclined to act more aggressively, deviating from last-resort motivations, it should also be noted that there are a number of instances in which state-sector expansion has deviated from last-resort considerations at the invitation or insistence of private-sector firms—instances, that is, in which private sector firms actively encouraged the state to play a role in some project, and not because of any incapacity on their part. For example, Tubacero, S.A., encouraged Altos Hornos to purchase a minority holding in its stock when the giant state steel company initiated plans to manufacture products in direct competition with Tubacero. The partnership eliminated the threat of competition.[63] A related case is that of Borg and Beck, an auto parts firm in which SOMEX recently increased its holding at the request of both the Mexican and foreign private partners, each of which, for slightly different reasons, wanted the state bank to act as a buffer in its relationship with the other. A more complex and unusual example is provided by another state-promoted mining venture, the recently opened Consorcio Minero Benito Juárez-Peña Colorado, in which ownership is shared among the public and private steel firms which will purchase its iron ore: Altos Hornos (47.6 percent), Hojalata y Lámina (27.1 percent), Siderúrgica Tamsa (15.7 percent), and Fundidora Monterrey (4.8 percent).[64] In this venture, strong state participation may have been necessary to promote an enterprise of such magnitude (711 million pesos), and the state has majority control of the venture, but only because of an additional 4.8 percent of the stock which is held by the federal government, not Altos Hornos. The intention here seems to be to use the government itself as a buffer and a mediator in any conflicts that may arise between the private sector firms and the powerful and largely autonomous state steel firm.

Some Theoretical Conclusions

THE PROBLEM OF ORIENTATIONS: THE FILLED-IN
CHARACTER OF STATE "INTEREST"

In the pursuit of economic growth in this century, primary reliance in Mexico has been laid on the private sector. However, because of the devastation of the Revolution, because of the context of dependency in which the country has found itself, and because of its "late, late" start towards industrialization, the Mexican state has come to act forcefully in the economy as banker and as entrepreneur to solve problems that the private sector has been unable or unwilling to handle. This characterization, while basically adequate as a description, is seriously flawed as an explanation because of its functionalist character. It gives no account of either the state's ability (power) or inclination (orientation, interest) to play the historical role that it has. In seeking a more adequate explanation, what can be learned from the historical sketch we have just provided? How is state action to be explained?

The dominant type of explanation for why the state acts as it does is that provided by the group theory approach,[65] to which (though there are important differences) "instrumentalist" approaches in the Marxist theory of the state bear strong resemblance.[66] These explanations are "exogenous" in that they look to explain state action by reference to external "pressures" of various kinds that may be brought to bear on the state and to which the state, for various reasons, may respond. Often the state is conceived (at least implicitly) as a "neutral" institution, buffeted by various groups and social classes, though some accounts in this approach will stress the disproportionate advantage of some groups to exert pressure successfully. Neither the state nor the various institutions and agencies which comprise it are seen as having an interest or orientation of their own. Such exogenous approaches clearly have their place in explaining state actions; externally applied pressures do limit and shape state actions. However, the insufficiency of exogenous approaches can clearly be seen when they attempt to explain why the Mexican state originally adopted the orientation that it did with regard to economic growth. Beginning in the 1920s, the Mexican state took on the task of developing a national bourgeoisie, and in no way can the very frail and nascent national bourgeoisie of that time be seen as a pressure group sufficiently powerful to induce the state to assist in its development. In this case, it is clear that political institutions acted out of orientations of their own to solve problems that were thrown up by historical circumstance. These orientations cannot be understood solely in terms of group pressures.

Further, in those cases where such exogenous explanations might be useful, there are limitations posed by a theoretical difficulty. Some pressures do not involve manifest channels or linkages of any sort; in various ways, the state comes to depend or rest on certain classes or groups for its power and for its legitimacy.[67] We can say that these classes or groups constitute the "social foundations" of the state. For example, the state may depend on a certain class for its tax revenues, or its industrialization strategy may depend on certain private sector investments, as has been the case in Mexico. The state may shape or trim its actions—without any direct pressure being brought to bear— to maintain the support (or at least the acquiescence) of groups that constitute its social foundations. Cárdenas' creation of the Ejidal Bank was not simply a response to peasant pressures but part of his effort to organize and mobilize the peasantry during his conflict with Calles. In triumph, his regime rested on altered social foundations. Attention to the social foundations of the state is necessary, moreover, not only for an understanding of the linkage-less pressure that a class or social group or foreign institution (a transnational corporation, the IMF, etc.) may bring to bear, but also for an adequate understanding of the direct pressures that such a group may mount, since the social foundations of the state constitute the basis on which are constructed the power groups to influence state action through manifest channels or linkages.

Without denying the utility of exogenous approaches (especially those informed by an understanding of the social foundations of state power), it is nevertheless essential to consider "endogenous" approaches as well, those which take seriously in explaining state action the interests of political institutions themselves—the orientations that are formed within state agencies to guide their activities in the absence of, and even sometimes in the face of, external pressures. A word needs to be said first about the problems raised in applying the concept of "interest" to the state. When "interest" is used in discussing the guiding orientations of firms in the economy, it is often a conceptual tool of considerable probity for understanding and anticipating the general directions of corporate action. Saying that the interest of a corporation lies in long-run profit maximization may not allow us to predict the precise details of strategy, but it does provide us with a broadly accurate indicator of general corporate policy. The question is, can we use the concept of "interest" to indicate and anticipate the general directions of state action? There are special difficulties here. The concept of "interest" serves for corporations because corporations have a reasonably definable essential nature which allows us to form a central, common characterization of their general orientations to action. States, however, differ so much from one another that it is difficult to identify an essential nature around which we could frame a concept parallel to "interest." It was this that led Max Weber to drop from a concern with purposes to a concern with means in stipulating that the state is "that institution which successfully claims a monopoly of the legitimate use of physical force within a given territory."[68] We can see in this, however, a lowest-common-denominator task or state interest: a concern for the maintenance of sovereignty against internal and external threats. But while the defense of sovereignty is one guiding orientation of all states, it is hardly the only one for most states and is of limited utility in understanding state interventions into the economy. In addition to the defense of territorial sovereignty, any particular state over the course of its history comes to perform an immense array of tasks: tasks concerned with economic growth, welfare, education, and the arts, for example. No two states will have taken on quite the same array. Understanding orientations that guide state action, then, requires an understanding of how each state has its essential nature or orientations *filled in,* and filled in in a way that depends on the society's particular historical trajectory.

The strengths and weaknesses of the currently prominent "endogenous approaches"—the structuralist approach within the Marxist theory of the state[69] and the bureaucratic politics approach[70]—warrant brief attention here. Although both assume that the state and its component agencies and bureaus have their own orientations, neither gives an adequate account of how these orientations arise. The structuralist accounts view the state as acting in accord with an internal logic that arises from the need for an institution to resolve the contradictions of capitalist production, particularly those that arise between the various fractions of the capitalist class. Like Gerschenkron's account, however, the structuralist approach risks slipping into the functionalist problem mentioned in the introduction in that it explains neither the power nor the orientation of the state. And although there is value in pointing to certain critical tasks that the state is likely to take on, structuralist approaches have tended to be excessively abstract and inattentive to the specific shape those contradictions or problems take on in a particular society.[71] By focusing on universal tasks assumed by the state under capitalism, these approaches become too deterministic and are only capable of accounting *post hoc* for the distinct timing and manner of state action. Bureaucratic-politics accounts look to explain state action by examining the organization of the state bureaucracy and the dynamics of the conflicts within and among its various agencies, looking for reasons why some agencies and outlooks prevail. Implicit here is the notion that various agencies have different orientations—but the bureaucratic-politics accounts often fail to explain how these state agencies take on the rationale or orientation that they do. How, then, does the state take on its guiding orientations?

In general, we can distinguish at least three ways in which the orientation of a state can be "filled in," all of which are exhibited in the interventions of the Mexican state in the economy of Mexico. First, one or more agencies of the state may be created or captured by a class, class fraction, or other group in such a way that it can use the agency simply and directly as an instrument for pursuing its own interests.[72] The post-Revolutionary consolidation of the Mexican state is to be understood in this way. It was the middle-class constitutionalist element from Sonora (with the assistance of nationalist economists, both orthodox and Keynesian) and not the agrarian radicals, who organized Mexico's major political institutions and imbued them with an orientation, particularly strong in the Treasury and the agencies associated with it, towards an industrialization strategy that placed primary reliance on the private sector, an orientation that strongly shaped the subsequent history of Mexico.

A second important possibility is that in a certain context particular problems or crises arise which the state may see as necessary to confront and solve. A new agency may be created or an existing one adapted to deal with the particular problem in a certain way. The mere existence of a problem or crisis, however, does not "cause" the creation of a state institution to deal with it. Whether or not the state will respond will itself be shaped by already existing orientations. In the Mexican case, the orientations of the Revolutionary groups that captured and set up the new political institutions were of primary importance in shaping the direction of future state expansion and action. Thus, the state's entry into investment banking to finance private sector activity in the late 1920s and 1930s, for example, was not simply a mechanistic response to the problem of capital accumulation in the aftermath of the Revolution. Instead, it was shaped by the orientations given the state by the nationalist, development-oriented, middle-class elements of the Carranza, Obregón, and Calles regimes. However, once a new agency is set up to deal with a problem it will develop a characteristic way of dealing with other problems that fall within its purview. An orientation thus becomes institutionalized, growing more or less stable, and is generally susceptible to redefinition only slowly and on the margin.

NAFIN, to take one interesting example, was originally created out of the continuing concern of the state to develop an adequate

financial system; it was particularly charged with the development of
a stock and bond market. But as the international economy changed
(with the Depression and World War II) and import-substitution industrialization became both a necessity and an opportunity, NAFIN
was reorganized to serve as an industrial development bank. The orientation that came to guide the bank during the 1940s has more or less
continued to inform its activities, though there have been some
changes (a greater concern with regional development and with small
businesses, for example). As the state has acquired or created various
industrial enterprises—Atenquique, DINA, and the rest—in response
to private sector incapability or failure, new entities have been added
to the state with their own distinctive tasks and orientations, and these
institutionally based orientations are thus added to the state's repertoire. Altos Hornos and SOMEX were acquired by the state acting out
of last-resort considerations, but these entities themselves, acting in
response to their own problems, needs, and guiding orientations, have
acquired or initiated other ventures in ways that move beyond the
strict definition of last-resort considerations. Hence, Altos Hornos'
expansion for upstream and downstream integration, or DINA's acquisition of Motores Perkins.

Changes in government personnel are a third way in which the
orientations of the state can be filled in. In Mexico, despite the enduring rule of the Partido Revolucionario Institucional (PRI), there is a
substantial turnover in personnel with the change of president every
six years. A new president and his chief ministers may bring with
them new, creative shaping visions that change the orientations of the
state, often by adding new tasks to its repertoire. For example, the
López Mateos administration brought with it a concern for strong
state action to restimulate import substitution. By contrast, the Díaz
Ordaz administration that followed was more outward looking, more
inclined to promote growth through exports. And the Echeverría administration had a decidedly more statist orientation than its predeces-
sors, as was to be seen in the aggressive dynamism it encouraged in the
Comisión de Fomento Minero, in the Ministry of National Patrimony,
in SOMEX, and elsewhere. It should be emphasized, however, that in
the ministries and agencies concerned with economic growth there has
been an unusual degree of continuity—of personnel, but particularly
of outlook. Furthermore, the changes in orientation that were possible
through changes in personnel were often severely limited by the tasks
and orientation that the Mexican state had already taken on—and by
the economic, social, and political context in which the state found
itself at the time of the attempted changes.

In conclusion, three points should be noted. First, the orientation of a state institution may be treated as a given in explaining any particular action that it undertakes, but it must always be kept in mind that this orientation evolved historically and may be altered as a result of the action in question. That different tasks and concerns become institutionalized in different agencies with divergent orientations opens the possibility of conflict among government agencies, conflict of the sort on which "bureaucratic politics" approaches have focused attention.

Second, the evolution of state orientations followed a certain developmental sequence in Mexico, and this particular historical pattern must be understood if present state orientations and possibilities for change are to be fully explained. Initially, certain basic orientations (such as economic growth through primary reliance on the private sector) were set by the groups who captured or created Mexico's political institutions after the Revolution. These initial orientations help explain why certain other institutions (the Central Bank, the Treasury, the Ministry of Public Works, NAFIN, and other state development banks) were set up to solve crises or problems (like that of capital accumulation) that were thrust on the state. These new state agencies, often taking on a certain life of their own, not only institutionalized specific, new orientations (long-term credit to the private sector, entrepreneurship and public investment when the private sector was unable or unwilling to meet national needs, the bail-out of failing firms) but often came to take on their own orientations as their managers (*políticos* or *técnicos*) sought to expand their scope of activity (vertical or horizontal integration, acquisition of competitors, and so forth). At certain moments in Mexican history, regime changes were able to alter the character of existing orientations or to create new institutions with their own particular orientations—for example, the Ministries of Industry and Commerce and of National Property in 1959, and the Ministry of Patrimony and Industrial Development, which consolidated these two, in 1977.

A third, related point is this: these different ways that the Mexican state's orientations were filled in were not of equal importance; at any given historical moment, the prior development of political institutions with their own orientations posed certain limits for changing their character. Thus the state institutions set up by the victors in the Revolution in the early 1920s defined a certain character and direction for Mexican economic growth. The ability of new regimes (Cárdenas, Echeverría) to drastically alter this direction has been severely limited. On the other hand, certain incremental changes may, over time, create the possibilities for major changes. As we will suggest below, the present role the state has come to play as an investor in the economy may create strains with the private sector leading not merely to a crisis but to the possibility of a changed relationship between the state and the private sector in future economic development.

THE DEFINITION OF PROBLEMATICS

The Mexican state's response to economic problems and needs which the private sector was unwilling or unable to solve was in part dependent upon what was defined as a problem or a need (and what was defined as unwillingness or inability). Many of the problems had a certain "objective" character which would make them recognizable in other developing countries. There were, for example, certain universal prerequisites of industrialization and certain problems common to late starters (the problem of rapid capital accumulation, for example). Furthermore, the Mexican state had to deal with such post-Revolutionary problems as a disorganized financial system and an enormous external debt; with the problems and possibilities created by the Depression and World War II; with the danger of the "exhaustion" of the "easy" stage of import substitution in the late 1950s and early 1960s and the need for investment in the capital goods industry beyond the capacity of the domestic private sector; with the influx of transnational corporations in manufacturing in the 1960s and the political and economic problems this created; and, finally, with the growing balance of payments problems in the late 1960s and early 1970s and the need to find new sources of foreign exchange. In looking at the problems thrown up by late, dependent industrialization and by Mexico's place in the international political economy, it is important, however, to avoid a purely mechanistic or "economistic" view of the problems that have had to be confronted by the Mexican state. We also need to understand how such (often general) problems are historically defined, how their understanding has been shaped by the particular political dynamics and ideological currents in Mexico.

In the early 1950s, for example, Mexico made the political decision to respond to problems of inflation, an overvalued currency, and pressures from the IMF for stabilization with a devaluation, an orthodox monetary policy, and a development strategy based on low rates of inflation *(desarrollo estabilizador)*. This strategy then created a new set of internal problems such as the one we saw in the sugar industry. It led to a decision to control prices of basic commodities, such as sugar, and this, coupled with rising labor costs, created a situation in which the private sector was unwilling to invest in sugar production. This in turn was defined as both an economic problem (loss of export revenue and perhaps even a need for future sugar imports) and a political problem (unemployment in sugar regions and popular sector unrest if the prices of basic commodities could not be kept low). The state responded by taking over the sugar mills.

We have also seen how the state's orientation towards foreign investment (one rather distinct from that held in other Latin American countries facing similar situations) led to efforts to protect the national bourgeoisie through such schemes as Mexicanization. The way foreign investment was defined as a problem, and the political definition of a solution (forcing TNCs to sell shares to the Mexican private sector) created a new set of problems—the private sector's inability (or unwillingness) to raise the capital to purchase shares at the same time that Mexican policy required these TNCs to Mexicanize often left the state in a position in which it had to act as an institution of "last resort." The state bought the shares from the TNCs and thus found itself again expanding its role as an owner in the industrial sector.

THE LIMITS ON STATE POWER: GROWING FISCAL DIFFICULTIES

State intervention into the economy in late dependent industrialization does not come about simply because prerequisites need to be filled or because problems would be left unsolved if left to private sector institutional arrangements. The state must have the *power* to intervene, and a full explanation of state intervention must take power as a variable, not a given. We have argued that the Mexican state had the power to act as a banker and entrepreneur because of the way in which strong political institutions were created after the Revolution and because of the weak and disorganized nature of the private sector at this time. Furthermore, certain factors stemming from Mexico's place in the international political economy created possibilities for state action (the Depression and World War II opened up the possibility for pursuing import-substitution industrialization; the threat of conflict in Europe somewhat tempered U.S. reaction to the 1938 oil nationalizations) while others severely limited the power of the state (the needs the Obregón and Calles governments had for U.S. diplomatic recognition and refinancing the huge external debt not only would have made difficult a development strategy that challenged private capital but actually did force these regimes to stop their moves against U.S. oil companies; the devaluation in 1953 and the orthodox monetary policies that followed were in large part due to pressures exerted by the international financial community, particularly the IMF). We are, however, far from presenting a full explanation of the growth, maintenance, and limits of the power of the Mexican state.

We might, however, touch on two very current matters which any such explanation would have to take into consideration since they are imposing increasingly serious obstacles limiting the power of the Mexican state to intervene in the economy. One is increasing resistance from the very national bourgeoisie the state helped to create. Sometimes this resistance has taken dramatic, public form such as the determined opposition that President Echeverría faced from the Monterrey business groups, particularly the flight of capital that occurred in the last years of his regime. But there are other, less visible but surely important ways that the activities of the private sector—which now constitutes a crucial part of the social foundations of the state—limit state action. Foremost, perhaps, is the systematic connection between state spending and private sector investment. The state finances many of its activities through a complex scheme of reserve requirements in the banking system. Increased state expenditures lead to high interest rates and a tightening of credit for private investment, but this only increases the need for state expenditures as the state acts in "last resort" in the face of declining private sector investment. Primary reliance on the private sector has become, in recent years, an increasingly important obstacle to new state investments at the same time that private sector reluctance to invest has made such state intervention increasingly necessary. This problem was exemplified by the state-business-labor pact (Alianza para la Producción) organized by President López Portillo when he took office in December 1976. It has as one of its key terms an agreement by the state to cut its spending and, in return, an agreement by the private sector to increase its investments. The difficulties of this pact are highlighted by the impatience of key economic officials with the private sector—they consider the private sector to be dragging its heels and are urging more state investments.

A second increasingly serious obstacle to state intervention in the economy is the limitation placed on Mexico by its place in the international financial system. Partly to avoid dependence on the private sector while making the investments needed to overcome the potential exhaustion of the "easy stage" of import-substitution industrialization, the Mexican state borrowed larger and larger amounts from abroad to finance its activities. The increased willingness of transnational banks to lend to certain lesser-developed countries like Mexico in the late 1960s and early 1970s made possible the expansion of state economic activities engineered by the Echeverría regime. But this expansion created a new problem that was potentially limiting to state activities —the rapid growth of foreign debt in the 1970s.[73] Under pressure from the IMF, the World Bank, and private transnational banks, Mexico was forced to devalue twice in the last months of 1976 and had to make

promises to cut its federal expenditures. The internal pressures of the
national bourgeoisie, compounded by the external pressures set by
foreign indebtedness, have created a contradiction—the ability of the
state to continue to act as an institution of last resort, while at the same
time following a policy of primary reliance on the private sector, seems
to be severely threatened at this point in Mexican history.

THE CONCEPT OF "THE STATE"

What we have been calling the "state" is clearly no coherent, unified
entity but rather an amalgam of bureaus, agencies, commissions, and
the like, each with its own resources and distinctive orientations, and
all liable to compete and conflict with one another. Is there reason,
then, to speak of the state as a single entity, or should we drop such
a conception and speak only of its component parts? We feel it is
important to have some concept of the state which unifies all government institutions into a whole. By definition, this institution successfully claims a monopoly of the legitimate use of physical force within
a given territory and also has an historically filled-in character.

In understanding certain aspects of the power of the state, it is
important to look at its particular parts—its agencies, ministries, enterprises, and so on. Understanding the state's success as an investment banker, for example, demands understanding something about
the organization and technical competence of such specific institutions
as NAFIN and SOMEX. Understanding the ability of these banks to
intervene in the economy demands an understanding of their relationship to other government agencies. NAFIN's historical relationship
with the Treasury and the Bank of Mexico is important in explaining
the autonomy it has enjoyed from cross-currents of political pressure.
And the more recent close ties between SOMEX officials and those at
NAFIN shape SOMEX's opportunities for industrial investment.

But as important as this understanding of the individual parts and
their particular relations may be, we can also see the danger of reducing the state to the sum of its parts. Important limits are placed on the
power of each component entity by the general fiscal difficulties of the
state that have been mentioned above. And these fiscal difficulties
cannot be understood without looking at the state as a whole—seeing
its overall administrative, social, military, and economic responsibilities, as well as the limitations on its power to generate revenue through
taxes, the reserve requirements, or foreign borrowing by the position
of the state in the national and international political economy.

In looking at the problem of orientations, we see the same pattern
that was revealed in the discussion of power. It is clearly important to

look at the particular governmental institutions if we want to understand (a) what their orientations (interests) are; (b) how these orientations are acquired, maintained, or changed; and (c) how the relative power of a particular institution determines the extent to which its orientation can successfully guide action or, in some cases, shape the overall direction of state policy. But this, of course, brings us back to the importance of dealing also with the state as a whole. The overall character of the state's orientation may change over time (as the result of a regime change or a change in the relative power of a ministry), and this character—the state as an institution of last resort, for example—will shape or limit the orientation of any particular government institution.

The emphasis we place on the state—treating it as a whole or as an aggregate of individual parts—depends on what particular phenomenon we are trying to explain. In order to understand why the Mexican state has come to intervene in the economy as banker and entrepreneur we have found that we need to understand both how particular governmental institutions shape the nature of state policy and how the character of the state as a whole informs the power and orientations of its particular institutions.

To take up a distinct but related matter: a question frequently asked about a political economic analysis is whether the state was treated as an "independent" or a "dependent" variable. The thrust of this chapter is that this question misconceives the relationship of the state to society. The Mexican state did not mechanistically or passively respond to the "problems," "needs," or "prerequisites" of late dependent development; nor were state banking and entrepreneurial activities independent of these problems. State actions were, indeed, responses to problems of late dependent industrialization, but the ability to respond and the character of the response were shaped by the power and orientation of the state, themselves historical products. Each state action, in turn, created new situations which contained within them new problems and new possibilities which the state was then called on to confront. Thus the very problematics which the state faces are historical products shaped not only by certain common problems of late dependent development but also by the state's past actions in dealing with these problems. Our discussion of state action in the sugar industry and state actions to Mexicanize foreign industry well illustrate the dialectical character of state action.

The power and orientations of the state itself, while clearly determining the kind of action the state can and will take, are themselves historical products. Political institutions are created to deal with certain problems; the orientations they take on are changed or maintained through their confrontation with particular problems. Similarly the very power of the state changes as it acts upon society. The national bourgeoisie, in many ways the creation of the state, now acts in ways to limit the power of the state. Mechanisms set up to finance state investments to supplement private sector investment now risk hindering private sector investment itself.

Assuming the state to be an "independent" variable creates the risk of falling into a kind of voluntarism which fails to understand the real limits placed on the ability and will of the state to act. Assuming the state to be a "dependent" variable risks a determinism which is both blind to historical possibilities and provides only a mechanistic explanation for state action. The state must be conceived of as both an historical product and as a creator of history.

Acknowledgments

The theoretical arguments in this chapter benefitted greatly from ongoing collaborative work with Dr. Morris J. Blachman. The skillful research assistance of Bonnie Sharpe was important in collecting the case data. Funding from the following foundations made possible the larger research project of which this chapter is a part: the Tinker Foundation, the Social Science Research Council, the Carnegie Endowment for International Peace, the Doherty Foundation, and the National Endowment for the Humanities.

Notes

1. See, for example, Roger D. Hansen, *The Politics of Mexican Development* (Baltimore: Johns Hopkins University Press, 1971), especially chapter 4, "Fruition: For Whom?"; Pablo Gonzáles Casanova, *Democracy in Mexico* (New York: Oxford University Press, 1970); Susan Eckstein, *Poverty of Revolution* (Princeton: Princeton University Press, 1977); Judith Adler Hellman, *Mexico in Crisis* (New York: Holmes and Meier Publishers, 1978).

2. A 1971 ECLA (UN Economic Commission for Latin America) study, for example, showed that the Mexican state owned 26 enterprises in the manufacturing sector compared with 4 for Argentina, 3 for Brazil, 3 for Columbia, 4 for Chile, 5 for Peru and 6 for Venezuela. See "Public Enterprises: Their Present Significance and Their Potential in Development," *Economic Bulletin for Latin America*, vol. 16, no. 1 (1971), pp. 1–70, table 4. It should be noted that this ECLA study was conducted just as the administration of Luis Echeverría was taking office, an administration that dramatically increased the intervention of the state in the Mexican economy. For a survey of the new state enterprises, see "La transformación o creación de organismos descen-

tralizados, empresas de participación estatal, comisiónes y fideicomisos," *Linea: Pensamiento de la Revolución,* vol. 23/24 (1976), pp. 202–18.

3. The full thesis will be treated in a larger work now in progress.

4. Alexander Gerschenkron, *Economic Backwardness in Historical Perspective* (Cambridge: Harvard University Press, 1966), p. 7.

5. Gerschenkron emphasizes that the need for these special institutional devices arises in part from the larger plant sizes and higher ratios of capital to output dictated by the progress of industrialization in the world. *Ibid.,* p. 7.

6. For a discussion of the differences between "late" industrialization in Europe and "late, late" industrialization in Latin American, see Albert Hirschman, "The Political Economy of Import-Substituting Industrialization in Latin America," *Quarterly Journal of Economics,* vol. 82, no. 1 (1968), pp. 1–32.

7. Joseph E. Sterrett and Joseph S. Davis, *The Fiscal and Economic Condition of Mexico,* a report submitted to the International Committee of Bankers on Mexico, New York, 25 May 1928, pp. 227–28.

8. A full explanation—beyond the scope of this paper—would have to touch on the character and strength of the political institutions that were constructed as well as on the kind of autonomy afforded the state by the class structure and organization.

9. For a fuller discussion of the process of political centralization see Hansen, *Politics of Mexican Development,* and Robert E. Scott, *Mexican Government in Transition* (Urbana: University of Illinois Press, 1964).

10. Eric Wolf, *Peasant Wars of the Twentieth Century* (New York: Harper and Row, 1969), p. 21.

11. For example, the Rio Blanco mill in Veracruz, while only one of eleven firms in the textile industry, employed half of all the workers and was owned by a company of French merchants. See Wolf, *Peasant Wars,* p. 20.

12. *Ibid.,* p. 39. See also Arnoldo Córdova, *La ideologica de la revolución mexicana: la formación del nuevo régimen* (México, D.F.: Ediciones Era, 1973) for a detailed analysis of the character of the post-Revolutionary Mexican state.

13. Howard F. Cline, *The United States and Mexico,* rev. ed. (Cambridge: Harvard University Press, 1963), pp. 192–94.

14. Wolf, *Peasant Wars,* pp. 38–39.

15. However, its expression has taken a number of different forms. Note, for example—it is particularly important in view of the discussion that will follow—that an insistence on Mexican ownership implies nothing about whether that ownership will be public or private. At a minimum, Mexican nationalism has meant a firm insistence on Mexican control over national resources, national autonomy in both economic and political affairs, a concern that economic growth be responsive primarily to internal rather than external conditions, and an effort to keep the benefits of such growth inside Mexico. For more detailed discussions, see William P. Glade, Jr., "Revolution and Economic Development," in William P. Glade, Jr., and Charles W. Anderson, *The Political Economy of Mexico* (Madison: University of Wisconsin Press, 1968), pp. 28–52; and Frederick W. Turner, *The Dynamics of Mexican Nationalism* (Chapel Hill: University of North Carolina Press, 1968), *passim.*

16. On these measures, see Harry K. Wright, *Foreign Enterprise in Mexico* (Chapel Hill: University of North Carolina Press, 1971); and Douglas Bennett, Morris Blachman, and Kenneth Sharpe, "Mexico and Multinational Corporations: An Explanation of State Action," in Joseph Grunwald (ed.), *Latin Amer-*

ica and World Economy: A Changing International Order (Beverly Hills: Sage Publications, 1978).

17. Charles W. Anderson, "Bankers as Revolutionaries," in Glade and Anderson, *The Political Economy of Mexico*, pp. 113–14. He continues: "Nurtured on the economics of the Díaz period, these latter-day *científicos* largely accepted the legitimacy of the intricate and many-faceted institutions of the modern economic system as it had been elaborated and developed in the advanced nations of Europe and North America. . . . [T]hey anticipated no radical departure in their planning from the economic institutions and practices prevailing in the industrialized nations. Accepting this model for the economic modernization of Mexico, they conceived their mission, in a sense, as that of implementing programs that were the unfinished business of the Porfiriato." *Ibid.*, pp. 114–15.

18. Secretaría de Hacienda y Crédito Público, Dirección General de Crédito, *Legislación Bancaria* (México, D.F., 1957), vol. 1, pp. 27–28; translated in Robert L. Bennett, *The Financial Sector and Economic Development: The Mexican Case* (Baltimore: Johns Hopkins University Press, 1965), p. 40.

19. On the formation of these two agricultural banks, see Anderson, "Bankers as Revolutionaries," pp. 122–23.

20. *Ibid.*, pp. 122–29.

21. On *financieras*, and more generally on the development of the banking system, see Dwight Brothers and Leopoldo Solis, *Mexican Financial Development (1940–1960)* (Austin: University of Texas Press, 1966).

22. For a current portrait of these groups, see Salvadore Cordero and Rafael Santín, "Los grupos industriales: una nueva organización económica en México," *Cuadernos del CES*, no. 23 (México, D.F.: El Colegio de México, 1977), pp. 1–98.

23. Sanford Mosk, *Industrial Revolution in Mexico* (Berkeley: University of California Press, 1950), especially chapter 2. However, in a number of regards Mosk's portrait of the "New Group" seems to have been mistaken.

24. Hansen, *Politics of Mexican Development*, p. 37. On the question of contemporary linkages between economic and political elites in Mexico, see the provocative conclusions of Peter Smith, "Does Mexico Have a Power Elite?" in José Luis Reyna and Richard S. Weinert (eds.), *Authoritarianism in Mexico* (Philadelphia: Institute for the Study of Human Issues, 1977), pp. 129–51.

25. Going back only as far as their grandparents, fully 44 percent of her sample of 200 industrialists were of foreign origin, and 20 percent were themselves born outside of Mexico. See Flavia Derossi, *The Mexican Entrepreneur* (Paris: Development Centre of the Organization for Economic Cooperation and Development, 1971), pp. 157, 143–44.

26. Anderson, "Bankers as Revolutionaries," p. 118.

27. On the petroleum case, see Lorenzo Meyer, *México y Estado Unidos en el conflicto petrolero (1917–42)* (México, D.F.: El Colegio de México, 1968). On light and power, see Miguel S. Wionczek, *El nacionalismo mexicano y la inversión extranjera* (México, D.F.: Siglo Veintiuno Editores, 1967). For an elaboration of the argument presented here, see Bennett, Blachman, and Sharpe, "Mexico and Multinational Corporations."

28. Nora Hamilton, "Mexico: The Limits of State Autonomy," *Latin American Perspectives*, vol. 2, no. 2 (Summer 1975), pp. 86–87.

29. *Ibid.*, p. 96.

30. Nacional Financiera is one of the most well-studied investment banks

in a developing country. Our discussion will only highlight selected aspects of NAFIN's activities. For more extensive discussions, see Calvin Blair, "Nacional Financiera: Entrepreneurship in a Mixed Economy," in Raymond Vernon (ed.), *Public Policy and Private Enterprise in Mexico* (Cambridge: Harvard University Press, 1964); José Hernandez Delgado, *The Contribution of Nacional Financiera to the Industrialization of Mexico* (México, D.F.: Nacional Financiera, 1961); Robert T. Aubey, *Nacional Financiera and Mexican Industry* (Los Angeles: University of California, Latin American Center, 1966); and Rosa Olivia Villa M., *Nacional Financiera: banco de fomento del desarrollo económico de México* (México, D.F.: Nacional Financiera, 1976).

31. Villa M., *Nacional Financiera,* p. 41, table 4.

32. Blair, "Nacional Financiera," pp. 213, 194.

33. Villa M., *Nacional Financiera,* p. 8. She cites "Exposición de motivos de la ley orgánica de la institución nacional de credíto denominada 'Nacional Financiera' de 30 diciembre de 1940," *Legislación constitutiva de Nacional Financiera, S.A.* (México, D.F.: Nacional Financiera, S.A., 1976), p. 84.

34. After surveying NAFIN's activities, Blair concluded: "Nacional Financiera has been something more than just another source of finance capital. It has advised, promoted, invested in and directed business enterprises often enough to be identified as a genuine entrepreneurial agent. In the Mexican environment, with its scarcity of investment capital and managerial talent for large-scale industry, and its traditional concentration of private capital in commerce and real estate, NAFIN has undoubtedly offered elements of entrepreneurship which the Mexican private sector had been unprepared to offer." Blair, "Nacional Financiera," p. 232.

35. Norman Schneider, *Government Competition in the Mexican Steel Industry* (Davis: University of California, Institute of Governmental Affairs, 1967), pp. 15–18.

36. For versions of the Altos Hornos story, see Schneider, *ibid.,* pp. 18–20; William E. Cole, *Steel and Economic Growth in Mexico* (Austin: University of Texas Press, 1967), pp. 11–15; Mosk, *Industrial Revolution in Mexico,* pp. 139–45; and Blair, "Nacional Financiera," pp. 215–16.

37. Raymond Vernon, *The Dilemma of Mexico's Development* (Cambridge: Harvard University Press, 1963), p. 97. It surely understates the matter to call the government participation merely "a form of risk insurance."

38. On these, see Mosk, *Industrial Revolution in Mexico,* pp. 163–66 (paper), and 153–60 (cement); Villa M., *Nacional Financiera,* pp. 43, 68 (paper); and Blair, "Nacional Financiera," p. 216 (cement).

39. See Blair, "Nacional Financiera," pp. 227–28, though his account is based on some inaccurate surmises. Further information on this and a number of other cases come from interviews conducted by the authors in 1976 and 1977 with former government officials and members of the private sector.

40. Shortly after the Alemán administration came into office, an amendment to NAFIN's organic law stipulated that NAFIN should not intrude upon activities that were the rightful domain of private initiative, and "contained the explicit assurance that NAFIN would make every effort to obtain private cooperation in any promotions which it might undertake and, before offering finance, would see that the private promoters put up as much capital as could reasonably be expected under the circumstances." Blair, "Nacional Financiera," pp. 220–21.

41. Glade, "Revolution and Economic Development," p. 93. And in the same vein, Calvin Blair concludes, "It is not certain whether NAFIN's major

investments could have been made by private Mexican capital. In theory there were no insurmountable obstacles, but most of the projects required a great deal of official representation abroad, borrowing money and negotiating with the United States government for necessary material and equipment. It is not likely that private entrepreneurs could have gotten this outside help without significant government backing." Blair, "Nacional Financiera," p. 212.

42. On the current holdings of Bruno Pagliai, see Salvadore Cordero and Rafael Santín, "Los grupos industriales," p. 37.

43. Victor Manuel Villasenor, *Memorias de un hombre de izquierda*, vol. 2, *De Avila Camacho a Echeverría* (México, D.F.: Editorial Grijalbo, 1976), p. 243. Villasenor was director of DINA from 1958 to 1970.

44. The state's takeover of Toyoda de México, a textile machinery firm with Japanese technology and capital, now called Siderúrgica Nacional (and, with DINA and CNCF, part of the Sahagun complex) followed a roughly similar course. See Blair, "Nacional Financiera," p. 228; and Victor Manuel Villasenor, "Avila Camacho," p. 298.

45. The canning and fishing firms were a recurrent source of problems. Because of the difficult rural situation in Mexico, it is not surprising that these firms were unable to assure reliable sources of raw materials, particularly when there were problems in trying to extend credit to peasants and fishermen.

46. Including, for example, Aceros Esmaltados, S.A. (a major stove manufacturer), Vehiculos Automotores Mexicanos, S.A. (a joint venture in which American Motors is minority partner, manufacturing American Motors vehicles), Sosa Texcoco, S.A. (a large chemical firm), and Manufacturera Mexicana de Partes de Automóviles, S.A. (an important manufacturer of automobile parts). The acquisition by the government of Banco Internacional, now affiliated with NAFIN, followed similar motives.

47. *Comercio Exterior*, November 1975, p. 1212.

48. Samuel I. del Villar, "Depresión en la industria azucarera," *Foro Internacional*, vol. 6, no. 4 (1976), pp. 538–39.

49. *Ibid.*, pp. 550–51.

50. For an explanation of the changing course of Mexican policy towards direct foreign investment, see Bennett, Blachman, and Sharpe, "Mexico and Multinational Corporations." For a more extensive discussion of the Mexicanization policy, see Douglas C. Bennett and Kenneth E. Sharpe, "El control de las multinacionales: las contradicciones de la mexicanización," *Foro Internacional*, vol. 21, no. 4 (April-June 1981).

51. *Mercado de Valores*, 27 August 1971.

52. For a brief discussion of NAFIN's role in Mexicanization touching on some of these cases, see Villa M., *Nacional Financiera*, pp. 46–50.

53. Carlos Avila Martinez, "Comisión de fomento minero," in Secretaría del Patrimonio Nacional, *Economía publica: soberania y justicia social*, (México, D.F.: Secretaría de Patrimonio Nacional, 1976), pp. 58–59. The CFM has also come to intervene in the mining industries for other reasons, which will be mentioned briefly below.

54. A figure that includes 71 decentralized entities, 351 firms with majority state participation, and 48 firms with minority state participation, but does not include an additional 47 "juntas federales de mejoras materiales"; Secretaría del Patrimonio Nacional, *Directorio de organismos descentralizados y empresas de participación estatal* (México, D.F., 1976).

55. Blair, "Nacional Financiera," p. 226.

56. *Ibid.*, pp. 234–35.

57. To be sure, some of Altos Hornos' acquisitions have followed last resort lines. For example, Rassini Rheem, a manufacturer of springs for the automobile industry, was originally organized by private Mexican interests, though after 1962 it involved some foreign capital. Through the middle 1960s, the firm lost a great deal of money and incurred substantial debts both to Altos Hornos and to Rheem International, the foreign partner. In 1969, when it was on the verge of collapse, Altos Hornos and Rheem took it over in approximately equal shares.

58. The takeover of FANASA's plant by DINA was rather more complex than this would indicate, since FANASA was originally taken over by SOMEX, its principal creditor. SOMEX, however, sold FANASA's machining operation to DINA-Rockwell, and has rented the assembly operation to DINA-MAN. To make matters still more complicated, DINA had difficulties with the management of DINA-MAN and has now subcontracted with Vehiculos Automotores Mexicanos, the automobile company owned by SOMEX, to operate the firm. What is particularly to be noted in these complex arrangements is an unusual degree of cooperation among a number of state enterprises, in this case the state's two automobile firms, DINA and VAM, and the state's two major industrial development banks, NAFIN and SOMEX, which own those auto firms.

59. Sociedad Mexicana de Credíto Industrial, *SOMEX en marcha 1971–1976* (México, D.F.: Sociedad Mexicana de Credíto Industrial, 1976), p. 44.

60. The rationale for this policy grew out of the concern in the Revolutionary ideology for Mexican control of Mexican natural resources. It was the López Mateos administration that saw Mexicanization as the particular policy strategy to pursue, but that policy had an economic rationale as well; Mexicanization was seen as a way to halt the net disinvestment by foreign companies in mining and to redevelop this crucial but then declining sector. See Wionczek, *El nacionalismo mexicano,* pp. 300–305.

61. *Mercado de Valores*, 2 July 1973, p. 914.

62. In 1970, CFM participated in only 15 enterprises, and mostly as a minority shareholder; in 1975, CFM was involved in 38 ventures, many of them new investments of great magnitude, and often as majority shareholder. See Carlos Avila Martinez, "La minería en México 1970–1975," in Secretaría del Patrimonio Nacional, *Economía Publica,* p. 79.

63. See *Expansion,* 19 April 1972.

64. *Mercado de Valores,* 5 January 1976, p. 6.

65. The literature is voluminous, but see, for example, David Truman, *The Governmental Process* (New York: Alfred A. Knopf, 1951); and Earl Latham, "The Group Basis of Politics: Notes for a Theory," and Stanley Rothman, "Systematic Political Theory: Observations on the Group Approach," both in Frank Munger and Douglas Price (eds.), *Readings in Political Parties and Pressure Groups* (New York: Thomas Y. Crowell, 1964).

66. See, for example, Ralph Miliband, *The State in Capitalist Society* (London: Weidenfeld and Nicolson, 1969); and William Domhoff, *The Higher Circles* (New York: Vintage Books, 1970), especially part II.

67. This point is to be distinguished from a related and also serious methodological problem. The empiricist methodology of group theory demands the identification of the mechanisms (channels or linkages) through which pressures are exerted. But some of the channels may be informal (involving friend-

ships and social ties) or they may be private and secret; in both cases, they may be empirically inaccessible. Such explanations are thus inherently difficult to establish and even more difficult to disprove. This problem greatly affects research on Mexico and presents even greater difficulties in the more closed and authoritarian regimes in other parts of Latin America.

68. Max Weber, "Politics as a Vocation," in Hans Gerth and C. Wright Mills (trans.), *From Max Weber: Essays in Sociology* (Glencoe, Ill.: The Free Press, 1949).

69. See particularly Nicos Poulantzas, *Political Power and Social Classes* (London: New Left Books/Sheed & Ward, 1973); and Louis Althusser, "Ideology and Ideological State Apparatuses," in *Lenin and Philosophy and Other Essays* (New York: Monthly Review Press, 1971).

70. A good view of the bureaucratic politics approach can be obtained from Morton H. Halperin and Arnold Kanter, *Readings in American Foreign Policy: A Bureaucratic Perspective* (Boston: Little, Brown, 1977).

71. For an elaboration of this line of criticism, see Ralph Miliband, "Poulantzas and the Capitalist State," *New Left Review*, vol. 82 (1973), p. 84.

72. For discussions concerning this possibility in the United States, see Grant McConnell, *Private Power and American Democracy* (New York: Alfred Knopf, 1967), and Theodore Lowi, *The End of Liberalism* (New York: W.W. Norton, 1969).

73. See Rosario Green, *El endeudamiento publico externo de México, 1940–1973* (México, D.F.: El Colegio de México, 1976).

6

The State and Organized Labor
in Brazil and Mexico

KENNETH PAUL ERICKSON
and KEVIN J. MIDDLEBROOK

The organized labor movements in Brazil and Mexico generally play a subordinate role in decisions that most directly affect workers—decisions regarding wage levels, income distribution, and the direction of political and economic change. In both Brazil and Mexico, labor's subordinate position is the result of policies devised by the governing elites to establish political control over the working class. These policies have created a network of corporatist institutions and restrictive procedures that structure the political participation of labor organizations and thus reduce their political autonomy and economic bargaining power. Although there are important similarities in the corporatist institutions that regulate labor participation in these two nations, one can nonetheless observe major national differences in the structures and techniques that incorporate the organized labor movement into national politics—differences that result from the very different historical evolution of the two countries. This chapter examines these similarities and differences in an analysis that places principal emphasis on the relationship between organized labor and the state. It considers the historical pattern of socioeconomic and political change in these two countries, highlighting both labor's influence on the outlines of national development and the way in which the pattern of development has affected workers and their organizations.

In any nation that develops modern industrial activities, the manner in which the emerging labor movement is incorporated into the national political system will have enduring consequences both for the structure of the system as a whole and for labor's future economic and political participation within it. Indeed, the expansion of political participation and the incorporation of mass political actors into national politics constitute a critical moment in a country's political development.[1] If this political incorporation proceeds in a form largely controlled by members of the nation's governing elites, as occurred in Brazil and Mexico, it redefines the balance of political forces in their favor, provides an important basis for future elite coherence, bolsters national political stability, and thus lays the basis for an expansion of state power.[2] The form of incorporation likewise structures relations between labor and capital and helps determine the range of economic options available to the policy-making elite, significantly shaping the subsequent pattern of economic growth and income distribution. The institutional incorporation of labor in Brazil and Mexico reduced the ability of labor organizations to defend workers' economic and political interests and thus facilitated rapid economic growth processes characterized by severe income inequality. This chapter analyzes the development of the state and party institutions through which organized labor's political incorporation occurred, the specific mechanisms used to control labor economically and politically, and the possible sources of future tension and change in these national patterns.

The Development of the Interventionist State in Brazil and Mexico

Labor relations in contemporary Brazil and Mexico offer many similarities, but the two countries arrived at this situation from very different points of departure. Although both modern states trace their origins to twentieth-century revolutions, the character and social content of these two historical processes contrast sharply. In Brazil's "Revolution of 1930," a group of self-styled "nation-builders" challenged the power of the dominant agricultural elite and significantly altered national political institutions. Rejecting the liberal political values and institutions of the Old Republic (1891–1930), President Getúlio Vargas (1930–45, 1950–54) and his associates relied heavily upon corporatist doctrines as they built a strong state and restructured national political life. The centerpiece of Vargas' Estado Novo (1937–45) was an elaborate corporatist system of state-labor relations designed to coopt and control the fledgling industrial labor movement by linking labor organizations directly to state administrative structures. This elite-dominated system, created expressly to prevent autonomous labor organization and mobilization, consisted of a hierarchically ordered, functionally specific *sindicato* ("trade union") system, a network of labor courts, and a social welfare system. The labor legislation of Vargas' Estado Novo gave Brazilian workers the right to organize for the first time, but it also required that labor organizations be formed under the express tutelage of the political elite. The system simultaneously sought to preserve the fundamental characteristics of the established socioeconomic order while laying the basis for future industrial modernization and growth. These labor laws were left intact under the democratic constitution of 1946 and served these same purposes very effectively until challenged by increasing political competition and growing labor mobilization in the early 1960s. Precisely to put down this challenge, a conservative civil-military movement overthrew the democratic regime in 1964 and replaced it with a military-dominated system that still holds power. Since 1964, Brazil's corporatist system of labor relations has continued to provide the organizational basis for state control of the labor movement, at tremendous cost to the workers' economic well-being. But by the mid 1970s, as discussed in the last section of this chapter, Brazilian workers again began challenging their legal and institutional straitjacket under conditions more favorable to their long-term success.

In contrast to the conservative intent and effect of Brazil's elite-dominated Revolution of 1930, the Mexican Revolution (1910–17) was a broad revolutionary process that mobilized large numbers of workers and peasants and fundamentally redefined the social bases of political legitimacy.[3] The organized labor movement emerged as a significant actor in postrevolutionary political events and helped shape the new political order. Most important, President Lázaro Cárdenas (1934–40) institutionalized labor's political role by including the Confederation of Mexican Workers (Confederación de Trabajadores Mexicanos, CTM) as one of the principal sectors of the "official" party so that, in the face of conservative opposition, he could mobilize organized popular support behind further social and economic reforms. In contrast to the socially conservative corporatist doctrines that guided the founders of the modern Brazilian state, Cárdenas' postrevolutionary actions were influenced by the "popular front" strategy of contemporary Europe, which advocated a multiclass alliance to promote progressive socioeconomic and political change.[4] Similarly, the architects of the state administrative apparatus which emerged during the 1920s and 1930s rejected nineteenth-century liberal doctrines and explicitly advocated and practiced an interventionist role in socioeconomic affairs. This approach justified official regulation and mediation of labor-management relations as necessary both to advance workers' constitutionally guaranteed social rights and to conciliate conflicting interests and thus moderate potentially divisive social conflict.

These structures and practices, adopted in the name of furthering Mexican workers' interests, ultimately served to erode the labor movement's political autonomy and its capacity to protect workers' socioeconomic welfare. Organized labor's political incorporation into an increasingly centralized, executive-dominated political system meant the subordination of labor interests in the national decision-making process. As a result of their perceptions of the requirements for economic growth and national industrialization, Cárdenas' immediate successors—Presidents Manuel Ávila Camacho (1940–46) and Miguel Alemán (1946–52)—differed dramatically from Cárdenas in their attitudes and policies towards organized labor. This policy shift resulted in a severe decline in workers' real wages and culminated in the forcible elimination of independent tendencies within the organized labor movement in the late 1940s and early 1950s. Throughout the post-World War II period, the Mexican political elite has effectively controlled the organized labor movement, drawing upon it as a source of mobilized support in times of political crisis and as a means through which to regulate labor's economic demands in order to facilitate national industrialization and economic growth. The remainder of this section examines the pattern of labor's political incorporation in Brazil and Mexico.

BRAZIL

Brazil's Revolution of 1930 both embraced the past and made a break with it. It created new political institutions and attributed broad new socioeconomic functions to an expanded state apparatus, but it justified these changes in the name of preserving the old social order. In the political domain, Vargas and his aides perceived themselves as modernizing nation-builders, and they effected permanent changes in state structures and functions. In the Old Republic, rural oligarchies from the most powerful states had controlled the national political institutions and tailored policies to suit their specific regional, rural interests. After 1930, Vargas and the new political elite conceived the national interest in terms that included, in theory and increasingly in practice, Brazil's entire half-continent. This conceptual transformation required changing the role of the state. Rather than simply serving as a referee among contending regional economic and political groups, the federal government became the dominant political actor. It asserted its right to define the national interest and, accordingly, imposed its own rules upon those economic and political groups. The once highly autonomous state governments were soon brought under firm centralized control, as was symbolized dramatically by the 1937 ceremony at which Vargas burned the state flags.[5]

In the economic domain, the interventionist state sought to cushion Brazilian agriculture from the blow of the Great Depression and, as the 1930s wore on with no improvement in the world market, it designed new policies to spur domestic industry and to protect it from foreign competition. In sectors where private domestic entrepreneurs were reluctant or unable to invest, the state itself took a leading role in industrial and infrastructure development. Such was the case in the federal government's formation of the National Steel Company.

In the social domain, the state for the first time recognized a public obligation to care for and protect the poor and underprivileged. Faced with growing rural-to-urban migration and the erosion of such traditional forms of social welfare as ritual kinship, the Vargas government designed the institutional framework for Brazil's modern social welfare system.

Institutional innovation, the expansion of the state's economic role, and the inclusion of previously excluded strata unquestionably marked a break with the past. Paradoxically, however, the guiding corporatist political values of the Revolution of 1930 represented a return to the past. The ideologues of the Vargas regime argued persuasively that the Old Republic's liberal values, federal structure, and weak national government were foreign imports from the Anglo-Saxon world that ill-suited Brazil's reality and needs. Brazil of the 1930s offered a receptive environment for the corporatist doctrines which they espoused. Although Vargas and his aides were well aware of contemporary corporatist experiments in Italy and Portugal, domestic factors were largely responsible for their adherence to corporatist doctrines. Brazilian Catholic lay associations and religious figures had popularized corporatism after Pope Leo XIII (1878–1903) espoused it in 1891 in his well-known encyclical, *Rerum novarum*. On the secular plane, Alberto Tôrres—a prominent law professor, political commentator, and politician during the early decades of this century—inspired a nationalist school of thought which contrasted Brazil's corporatist intellectual heritage with "imported" liberalism. Significantly, one of Vargas' key advisers in the Ministry of Labor (and one of Alberto Tôrres' most noted students) was Francisco José de Oliveira Vianna, a prolific exponent of corporatism.[6] His writings stressed an organicist conception of politics and society in which the state would oversee and order a complex, functionally specialized, hierarchical array of separate social groups. In this way it would impose the nation's general will over the views of particular interests.

The corporatist approach offered the Brazilian ruling class the hope of modernizing and industrializing the national economy without losing control to restive workers. Indeed, the Russian Revolution, rising class conflict in Europe during the 1920s and 1930s, and increasingly successful political and union organization by the left in Brazil in the late 1920s caused the Brazilian political elite to view industrialization and urbanization with some trepidation. Corporatist doctrines now presented an appealing mechanism through which to foster class collaboration and harmony, for they claimed to replace class conflict with harmony by interposing the state between labor and capital. In his defense of Vargas' authoritarian Estado Novo, Francisco Campos (Vargas' Minister of Justice) argued that this arrangement was the only means by which class conflict could be prevented from ultimately degenerating into either a communist or a fascist regime.[7] Of course, the political and economic crisis created by the Great Depression further undermined faith in liberalism and lent convincing support to the corporatist alternative.

The institutions created in the 1930s reflected both these specific political concerns and the central tenets of the corporatist philosophy espoused by Vargas and his adherents. Shortly after Vargas took power he created the Ministry of Labor, Industry, and Commerce as the state's principal mechanism for supervising labor organizations and conciliating and arbitrating disputes between labor and capital. To this end, Oliveira Vianna shaped the *sindicato* system so that an employers' organization paralleled each employees' union, with most contact between the two occurring through state administrative agencies. The regional offices of the Ministry of Labor maintained general administrative and political supervision over labor-management relations. In a further effort to eliminate sources of direct labor-management conflict, the Estado Novo created a complex system of labor courts. Rather than resolving conflicts through strikes and trials of strength, Oliveira Vianna argued, disputes should be adjudicated administratively so as to better serve the national interest. Local-level courts resolved individual conflicts between workers and their employers; regional-level courts handled collective negotiations involving matters such as wage conflicts; and a federal labor court ruled on appeals. The corporatist structure of these labor courts integrated workers and employers into a state-dominated administrative system because workers' and employers' representatives shared the bench with professional magistrates. The Vargas regime also created a network of social welfare agencies to deliver health care, provide housing, and administer worker pensions. Established in order to maintain social harmony through distributive social justice, these welfare agencies nevertheless failed to live up to their promise during most of their history, largely because of inadequate funding.[8]

Vargas chose not to develop an "official" political party to mobilize support for his regime. From his point of view, the Estado Novo embodied the nation's constituent interests—so there was no need for a party. He may also have feared that in a country as vast and as socially and politically unintegrated as pre-World War II Brazil, regional party branches might tend to escape central control. Only in 1945, as Vargas entered the last year of his presidential term and it became clear that the war's end would mean a return to electoral democracy, did Vargas turn to party-building. And when he did, he created not one but two parties. Both were based on the personalistic and clientelistic ties which the corporatist structures of the Estado Novo had encouraged. Ministry of Labor officials—who had already cultivated a mass clientele through the legalization of unions and the distribution of social welfare benefits and services—founded the Brazilian Labor Party (PTB). In similar fashion, a Social Democratic Party (PSD) was organized among landholders, business interests, and the urban middle class through patronage made available to them at local, state, and national levels. These two parties remained among the most important in Brazil during the democratic period between 1946 and 1964, and in 1950 they backed Vargas when he won the presidency in a popular election.

The constitution of 1946 introduced democratic elections and political competition in a multiparty system, but it also retained the corporatist system of state-labor relations. The Brazilian polity was thus based upon two contradictory principles, one designed to foster political competition and the other designed to prevent it. For the next eighteen years, the contradiction between these principles took the form of political conflict in which militant labor leaders and the populist politicians who were allied with them sought to mobilize the labor movement against the restrictions imposed by the state-dominated *sindicato* system.[9] In the early populist period (through the 1950s), labor leaders pledged support to politicians in exchange for material benefits for themselves or the union members they represented. During the early 1960s, however, increasingly militant labor leaders turned populist politics to their advantage by exchanging their support for political gains which ultimately enabled them to take the initiative in advancing their demands. Specifically, they won representation for organized labor on national policy-making bodies and came to exert considerable influence over populist politicians such as President João Goulart (1961–64).

By the early 1960s, prominent conservative civilian and military figures were decrying the growing influence of labor leaders, the rise in working-class militancy, and the soaring strike rate. At the root of these related processes, they claimed, lay the increasing control that radical nationalists had come to exercise over the nation's most important union organizations. President Goulart, who could have employed corporatist controls to block these radical union leaders, had instead used his position to expand their base within the labor movement. He even enabled several of them to become executive directors of some of the largest state-administered social welfare agencies. These radical leaders then used their government offices to distribute patronage, employment, and services in order to expand their own clienteles and increase their own political influence. Populism in general, and populist President Goulart in particular, were pointed to as the cause of the growing mass mobilization which emerged during the early 1960s. A few weeks after a restively tense and militant mass rally in March 1964, a civil-military alliance overthrew Goulart and set about applying the corporatist system of labor controls in order to reestablish a political order acceptable to conservative interests. Authoritarian rule since 1964 has had a profound impact on Brazilian workers, as the final section of this chapter shows.

MEXICO

Active state intervention in socioeconomic affairs and the expansion of centralized political power are prominent characteristics of twentieth-century Mexican development. The concept of a strong state first evolved in coherent form under the rule of Porfirio Díaz (the Porfiriato, 1877–1910), when effective central control was the perceived prerequisite for national economic growth and the society's moral progress.[10] Although the revolution that began in 1910 repudiated the Díaz dictatorship and its positivist conception of socioeconomic change, the constitution adopted in 1917 nonetheless provided the legal basis for further expansion of centralized political power. This constitution, which is still in effect, placed preeminent authority in the hands of the Mexican chief executive and effectively limited the powers of the legislative and judicial branches. And even though Mexico is a federal republic, the constitution's legal and budgetary restrictions substantially limit the autonomy of state and municipal governments.[11] This constitutional distribution of power was justified as necessary to guarantee the implementation of social reforms proclaimed during the revolution and to establish the political stability needed for national economic development.[12] The formation of an "official" political party in 1929 further consolidated central political power by creating an institutional framework closely tied to the federal executive that was capable of controlling contending political elites. The party provided a channel for gradual, continuous leadership selection and cooptation, and its domination of national electoral politics facilitated the further consolidation of presidential control over the national legislature and state governments.[13]

Pursuing an interventionist logic in national economic development, state policymakers in the 1920s and 1930s laid the bases for agricultural modernization and industrialization.[14] President Calles (1924–28) greatly strengthened the key Ministries of the Treasury and of Public Works. The Banco de México was founded in 1925, and in 1934 Nacional Financiera was formed as the state development bank. In addition to these institutional changes, the state undertook major economic infrastructure projects in the form of dam construction, agricultural irrigation, and road building. The state also encouraged basic industry, and under the Cárdenas administration it became the major or sole owner of the light and power industry, the petroleum industry, and the national railroads. Public policy provided such incentives as protective tariffs, import quotas, and beneficial tax arrangements to promote industrialization by the national private sector. Later, the state also enacted restrictions on foreign investment in order to further national industrialization. These measures built upon important foundations laid in the Porfiriato to foster economic development (for example, the construction of a national railway system), but they also represented a major increase in state intervention in national socioeconomic affairs.[15]

The Mexican state's interventionist role also reflected the maturation of postrevolutionary political beliefs advocating extensive state involvement in all aspects of national life.[16] The 1910–1917 revolution produced a new conception of the Mexican state: as a representative of all groups and classes, the modern state was given responsibility for the moderation and conciliation of conflicting interests. The organization and integration of newly mobilized workers and peasants into the national political system were primary concerns of postrevolutionary governments, and these tasks required active state mediation of mass participation. Moreover, the official recognition of popular demands for widespread social reforms and the inclusion of these reforms in the 1917 constitution reaffirmed the state's interventionist role. The constitution thus represented

> a will which the people transmitted directly to the state, authorizing its intervention in social life as it was considered necessary, on the supposition that the state fulfilled a program which society had entrusted to it; any act of power was automatically justified. The popular will had been fixed in the constitution and had then been passed to the state in such a manner that the will of the state was at the same time the will of the people.[17]

With social reforms consecrated as constitutional guarantees, the state's extensive interventionist role was formally recognized as the means to insure their implementation.

Given the relative organizational and political weakness of the labor movement during the revolutionary period, the need to guarantee the implementation of constitutional provisions designed to protect workers' rights (Article 123) served as an important justification for initial state supervision of labor affairs. The political elite's recognition of the conflictual nature of worker-employer relations and the elite's perceptions of the state's necessary role in interest conciliation and conflict moderation to balance the interplay of social forces were important legitimating bases for state intervention in this area. It was in this context that the first labor-related state administrative structures emerged to enforce constitutional reforms and moderate labor-management conflicts. However, the development of an organized labor movement, national economic growth and diversification, and increasingly centralized political power resulted in the expansion of the state's role as guarantor of social peace and interest conciliator in the labor sector. These changes resulted in the extension of federal labor regulation over an increasingly wide array of economic activities as well as an expansion in the powers exercised by those state administrative structures related to labor affairs. In this way the Mexican state worked actively to organize the labor sector and integrate labor groups into the national political system through ties to its administrative apparatus. Indeed, an important dimension of the overall trend toward increasingly centralized political power in the Mexican system was this expansion of the jurisdictional scope and authority of federal administrative authorities. Over time the state has also extended an increasingly widespread array of social welfare measures to the labor sector, while simultaneously using a variety of informal and formal mechanisms to regulate various aspects of labor's economic and political participation.

Evolution of State Administrative Structures. A variety of administrative structures in Mexico deal with labor-related measures such as profit-sharing, minimum wages, health care, housing, and credit. However, the Ministry of Labor (Secretaría del Trabajo y Previsión Social) and the labor conciliation and arbitration boards (Juntas de Conciliación y Arbitraje) are the principal bodies responsible for implementing labor policy and resolving labor conflicts.[18] Two major trends have characterized the organizational development of these administrative structures. First, there has been a continual expansion in their jurisdictional scope as increasing numbers of labor-related activities have been brought under state control. This reflects a functional response to an increasingly complex national economy and the growing power of Mexico's organized labor movement, as well as the maturation of sociopolitical doctrines advocating widespread state interventionism as the hallmark of the modern state. Second, the federal government has progressively expanded the degree of centralized control exercised over labor activities, principally by extending its jurisdiction over labor affairs and thus eroding local-level authority in these matters.

The early history of labor-related administrative structures reflected the political turbulence of the revolutionary period and the general uncertainty which prevailed regarding the shape of the postrevolutionary state. The first office specifically charged with overseeing labor activities, the Labor Department (Departamento del Trabajo), was created in 1911. It appeared at the beginning of the Mexican Revolution in response to increasing agitation by industrial laborers for social reforms and the federal government's subsequent recognition of the severe economic problems and deplorable working conditions of rural and urban workers.[19] However, the overall organizational and political weakness of the labor movement at the time, the consequent lack of concerted pressures for additional governmental policies to benefit labor, and the violence of the revolutionary struggle meant that little significant legislative or administrative action was undertaken until the new constitution went into effect. Only with the return of national political order and the reorganization and functional differentiation of the state bureaucracy did this situation substantially change. Labor affairs were formally integrated into the new state apparatus with the creation of the Ministry of Industry, Commerce, and Labor (Secretaría de Industria, Comercio y Trabajo) in 1917. In 1918 a special labor office (Dirección del Trabajo) was created within this newly established ministry.

The relative uncertainty of the state's role in labor affairs during the revolutionary period was also evident in the limited responsibilities entrusted to the first labor offices. The original Departmento del Trabajo was primarily concerned with the publication of data relating to labor affairs. The legislation which created the department permitted it to act as an intermediary in contracting workers and as a mediator in labor-management conflicts, but in neither case was this action possible without the express request of the workers and the employers involved. Many of the most important precedents regarding labor legislation prior to the elaboration of the 1917 federal constitution appeared as part of legislative initiatives intended to resolve very specific problems. Only in late 1917 was federal labor jurisdiction expanded to permit the Ministry of Industry, Commerce, and Labor to deal with general industry-related matters, worker and employer organizations, insurance, industrial and commercial education, strikes, and industrial statistics.[20]

Three developments shaped the evolution of the federal labor office and the expanding jurisdictional scope of its actions. First, the adoption of Article 123 at the 1917 constitutional convention marked a turning point regarding the scope of Mexican labor legislation and the role played by the state administrative structures charged with overseeing labor affairs. Article 123 raised a number of social reforms —working hours and workplace conditions, occupational health and safety measures, minimum wages and overtime pay, educational facilities for workers, labor unions and the right to strike, work contracts, and consumer cooperatives—to the level of constitutional guarantees. The broad social rights guaranteed by Article 123 created a philosophical contradiction between the federal government's responsibility for implementing these provisions and the preservation of states' rights. Although the constitutional convention rejected a proposal which would have given the federal legislature exclusive jurisdiction over labor matters, the need to protect the rights of workers proved to be the more dynamic element and led to effective federalization of labor legislation.

A second major factor behind the expansion of federal control over national labor activities derived from changes in the Mexican organized labor movement and its relationship to the government. Between 1920 and 1928 the labor movement was effectively dominated by the Mexican Workers' Regional Confederation (Confederación Regional Obrera Mexicana, CROM) and its *jefe máximo*, Luis Morones. In 1920 the CROM had offered important political support to Alvaro Obregón in his campaign for the presidency, and the confederation thereafter enjoyed official backing in its actions against employers and rival labor organizations. CROM leaders were also given important positions in the government, and in 1924 Morones was appointed Minister of Industry, Commerce, and Labor. The result of this CROM-government pact was the rapid expansion of *de facto* central control over national labor affairs.[21] Even though the political importance and organizational strength of the CROM declined rapidly after 1928, the growing power of the Mexican organized labor movement and its ability to cause widespread economic disruption in critical industrial activities were major factors justifying jurisdictional expansion and centralized state control over labor affairs.

The passage of the 1931 federal labor law was the third milestone in the expansion of federal jurisdictional and centralized administrative authority over labor affairs. It represented the maturation of a philosophical justification of active state intervention in socioeconomic affairs articulated earlier in the 1917 constitution. This orientation rejected a liberal conception of state action and justified legislation designed to regulate and protect workers' interests.[22] A coordinating role in labor affairs and the active mediation of social conflicts were associated with the characteristics of the modern state.[23] The realization of this philosophical position demanded that state administrative structures adapt to new demands. Moreover, increasingly complex economic questions and industrial problems, the continued growth of a national organized labor movement, and union tactics such as solidarity and sympathy strikes called for state structures capable of dealing with labor problems which often involved large geographic regions or critical economic sectors. Thus in 1932 a separate Labor Department (Departamento Autónomo del Trabajo) was created under the direct responsibility of the federal executive. In 1940 this office was elevated to cabinet rank with the creation of the Ministry of Labor and Social Welfare (Secretaría del Trabajo y Previsión Social). The Ministry's active participation in social welfare activities and its role in resolving labor-management disputes constitute major dimensions of the Mexican state's broader participation in regulating and mediating social conflicts.

The organizational history of the Ministry of Labor and Social Welfare in many ways reflects a normal evolution in response to new functional requirements posed by economic development and a growing and increasingly diversified labor force. The scope of its activities has expanded over time in response to the adoption of new social welfare programs and the extension of federal labor jurisdiction over additional industrial activities. The Juntas de Conciliación y Arbitraje, on the other hand, manifest much more formally corporatist state intervention in labor affairs. The Juntas' tripartite composition (labor, business, and government representatives) clearly places the state in an arbitrating role in labor-management disputes. Changes in the state's orientation towards labor activities are clearly embodied in the evolution of the Juntas' organizational structure and their role in mediating labor management disputes.

Mexico's first labor conciliation and arbitration boards appeared at the state level after the outbreak of the revolution in 1910 as part of the early labor legislation enacted by some state governments. The groups charged with administering this legislation varied considerably, ranging from political bodies to civil courts to specially created administrative or judicial organizations. The conciliation and arbitration system was adopted at the 1917 constitutional convention as a means of introducing social justice criteria into the administration of labor legislation and moderating increasingly disruptive conflicts between workers and employers. Advocates of the system argued that labor justice had to be kept out of the civil courts and that the dictates of practical knowledge should be applied to each specific case.

Article 123 placed considerably more emphasis on social reforms intended to raise workers' living standards than on the development of administrative mechanisms charged with implementing them. The failure to resolve questions regarding the conciliation and arbitration boards' jurisdiction and legal powers resulted in a prolonged series of legal battles between 1917 and 1924.[24] Finally, in 1924 the Supreme Court reversed its earlier findings and declared that the Juntas' decisions were binding if the applicable state legislation provided for it. This decision laid the basis for a rapid expansion of centralized state authority over labor affairs through the creation of a federal conciliation and arbitration board system with subsidiary regional branches in 1927. While this action remained of questionable legality until the passage of the necessary constitutional reforms in 1929, it effectively forced the question of federal jurisdiction over labor matters and opened the way for the later passage of the 1931 federal labor law.

Despite the 1927 effort to expand federal jurisdiction over labor activities, the initial legislative proposals for a federal conciliation and arbitration system showed considerable concern for local autonomy and the preservation of local-level control over the labor justice system. This was reflected in a number of the specific provisions regarding the Juntas which were eventually adopted in the 1931 federal labor law. But subsequent modifications in the system tended to reduce both the importance of local organizations and the role of local-level authorities.

In addition to their designated jurisdictional authority over labor-management conflicts, the conciliation and arbitration boards perform a variety of other functions. For economic activities coming under local (state) jurisdiction, the boards register labor unions and collective contracts and record workplace conflicts. (The Ministry of Labor registers unions, contracts, and conflicts in activities that fall under federal jurisdiction.) Without such registration, unions, contracts, and conflicts have no legal standing. The boards also have responsibility for overseeing the enforcement of collective labor contracts and legal requirements concerning workplace conditions, minimum wages, and so forth. However, the Juntas' primary function is to resolve individual and collective labor disputes. They do not constitute a compulsory arbitration system because parties in dispute can seek a solution under a privately chosen arbiter. Nonetheless, in practice the boards constitute the primary mechanism for resolving individual labor conflicts when the parties cannot reach agreement by themselves. In the case of collective disputes such as strikes, the boards are charged with seeing that strike petitions and the parties' behavior meet the requirements specified by law.[25] In the event that the necessary conditions and requirements are not fulfilled, Ministry of Labor officials frequently intervene to carry on substantive negotiations or to make political decisions, and the Juntas' functions are limited to these formal legal procedures. For this reason, the conciliation and arbitration boards' principal role centers on individual rather than collective conflicts.

Evolution of Party-Labor Linkages. The evolution of organized labor's ties to the state administrative apparatus was paralleled by labor's changing relationship with the Mexican party system. Both relationships showed increasing centralization over time as the structural dimensions of Mexico's "revolutionary coalition" took shape. While organized labor secured an institutionalized role within this coalition as the most significant mass political actor, the eventual result was a decrease in labor's autonomy in the national decision-making process and in its own mobilizational capacity. This change in labor's mobilizational and political role was closely linked to the labor movement's shifting economic fortunes and the ability of rank-and-file workers to defend their socioeconomic welfare.

Three stages characterized the evolution of this labor-party relationship in Mexico. The labor movement's initial relationship with political parties during the prerevolutionary and early revolutionary periods was tenuous and undefined.[26] Several factors which had shaped the emergence of Mexican labor unions in the prerevolutionary period played an important role in this regard. During the Porfiriato, labor unions per se had been outlawed and strikes repressed. Labor activities and worker organizations were generally confined to mutual-aid societies. Because most political parties had also been prohibited, there were few opportunities for party-union ties to develop. The Flores Magón brothers' Partido Liberal Mexicano succeeded in developing some worker support, especially in the mining areas of northern Mexico, but little organizational work could be accomplished under the watchful eyes of the Porfirian dictatorship. The predominance of anarchosyndicalist doctrines in many of the urban areas (where labor unions actively took part in the political struggles of the revolutionary period) further weakened potential labor-party linkages. The most important labor organization of this period, the Casa del Obrero Mundial, followed the anarchosyndicalists' apolitical orientation by eschewing direct political action. Finally, the generally low level of political mobilization also hindered the development of labor-party linkages in the early years of the revolutionary period. This condition gradually changed as a result of the revolutionary transformation, when political parties and labor unions expanded their mass followings and developed firm organizational bases.

The second principal stage in the evolution of labor-party linkages involved early incorporation. The creation of the CROM in 1918 and its rapid organizational and membership expansion under direct government tutelage led to the subordination of a major portion of the national organized labor movement to the state. In the late 1910s and early 1920s labor groups had maintained alliances with a large number of small, often geographically limited political parties. But the CROM managed to centralize labor's political activity and, increasingly, to channel it through the party of CROM leader Luis Morones, the Partido Laborista Mexicano (PLM).[27] Significantly, this party linkage did not expand labor's political mobilization, for Morones blocked strikes and restrained militant activity in exchange for high office and financial rewards for himself and his associates.

The most significant efforts to develop labor's organizational strength and party-linked mobilizational capacity occurred under Cárdenas' direction in the late 1930s. The government-affiliated Revolutionary National Party (Partido Nacional Revolucionario, PNR) created in 1929 had not immediately encompassed the bulk of the organized labor movement because the PLM had not joined in its formation. Morones' leadership position was in eclipse by 1929, and the organized labor movement was severely factionalized. The initial step in consolidating labor unity was the creation of a new central organization, the Confederation of Mexican Workers (CTM), in 1936. Cárdenas prevented the combined organization of workers and peasants, but during the period of "popular front" mobilization he relied heavily on the CTM for mass support for reform policies such as the expropriation of foreign-owned petroleum companies in 1938. In exchange for this support Cárdenas pursued pro-labor wage policies and encouraged workers' efforts to organize and strike in support of their economic demands. In 1938 Cárdenas formally recognized organized labor's political position within the governing revolutionary coalition by including the CTM as the labor sector in the reorganized government-affiliated party, the Mexican Revolutionary Party (Partido Revolucionario Mexicano, PRM).[28]

The organization of the CTM and its inclusion in the "officialist" PRM are frequently interpreted as the turning points in the evolution of labor-party ties in Mexico. However, the third stage in this process did not emerge until the consolidation of this linkage in the early 1950s.[29] The Cárdenas coalition was subject to severe internal tensions and secessionist tendencies, many of which were exemplified by internal struggles and divisions within the CTM. These divisions within the organized labor movement worsened under Manuel Ávila Camacho's presidency (1940–46) as World War II inflationary pressures challenged the government-CTM wartime policy of wage restraint. By 1947 the CTM's position had been substantially weakened, and an effort to organize a new majority labor organization gained force in the form of the Workers' Unity Confederation (Confederación Unica de Trabajadores, CUT). By 1948 the CUT apparently represented more workers than the CTM, especially in the most strategic economic sectors.[30] But President Alemán's (1946–52) economic plans required an organized labor movement willing to enforce a policy of wage restraint as a critical ingredient for rapid national industrialization. Thus the Alemán government forcibly disbanded the CUT's core support base, the "Coalition of Industrial Unions" formed by the railroad, petroleum, and mining-metallurgy workers' unions. Between 1948 and 1952 opposition leaders were purged from these three strategically located unions, as well as from other labor organizations. By the early 1950s the CTM's hegemonic position had been reestablished, and organized labor's subordinate ties to party and government had been consolidated.

State Controls and Union Activity

Trade union activities in both Brazil and Mexico are subject to extensive regulation and supervision by the state. In both countries this relationship between the state and labor unions reflects Latin America's heritage of Roman law, in which groups' legitimacy depends upon juridical recognition by the state.[31] Perhaps more importantly, however, this relationship is the result of the historical evolution of the interventionist state and the organized labor movement in Brazil and Mexico. While the right to organize was among the principal victories won by workers in post-1930 Brazil and post-1917 Mexico, labor unions were subject to an extensive set of guidelines and requirements which governed their formation and activities. The development of state controls over this central dimension of national socioeconomic and political life was both a reflection of, and a major contribution to, the consolidation of the interventionist state in Brazil and Mexico.

Labor legislation in Brazil and Mexico provides for state regulation of three main aspects of trade union life: union formation; internal union activities, including elections and leadership selection; and union collective actions, such as strikes. However, despite these broad parallels and similarities, Brazil and Mexico evidence significant differences in both the specific details of state controls over labor unions and the rigidity with which these control mechanisms have been applied. This section examines these similarities and differences and evaluates their consequences for organized labor.

FORMATION AND STRUCTURE OF LABOR ORGANIZATIONS

The keystone of state control over labor unions in Brazil and Mexico is the authority to grant legal recognition to labor unions. In Brazil, this power is wielded exclusively by the national Ministry of Labor. In Mexico, as a reflection of the 1917 constitution's formal commitment to federalism and the continuing role which individual Mexican states play in the national political process, jurisdiction over labor matters is divided between the federal government and the states. Economic sectors of strategic importance—such as railroads, shipping, heavy industry, petroleum and petrochemicals, mining and metallurgy, textiles, and food processing—fall under federal jurisdiction; they are regulated and supervised by the Ministry of Labor. Economic activities that fall under local jurisdiction generally employ smaller numbers of workers and are of lesser consequence in the national economy. Recognition of unions in these activities is exercised by the state-level Juntas de Conciliación y Arbitraje.[32]

In both Brazil and Mexico, the requirements and documentation for official union recognition are similar: achievement of minimum membership levels and representational standards within a stated geographic or functional area, and the submission of proposed union by-laws and internal statutes, membership lists, and minutes from the initial organizational meeting.[33] While these formal requirements are quite simple, the union registration process can be prone to bureaucratic error, politically inspired delay, and corruption. Without such legal recognition, workers' organizations in both countries cannot enjoy the extensive protection granted to unions and their officers by the federal labor laws. Without recognition, unions have no authority to negotiate collective contracts with employers, to file strike demands, or otherwise to represent rank-and-file interests before employers, public administrative agencies, or judicial authorities. And, significantly, legal recognition can be withdrawn when a union ceases to fulfill the substantive purposes and procedural requirements which it was initially required to meet.

Despite these general similarities, Brazil and Mexico differ in the specific controls at the disposition of the state, and their labor movements have distinctive organizational shapes because of differences in their national labor laws and enforcement policies. Brazilian regulations are more minutely restrictive, and labor authorities have interpreted them more rigidly in most (but not all) periods. For example, in stimulating union formation during the formative years of the system between 1930 and 1945, the Vargas government withheld legal recognition from some unions influenced or controlled by political opponents who could not be coopted. The state increased its leverage over workers' organizations by adopting three successive basic labor laws in the 1930s (in 1931, 1934, and 1939), which required unions to reapply for official recognition under changing criteria.[34] Since that time, the government has not withdrawn recognition from unions it seeks to punish or control. Instead, it relies on a variety of selective incentives and controls, the most formidable of which is "intervention" by the Labor Ministry to purge a union's officers and appoint one or more interventors to run the union in a manner more to the liking of the government.

While state control over union formation has also been used in Mexico to serve the government's political ends, this policy has been employed less generally than in Brazil. The use of this control mechanism has varied considerably over time, and it has been used selectively as an additional means of building political support or limiting the activities of regime opponents in the labor movement. For example, during the 1936–1938 period Cárdenas used the power of union recognition to stimulate labor union formation as a means of expanding his popular support base. Many of these unions, especially in rural areas, lacked strong membership support and subsequently disappeared in the years after Cárdenas left office. Between 1973 and 1978 the opposition-oriented National Metalworkers' Confederation was unable to secure official registration despite its having fulfilled the necessary criteria stipulated in the federal labor law.

Like their Brazilian counterparts, Mexican labor authorities have usually found it unnecessary to withdraw official recognition from unions because other, less drastic control mechanisms have operated effectively. In many of the cases in which recognition has been withdrawn, the union in question had in fact ceased to fulfill the necessary requirements for registration—its membership had fallen below the minimum required level, it no longer represented a majority of the employees in a specific workplace, and so forth. But in some cases more explicitly political criteria have been applied. For example, in a 1943–1945 conflict among internal factions within the national railroad workers' union, official recognition was granted to secessionist organizations representing boilerworkers and engineers when the Ministry of Labor wished to undermine the national union's Communist-influenced leadership. Later, when wartime economic stability was threatened by growing strife within the union, these opposition groups lost their legal recognition and were suppressed.[35]

The use of union recognition as a state control mechanism has occurred less frequently in Mexico than in Brazil because of two factors normally affecting the formation of Mexican labor unions. First, labor unions in Mexico are usually organized either as additional sections of existing sector-specific national industrial unions or as affiliates of established state or national labor federations and confederations. These labor organizations normally reach agreements with employers to organize workers at the time a new enterprise or production facility is founded. In the case of economic activities not represented by a single national industrial union, this decision is the result of political maneuverings and negotiations among labor officials, the employer, and the various "officialist" labor organizations seeking to represent the work force in question. But once agreement among these actors has been reached, the labor authorities' principal concern—the new union's political orientation—has been settled. In these cases official union registration is a mere administrative formality.

Second, in comparison to the coherent, narrowly interpreted corporatist doctrines which have influenced the state's recognition of labor unions in Brazil, Mexico's governing revolutionary coalition has favored a broader, more inclusive strategy with regard to the formation of labor unions. This difference was in part reflected in Mexico's 1931 and 1971 federal labor laws, which established registration criteria formally designed to encourage union organization. Moreover, successive Mexican presidents have stimulated limited organizational pluralism in the labor sector as a means of enhancing the state's own relative autonomy vis-à-vis different labor groups. Thus historically there has been considerably more heterogeneity in the organization and orientations of Mexican labor groups than in the more closed Brazilian system. Not only do diverse local, regional, and national labor organizations exist, but employer-dominated "white unions" *(sindicatos blancos)* and opposition-oriented "independent unions" *(sindicatos independientes)* are also tolerated. The state uses its authority to withdraw legal recognition from a union only as a last resort when other, more flexible means have failed to restrain the organization's open political opposition.

Union pluralism was permitted in Brazil for just one brief period, under the 1934 labor law. This brief departure from the strong centralizing forces of the Revolution of 1930 was due to a short-lived democratic interlude in which an elected, heterogeneous legislature included provisions permitting union pluralism in the Labor Ministry's draft labor law before approving it. Labor Ministry officials argued that these provisions reduced state control over the labor movement and permitted opposition forces to organize among the workers. When the labor law was revised in 1939, Labor Ministry officials wrote the new draft and Vargas—now dictator under the authoritarian Estado Novo—simply decreed it into law.

Official incentives exist in support of union formation in Brazil, but their purpose is to prevent pluralism. Indeed, Brazilian corporatist theory explicitly encourages workers to mobilize in their official unions, and both labor law and Labor Ministry programs provide incentives for individuals to join unions—incentives that even increased under military rule in the late 1960s and early 1970s. In an apparent paradox, governments that openly repress union leaders or militant workers have at the same time encouraged unionization. This ceases to be a paradox when one considers that officially recognized unions fill the legally permitted organizational space and thus block opposition forces from creating union organizations to mobilize against government policies. So effectively does the corporatist network monopolize the available organizational space that, in cases in which independent Brazilian labor leaders have succeeded in mobilizing workers, they have had to work through the official unions. Prominent examples include the unions affiliated with the General Labor Command (Comando Geral dos Trabalhadores, CGT) in the early 1960s and the increasingly militant industrial unions in the late 1970s and early 1980s.[36]

Different mechanisms and patterns of state control over union formation have therefore given different and distinctive organizational shapes to organized labor in Brazil and Mexico. The corporatist doctrines of Vargas' Estado Novo were inspired by the specter of class conflict, and Brazilian labor law therefore seeks to block the organizational unity of the labor movement. It divides labor by requiring that unions organize only within geographically circumscribed, narrowly defined industrial or sectoral categories. Because it makes no provision for a single national confederation of workers, the law is construed as prohibiting such a body. The law divides all economic activities into eight branches and does not provide for organizational links between workers in one branch and those in another branch. There are thus eight isolated confederations, corresponding to the following sectors: industry; commerce; river, maritime, and air transport; land transport; communications and advertising; banking and insurance; education and culture; and agriculture. Except for activities whose geographical limits are by nature imprecise (for example, maritime, railroad, and air transport), each union's territorial base is restricted to one, or at most a few, counties *(municípios)*. State-level federations (joining at least five unions in the same economic sector) can be formed, but they are not allowed to engage in collective bargaining with employers. This corporatist hierarchy is, therefore, an intentionally truncated pyramid with no single, overarching organization at the top to link existing industry-specific confederations and represent the labor movement as a whole.

In the rapid political mobilization of the early 1960s, Brazilian labor leaders organized the General Labor Command as an extralegal umbrella organization designed to cap the pyramid and fulfill this unifying task. The CGT and affiliated inter-union organizations in Brazil's major cities played an instrumental role in coordinating the political strikes and labor mobilizations that influenced national politics between 1962 and 1964. During this period the CGT-affiliated leaders pressed President Goulart and his labor ministers for official recognition, citing their movement's ability to mobilize a militant mass base on behalf of the president. CGT-affiliated leaders of the National Confederation of Industrial Workers (CNTI) also used a major industrial general strike in São Paulo in October 1963 to pressure both employers and the state to grant the CNTI collective bargaining rights so that it could legally represent all industrial workers in any given state. In this way the workers would no longer have to bargain separately through their narrowly defined unions. Through the CNTI, most workers—particularly those in smaller unions— would have had a far more effective bargaining agent than they currently had, one equipped with a team of lawyers, accountants, economists, and industrial-safety experts. Before labor organizations could press this demand further, however, the military overthrew President Goulart in April 1964 and intervened in many officially recognized union bodies to oust the most militant labor leaders.

The overall structure of the Mexican labor movement differs substantially from the Brazilian model. As a result of postrevolutionary mobilization and political beliefs favoring a degree of organizational pluralism, Mexican unions tend to be organized in one of two principal ways.[37] First, the strongest unions are organized by specific industry or economic activity. "Industrial" unions are formed by workers employed in two or more firms in the same economic activity; "national industrial" unions are formed by workers employed in one or more enterprises in the same economic activity, located in two or more states or federal territories. Both are usually divided into local "sections" corresponding to specific workplaces. Examples of national industrial unions are those for workers in the railroad, petroleum, petro-chemical, mining and metallurgy, and sugar industries. They are the sole unions representing workers in these activities, and the national union cuts across administrative and geographical boundaries.

Second, state and regional federations are organized along federal jurisdictional lines without regard to functional specificity. These federations' membership is heterogeneous in terms of union size, economic activity represented, and the kind of local union included. Guilds (workers of the same profession, activity, or speciality), company unions (workers employed in a single firm), and "mixed" unions (workers employed in various activities in a single municipality where the number of workers in any single activity is less than twenty) are grouped together. State and regional federations may also be organized in local-level sections where this heterogeneity in size, economic activity, and union structure also exists. Different national-level confederations may have their own state and regional federations operating within the same geographical or jurisdictional area, competing for the same heterogeneous union membership.

Industrial unions, national industrial unions, and state and regional federations may all be affiliated with national-level labor confederations such as the CTM. The great majority of Mexican labor organizations are also affiliated with the umbrella-like Labor Congress (Congreso del Trabajo, CT). As a reflection of their strategic economic position and greater organizational and mobilizational capacities, industrial and national industrial unions often affiliate directly with the CT. State and regional federations' affiliations with the CT are normally mediated through one of several national labor confederations. While the CTM is its single most important member, the Labor Congress groups together labor organizations of very diverse political orientations and includes a number of opposition-oriented independent unions.

INTERNAL UNION ACTIVITIES

State labor authorities have the power to regulate and oversee various dimensions of a labor union's internal organizational life in both Brazil and Mexico. However, just as Brazilian labor law and Labor Ministry officials have given the labor movement a more restrictive organizational structure than their Mexican counterparts, so too have they exercised closer control over internal union activities. Indeed, Brazil's Consolidation of Labor Laws and related legislation and regulations provide for extensive supervision of union personnel, finances, and activities by Labor Ministry officials and even by the police. The use of political patronage complements administrative controls in matters such as the selection of union officers. Not only must the Labor Ministry ratify union officers when they are elected, but it also sets the rules governing election procedures and enforces them by observing union balloting. The authors of the labor law justified this control as necessary to protect union members from electoral fraud, but particularly since 1964 such measures have served to screen out militants who are alleged to be subversives. Since 1965 prospective candidates have been unable even to secure a place on the ballot without first passing the scrutiny of the Labor Ministry and the political police. They must also declare "that they will zealously work for faithful obedience to the Federal Constitution and national laws and that they will promise to respect the duly constituted authorities and carry out their decisions."[38]

In the democratic period prior to 1964, official patronage coopted labor leaders into the system. Politicians appointed key labor leaders to state or parastate positions, helped them obtain bank credit for themselves or their constituents, and directed government agencies to improve health services or schools in areas where their unions were located. Such patronage politics not only won cooperation from the labor leaders, but it also generated electoral and other support for the politicians who provided these benefits. For example, in 1961 President Goulart applied a combination of patronage benefits and the threat of administrative controls to reward labor leaders who had supported him with political strikes and massive turnouts at demonstrations during the succession crisis in August and September of that year. Goulart had been vice-president when President Quadros resigned, and key military officers tried unsuccessfully to block his accession to the presidency. In the elections for officers of the powerful National Industrial Workers Confederation (CNTI) in December, Goulart helped his labor supporters, an ascendant faction of radical nationalists, wrest control from the incumbents, who had not supported him during the succession crisis. Goulart's personal labor advisor dispensed patronage appointments and cash bribes to influence delegates' votes at the CNTI convention, and he threatened ministerial intervention in the CNTI if the radical nationalist slate failed to defeat the confederation's incumbent leaders. With the signals clear for everyone to see, all but one of the thirteen undecided delegates ultimately cast their ballots for the challengers' slate, which won handily.[39] In 1964 and 1965 these radical nationalists were among the principal victims of the wave of state interventions in labor unions.

Intervention is the Brazilian state's ultimate weapon for maintaining control over internal union activities. The Labor Ministry is empowered, at moments when the "normal" operation of a union is threatened, to oust its elected officials and replace them with one or more government-appointed interventors to correct the situation. The Ministry generally intervenes in several unions each year in cases involving electoral fraud or the mishandling of union funds. However, this power is most often employed to oust union leaders who pose an open challenge to government policy. On two occasions the government has intervened massively in labor unions during generalized political purges. In 1947 and 1948, when a rising wave of labor activism coincided with rapid growth in the Communist Party's strength and popularity, the government banned the Party, expelled its members from legislative posts to which they had been elected, and repressed many of the mass organizations with which they had been associated. The Ministry closed the Confederation of Brazilian Workers (CTB) and intervened in at least 200 of the 969 recognized labor organizations, replacing the unions' elected officers with its own appointees.[40] Again, after the coup of 1964, the conservative civil-military government moved to oust radical nationalists from elective public office, the bureaucracy, political parties, and a broad range of interest groups such as labor unions. In 1964 and 1965 the government intervened in at least 532 labor organizations, and the largest and most dynamic unions were the special targets of government action. The Labor Ministry intervened in 70 percent of those unions with more than 5,000 members, 38 percent of those with 1,000 to 5,000 members, and only 19 percent of those with fewer than 1,000 members. And, reflecting the political importance of higher-level organizations, it intervened in 67 percent of the confederations, 42 percent of the federations, and only 19 percent of the local unions.[41]

Government control over internal union activities in Mexico depends more on political arrangements than on the broad range of administrative controls available to Brazilian labor authorities. State regulation of internal union affairs is limited principally to the validation of union elections. Although this mechanism has frequently been used to protect incumbent "officialist" labor leaders from opposition movements, the Mexican state has never exercised as extensive control over the leadership selection process as in post-1964 Brazil. Only at the request of some union faction does the state investigate charges of union corruption, internal violence, and so forth. In some cases, such as the 1948 purge of the railroad workers' Communist-influenced leadership and the 1959 repression of the railroad workers' strike, military and police forces have been used to impose pro-government union leaders. But the more important control mechanism in Mexico is the selective cooptation of labor leaders via economic and financial re-

wards and/or political mobility through the government-affiliated Institutional Revolutionary Party (Partido Revolucionario Institucional,
PRI). Both techniques are widespread and effective. Political rewards
to loyal labor leaders occur through PRI-controlled nomination and
election to municipal, state, and national office. Positions as federal
deputy or senator are normally the highest political reward to which
"officialist" labor leaders can aspire, and these offices frequently offer
opportunities for economic self-enrichment.

Local-level union life in each country also has its own national
characteristics. Brazilian labor law and administrative practice seek to
foster class harmony and therefore channel union activities into pur-
suits that do not build class consciousness or lead to class conflict. This
approach is explicit in the first of the duties that the Consolidation of
Labor Laws enumerates for the unions: "to collaborate with the public
authorities in the development of social solidarity."[42] One of the most
effective tools to orient and influence union activities is Labor Ministry control over union finances. Ministry officials not only examine
union books, but they can even veto the distribution of the greatest
source of funds for most unions. The trade union tax *(imposto sindical)*,
amounting to one day's pay per worker per year, is a payroll tax levied
directly by the federal government and subsequently distributed to
recognized unions, federations, and confederations. These funds
amount to some 60 percent of union income, and the law restricts their
use to social service activities of a type associated with the mutual-aid
societies of preindustrial Brazil: primary and vocational schools; li-
braries; job placement services; maternity, medical, dental, and legal
services; credit and consumers' cooperatives; holiday camps and sports
activities; and so forth. They may not be used for strike funds, rallies,
or other mobilizing activities. Although the tax was renamed "trade
union contribution" in 1966, it remains a tax, unchanged in all substantive respects.

Unions in Brazil generally lack vitality at the plant level. The
Brazilian labor law provides for local unions only by geographic area
(generally a *município*), and it offers no legal protection for shop stewards. Thus most unions do not have factory-level subunits, because
employers are not barred from firing plant-level activists and because
trade union tax funds cannot be used to support plant-level activities.
In all but a few exceptional cases, therefore, the central union hall
serves members from the entire *município*, and its principal function
is to dispense medical, dental, legal, and other services. Only in some
of the best organized and most modern sectors, as in the automobile
factories outside of São Paulo, does one find the stirrings of plant-level
activity. Indeed, plant-level activity has been so stunted by the combi-

nation of legal restrictions, employer hostility, and government repression that it was considered a significant victory when, in 1977, the São Bernardo automobile workers got Ford to allow the union to place a bulletin board in the plant.[43]

Mexican labor law and state policies also create the context in which local labor organizations maintain control over rank-and-file workers, but the mechanisms and processes are different from those in Brazil. The compulsory collection of membership dues is widespread in Mexico, but it is in all cases a checkoff system stipulated by the specific collective contract rather than by federal or state labor law. State authorities play no direct role in this process, for the employer deducts workers' dues from their paychecks and surrenders the funds to the recognized union leadership.

Mexican union leaders can also utilize a variety of practices and procedures—including bribery, electoral fraud, and the manipulation of general assembly meetings—to punish rivals and silence dissidents.[44] Labor leaders' use of legal provisions to maintain their position generally requires collaboration with employers at the plant level. The operation of closed or union shop provisions ("exclusion clauses," *cláusulas de exclusión*) is an important example of the way in which such mechanisms coincide with structural socioeconomic factors to make control by "officialist" labor organizations viable at the local level. Collective contracts in the principal economic sectors frequently require employers to hire only union members ("entry exclusion clause") and to dismiss any worker who loses his union membership ("separation exclusion clause").[45] Where employers and union leaders collaborate to manipulate internal procedures to deprive a worker of his union membership, the threat of dismissal in a high unemployment economy constitutes a powerful mechanism by which to eliminate internal opposition to "officialist" control of workplace labor relations and the local union apparatus.

LABOR STRIKES

In addition to controls over union formation and internal union activities, organized labor in both Brazil and Mexico is subject to extensive regulation of its most important political and economic weapon—the strike. In both countries labor legislation requires formal state recognition and approval of strike actions. These regulations govern the strike's specific goals, the procedures concerning the filing of strike petitions or papers, the formal notification of both employers and labor authorities in advance of the strike, the tactics which striking workers can use, and the conciliation and arbitration procedures which striking workers must follow.[46] Not only is the state empowered to declare strikes illegal and to use force to end them if these various conditions are not met, but the very detail and length of the administrative procedures involved allow ample opportunities for the state selectively to stifle or to support a strike.

In Brazil, the administrators and police of the Old Republic routinely repressed strikes through 1930, and corporatist legislation and Vargas' authoritarian rule effectively barred nearly all strikes for the next fifteen years. The constitution of 1946 guaranteed the right to strike for the first time, but even this guarantee was open to interpretation. In a characteristic example of Brazilian ambivalence towards the strike, the Congress between 1946 and 1964 never passed the necessary enabling legislation *(regulamento)*, and it also failed to repeal an earlier law prohibiting strikes. In this situation in which the constitution and specific laws contradicted each other, both advocates and opponents of strikes naturally argued that the law supported their position. Ironically, the military ultimately succeeded where eighteen years of democratic government had failed, for President Humberto Castello Branco forced strike regulation through the legislature soon after the 1964 coup. While prohibiting political and solidarity strikes, the new legislation permitted most economic strikes. Its provisions are mere window-dressing, however, for post-1964 military governments have effectively prevented or suppressed strikes by other means.

Political decisions to enforce or to ignore strike legislation in Brazil have been as important as the controls themselves. During the populist period from 1946 to 1964, successful strikes generally had the political backing of important politicians, and the more important the strike, the higher the level of political backing. In 1962, for example, President Goulart instructed the Labor Ministry to refrain from pronouncing a key political/economic strike illegal so that public-sector rail and port workers who supported him would not lose any pay while participating in it.[47]

Despite the existence of a right-to-strike law since 1964, the military has relied on other laws to prevent, contain, or repress most strikes since that time. A 1966 presidential decree removed effective wage-bargaining rights from the unions by establishing a mandatory wage-setting formula, one that sharply reduced the purchasing power of workers' paychecks. The government considered raises above the level set by the formula to be illegal, so little was left for union leaders to discuss at the annual contract talks and strikes for higher wage increases became automatically illegal. Moreover, the National Security Law of 1969 barred strikes in "essential" activities and stipulated long prison terms for violators. Strike data for the industrial state of

São Paulo show how thoroughly the government's enforcement of the strike law and complementary forms of intimidation reduced work stoppages. Before the passage of the strike law, there were 180 strikes in 1961, 154 in 1962, and 302 in 1963. The total dropped to 25 in 1965, 15 in 1966, 12 in 1970, and zero in 1971.[48] A few strikes occurred in the mid-1970s. Beginning in 1977 the system of controls began to break down under the pressures of increasing union mobilization, a topic discussed below.

The Mexican labor movement won the right to strike as part of the extensive labor legislation enacted as Article 123 of the 1917 constitution, but the selective application of strike regulations has produced significant variations over time in the incidence and success of strikes. Cárdenas' policies favoring labor mobilization resulted in major increases in the number of strikes during his presidency.[49] But during the 1941–1975 period the total number of strikes declined sharply. While there has been some variation in the overall level of strike activity during this period—showing a substantial increase under President López Mateos' (1958–64) pro-labor administration—the government has effectively prevented or restricted strikes in the important economic sectors that are subject to federal jurisdiction. Indeed, an examination of strike patterns from 1941 to 1975 shows that strike activity in these key industries has been minimal across all presidential terms. Moreover, in neither local- nor federal-jurisdiction industries has there been a close relationship between the level of strike activity and changes in economic indicators such as the cost-of-living index and the pattern of real wages.[50] State controls over Mexican unions have effectively prevented these organizations from striking to protect their members' real wage levels during periods of rapid inflation.

SOCIAL WELFARE BENEFITS

The politicization of social welfare measures and the differential distribution of these benefits to labor unions have constituted important means of controlling organized labor in both Brazil and Mexico. This approach has been particularly important under populist presidents who directed special attention towards workers. In Brazil, for example, the technocrats who set up the social welfare system *(previdência social)* in the 1930s genuinely wanted a sound insurance system that would meet the needs of the nation's workers for housing, health services, and pensions. Within a very few years, however, it became clear that the system could not work as planned because neither the government nor the employers were paying their full statutory contributions. The system therefore lacked the financial resources to provide services to all insured workers who deserved them (and had paid for them). In place of the original criterion of genuine but routine need, other criteria—such as connections with politicians or welfare officials, and emergency need—came to determine the distribution of benefits. When the Congress passed a new social welfare law in 1960 that created equally shared tripartite control by the system's three contributing groups—labor, employers, and the government—populists like President Goulart directed the government delegates to collaborate with the labor union representatives on most issues, thereby transferring effective control over who would be indulged or deprived to the officers of the nation's key labor confederations, many of whom were CGT militants. Moreover, since the social welfare system employed about one-seventh of all federal civil servants, these labor leaders were able to increase their political power by carefully distributing the patronage employment now available to them. After the military ousted Goulart in 1964, the new government purged the labor representatives on the social welfare executive bodies and rewrote the law to restructure the system, eliminating labor and employer representatives and placing control firmly in the hands of government technocrats.[51]

In 1971 social welfare coverage was expanded to the Brazilian countryside, nearly doubling the number of participants. By 1975 the total number of insured and their dependents exceeded 96 million, or about 92 percent of the nation's 104 million inhabitants. Although rural beneficiaries receive significantly smaller payments and fewer services than their urban counterparts, the benefits are nonetheless meaningful to them and serve to bring them and their unions under the state's administrative control. All public medical services in rural areas are dispensed by the officially recognized unions, which do this on contract with the welfare agencies. The political significance of this is neatly summed up in an insightful study of social welfare policies in Brazil:

> It reinforces the salience of the official *sindicato* structure by increasing the direct dependence of rural workers on these organizations. At the same time it heightens government control over the rural syndicates [unions]. In both the rural and urban sectors, the present regime has revived the Vargas policy of transforming officially recognized unions into quasi-governmental dispensers of prized social services dependent on the state, thus hampering their ability to act as autonomous organizations defining and articulating the interests of their members.[52]

This same process is at work in the urban areas. There, too, the Labor and Social Welfare Ministries have sought to reduce the government payroll by contracting out to labor unions some of the medical and dental services formerly offered by the social welfare system's clinics. Labor Ministry officials also retain leverage because they can reward friendly union leaders by distributing services that fall outside the social welfare system. These include scholarships, positions in training programs, and loans to workers and their children.

The politicization of social welfare benefits in Mexico reflects the central role which government-backed labor confederations play in state-labor relations. In those social welfare programs which have been created as a direct result of negotiations and lobbying by "officialist" organizations such as the CTM, these same unions tend to dominate (if not wholly control) labor representation on the decision-making organs of these social welfare agencies. As a result, "officialist" labor organizations tend to benefit disproportionately in the actual distribution of benefits to workers. Control over the distribution of publicly financed material benefits contributes significantly to these organizations' continued viability, and social welfare policies thus constitute a flexible means of sustaining the established system of labor controls.

The formation of the "Workers' Bank" (Banco Obrero) in 1977 is among the most recent examples of the state's use of social welfare programs to reward the "officialist" labor movement for its support in a period of economic and political uncertainty.[53] Following the 1976 devaluation of the *peso* and in the face of the highest rates of inflation in recent Mexican history, the López Portillo government (1976–82) instituted a policy of wage restraint in organized labor's contract negotiations. The key to the success of this wage policy (and thus the government's ability to slow domestic inflation) was the "officialist" organized labor movement's—and especially the CTM's—willingness to hold affiliates' wage demands within the limits set by the wage ceiling. Among the concessions which the CTM received in exchange for this support for the government's economic policy was the creation of the Workers' Bank. The Minister of Labor specifically noted that the bank was part of the López Portillo administration's "Alliance for Production" to resolve problems such as unemployment, low productivity, and workers' low living standards.

The CTM played the principal role in the creation of this financial institution and continues to have a central part in the bank's operations. The chairman of the bank's organizing committee and later president of its administrative council was leader of the powerful CTM-affiliated sugar workers' union. The other members of the organizing committee were the heads of many of the country's most powerful and prestigious unions; those eight union leaders signing the bank's incorporating documents were all major "officialist" labor leaders. At the bank's inauguration ceremonies, long-time CTM leader Fidel Velázquez argued that unions affiliated with the financial institution should all be members of the Labor Congress. Moreover, CTM affiliates provided the vast majority of the institution's initial operating capital. Of the major initial contributors, only the CROM was not linked to the CTM; it was also the only labor organization not affiliated with the CTM to hold a position on the administration council. In a role whose title certainly does not adequately capture his importance to the operation of the bank, Fidel Velázquez acts as the institution's "general advisor." The CTM's chief economic advisor is the bank's technical advisor and associate director. Unorganized workers remain excluded from participation in the bank—despite its motto, "A Bank for All."

The Future: Continuity or Change?

Organized labor in both Brazil and Mexico has generally played a subordinate role in the processes of economic and political change since the 1940s. The character of the labor movement's linkages to the national political system and specific controls over union actions have often operated to undermine labor's organizational autonomy and socioeconomic welfare. The preceding sections show that the institutions, laws, and processes which sustain state-labor relations systems in these two countries are well-established and firmly supported by political and economic elites and even by many labor leaders who themselves benefit from these arrangements.

In both nations, nevertheless, there are indications that the economic and political role of organized labor may undergo significant change. Signs of change are more apparent in some economic sectors than in others, suggesting that workers may first assert themselves and increase their political autonomy in such strategic sectors as metallurgy and automobile manufacturing. There is no indication that the corporatist structures examined in earlier sections of this chapter will soon be completely overthrown in either Brazil or Mexico. Several major factors condition the evolution of state-labor relations in contemporary Brazil and Mexico: structural changes in the national economy and society, including the emergence of groups of workers with distinctive occupational characteristics and unusually high mobilizational capacities; shifts in the political cohesion of national political elites and their attitudes towards labor's participation in workplace negotiations and in the political system; changes in the internal characteristics of labor organizations, such as the age and dynamism of the leadership; and exogenous factors such as the OPEC oil shocks of the 1970s that squeezed Brazil economically and dramatically increased the value of Mexico's expanding oil reserves.

BRAZIL

These factors have conditioned the abrupt and startling recent developments in Brazil. As the Brazilian data and examples cited earlier make clear, the military government that took power in 1964 tightened corporatist controls over working-class organizations and supplemented these controls with direct repression. Then, taking advantage of the workers' inability to resist, technocratic policymakers imposed policies to reduce workers' real wages and to transfer the resources gained in this way into capital accumulation by the industrial bourgeoisie or into luxury consumption by middle and upper social strata. For example, the technocratic formula that set annual wage increases from 1966 to 1980 should theoretically have at least kept real wages (purchasing power) on an even level from one year to the next. In practice, however, the government officials who applied the formula consistently understated the figures for inflation and productivity increases, so that in nearly every year after 1966 the formula served to put real wages another step further behind inflation.[54]

The impact on most workers' lives was devastating. For the 40 percent of Brazilian workers who earned salaries at or near the minimum wage, the purchasing power of the base wage dropped by one-quarter to one-third by the early 1970s. The decline was even greater for food purchases. One study found that in 1965 a minimum-wage earner had to work 87 hours to buy a market basket with the minimum monthly nutritive requirements for one person; by December 1973 the same market basket required 159 hours of work![55] Workers' diets necessarily deteriorated, and epidemic diseases such as polio, meningitis, and encephalitis ravaged working-class neighborhoods. During the years of the "economic miracle" from 1968 through 1974, gross domestic product increases averaged 10 percent annually, employment soared, and wage earners often were required to put in long overtime hours. Declining nutrition, combined with overtime-induced fatigue, probably contributed to the steady rise in the workplace accident rate from 14.6 percent of the labor force in 1969 to 19.4 percent in 1973.[56] One comparative study found that Brazilian workplace-injury rates were at least five times those for the United States.[57] To compound working-class misfortunes and insecurities, in 1966 the government

abolished a law that guaranteed job stability, opening the door to very
high involuntary turnover rates. A 1970 survey in São Paulo found
that 56 percent of the workers had not been in the same job for even
two years.[58]

Workers, not surprisingly, sought to escape these controls and to
reverse the deterioration in their living standards. This was not easy,
given the range of administrative, juridical, political, and police controls that the government exercised over workers' organizations. The
first major act of worker resistance came in 1968 when metalworkers
in factory suburbs outside São Paulo and Belo Horizonte struck to
prevent further erosion of their economic position. The strikes directly challenged the government's wage-squeeze policies and the very
basis of state control over the labor movement. Police and military
units forcibly suppressed these strikes.[59] This violent repression in-
timidated and demoralized for several years both the rank and file who
wished to resist and the potential leaders who could have organized
such resistance. By 1972, however, workers began to develop ways of
defending their interests while minimizing the likelihood that their
actions would lead to direct repression. In the boom years of the early
1970s, workers began to carry out carefully defined job actions against
specific employers rather than against all employers in a given industry. The actions chosen were not in themselves against the law.

Because it was illegal to strike for wage rates higher than those
permitted by the official formula, workers at first did not confront the
question of their base pay. The formula, however, applied only to the
standard forty-hour work week; it did not set the rates for overtime.
With employment rates running very high during this period of rapid
economic growth, employees in a number of plants refused to work
overtime without significant increases in overtime pay scales. Likewise, they struck or staged work-to-rule slowdowns to win improvement of working conditions that did not meet the standards of the
labor code and to force employers who fell into arrears to pay the back
wages. At least 34 such job actions occurred from 1973 through May
1977.[60] Finally, in May 1978 metalworkers in the São Paulo factory
suburbs held a major strike that effectively broke the official strike ban
and opened the floodgates of pent-up worker resentment. From 1978
through 1980, hundreds of strikes involving millions of workers took
place. The factors that gave rise to these strikes may imply significant
changes in state-labor relations in Brazil.

The Brazilian economy changed in major ways during the 1964–
1978 period. This economic transformation projected metalworkers
into a pivotal position both in the economy and in recent efforts to
change the political system. As recently as 1965 there were only

900,000 industrial workers directly engaged in production in Brazil, and most of them were located in relatively small enterprises and in traditional industrial activities (for example, food processing, beverages, textiles). But by 1974, because of dramatic growth in modern industrial sectors (especially consumer durables and capital goods industries), metalworkers directly engaged in production numbered 943,000 and constituted about one-third of the manufacturing labor force of 2.8 million. These metalworkers are concentrated in such a way as to increase their mobilizational capacity and hence their potential power. About half of them work in the greater São Paulo industrial area and they are frequently employed in very large enterprises. For example, in 1978 Volkswagen, Ford, and Mercedes-Benz employed a total of about 80,000 workers; nearly half of them worked in the giant Volkswagen facilities.[61]

The metalworkers' union in the industrial suburb of São Bernardo has most frontally and visibly defied the state's repressive restrictions on labor.[62] It is the site of many of the automobile plants established since 1958, and workers in São Bernardo have from the mid-1970s sought to devise practices that would expand union autonomy. São Bernardo metalworkers set off the 1978 strikes, and they struck for over two weeks in 1979 and for 41 days in 1980. The union represents 140,000 workers, and solidarity and militancy were high enough in the 1980 strike that 40,000 to 80,000 of them regularly turned out for union assemblies in a local stadium, even in the face of such explicit threats as treetop level overflights by air force helicopters bristling with machine guns.[63] The density and sheer numbers of workers in metalworking and in modern productive sectors have thus created conditions for working-class self-assertion that are comparable to those of the now industrialized countries in an earlier period when their labor movements effectively asserted themselves.

The political climate and the attitudes of dominant elite sectors also changed greatly in the mid-1970s. Many industrialists in the private sector, citing a threatening expansion of state-owned economic enterprises and the slowdown of the "economic miracle" after 1974, found cause to qualify their enthusiasm for military rule. In the same period, the armed forces became increasingly concerned about the price that the military-as-institution would have to pay for direct rule. Continued military rule generated hostility towards the armed forces among those Brazilians who were tortured or repressed from the late 1960s on, and it created only short-lived gratitude among its civilian beneficiaries. Perhaps most important, military rule sharpened political divisions within the military institution itself.

Presidents Ernesto Geisel (1974–79) and Joao Baptista Figuciredo

(1979–   ) therefore relaxed the regime's most repressive political controls in order to prepare for an unspecified day in the future when the presidency would be transferred back to civilian politicians. Censorship of newspapers was first relaxed and then lifted completely (though censorship of radio and television remains in effect), torture by police and security officials eased gradually and then ceased, and the political opposition was allowed to win some elections (though Geisel tailored the rules of the electoral game so as to limit the opposition's area of activity). Important sectors of the population, including some military figures, took advantage of the liberalized environment to call for an end to military rule and for the redemocratization of the country. While the political liberalization that has taken place since 1974 is still quite limited, it has given rise to a broad-based movement which by 1978 included not only opposition politicians but also major spokespersons from legal, religious, university, industrial, commercial, feminist, and labor organizations. It is the entry of the workers into the national debate on democratization that marked a new phase in this process.

As of August 1977 the political liberalization process had scarcely affected labor. Indeed, on 1 May 1977 (Labor Day) one of the nation's two leading newspapers conveyed the spirit of the times when it headlined its obligatory feature story on labor, "The Worker: The Unknown One."[64] Press coverage on workers and unions was minimal in the early- to mid-1970s. But by September 1977 the situation had changed dramatically, leading another journalist to write, "A new star is rising on the national political stage: the unionized worker."[65] Brazil's recent economic transformation gave industrial workers the numbers and geographic concentration necessary to assert themselves, and political decompression created the context that allowed labor leaders to catapult a working-class presence into the national debate on redemocratization. Political infighting within the government gave the workers their entering wedge. Minister of Finance Mário Henrique Simonsen unknowingly provided the catalyst. Simonsen, seeking to restrain the political ambitions of Antônio Delfim Netto (his predecessor as minister of finance and "father" of the "economic miracle"), leaked to the press an official report showing how Delfim had manipulated the inflation figures for 1973.[66] The bogus figures, of course, were used in the national wage formula, effectively costing workers over one-third of the wage increases legally due them.

Officers from the São Bernardo metalworkers' union and other unions in greater São Paulo immediately demanded wage increases as mere restitution of wages illegally withheld from them. Although there never was a dispute about the facts, government officials invoked the higher priority of national inflation-control policies and announced that employers who granted restitution raises would not be allowed to pass along the increased costs in the prices of their products. Under this condition, of course, employers did not grant restitutive wage increases. But workers did make significant gains on other levels. Labor leaders at last entered into the national debate on the redefinition of the political system. For example, in the following months they succeeded in organizing a widely publicized meeting between union heads and the ministers of finance, planning, labor, and industry and commerce; they were sought after and consulted by party politicians; and their newly acquired prominence led President Geisel to institute weekly meetings with labor delegations. Perhaps most important, labor leaders made headway in their efforts to break down the constraints of the labor code, particularly those provisions which required all contact between employers and workers to be carried on through corporatist institutions controlled by the state. The São Bernardo metalworkers' union set an important precedent in October 1977 when its leaders initiated direct public contacts with the president of the automotive parts manufacturers' organization, without inviting Labor Ministry officials. It was in this period that the union compelled the Ford Motor Company to allow workers to hold union meetings on plant premises for the first time and to put up a union bulletin board.

Union leaders' success in representing their workers in high-level political and industrial negotiations was paralleled by, and in many ways a reflection of, successful labor organization at the rank-and file level. Even though the labor law provided no recognition or protection for shop stewards or plant-based union sections, metalworkers managed to organize ad hoc factory committees. In late May and early June 1978, these two levels of activism together produced one of the most significant and unusual strikes in Brazilian history. Workers at one transnational automotive firm in São Bernardo sat down on the job, demanding an immediate raise to help them cope with the rising cost of living. The strike ultimately spread to include 275,000 workers in 255 enterprises in greater São Paulo, and the resultant contracts raised the wages of 1.1. million wage earners by about 25 percent.[67] Rather than a single general strike, this was a series of related actions that took place domino-fashion over a two-week period. In each case the workers in a given factory, organized by their factory committees, made demands specific only to their workplace. The official unions adopted a hands-off position in order to prevent the government from charging them with organizing illegal strikes as grounds for intervening. Only after the employers requested that the union represent the workers did union leaders coordinate the factory-level actions and negotiate with the employers' organizations—again, independently of the state.

Some government officials sought to break the strikes. The labor minister, for example, declared the strikes illegal and announced that employers would be justified if they called in the police "to safeguard the right to work." He thus implied that small numbers of agitators were keeping workers off the job. The government forbade coverage of the strikes by radio and television, though it did not censor newspapers and magazines. A background report from a source in the presidential palace sought to link the strikes with subversion: "Today a strike, tomorrow agitation, afterward even worse things!"[68] The minister of finance held a meeting of the Interministerial Price Council, which resolved to order fines for employers who increased their prices after making wage concessions to their workers.

In the end, liberal elements within the regime prevailed. This was largely due to their concern over the ongoing liberalization process and, in particular, to the fact that the nation was preparing for parliamentary elections on November 15, 1978. Because the governor of São Paulo did not wish to undermine the campaigns of his future parliamentary allies in the governing party, he announced that he would only mobilize the police if the strike threatened public order or if employers made a written request for police protection. The workers ensured that the strike was peaceful, and no employers dared call for the police and thereby single themselves out for reprisals by workers or opposition politicians. Even the commander of the São Paulo–based Second Army noted that the strikes were peaceful, so there was no need for the army to take action.

These metalworkers' wildcat strikes sparked an escalating strike movement that spread out geographically from greater São Paulo to the interior of the state and then to the country as a whole. One careful analysis of the national press in 1978 counted 112 strikes in greater São Paulo, 9 in the interior of the state, and 17 in other states. For 1979, the same survey found 52 strikes in greater São Paulo, 26 in the interior, and 149 in other states. The movement spread not only geographically but also from modern manufacturing industries to more traditional sectors and to nonindustrial activities. Some 76 percent of the 1978 strikes were held by factory workers. But only 27 percent of the 1979 strikes were by factory workers; the other 73 percent involved workers in nonfactory activities.[69]

One Brazilian scholar observed that the evolution of the strike movement and of state-labor relations from 1978 through 1980 illuminated a dual crisis of trade union organization in Brazil. From the perspective of the state, the official union network appeared to be in crisis because it no longer served the state's goal of controlling the organized labor movement. Indeed, many of the strikes during this period occurred without the participation of—and often over the objections of—the union officers, rendering the established union system almost irrelevant. On the other hand, from the perspective of the workers, the union organizations themselves were also in crisis for they were structured and constrained so that they failed to serve the interests of their members. Moreover, it was all but impossible for workers to restructure the unions in a more appropriate manner. The centralizing tendencies of the labor law and the unions' willful domination by a government determined to prevent workers from interfering with official economic plans necessarily undermined factory-level union locals and eroded whatever legitimacy union organizations might have had. Bargaining relationships based on mutual respect between employers and workers thus had no opportunity to develop, and conflict within the legally prescribed centralized format almost inevitably escalated into bitter confrontation in which neither the employers' nor the workers' organizations were structured or prepared to make concessions in order to negotiate a peaceable and workable resolution.[70]

The evolution of the São Bernardo metalworkers' strikes from 1978 to 1980 illustrates this process. As noted earlier, the 1978 strikes began as grassroots movements at the plant or company level. While the unions ultimately handled negotiations with employers in the industry, workers' committees at the factory level resolved many specific grievances and sometimes reached final contracts with their employers. Indeed, the success of decentralized negotiation that built upon experience accumulated during the mid-1970s led some observers to conclude that the ad hoc factory committees might transform themselves into company-level bargaining agents, at least for the largest employers. These speculations proved groundless because the Brazilian labor law provides only for industry-wide contracts, leading both the metalworkers' union and the companies to begin preparations for centralized negotiations in 1979. The negotiating strategy ultimately adopted by the workers was highly centralized, with the union represented by its elected directorate and especially by its highly mediagenic president, Luís Inácio da Silva (known to the nation by his nickname, Lula). When the union declined the employers' contract offer, the Ministry of Labor intervened to oust Lula and the union directorate. The workers refused to call off the strike, however, and the government and employers ultimately had to negotiate a contract with the ousted leaders. After the workers accepted it (on Lula's recommendation), the Ministry lifted the intervention and the elected officers returned to their positions.

On the basis of these experiences, the metalworkers' union planned for the 1980 contract negotiations in painstaking detail. The officers prepared the workers with nearly 300 plant-level meetings to discuss strategy and tactics, and they created an advisory "wage commission" of 400 members to serve as a liaison between the negotiating team and rank-and-file workers. This commission ultimately coordinated strike operations when the government again intervened in the union. The operation of the wage commission offers another example of the way in which the system of Brazilian state-labor relations undermines trade union organizations. Its members had initially been selected at plant-level meetings, but they had to develop ties with rank-and-file union members via neighborhood organizations and churches rather than through factory-based union locals. Because the labor relations system does not sanction local union sections and because the state can always intervene to take over union facilities, the union leadership was forced to rely on organizations that were sympathetic to the workers but whose interests were not fully identified with those of workers on the job.[71] Once the strike movement extended beyond the workplace, it quickly expanded into what government spokespersons claimed they wished to avoid: an increasingly politicized challenge to the authoritarian regime, to which students, Catholic lay organizers, opposition politicians, and many others lent their moral, material, and organizational support.

During the bitter forty-one–day strike in April and May 1980, top-level presidential advisors orchestrated a combination of employer intransigence and governmental intimidation and repression. The armed forces and police sought to provoke violence. Labor Ministry officials not only intervened in the metalworkers' union to oust Lula and the other elected officers, but they also indicted them under the harsh National Security Law. By juggling prosecutors and using a military court judge who commented, "I took part in the trial with my mind already made up," the government obtained convictions with sentences ranging up to three and one-half years of imprisonment, in addition to a ban on future union or political organizing for seven years. The union officers in question have appealed their convictions.[72]

However dramatic and intentionally symbolic, these repressive actions by the state are unlikely to put an end to labor mobilization or the union movement's slowly growing margin of autonomy from the state. Of course, little is certain in the present contradictory moment of liberalization within an authoritarian military regime, but there are a number of indications that key government policymakers are far from unanimous about crushing the independent union movement. It is thus possible that continued liberalization will occur in the labor sector. General Golbery do Couto e Silva, the architect of the political liberalization process, recently outlined the government's strategy for keeping and expanding its margin of maneuver vis-à-vis the opposition during the gradual process of liberalization. The strategy is based on a conditioned-reflex approach that aims "to set limits to the actions of adversaries" by unexpected blows timed to suit the government's convenience and to keep the adversaries off balance.[73] Golbery singled out the workers' movement as having gone astray into political disputes, thus suggesting that the repression was aimed specifically at Lula, the moving spirit and charismatic president of the recently created Workers' Party. Ironically, it is precisely the system of official legal-institutional controls that has accelerated and intensified the politicization of labor leaders in modern industrial sectors, for workers perceive that only through political action can they loosen institutional restraints so that their unions will be able to defend their members' interests. As Lula acknowledged in a 1979 interview, the very experience of exercising union office in this context led him to give up his apolitical orientation and to form the Workers' Party.[74]

The growing numbers and strength of workers in the manufacturing sector make their permanent repression a prospect too costly for Brazil's military rulers to consider without at least weighing alternative responses. The repression of the 1980 strike thus may prove to have been one of the blows Golbery envisaged to set limits to the opposition's action rather than an attempt to crush the workers' movement outright. Indeed, the government has sought   even if hesitantly and somewhat equivocally—to introduce reforms in the corporatist trade union system. One study notes that although the proposed draft bill to revise the labor laws "obviously falls far short of labor demands, . . . the concessions made by the government at this stage do suggest that there is room for meaningful negotiation." In this draft bill, the Labor Ministry would not have the power to intervene directly in the unions (though it could bring action through the Labor Courts). The terms of the draft permit unions to negotiate individually with specific employers, recognize shop stewards and factory committees, and provide other measures likely to strengthen the autonomy and increase the legitimacy of the unions.[75] In late 1980 the government allowed Volkswagen to create a labor-management council, with worker representatives divided between union and nonunion members. This represented an attempt by the state and employers to permit some of the functions of factory committees while keeping the initiative out of the hands of the union. Both labor and management are carefully observing the consequences of this experiment. In February 1981 the Labor

Ministry announced that its agents in charge of the intervened metal-workers' unions in greater São Paulo would be replaced by boards composed of members of those unions. Significantly, Ministry officials selected board members who were not government stooges but rather well-known union militants.[76]

Relations among labor, employers, and the state in Brazil since the late 1970s present so many contradictory aspects that one can envision a future either of unchanging state domination of labor or of dramatically increased union autonomy.[77] Contradiction and inconsistency have characterized the entire process of modernization and economic development in Brazil, so it would not be surprising if the future labor relations system combines elements of both state control and union autonomy, with the mix differing from region to region and from industry to industry. Indeed, the proposed revisions to the labor law seem to seek this kind of administratively inconsistent but politically likely result.

MEXICO

Both specific political factors and long-term structural economic changes have shaped recent developments in the Mexican organized labor movement. For example, presidential policy towards organized labor has historically been a major determinant of the incidence of labor strikes and fluctuations in real wage levels. Echeverría's effort to increase political participation and to restructure the organized labor movement was principally responsible for the heightened degree of labor mobilization, the increased number of strikes, and the rise of real wages which characterized the 1970–1976 period of "labor insurgence."[78] Increases in labor mobilization were particularly notable in such economic sectors and industrial activities as the automobile industry, where long-term structural transformations had undermined traditional means of control by "officialist" labor leaders. But despite a reversal of official labor policy under the José López Portillo administration (1976–82) and a renewed emphasis on labor peace and wage restraint, in the automobile industry there is no possibility of reimposing traditional labor control mechanisms in unions which have become independent of government-backed labor confederations.[79]

Changes within the Mexican organized labor movement effected by presidential policy towards labor will in the future be conditioned by the broader consequences of the 1977 political reform.[80] Organized labor may in the future face a very different relationship to the political party system as a result of this political liberalization process and an expansion in the number of officially recognized political parties.

Opposition, especially leftist, political parties have not enjoyed freedom to campaign, organize, and publicize their policy positions since the Mexican Communist Party was active in the 1930s and 1940s. The current political reform offers opposition political parties new opportunities to organize openly among workers and peasants. In turn, labor unions will have an opportunity to develop important new political allies. An ability to form alternative labor-party linkages has not effectively existed in Mexico since Vicente Lombardo Toledano failed to establish a Popular Party–General Union of Workers and Peasants linkage in the early 1950s. A change of this kind would represent a major transformation in the structure of the Mexican political system and labor's pattern of political incorporation. At least in principle, an alliance of this kind would create the possibility of new freedom of maneuver and negotiation for important segments of the organized labor movement.

Changes in the structure of the national economy and the socioeconomic characteristics of the urban industrial labor force have also had major consequences for the organized labor movement in Mexico. Capital-intensive, technologically advanced industries such as automobile manufacturing, steel and metalworking, electrical products, machine tool manufacturing, and so forth evidence distinctive contrasts to more traditional manufacturing activities such as textiles, shoes, and food processing. Similarly, employees in these modern industrial sectors show characteristics which distinguish them from the national labor force in general: higher worker concentrations per firm, larger capital investment and higher production value per worker, and higher total remunerations. Comparative studies show that mass production industrial activities such as these are generally characterized by a potentially more conflictive working environment due to a high degree of repetitiveness in work tasks, relatively unskilled and highly standardized work techniques, and the considerable subdivision of the productive process.[81] At the same time, the centrality of labor in such technologies, the greater worker concentration per firm, and workers' relatively higher remunerations increase labor's bargaining leverage and mobilizational capacity in these advanced industrial sectors. Of course, tensions generated by macrosociological changes such as these can be accelerated or accentuated by variations in the national political elite's attitude and policy towards organized labor, but changes such as these also create an independent source of pressure towards change within the organized labor movement.

These changes have been more gradual in Mexico than in Brazil, but they are no less significant. For example, the development of the Mexican automobile industry after the mid-1960s produced major changes in the character of the industrial labor force and resulted in challenges to "officialist" union control in nearly all of the major automobile manufacturing firms. Faced with larger worker concentrations per firm and new kinds of workplace problems, the old-line labor leaders' control techniques proved inadequate and they were unable to maintain control. By 1973 workers in three of the industry's firms had broken with the CTM and formed "independent" unions; in all but one of the industry's remaining four principal firms, major opposition movements had also emerged to challenge "officialist" control. Where successful, these opposition movements produced unions which were much more aggressive in protecting rank-and-file interests. In comparison to "officialist" unions in the automobile industry, they generally secured more advantageous contract conditions, were more aggressive in their defense of employees' interests in cases before labor conciliation and arbitration boards, and were more inclined to use the strike to advance their demands.

Internal developments within the labor movement may also play an important part in determining the future course of change in state-labor relations in Mexico. For example, in the relatively near future the "officialist" labor movement will face its first major leadership transition since the 1940s. One result of Mexico's twentieth-century social revolution and the relatively late emergence of a major industrial labor movement has been the continuity of labor leadership. The two earlier leadership changes of importance—the decline of a discredited Luis Morones in the late 1920s and the gradual isolation and eclipse of Vicente Lombardo Toledano in the late 1940s—were in fact closely related to the political consolidation of labor leadership by those individuals who currently dominate the "officialist" organized labor movement. Among those labor leaders who challenged Morones' faltering control in the 1920s were the "the five little wolves"—Fernando Amilpa, Luis Quintero, Jesús Yurén, Alfonso Sánchez Madariaga, and Fidel Velázquez. These leaders acted in uneasy coalition with Lombardo Toledano throughout the 1930s and early 1940s, but this alliance failed to hide significant differences in tactics and goals. By 1941 Fidel Velázquez had emerged as secretary-general of the CTM, and thereafter this group maintained effective control of the politically most important sectors of the labor movement. Velázquez has been reelected secretary-general of the CTM since 1950.

What remains of this leadership is now well advanced in age. Indeed, Amilpa, Quintero, and Yurén have died. The most important labor leader in Mexican history, Fidel Velázquez, is now 81. His designated successor is even older, and those individuals who constitute the front-line leadership in the CTM and its major affiliated unions are generally in their sixties and seventies. There is thus a critical and generally recognized generational gap between them and those who might serve as future CTM leaders. Furthermore, some of those individuals who have been singled out as probable future leaders lack direct ties to broad-based constituencies in the organized labor movement.

However, the more general problem concerns the pattern of alliances and loyalties which characterizes the Mexican labor movement. The "officialist" organized labor movement is bound together by an intricate series of patron-client relationships and group ties built upon mutual favors and personal loyalties. Fidel Velázquez has succeeded in harmonizing and maintaining a diversity of personal interests and constituencies. It is unlikely that any of the major CTM leaders now on the scene, either among those of equal age or among the younger leaders who have been indicated as future leaders, will adequately replace him. The severe internal factionalism which broke out following the death of Jesús Yurén (a close associate of Fidel Velázquez and long-time leader of the "Federal District Workers' Federation," FTDF) and the schism which ruptured the FTDF and resulted in the creation of a rival federation competing for the same union constituency may well forebode a similar outcome following Velázquez' death.

Given the importance of the "officialist" labor movement to Mexico's contemporary political and economic system, one might expect the Mexican government to confront this eventuality by backing an emergent leader or faction so as to preserve overall unity in the organized labor movement. However, a response of this kind may well be at odds with broader forces of change affecting the future of Mexican organized labor. Among the most important of these are changes in the characteristics of the labor force which may do much to undermine structures and techniques that have traditionally characterized Mexican unionism. As indicated above, increases in literacy, skill levels, and the size of worker concentrations—especially in the most dynamic economic sectors which are politically and economically strategic— may undermine the traditional mechanisms which have been critical sources of control over the labor movement. Thus the challenge posed by leadership transition may also coincide with a broader crisis in the control structure of the "officialist" labor movement, offering new opportunities for more mobilized, autonomous labor actions.

Finally, exogenous factors such as Mexico's petroleum boom will affect the future of the organized labor movement in at least two ways.[82] First, the boom is likely to produce significant long-term economic strains in the form of increased inflation. This, in turn, will place new pressures on the "officialist" labor movement's traditional policy of wage restraint. Labor leaders, even in these progovernment organizations, will feel increasing pressures to respond to rank-and-file demands as they did in the mid-1940s, early 1950s, and early 1970s when Mexico also experienced high rates of inflation. Second, the accompanying economic boom may also produce shifts in the relative power of existing labor unions. The most important case here will be the national petroleum workers' union. This has traditionally been a conservative political actor, but existing internal opposition groups may become more active as new employment opportunities and new economic and financial resources become more plentiful and the union's power grows. The success of such internal opponents in affecting the national union's actions will in part depend upon the consequences of the 1977 political reform and the future development of opposition political parties which can serve as the focus of such internal union dissidence.

Acknowledgments

The authors would like to thank Gary Gereffi, Hobart A. Spalding, Jr., and Van Whiting for comments on earlier versions of this chapter. The authors are jointly responsible for the analysis and conclusions presented here, but Erickson assumed primary responsibility for the sections on Brazil and Middlebrook for the sections on Mexico. Erickson gratefully acknowledges a PSC-CUNY Research Award (grant no. 13002) from the City University of New York, which supported much work on this project, including a data-gathering visit to Brazil in June and July 1980. Middlebrook gratefully acknowledges the financial assistance of the Fulbright-Hays Commission and the Joint Committee of the American Council of Learned Societies and the Social Science Research Council, which made possible the larger research project of which this chapter is a part. The authors alone are responsible for the conclusions presented in this chapter.

Notes

1. See, for example, Myron Weiner, "Political Participation: Crisis of the Political Process," chapter 5 in Leonard Binder *et al.*, *Crises and Sequences in Political Development* (Princeton: Princeton University Press, 1971); and Samuel P. Huntington and Joan M. Nelson, *No Easy Choice: Political Participation in Developing Countries* (Cambridge: Harvard University Press, 1976), especially chapters 1 and 2. Also see Samuel P. Huntington and Jorge I. Domínguez,

"Political Development," in Fred I. Greenstein and Nelson W. Polsby (eds.), *The Handbook of Political Science* (Reading, Mass.: Addison-Wesley, 1975), vol. 3, pp. 33–47.

2. See Samuel P. Huntington, *Political Order in Changing Societies* (New Haven: Yale University Press, 1968), chapters 1 and 7, for the general relationship between organized political participation and political power.

International linkages may also affect the conditions under which the emerging industrial labor force is incorporated into the national political system, as well as the content of official policies towards labor. See Kenneth Paul Erickson and Patrick V. Peppe, "Dependent Capitalist Development, U.S. Foreign Policy, and Repression of the Working Class in Chile and Brazil," *Latin American Perspectives,* vol. 3, no. 1 (Winter 1976), pp. 19–44; and Hobart A. Spalding, Jr., *Organized Labor in Latin America: Historical Case Studies of Urban Workers in Dependent Societies* (New York: New York University Press, 1977), *passim.*

The term "state" is used in this chapter to refer to both the principal political authorities ("the government") and the institutions and bureaucracies that represent centralized power and authority and are responsible for the administration and enforcement of governmental policies.

3. Changes in the standard indices of social mobilization do not fully capture the impact of the revolutionary experience on the political mobilization of urban and rural workers and peasants. See Wayne A. Cornelius, "Nation Building, Participation, and Distribution: The Politics of Social Reform Under Cárdenas," in Gabriel A. Almond, Scott C. Flanagan, and Robert J. Mundt (eds.), *Crisis, Choice, and Change: Historical Studies of Political Development* (Boston: Little, Brown, 1973), especially pp. 396–97; and Ramón E. Ruiz, *Labor and the Ambivalent Revolutionaries: Mexico, 1911–1923* (Baltimore: Johns Hopkins University Press, 1976).

4. Nathaniel and Sylvia Weyl, *The Reconquest of Mexico: The Years of Lázaro Cárdenas* (New York: Oxford University Press, 1939), pp. 345–46.

5. This process provoked a brief civil war in 1932 when the state of São Paulo tried to secede.

6. For a summary of Oliveira Vianna's thought and citations to his writings, see Eli Diniz Cerqueira and Maria Regina Soares de Lima, "O modêlo político de Oliveira Vianna," *Revista Brasileira de Estudos Políticos,* no. 30 (January 1971), pp. 85–109. For a more extended discussion of corporatist thought in Brazil, see Kenneth Paul Erickson, *The Brazilian Corporative State and Working-Class Politics* (Berkeley: University of California Press, 1977), pp. 1–5, 15–29.

7. Francisco Campos, *O estado nacional: sua estructura, seu conteudo ideologico,* (Rio de Janeiro: José Olympio, 1940), pp. 23–40 and *passim.*

8. James M. Malloy, *The Politics of Social Security in Brazil* (Pittsburgh: University of Pittsburgh Press, 1979), pp. 105–13.

9. See Kenneth Paul Erickson, "Populism and Political Control of the Working Class in Brazil," in June Nash, Juan Corradi, and Hobart A. Spalding, Jr. (eds.), *Ideology and Social Change in Latin America* (New York: Gordon and Breach, 1977), pp. 200–36, for a discussion of populism in the Brazilian context.

10. Arnaldo Córdova, *La ideología de la revolución mexicana* (México, D.F.: Ediciones Era, 1973), pp. 46, 49–50, 53–63, 68.

11. Pablo González Casanova, *La democracia en México* (México, D.F.: Serie Popular Era, 1976), pp. 29–43, analyzes these questions in detail.

12. Córdova, *La ideología*, pp. 215, 262.

13. Daniel Cosío Villegas, *El sístema político mexicano* (México, D.F.: Cuadernos de Joaquín Mortiz, 1976), calls the president and the "official" political party the principal characteristics of the Mexican political system. The Revolutionary National Party (Partido Nacional Revolucionario, PNR), formed at Calles' initiative in 1929, was reorganized as the Mexican Revolutionary Party (Partido de la Revolución Mexicana, PRM) in 1938. In 1946, it was renamed the Institutional Revolutionary Party (Partido Revolucionario Institucional, PRI).

14. See Raymond Vernon, *The Dilemma of Mexico's Development* (Cambridge: Harvard University Press, 1963); Roger D. Hansen, *The Politics of Mexican Development* (Baltimore: Johns Hopkins University Press, 1971); Clark W. Reynolds, *The Mexican Economy: Twentieth Century Structure and Growth* (New Haven: Yale University Press, 1970); and Douglas Bennett and Kenneth Sharpe, "The State as Banker and Entrepreneur: The Last-Resort Character of the Mexican State's Economic Intervention, 1917–1976," *Comparative Politics*, vol. 12, no. 2 (January 1980), pp. 165–89.

15. James Wilkie, *The Mexican Revolution: Federal Expenditure and Social Change Since 1910* (Berkeley: University of California Press, 1973); and Mario Huacuja R. and José Woldenberg, *Estado y lucha política en el México actual* (México, D.F.: Ediciones "El Caballito," 1976), point to the economic crisis of the 1930s as a critical factor in the expansion of state economic participation.

16. The most thorough examination of this ideological orientation is presented in Córdova, *La ideología;* the following section draws upon his argument.

17. Córdova, *La ideología*, p. 247.

18. Like several other bureaucracies which deal with specific labor-related matters, the Juntas de Conciliación y Arbitraje are an administrative dependency of the Secretaría del Trabajo y Previsión Social. They are analyzed separately here because of their special relevance to labor conflicts.

19. On the early origins, purposes, and functions of these structures, see Felipe Remolina Roqueñi, *Evolución de las instituciones y del derecho del trabajo en México* (México, D.F.: Junta Federal de Conciliación y Arbitraje, 1976); and Juan Francisco Rocha Bandala and José Fernando Franco, *La competencia en materia laboral: evolución* (México, D.F.: Ed. Cárdenas, 1976). These structures' evolution is evaluated in detail in Kevin J. Middlebrook, "State Structure and Labor Participation in Mexico," paper presented at the Seventh National Meeting of the Latin American Studies Association, November 1977.

20. Remolina Roqueñi, *Evolución*, pp. 12–14, 26–27.

21. One specific consequence was a marked decline in the number of strikes. See Barry Carr, "Labour and Politics in Mexico, 1910–1929," Ph.D. dissertation, Oxford University, 1974, p. 274. Carr also provides a general discussion of the CROM, pp. 131–283.

22. Remolina Roqueñi, *Evolución*, p. 81, citing from the report by the congressional study commission on the measure creating the Departamento Autónomo del Trabajo.

23. For example, see p. x of the "Exposición de motivos," in Secretaría de Industria, Comercio y Trabajo, *Proyecto de ley federal del trabajo* (México, D.F.: Talleres Gráficos de la Nación, 1931).

24. See Middlebrook, "State Structure," for additional details on these developments.

25. Alberto Trueba Urbina and Jorge Trueba Barrera, *Nueva ley federal del*

trabajo reformada (México, D.F.: Ed. Porrua, 1976), articles 44, 450–52, 469.

26. See Ruiz, *Labor,* and Carr, "Labour and Politics."

27. Vicente Fuentes Díaz, *Los partidos políticos en México* (México, D.F.: 1946), vol. 2, pp. 21–24; and Spalding, *Organized Labor,* pp. 104–12.

28. Joe C. Ashby, *Organized Labor and the Mexican Revolution Under Lázaro Cárdenas* (Chapel Hill: University of North Carolina Press, 1963).

29. For additional detail on developments during this period, see Kevin J. Middlebrook, "The Political Economy of Mexican Organized Labor, 1940–1978," Ph.D. dissertation, Harvard University, 1981, chapter 2.

30. See Fernando Talavera and Juan Felipe Leal, "Organizaciones sindicales obreras de México, 1948–1970: enfoque estadístico," *Revista Mexicana de Sociología,* vol. 39, no. 4 (October–December 1977), tables 14, 15.

31. See Ronald C. Newton, "On 'Functional Groups,' 'Fragmentation,' and 'Pluralism' in Spanish-American Political Society," in Howard J. Wiarda (ed.), *Politics and Social Change in Latin America: The Distinct Tradition* (Amherst, Mass.: University of Massachusetts Press, 1974); and Howard J. Wiarda, "Toward a Framework for the Study of Political Change in the Iberic-Latin Tradition: The Corporative Model," *World Politics,* vol. 25, no. 2 (January 1973), pp. 206–35.

32. These jurisdictional responsibilities are detailed in Mexico's 1971 *Ley federal del trabajo,* article 527, and the *Diario Oficial,* February 7, 1975, p. 26. Those economic activities which fall under federal jurisdiction in Mexico now include railroads, mining-metallurgy, hydrocarbons, marine and maritime zone activities, textiles, electricity, cinematography, rubber, sugar, petrochemicals, steel, cement, automobile manufacture, pharmaceuticals, pulp and paper, vegetable oils and products, soft-drink bottling, and all companies operating under federal concession or contract or operated directly or in decentralized form by the federal government.

33. These various requirements governing the formation, registration, and dissolution of unions are detailed in Brazil's *Consolidaçao das leis do trabalho,* articles 511–610, and Mexico's *Ley federal,* articles 362–80.

34. Erickson, *The Brazilian Corporative State,* pp. 20–21, 27–46, 157–68.

35. Middlebrook, *The Political Economy,* chapter 3.

36. Erickson, *The Brazilian Corporative State,* pp. 42, 110, 131–50.

37. For additional details, see Francisco Zapata, "Afiliación y organización sindical en México," in José Luis Reyna *et al., Tres estudios sobre el movimiento obrero en México* (México, D.F.: El Colegio de México, 1976), pp. 79–148.

38. Erickson, *The Brazilian Corporative State,* pp. 34–46, 158–59.

39. *Ibid.,* pp. 106–7; see also pp. 8–10, 83–93, 145, 147.

40. Timothy Fox Harding, "The Political History of Organized Labor in Brazil," Ph.D. dissertation, Stanford University, 1973, pp. 171–224.

41. Argelina Maria Cheibub Figueiredo, "Política governamental e funções sindicais," M.A. thesis, University of São Paulo, 1975, pp. 40–76.

42. *Consolidação,* article 514.

43. *Isto É,* 14 September 1977, p. 18.

44. For a discussion of these various control techniques, see Manuel Camacho, "Control sobre el movimiento obrero en México," *Foro Internacional,* vol. 16, no. 4 (April–June 1976), pp. 496–525.

45. For a discussion of the legal dimensions and evolution of the *cláusula de exclusión,* see Mario de la Cueva, *Derecho mexicano del trabajo* (México, D.F.: Ed. Porrua, 1964), vol. 2, pp. 369–76.

46. For details regarding these requirements, see Brazil's *Consolidação,* arti-

cles 722–725, and Lei 4,330 of 1 June 1964; and Mexico's *Ley federal,* title 8, articles 440–71.

47. Erickson, *The Brazilian Corporative State,* pp. 97–130, especially p. 109.

48. Kenneth Scott Mericle, "Conflict Regulation in the Brazilian Industrial Relations System," Ph.D. dissertation, University of Wisconsin, 1974, pp. 129–32. The National Security Law is Decreto-lei 898 of 29 September 1969, later replaced by Lei 6,620 of 17 December 1978.

49. González Casanova, *La democracia,* pp. 233–34.

50. Middlebrook, "State Structure," part II, presents a detailed analysis of labor strikes in Mexico during the period from 1941 to 1975.

51. Erickson, *The Brazilian Corporative State,* pp. 33–34, 62–74, 83–93, 159; Malloy, *The Politics of Social Security,* pp. 124–30.

52. Malloy, *The Politics of Social Security,* pp. 126–33; quotation from p. 133.

53. Middlebrook, "The Political Economy," chapter 4, provides additional details regarding the founding and operation of the Banco Obrero.

54. For more detailed description of the wage formula, see Erickson, *The Brazilian Corporative State,* pp. 160–65.

55. DIEESE, "Salário mínimo, 1/74," 25 April 1974 (mimeo), p. 8.

56. Ângela Mendes de Almeida and Michael Lowy, "Union Structure and Labor Organization in the Recent History of Brazil," *Latin American Perspectives,* vol. 3 (Winter 1976), pp. 115–16.

57. Richard Ginnold, "Job Hazards in the U.S. and Brazil—How Do They Compare?" typescript, School for Workers, University of Wisconsin Extension, Madison, 1977, pp. 1–3.

58. Mericle, "Conflict Regulation," pp. 185, 280–85.

59. Francisco C. Weffort, *Participação e conflito industrial: Contagem e Osasco, 1968* (São Paulo: Cebrap, 1972); and *Greves operárias, 1968–1978,* special issue of *Cadernos do Presente,* no. 2 (July 1978).

60. José Álvaro Moisés, "Current Issues in the Labor Movement in Brazil," *Latin American Perspectives,* vol. 6 (Fall 1979), pp. 62–66.

61. "Uma nova classe operária," *Veja,* 8 March 1978, pp. 84–87; 1974 data from *Anuário Estatístico do Brasil,* 1978, p. 441; José Álvaro Moisés, "Qual a estratégia do novo sindicalismo?" paper presented at the meeting of the Grupo de Trabalho de Movimentos Laborais, Conselho Latino Americano de Ciências Sociais (CLACSO), Mexico City, 4–7 November 1980.

62. See John Humphrey, "The Development of Industry and the Bases for Trade Unionism: A Case Study of Car Workers in São Paulo, Brazil," Ph.D. dissertation, University of Sussex, October 1977.

63. See the press from 31 March through 13 May 1980, or the collection of press articles in Centro Ecumênico de Documentação e Informação, *1980: ABC da greve* (Rio de Janeiro: CEDI, 1980), pp. 19, 23.

64. "Trabalhador: o desconhecido," *O Estado de S. Paulo,* 3 May 1977, p. 16.

65. "Uma estrela sobe," *Folha de São Paulo,* 30 September 1977, p. 2.

66. *Folha de São Paulo,* 10 August 1977, p. 20.

67. Data from "Efeitos da negociação," *Veja,* 20 September 1978, p. 89. Description of strike from selected issues of *Veja, Isto É,* and other daily and weekly newsmedia from Brazil between May and October 1978.

68. Quotations from *Isto É,* 31 May 1978, p. 67, and *Veja,* 24 May 1978, p. 95, respectively.

69. Maria Hermínia Tavares de Almeida, "Tendências recentes da negociação coletiva no Brasil," *Dados,* vol. 24, no. 2 (1981), pp. 168–72.

70. For an insightful discussion of the dual crisis, see Almeida, "Tendências recentes," pp. 172–77.

71. Almeida, "Tendências recentes," pp. 172–76; Moisés, "Qual a estratégia," pp. 4–5.

72. Moisés, "Qual a estratégia," pp. 3–4, 5–7, 8, 10; quotation from *Latin America Weekly Report,* 6 March 1981, pp. 1–2.

73. Text of speech to Superior War College on 1 July 1980, printed in *O Estado de S. Paulo,* 19 October 1980, p. 152, and 26 October 1980, p. 132; quotation from 26 October.

74. Luís Inácio da Silva, *Lula: entrevistas e discursos* (São Bernardo: ABCD, 1980), pp. 232–33.

75. Amaury de Souza and Bolívar Lamounier, "Governo e sindicatos no Brasil: a perspectiva dos anos 80," *Dados,* vol. 24, no. 2 (1981), pp. 155–58; see also Almeida, "Tendências recentes," pp. 186–87.

76. De Souza and Lamounier, "Governo e sindicatos," pp. 156–57; Almeida, "Tendências recentes," p. 187; *Latin America Regional Reports: Brazil,* 13 March 1981, p. 5.

77. See Leôncio Martins Rodrigues, "Tendências futuras do sindicalismo brasileiro," in Henrique Rattner (ed.), *Brasil 1990: caminhos alternativos do desenvolvimento* (São Paulo: Brasiliense, 1979), pp. 121–42.

78. For an analysis of the "labor insurgence" phenomenon and a case study of changing labor relations within the Mexican automobile industry, see Middlebrook, "The Political Economy," chapter 5.

79. For an overview of the contemporary Mexican labor movement, see Raúl Trejo Delarbre, "El movimiento obrero: situación y perspectivas," in Pablo González Casanova and Enrique Florescano (eds.), *Mexico, hoy* (México, D.F.: Siglo Veintiuno Editores, 1979), pp. 121–51.

80. For a detailed examination of the 1977 political reform and its likely consequences, see Kevin J. Middlebrook, "Political Change and Political Reform in an Authoritarian Regime: The Case of Mexico," Working Papers No. 103, Latin American Program, Woodrow Wilson International Center for Scholars, Smithsonian Institution, Washington, D.C., 1981.

81. Michael Fullan, "Industrial Technology and Worker Integration in the Organization," *American Sociological Review,* vol. 35, no. 6 (December 1970), pp. 1028–39.

82. For an additional discussion of the socioeconomic and political consequences of the Mexican petroleum boom, see Kevin J. Middlebrook, "Energy Security in U.S.-Mexican Relations," in David A. Deese and Joseph S. Nye (eds.), *Energy and Security* (Cambridge, Mass.: Ballinger Publishing Co., 1980), especially pp. 161–69.

7

Income Distribution Trends in Mexico and the Kuznets Curves

DAVID FELIX

Analysts of the distributional consequences of economic growth in the LDCs are still wrestling with a dearth of systematic information on the long-run trends of the size distribution of income for individual LDCs. Those who are probing for long-term distributional patterns (e.g., for parabolic Kuznets curves)[1] have had to rely on rather inappropriate data—cross-country comparisons from single-year estimates or very short time series. These have resulted in conflicting growth-equity patterns, reflecting differences in the data sets and the methods used to adjust for the heterogeneity of structure and culture between the countries in the sets.

Four recent studies, mainly using data from the 1960s, illustrate these contradictions. Paukert simply classed a large number of LDCs and advanced countries in per capita income groups and found a strong parabolic relation between the ascending group incomes and various measures of income distribution.[2] Adelman and Morris, on the other hand, found that structural and policy differences rather than income level explained most of the variation of inequality within their data set, which included only LDCs.[3] Ahluwalia, using a regression equation, quadratic on income and augmented by proxies for various structural features, found the sign of the squared term on income to be significant and supportive of a parabolic growth-equity pattern.[4]

An initial version of this study was prepared in 1974 and circulated in mimeograph as "Trickling Down in Mexico and the Debate Over Long Term Growth-Equity Relationships in the LDCs." The main differences between the estimates in the two versions are explained in the Appendix.

Bacha, however, regressing the share of the lowest 40 percent on the log of per capita income for a similar sample of LDCs, found that the turning point for the share could be shifted from zero to infinity by a minor alteration in the selection from alternative country estimates in the data set.[5]

As an alternative approach, this chapter presents long-term estimates for a single LDC, Mexico. These show the Mexican trend diverging substantially from those traced by Kuznets for the now developed capitalist countries, as well as for those projected by Paukert and Ahluwalia for the LDCs. Mexico's above-average rate of growth of per capita income from the late nineteenth century to the mid-1970s has not sufficed to bring an unevenly upward trend of income concentration to a peak. While a turnaround may yet come, at the least the data suggest that rising levels of income have been a less powerful force for reversing the trend towards income concentration in Mexico than is indicated by the historic Kuznets pattern or by trend simulations derived from cross-sectional analysis.

Is Mexico merely a deviant case? This chapter hypothesizes the contrary: Mexico's political power alterations, including a leveling revolution, have seemingly created institutional changes more supportive of integrated growth and extensive trickling down than those in the majority of the market LDCs. Its prolonged trend towards income concentration suggests, therefore, that the market forces pushing in that direction are generally more powerful in the twentieth-century LDCs than they were in the nineteenth-century industrializing economies. The concluding section of this chapter speculates on why this may be so.

Trends in Mexican Size Distribution of Income, 1885–1975

Our estimates are composed of two segments. For the period from 1950 to 1975, fairly detailed estimates have been put together from comparable household income-expenditure surveys. This segment is then spliced to quasi-quantitative inferences, based on sketchy information, for the period from the Porfiriato to 1950.

INCOME DISTRIBUTION TRENDS, 1950–1975

For this period we have estimates for the years 1950, 1957, 1963, 1968, and 1975. Those for the fifties were made by Professor Navarrete in her pioneering monograph on Mexican income distribution.[6] The others are my computations from household income-expenditure sample surveys carried out in the subsequent years.[7] The data base for Navarrete's 1957 estimates was also a government income-expenditure survey,[8] with similar sampling methodology and definitions to those of the later years, i.e., with income and expenditure defined to include in-kind components. For 1950, however, Navarrete's data source was the 1950 census, which recorded only family cash income. To improve comparability with 1957, she multiplied the 1950 cash incomes of the lower-income brackets by the ratios of in-kind to cash income for similar income brackets in the 1957 survey. The 1957 to 1975 estimates thus form a standardized set, while that for 1950 had to be doctored into compatibility.

Table 1 presents two series of Gini coefficients,[9] each indicating rising overall concentration between 1950 and 1975. Series A is computed directly from incomes as reported in the surveys—except for the 1950 coefficient, which was computed from 1950 cash incomes augmented by Navarrete for in-kind income. Series B is computed from survey incomes adjusted for the substantial shortfall of the survey-reported income from the national accounts estimates of national disposable household income of the same years. The adjustment formulas and their rationale are detailed in the Appendix. Essentially, they allocate the survey income shortfall, which widened with successive surveys, in two directions. Part is allocated to the lowest two quintiles so as to bring their respective income-expenditure ratios up to those of 1957. The rest is allocated to the remaining income brackets following the adjustment formula used by Navarrete.[10]

Table 1 / Trends in the Gini Coefficient for Mexican Household Income, 1950–1975

Year	Gini Coefficient		Number of Income Classes Used to Compute the Coefficient
	Series A (Not Adjusted for Income Underreporting)	Series B (Adjusted for Income Under-reporting)	
1950	0.432	0.526	10
1957	.437	.551	10
1963	.543	.555	13
1968	.529	.577	12
1975	.570	.579	13

Sources: 1950 and 1957 computed from Ifigénia M. de Navarrete, *La distribución del ingreso y el desarrollo económico de México* (México, D. F., 1960), cuadros 9, 10. Remaining years computed from respective income-expenditure surveys. See Appendix Table A-1 for citations.

Table 2 / Percentage Distributions of Mexican Disposable Household Income, 1950–1975

Household Percentile	1950[a]	1957[a]	1963[b]	1968[b]	1975[b]
A. Not Adjusted for Underdeclared Income					
96–100	29.5	24.2	27.8	27.5	30.6
90–95	9.1	9.8	14.2	14.7	12.9
81–90	12.6	16.9	17.3	16.1	16.6
61–80	18.2	19.9	19.3	19.5	19.9
41–60	12.9	13.7	11.1	11.4	11.8
21–40	9.9	9.5	6.7	7.2	6.3
1–20	7.8	6.0	3.6	3.6	1.9
B. Adjusted for Underdeclared Income					
96–100	40.2	37.0	32.3	29.2	35.9
91–95	8.8	9.7	14.3	17.8	15.2
81–90	10.8	14.7	17.5	16.7	15.0
61–80	15.6	17.4	17.4	17.9	16.2
41–60	10.3	9.9	9.3	10.5	9.7
21–40	8.2	6.9	5.6	5.1	5.4
1–20	6.1	4.4	3.6	2.8	2.6

[a]Computed from Navarrete, *La distribución,* cuadros 9 and 10 (for part A) and cuadros 12 (for part B).

[b]Data in panel A computed from income and expenditure surveys; see Table A-1 for citations. For panel B, see the Appendix for details on the income adjustment procedure.

Table 2 shows that the chief relative gainers have been the 80th to 95th percentiles, and the chief losers have been the lowest 40 percent. The alternative estimates diverge somewhat as regards the top 5 percent; the share follows a U-shaped path in the unadjusted income estimates and shows a moderate downward trend in the adjusted ones. In both cases, however, the trend of the top quintile's share was strongly upward. The combined shares of the 40th to 80th percentiles, on the other hand, stayed more or less constant in both estimates, conforming to Kuznets' conjecture that his overall parabolic curve reflects primarily opposing trends in the shares of the bottom and top income groups. In postwar Mexico, however, the flatness of the middle groups' share is an average of a mildly rising share for the second quintile and a mildly declining share for the third.

The Mexican economy grew rapidly through most of the period from 1950 to 1975, and so did average real income for the majority of the income brackets. According to Table 3, only the lowest quintile suffered declining real income. There are, however, ambiguities relat-

Table 3 / Trends of Average Real Income by Household Income Group, 1950–1975

Percentile Income Class	1950	1957	1963	1968	1975
A. Income Not Adjusted for Underdeclaration					
96–100	100.0	90.2	131.6	160.6	161.2
91–95	100.0	119.0	199.4	279.2	220.9
81–90	100.0	146.9	187.2	219.6	201.1
61–80	100.0	120.0	143.1	184.4	157.2
41–60	100.0	116.0	116.3	152.0	131.4
21–40	100.0	106.6	92.6	127.7	111.0
1–20	100.0	84.0	60.9	80.1	41.7
National average	100.0	109.9	135.6	172.4	155.6
B. Income Adjusted for Underdeclaration					
96–100	100.0	112.6	125.1	149.9	179.2
91–95	100.0	134.6	273.4	449.5	372.8
81–90	100.0	169.1	242.8	307.5	270.3
61–80	100.0	140.4	172.3	243.0	200.9
41–60	100.0	120.0	127.9	203.9	172.4
21–40*	100.0	106.6	115.2	131.5	129.3
1–20*	100.0	84.0	88.1	87.8	78.9
National average	100.0	123.2	159.3	206.5	206.2

Source: Computed from Appendix Table A-6.
*Corresponds to row (2) of Appendix Table A-6.

ing to the absolute and relative income trends of the various quintiles. These have to do with price deflating and with using point income estimates rather than permanent income. The following observations attempt to resolve some of the ambiguities.

A single deflator, the cost of living index, is used to convert the nominal incomes of all income brackets to real incomes. It would be preferable, were they available, to use separate indices appropriate for rural and urban and for high, middle, and low income expenditure patterns. Despite the absence of such indices,[11] it is possible to narrow the ambiguities concerning the real income trends that relate to income deflation. In particular, the rising proportion of urban families in the next to lowest quintile—from around 20 percent in 1950 to 30 percent in 1975—probably calls for a small downward correction of the real income trends for that quintile in Table 3.[12] This is because poor rural families who migrate to the cities encounter higher prices for most of the basic goods and services in their budgets, perhaps 50 percent higher in Latin American countries, according to Kuznets.[13]

Reducing the income of the increment to the urban proportion of the 21–40 quintile accordingly lowers the 1975 figure in Table 3 for estimate A to 107, and for estimate B to 125. That is, it eliminates much of the rising real income trend for the 21–40 quintile in the A estimates, but merely flattens it slightly in the B estimates. Since the required correction for rural-urban price differences diminishes the higher the quintile, in accordance with the declining shares of food expenditure in their budgets, the corrections would probably augment the rising inequality trends of both the A and B estimates slightly.

Similarly, in postwar Mexico, inequality of permanent income probably rose more than is indicated by the point income estimates of Tables 1–3. This conclusion, which runs contrary to conventional expectations,[14] derives from the following a priori reasoning and evidence.

In a steadily growing integrated economy—that is, one with a constant rate of increase of per capita income, similar humped-shaped age-income profiles for all occupations,[15] a constant demographic age pyramid, and constant rates of mobility between occupations—the permanent income of young families would average higher than indicated by point income data, but the inequality estimates from permanent and point income data would coincide. However, point income estimates will overstate permanent income inequality when there is an acceleration of population growth or a proportionate increase of upward mobility rates across the occupational spectrum.

The gap between permanent and point income estimates could, however, be in the opposite direction in a growing dualistic economy. In such an economy there are large divergences between the age-income profiles of low and high income occupations, and interoccupational mobility occurs mainly between the more affluent activities. An acceleration of demographic and/or income growth under these conditions could result in the point income estimates understating the rising inequality of permanent income distribution. Tables 4–6 indicate that this probably was the case in postwar Mexico.

Table 4 shows that in 1968 the age distribution of household heads in all but the highest income quintile peaked between ages 30 and 39. Also, the percentage of household heads in the low-earning years of the "normal" age-income cycle, i.e., the under 30 and over 60 age groups, was approximately unchanged between each of the lowest three quintiles, declining only for incomes above the third quintile. Table 4, however, catches only the initial impact of the acceleration of Mexico's demographic growth from an average of 1.6 percent per annum in the interwar years to a peak of 3.6 percent in the 1960s. The proportion of household heads under age 30 will keep rising at least until the end

Table 4 / Distribution of Mexican Families by Relative Income and Age of Head of Household in 1968 (percentage of families)

Age of Head of Household	Percentile Income Bracket*					All Families
	0–20	21–40	41–60	61–80	81–100	
Under 30	15.8	13.4	13.5	11.2	8.8	12.6
30–39	28.1	29.7	28.1	27.0	24.2	27.4
40–49	22.4	23.5	26.3	26.5	29.7	25.7
50–59	17.8	15.0	15.3	19.0	23.1	18.1
60 and over	15.9	18.4	16.8	16.3	14.2	16.2
	100.0	100.0	100.0	100.0	100.0	100.0

Source: Banco de México, *La distribución del ingreso en México, 1968,* cuadro VI-3.
*Unadjusted income distribution.

of the 1980s. Has this rise been biasing our successive post-1950s income distribution estimates increasingly upward? That depends on the shapes of the age-income profiles of the various occupations generating household income and the extent of interoccupational mobility.

Assume, temporarily, that there is no interoccupational mobility. In that case, whether the permanent income of a quintile is higher or lower than its point income would depend solely on the shapes of the age-income curves for the various activities feeding income to the different quintiles. Table 5 shows that in 1963 these profiles fell in two sharply diverging classes. In the first class were the wage-earner categories, encompassing over half of those who were economically active in 1963. Age-income profiles in this group fell more precipitously after age 30 than did the national average profile. Moreover, the average income of all the wage-earning categories is also shown to have been well below the national average. The only important category with below-average income and a positive aging effect was agricultural self-employment, with 18.9 percent of the economically active. Thus if there were no interoccupational mobility, the lowest three quintiles of family income and part of the next higher quintile would be permanently populated mainly by income earners for whom the aging effect on income was persistently negative.

The other class was the 30 percent of the economically active who were in occupational categories—administrative and technical employees, nonagricultural workers, those who are self-employed, and employers—whose incomes were substantially above the national average and whose age-income profiles peaked after age 40 or 50.[16] Under our no-mobility assumption, these fully populated the top family income quintile and part of the next lower one.

Table 5 / Family Income Profiles by Age and Occupation of the Economically Active, 1963*

Occupation	I. Relative Income Age Profiles					II. Relative Family Income by Occupation at Each Age					III. Percentage of Economically Active
	Age Bracket					Age Bracket					
	21–30	31–40	41–50	51–60	Over 60	21–30	31–40	41–50	51–60	over 60	
All economically active	100.0	80.4	99.6	96.5	83.9	100.0	100.0	100.0	100.0	100.0	100.0
1. Wage earners	100.0	82.0	85.5	83.2	72.1	66.0	67.4	56.7	56.9	56.8	50.6
a. Agriculture	100.0	81.1	88.8	87.6	61.4	41.2	41.6	36.7	37.4	30.1	21.6
b. Nonagriculture	100.0	79.4	83.1	86.2	85.9	84.7	83.7	70.6	75.7	86.7	29.1
(1) Services	100.0	86.2	72.9	78.5	87.2	69.6	74.6	50.9	56.6	72.3	9.2
(2) Industry and commerce	100.0	77.4	91.0	88.2	71.8	90.9	87.6	83.0	83.2	77.8	19.9
2. Administrative and technical employees	100.0	74.2	101.9	110.3	64.8	198.1	182.8	202.7	226.6	153.0	17.3
a. Agriculture	100.0	79.5	55.6	80.6	33.7	122.6	121.2	68.4	102.5	49.2	1.3
b. Nonagriculture	100.0	79.8	99.2	112.3	88.3	205.8	204.5	204.9	239.7	216.5	16.0
3. Self-employed	100.0	108.5	129.7	105.7	112.4	77.9	105.2	101.4	85.3	104.4	30.3
a. Agriculture	100.0	84.7	110.3	95.7	128.4	70.3	74.1	77.9	69.7	107.6	18.9
b. Nonagriculture	100.0	115.7	142.7	126.2	88.9	93.8	135.0	134.3	122.7	99.4	11.4
4. Employers	100.0	521.1	283.9	560.1	302.7	62.0	401.9	176.6	359.9	223.6	1.8

Occupation	Family Head	Economically Active
Wage earners	50.8%	50.6%
Administrative and technical employees	15.4	17.3
Self-employed	31.8	30.3
Employers	2.0	1.8
	100.0	100.0

Source: Banco de México, Encuesta sobre ingresos y gastos familiares, 1963 (México, D.F.: Investigaciones Industriales Oficina Editorial, 1966), Séries 9, 15.

*Income of family to which those who are economically active contributed. The economically active exclude the unemployed, unpaid family workers, and all active paid individuals under 21. With these exclusions, the total of the economically active is 19.6 percent larger than the total families. The relative distribution by broad occupational category is, however, quite similar. Thus:

It follows that, with accelerating demographic growth augmenting the proportion of young families in the lowest three quintiles, point income estimates overstate the permanent incomes of the lowest three quintiles relative to those for the highest two. Therefore successive point estimates will understate the rise of permanent income concentration during the time span in which the percentage of young families in the lowest three quintiles is increasing.

Interoccupational mobility may either dampen or reinforce the preceding conclusions. Table 6 suggests that in the Mexican case it was reinforcing. The table reports on the extent to which sons deviated from their father's occupation, where occupations are grouped into eight categories and arranged in descending order of average occupational income. Upward and downward mobility is defined as any movement up or down the ordering.[17] Intergenerational mobility is a crude proxy for the nonexistent data on life-cycle mobility of the offspring, but it is strong enough to at least support broad inferences about the latter.

Overall, Table 6 shows rather moderate intergenerational mobility as of 1963, considering the country's high economic growth rates since the late 1930s. Only 19 percent of the economically active were engaged in higher earning occupations than their fathers, 11.2 percent were in lower yielding ones, while almost 70 percent remained in their fathers' occupations. The upwardly mobile were heavily concentrated in the top four categories (populated by less than one-fourth of the economically active), while the downwardly mobile gravitated to manual labor categories. More specifically, 76 percent of the upwardly mobile were in the top four occupations, while around 70 percent of the downwardly mobile were in nonagricultural manual labor categories.[18] The broad inference is that on the average upward mobility raised the life-cycle income of young entrants into the higher income occupations of Table 5, but not of those in the manual wage labor and agricultural categories. Upward mobility in the Mexican case reinforced the upward divergence of the inequality trend of permanent income from the point income estimates of Tables 1–3.

It is tempting to try to quantify that divergence, but easy to resist the temptation. In the first place, the age-income profiles of Table 5, obtained from survey income unadjusted for underreporting, probably understate both the levels and curvatures of the profiles of the affluent occupations more than of the low yielding ones.[19] Second, cross-sectional profiles for one survey year tell us nothing about the degree of stability of these profiles.[20] Finally, one would need more direct information on life-cycle occupational mobility than is given by Table 6. These gaps notwithstanding, Tables 4–6 suffice to establish

Table 6 / Intergenerational Occupational Mobility in Mexico, 1963

Occupations	Number of Occupational Categories	Percentage of of Economically Active Mexicans	Occupation of Economically Active in Relation to Father's Occupation (%)		
			Higher Yielding Occupation	Lower Yielding Occupation	Same Occupation
Managerial, professional, sales, and clerical	4[a]	23.1	63.0	10.2	26.8
Manual labor, nonagricultural	3[b]	28.4	14.7	27.5	57.8
Agriculture, hunting, fishing	1[c]	48.5	0.6	2.1	97.3
All occupations	8	100.0	19.0	11.2	69.8

Source: José Luis Reyna, "Occupational Mobility: The Mexican Case," in Stanley M. Davis and Louis W. Goodman (eds.), *Workers and Managers in Latin America* (Lexington, Mass.: D.C. Heath, 1972), pp. 116–17, Tables 18-4, 18-5.

[a]Categories are: occupations; managers and directors, except in agriculture; professionals and technicians; clerks and kindred people; salesmen.

[b]Categories are: labor force in mining; artisans and workers directly related to production; workers not directly related to production.

[c]Categories are: labor force in agriculture, hunting, and fishing.

the qualitative conclusion that our point income estimates of the post-war trends towards greater inequality are lower-bound estimates.

INCOME DISTRIBUTION TRENDS, 1885–1950

For this period, the trends in the size distribution of income have to be deduced from sketchier and less suitable data since household income-expenditure surveys are nonexistent. However, for the fast growth period, from 1939 to 1950, IBRD national income accounts provide the basis for some fairly persuasive inferences.[21] These are, according to Navarrete,[22] (1) per capita nonwage income rose faster than national per capita income; (2) the average real wage of agricultural workers—36 percent of all wage-earners and 19.6 percent of all those who were economically active in 1950—fell around 11 percent, while the average real wage of nonagricultural workers declined about 6 percent; (3) the heavy migration of rural labor to higher-wage urban employment and to field work north of the Rio Grande more than compensated for the intrasectoral decline of real wages, so that nationally real income per worker rose one-third; (4) the above trends necessarily imply a worsening of the size distribution of income.

There is no disagreement among Mexican economists about the general inferences, though there is some over the details. National income statisticians contend that Navarrete underestimated the rise of nonagricultural income from ownership and hence the decline of the wage share.[23] Her conservative estimates suffice, however, to push back the onset of Mexico's rising income inequality trend to the beginning of World War II.

Can it be pushed back further? Singer also reports a consensus among Mexican economists that the period from 1921 to 1940, in which statistical trails virtually peter out, was also one of rising income inequality.[24] Despite the lack of numbers, the qualitative case is persuasive. The preceding revolutionary decade had been one of violent socioeconomic upheaval, heavy losses to land-owning and mining interests, and increased militancy of urban labor. After 1921, with the new bourgeois elite firming its political control and with a moderate revival of GNP growth,[25] it is a reasonable conjecture that the upper income shares and the Gini coefficient, depressed by the revolutionary leveling, rebounded at least somewhat.

While there is no adequate basis for numerical estimates of either the extent of the revolutionary income leveling or of the postrevolutionary rebound, it is possible to construct an upper-bound estimate of prerevolutionary income distribution to serve as a quasi-quantitative benchmark. To do this, we use well-known socioeconomic features of the Porfiriato era to delineate a general shape of the Lorenz curve for 1910. We then give numerical content to this shape by working back to 1910 from 1975 estimates of disposable income and subsistence income by means of historical series of real GNP per capita. Since the objective is a maximal plausible concentration estimate, the curve shaping and the data filling are intended to err on the high side.

The Porfiriato gave Mexico its first postcolonial economic boom. From 1885 to 1910, output per head rose about 50 percent; the chief growth sectors were mining, transportation, public works, and manufacturing.[26] Foreign equity capital and loans financed over half the investment in this period, while private Mexican wealth accumulation centered largely in agriculture and urban property. Agricultural output grew slowly, but land concentration, encouraged by government policies, reached phenomenal proportions by 1910. The "enrichez-vous, messieurs" development strategy of the Porfiriato also included forced labor in the fields, suppression of unionism, a regressive tax structure, and minimal expansion of primary education and social services. In 1910, 80 percent of the population was still rural, and about the same percentage was illiterate. There is no question, therefore, that the Porfiriato boom was marked by rising income inequality.[27]

To simulate an upper-bound Lorenz distribution for 1910, we first assume: (a) that the lowest 60 percent of families merely obtained "subsistence" income;[28] (b) that each decile in the 60–90 percent range received 10 percent more income than the preceding decile (which gives the 9th decile an average family income only one-third above "subsistence"); (c) that 80 percent of the remaining share, garnered by the top decile, went to the top half of that decile. Assumptions (b) and (c) are chosen to generate the maximum concentration of income distribution above "subsistence" that is consistent with a modest curvature of the Lorenz distribution in the upper middle-income range. Under these assumptions, the degree of income concentration varies with the ratio of "subsistence" to average family income, which fixes the size of the residual going to the top decile.

To fix that residual we use as the starting point 1975 per capita disposable income, 10,840 pesos or US$867. Applying an annual growth rate of 1.7 percent for the period from 1910 to 1975 reduces 1910 disposable income per capita to $290 in 1975 prices.[29] "Subsistence" income in 1910 is taken to be the lowest adjusted family income of the lowest quintile in Table A-6, which is that of 1975. There are, however, two candidates in that table—2,394 and 1,628 pesos, each in 1950 prices. In 1975 prices, alternative (1) is equivalent to 11,395 pesos and alternative (2) to 7,749 pesos. Dividing by 5.3, the average family size of the lowest quintile, gives a per capita "subsistence" in 1975 prices of 2,150 pesos or US$172 for alternative (1) and 1,462 pesos or US$117 for alternative (2).[30]

In Table 7 the two alternative simulations of 1910 income shares and associated Gini coefficients are compared with the adjusted and unadjusted income equivalents for 1975. It is evident that even the Gini coefficient of Variant II falls short of the 1975 Ginis. The top 5 percent capture almost half of the total income in Variant II, but the effort is more than offset by the smaller share going to the top two quintiles.[31] This is plausible; the middle classes were much less prominent in the Porfiriato than in 1975.

Is Variant II truly an upper-bound estimate? From the contrast between I and II, it is apparent that the 1910 simulations are quite sensitive to the choice of "subsistence." Thus, reducing it to US$100 elevates the share of the top decile to 66.9 and the Gini to 0.602, so that the late Porfiriato would regain first place in the income concentration derby.

However, additional information can be brought to bear to limit the feasible "subsistence" choice set. One is that heterogeneity of both land tenure and of the labor income structure of the hacienda was not negligible, even in the Porfiriato.[32] To allow for this requires modifying assumption (b) by shifting the first inflection point of the Lorenz curve down from the 6th to a lower income decile, e.g., to the 4th decile. For any given "subsistence" value this has the following com-

Table 7 / Size Distribution of Income, 1910 and 1975

Percentile Income Class	Income Shares (%)			
	1910		1975	
	Variant I[a]	Variant II[b]	Unadjusted Incomes[c]	Adjusted Incomes[d]
96–100	34.4	48.9	30.6	35.9
91–95	8.4	12.2	12.9	15.2
81–90	7.9	5.4	16.6	15.0
61–80	13.7	9.3	19.9	16.2
41–60	11.9	8.1	11.8	9.7
1–40	23.7	16.1	8.2	8.0
Gini coefficient	0.367	0.547	0.570	0.579

[a]1910 "subsistence" income equal to alternative (1) income of lowest quintile for 1975 in Table A-6.

[b]1910 "subsistence" income equal to alternative (2) income of lowest quintile for 1975 in Table A-6.

[c]Series A income shares of Table 2 and Gini coefficient of Table 1.

[d]Series B income shares of Table 2 and Gini Coefficient of Table 1.

putational consequences: it lowers the per capita income of the lowest 40 percent around 5 percent below that "subsistence," it raises the shares of the 5th to 9th deciles at the expense of the top decile, and it lowers the Gini coefficient slightly. For a $100 "subsistence," the per capita income of the lowest 40 percent is $95, the share of the top decile declines to 64.9 and the Gini to 0.599. To exceed the 0.579 Gini for adjusted incomes in 1975 requires selecting a Porfiriato "subsistence" below $106, which implies an income below $100 for the lowest two quintiles.

The key limit to realism is now the income of the lowest 40 percent and its implications for consumption. Data from the end of the 1960s suggest that even a $117 "subsistence" may be straining the limit. Thus, the 1970 population census, which included questions on the type of food consumed in the week prior to the census day, records that 22 percent of all families had zero consumption of meat, eggs, milk, and fish.[33] And in the 1968 income-expenditure survey 65 percent of total food consumption by weight of the lowest quintile was in corn, beans, and cooking grease.[34]

For the lowest quintile, 1968 was a relatively good year; its per capita income in 1975 prices was $130.[35] In Mexico, corn and beans are, in the jargon of consumption theory, the two major "inferior" foods, for which quantity consumed rises when income declines.[36] Applying the negative corn and beans income elasticities to a $117 "subsistence" income raises the food consumption weight of corn and beans to 73 percent. Allowing for income curvature in the lowest 60 percent of the Porfiriato distribution further raises the corn-bean weight of the lowest two quintiles to 80 percent. The corresponding percentages for a $100 "subsistence" are 86 and 92. The lowest 2 quintiles thus approach a purely corn-bean diet, sans chile, squash, or pulque.

An additional insight on the limit imposed by realism is obtained from data on the ratio of the market value of food to the market value of total consumption expenditures, cash and imputed, associated with different "subsistence" incomes. In 1968, the value of food for the lowest quintile was 64 percent of its total consumption, while the elasticity of food to total consumption for the lowest two quintiles was 0.9.[37] The "subsistence" of less than $106, required to generate a 1910 Gini higher than that for 1975, implies a food-to-total-consumption ratio of above 0.66 for the lowest two quintiles. This means an average value of annual nonfood consumption—shelter, fuel, clothing, utensils, furnishings, and so forth—by the lowest two quintiles of less than $34 per person in 1975 prices.

Perhaps the coup de grace is the fact that accepting a $106 subsistence income as reasonable implies that the real income of the lowest quintile rose around 50 percent between 1910 and 1950, when annual per capita GNP growth was 1.3 percent, but fell 21 percent between 1950 and 1975, when the GNP per capita growth doubled.[38] There is direct evidence for the postwar decline, but no qualitative or statistical basis for inferring a prior rise as high as 50 percent.[39] It is thus much more plausible to choose a higher value for Mexico's 1910 "subsistence" income and accept its consequence, a higher overall concentration of income in 1975 than in 1910.

SECULAR GROWTH-EQUITY RELATIONSHIPS IN MEXICO
AND THE PARABOLIC KUZNETS CURVES

With Tables 2 and 7 providing numerical benchmarks, several generalizations about secular distributional trends in Mexico between 1885 and 1975 can now be deduced. Income concentration, as measured by Gini coefficients, rose in the Porfiriato and fell during the Revolution, but a renewed rise brought it beyond the pre-Revolutionary peak by the late 1960s or early 1970s. However, behind this rising trend are diverging paths of the relative shares of various income groups. (a) The share of the lowest 40 percent has fallen strongly and persistently, with no sign of bottoming out in the postwar years. (b) The share of the top decile has also trended downward slightly, with the secular fall of the share of the upper half of the decile offsetting the rising share of the lower half of the decile. (c) The share of the top quintile has, however, been tending upward. (d) The 7th to 9th deciles and the 91st to 95th percentiles have been the strongest relative gainers, while the combined share of the 5th and 6th deciles probably fell during the Porfiriato, rose until World War II, and fell back thereafter, with the oscillations around a horizontal secular trend line.[40]

In general, Mexican income distribution in the period from 1885 to 1975 followed neither the humped Kuznets curve for overall income concentration or for the share of the top 20 percent nor the Kuznets U-curves for the shares of the lowest 60 percent and its subdivisions. As of 1975, it had traced out only the left or unequalizing phases of the postulated curves. Moreover, Mexico's unequalizing phases have already endured longer than the five to six decades that Kuznets suggested was typical of nineteenth-century industrialization in Europe and the United States. They have endured longer even though that overworked proxy for general structural transformation, output per capita, has risen substantially higher in Mexico since 1885 than the

Table 8 / *Turning Point Incomes and Relative Shares from Cross-Country Kuznets Curves Compared with Mexican Income and Relative Shares in 1975*

Income Class	GNP per Capita at Turning Point (U.S.$ at 1965–71 prices)[a]		Income Shares at Turning Point (%)		Mexican Shares in 1975 (%)	
	LDCs and Advanced Market Economies	LDCs only	LDCs and Advanced Market Economies	LDCs only	Unadjusted Income	Adjusted Income
81–100 percentiles	364	363	57.6	58.7	60.1	66.1
41–80 percentiles	291	—[b]	30.9	—[b]	31.7	25.9
Lowest 60 percentiles	412	364	23.3	22.4	18.4	17.7
Lowest 40 percentiles	468	371	11.3	10.8	7.9	8.0
Lowest 20 percentiles	593	381	3.8	3.7	1.9	2.6

Sources: Cross-country turning point data computed from regressions in Montek Ahluwalia, "Inequality, Poverty and Development," *Journal of Development Economics*, vol. 3 (December 1976), Table 1. Mexican shares are from Table 2.

[a]Mexico's 1975 GNP per capita (1965–71 prices) = $620.

[b]No statistically significant regression value.

increases associated with the unequalizing nineteenth-century phases delineated by Kuznets.

A comparison of the Mexican data with Ahluwalia's cross-country regressions—which produce parabolic Kuznets curves with per capita income, not time, on the horizontal axis—turns up other interesting contrasts. Table 8 gives the income per capita and the income shares at the turning points of each of the Ahluwalia curves, along with the corresponding Mexican relative shares for 1975. Although Mexican per capita GNP in 1975 was higher than any of the turning point values in the table, the Mexican share is consistently lower than the turning point of each of the U-shaped (lower income) Kuznets curves, and is higher than that for the hump-shaped top quintile curve.

Table 9 shows that the elasticities of real income with respect to GNP per capita also move in opposite directions. Those for cross-country Kuznets curves rise, which is to be expected, since the curves are U-shaped. However, the Mexican elasticities, based on time series data, declined for the equivalent increases of GNP per capita. That is, the downward sweep of the income shares of the lowest three quintiles in Mexico accelerated after 1950, indeed probably after 1940.[41]

Table 9 / Arc Elasticities of Real Income with Respect to GNP per Capita: Cross-Country Kuznets Curves and Mexican Time Series

Increase of GNP per Capita[a]	Income Class		
	Lowest 60%	Lowest 40%	Lowest 20%
From $200 to $330[b]			
LDCs and advanced market economies	0.93	0.86	0.76
LDCs only	0.87	0.82	0.80
Mexico	0.92	0.77	0.58
From $330 to $620[c]			
LDCs and advanced market economies	1.02	0.99	0.92
LDCs only	1.09	1.10	1.09
Mexico	0.47	0.11	−0.35

Sources: Cross-country arc elasticities are computed from regressions in Ahluwalia, "Inequality," Table 1. Mexican 1910–1950 elasticities are based on an assumed $117 "subsistence" in 1910 with Lorenz curve inflection at the 40th percentile; GNP growth rates from Enrique Pérez López, "The National Product of Mexico: 1895–1964," Tables 1, 3, in *Mexico's Recent Economic Growth: The Mexican View*, Institute of Latin American Studies, Latin American Monograph No. 10 (Austin: University of Texas Press, 1967). Mexican 1950–75 elasticities are derived from Table A-6 quintile real incomes and GNP growth estimates from official national accounts.
[a]Measured in U.S. dollars in 1965–71 prices.
[b]Increase of Mexican real GNP per capita, 1910–50.
[c]Increase of Mexican real GNP per capita, 1950–75.

Growth-Equity Theorizing and the Mexican Case

Is Mexico an anomaly or a serious warning against projecting Kuznets curves on the LDCs? Kuznets himself was uncertain whether his historic curves would be replicated by LDCs that were industrializing from diverse initial conditions in quite different technological contexts from that of the nineteenth century. Ahluwalia concluded his "primarily exploratory paper" with doubts that growth-equity time paths of LDCs can be "adequately captured" by cross-country analysis.[42] This concluding section ventures beyond skepticism and argues that the Mexican experience provides insights on why historic and cross-country Kuznets curves and their theoretical rationalizations are unreliable bases for generalizing about growth-equity time paths of twentieth-century industrializing LDCs.

There appear to be three main theoretical supports for the universality of Kuznets-type curves. One focuses on intersectoral shifts between agriculture and industry. The second emphasizes the role of the accumulation and diffusion of human capital in propelling the growth and diffusion of output per capita. The third postulates a causal chain from economic growth to mass political mobilization to egalitarian policies. What we want to show is that each of these theoretical supports is flawed, and that the Mexican experience highlights some of the flaws.

The intersectoral shift explanation postulates that during early industrialization labor productivity is higher and output grows faster in industry than in agriculture, drawing rural migrants to industry and supportive urban services. Hence even if income distribution is similar in the two sectors, overall income inequality increases for a time as labor shifts from the initially more numerous rural to the more productive urban sector. A turning point eventually comes because diminishing the agricultural share of the labor force reduces the negative impact of the urban-rural productivity gap on overall income distribution, while emerging rural labor shortages eventually force mechanization and other labor-saving improvements in agriculture that narrow the productivity gap.

The model can be embellished. If inequality is greater for urban than for rural incomes an intersectoral labor productivity gap is not essential for generating parabolic growth-inequality curves. Conversely, the interaction of intersectoral differences of inequality and of labor productivity affects the steepness and length of the unequalizing phase. When it is thus embellished, the model generates families of parabolic curves.[43] However, although it describes a dynamic process, the model has no explicit time dimension. Timelessness protects it from decisive refutation, but it also weakens its explanatory power. Mexican income inequality may yet reach a turning point. *Quién sabe?*

Placing the model in an historical time frame reveals another weakness: its failure to explore complications resulting from the varying evolution of property rights, technology, consumer demand, demography, and labor markets accompanying the growth process on the model's parameters. Yet if these evolve so as to produce rising inequality in one or both of the sectors concomitant with rising output and labor productivity, there need be no turning point even within the algebra of the model. The model thus obtains its turning points with the aid of two implicit assumptions: that the institutional matrix determining private property rights is not evolving in an unequalizing direction, and that economic growth eventually produces full employment, chronic excess demand for labor, and broadly rising urban and rural real wages. The universal validity of neither assumption is obvious. The above-mentioned trends can go in directions that heighten dualism and labor surpluses despite prolonged economic growth, as they have in Mexico both prior to and after the leveling Revolution.

Thus the Porfiriato railroad boom, by sharply raising the expected returns from lands serviced by new roads, encouraged massive land grabbing of communal village holdings through legal chicanery rather than free market purchases—and with the enthusiastic support of the government.[44] Labor shortages on the export-oriented plantations of southern Mexico were overcome by the use of impressed labor—*los enganchados*—dragooned from other regions of Mexico, again with strong government backing.[15] These and other Porfiriato responses to expanding economic opportunity—such as debt peonage, which occurred also in the pre-World War I history of many other LDCs—would have been readily recognized by Marx as primitive capital accumulation at work.

The 1917 Constitution outlawed such barbarities, and laws and instruments for carving up the *latifundia* and promoting peasant agriculture were instituted during the interwar years. But after the heady days of Cárdenas, the maximum legal limits on the size of farms and prohibitions against the alienation of ejidal property came to be increasingly evaded by various subterfuges, while government agencies supplying credit and technical assistance to small farmers were allowed to fall into corruption and decay. Since 1940 the lion's share of lands made arable by government water projects and accessible through public road building has been appropriated by large holders. The consequence has been a rising concentration of land ownership, a rising share of landless workers in the rural labor force, and a rising rate of rural underemployment.[46]

Farm output per worker rose 4.3 percent per annum between 1940 and 1960, exceeding the growth of labor productivity in industry.[47] But the large-farm group, which provided almost all the increase of output and labor productivity, has employed a miniscule percentage of the postwar increment to the rural labor force. Most of that increment has been absorbed by the slowly improving *ejidos* and the stagnating *minifundia,* so that by 1970 some 68 percent of the rural labor force were classified as underemployed. Expansion and mechanization of the large farms has been strongly encouraged by tax incentives and subsidized credit and fertilizer prices, as well as by the agri-business orientation of rural public works programs. Critics contend that the policy biases have promoted allocative inefficiencies: lower utilization rates of land and equipment on the large farms than on the *ejidos,* as well as rising underemployment.[48]

In any event, two of the conditions that are necessary for the intersectoral shift model to generate a turning point have not been met. Rural labor surpluses have grown with the rise in output and labor productivity since 1940, and the postwar trend of rural inequality has been upward rather than stable.[49] Responsibility may fall more heavily on the agri-business bias of post-Cárdenas agricultural development strategy than on "natural" market dynamics. But since similar biases have characterized the agricultural policies of many LDCs—especially in Latin America—the validity of using the model to predict Kuznets curve trends depends more on the pressures guiding LDC development policies, about which the model has nothing explicit to say, than on the push of competitive market forces, on which it takes its stand.

Overall inequality of urban incomes seems to have followed a relatively horizontal trend in postwar Mexico, and to have been overtaken in the past decade by rural inequality.[50] However, employment expansion in the industrial sector has been rather unspectacular, with a tendency to diminish. Thus, while the annual growth of industrial value added increased from 7 percent in 1950–60 to 8 percent in 1960–70, the employment elasticity with respect to industrial output fell from 0.62 to 0.53.[51] Secondary and tertiary sector employment grew in the latter decade at slightly more than the demographic growth rate, far from sufficient to offset the 1.45 percent annual decline of primary sector employment.[52] By 1970, the "underemployed" had risen to 44.5 percent of the economically active population; two-fifths of this group was in the nonagricultural sectors.[53] The economically active population has been growing at an even faster rate in the 1970s, while job creation slowed further—hence the "underemployment" percentage undoubtedly rose further in the 1970s.[54]

This could cause a shift of urban income distribution from constancy to rising inequality, for the postwar constancy of urban income distribution has been the outcome of offsetting trends in the income shares of subgroups. The share of the top 5 percent declined somewhat, that of the lowest 60 percent declined more, while the shares of the 60th to 95th percentiles rose substantially. Most urban salaried employees and unionized workers in the public and private sectors are in this last income group, along with many self-employed professionals and owner-employers of small businesses. The wage-salary members of this group have benefited not only from excess demand in the labor market for specialized skills, but also from the narrow incidence of the *conquistas sociales* in postwar Mexico. That is, social welfare programs and government supported increases of wages, salaries, and private fringe benefits have favored chiefly the more affluent sectors of the urban labor force.[55]

Constancy may give way to rising inequality in the distribution of urban incomes if the forces generating increasing urban underemployment persist, since that would further depress the relative share of the lowest 60 percent. Income concentration could also rise if the *conquistas sociales* are curbed, not in order to redistribute them more equitably, but to reduce their overall impact on labor costs and the government budget, as the López Portillo regime seems to have been intent on doing as part of its anti-inflation program. There is thus a fair likelihood that rising inequality may supersede the postwar constancy of urban income distribution, which would remove yet another key requirement for generating a Kuznets curve turning point in accordance with the intersectoral shift model.

The proposition that human capital accumulation generates Kuznets curves requires a belief in the general validity of the marginal productivity theory of factor pricing plus the acceptance of three special assumptions. One is that human capital is necessarily more dispersive than physical capital accumulation, since there are tighter limits to individual accumulation of the former than of the latter. The second is that long-run marginal product curves for classes of labor skills—at least relatively aggregated ones—are rather flat, so that wage differences between skill classes tend to diminish slowly despite the disproportionate growth of the skill classes. In effect, skill supply creates its own demand. The third assumption is that the elasticity of substitution between formal education and job experience in the production of human capital is less than one; the more schooling the higher the income, so individuals find it rewarding to extend schooling up to the point where the discounted value of the delayed but higher income stream to be derived from more schooling equals that to be derived from taking a job sooner. At first, new skills in a newly developing economy adhere to a minority of the work force and income inequality increases, but as the skills spread the turning point eventually comes.

As it has not yet come in Mexico, one can blame perverse educational policies or fault the economics of the theory. The former implies that the human capital model's prediction of Kuznets curves depends, as does the intersectoral shift model, on supportive policy decisions about whose political determinants neither model has anything explicit to say. The latter implies that even with egalitarian educational policies the model's specification of economic dynamics is flawed.

Mexican data partially support each view. Until the educational upsurge under Echeverría, the postwar ratio of educational expenditures to GNP, though rising, had hovered below the average for Latin America, although the skewing of educational outlays towards the urban sector and towards university education has been at the Latin American average. Income inequality has also been rising in many other Latin American countries,[56] suggesting, if one accepts the underlying economics of the model, that the skewed composition has had a stronger influence on the course of income distribution than has the rising level of educational services.

But the model's underlying economics is also debatable. The stock of human capital and its accumulation are merely grandiloquent metaphors. What are measurable are logical derivatives of the theory, mainly positive correlations between income differences and years of schooling, and the relative constancy of income differences between skill levels within countries. Such statistical regularities can be accounted for by other theoretical structures than neoclassical human capital theory. There is the thesis that, rather than merely augmenting skills, schooling filters the naturally more able or disciplined from the rest. In another variant, school systems are also social filters, sorting the young by socioeconomic background and cultural finish and enabling firms more efficiently to select recruits that fit the various social class layers of the firm's hierarchy of commanders and subordinates.[57] One important corollary of screening is that raising the general level of schooling proportionately causes firms to raise the educational requisites for each layer of its job hierarchy in order to preserve the effectiveness of schooling as a filter of the desired qualities. A corollary of social filtering is that democratizing higher education induces firms to use other screening tests, such as prestige rankings of the higher institutions, to preserve their social class hierarchy. When filtering is a major function of schooling, the accumulation of human capital via schooling may not generate Kuznets curves even if the composition of educational services is not badly skewed.

In Mexico, years of schooling correlate positively with income and the rate of growth of employment has also been greater the higher the schooling level.[58] But most university students have also come from families in the top quintile,[59] while a recent study of criteria used to hire staff employees in 33 large Mexican firms found the following:[60]

1. The firms were interested in years of education and diplomas, but indifferent to academic performance.
2. Educational qualifications for menial staff positions have tended to be raised when the supply of applicants has risen.
3. Ex-post evaluations of the employed by their supervisors show little correlation between educational level and job performance.
4. Secondary and university graduates of working class origin are deprecated by personnel executives as "educated people without culture," and the rise in their numbers has led some of the firms to give preference to applicants from fee-paying private universities.
5. For semiprofessional positions the firms preferred applicants with a couple of years of university education over graduates of middle-level technical schools, since the latter lacked "cultural development."

Only some of these data fit the economics of the human capital model, whereas all conform to the filtering thesis. Moreover, the heavy emphasis on cultural screening uncovered by the IDS study should not be surprising. Prejudice against *"indio"* traits are quite strong among the middle and upper classes of Mexico and other mestizo countries. Yet one could still contend plausibly that the emphasis would fade and the economics of the human capital model would dominate were job openings to catch up with the number of applicants. After all, British inequality, according to Kuznets, peaked before 1900, though the cultural gulf separating Disraeli's "two nations" was still in full flood.

The ultimate fall-back for both the human capital and intersectoral shift models is, therefore, the proposition that the persistence of labor surpluses in Mexico and other rapidly growing LDCs has been due to perverse *conquistas sociales* and import substitution policies which promote the adoption of excessively labor-saving techniques. LDCs that, like Mexico, pursued such policies to enlarge economic opportunities by broadening their productive structure have paradoxically retarded the advent of full employment and prolonged the unequalizing phases of their Kuznets curves. The two models are transformed by this fall-back from descriptive to purely normative models. However, the retreat can be to either of two conflicting normative refuges: to the benign neoclassical assessment of free market dynamics or to planning models that require redirecting these dynamics through controls, taxes, and subsidies in order to eliminate labor surpluses.

The benign neoclassical view gets rid of the possibility of chronic labor surpluses by its specifications of the production function governing the choice of techniques by the individual firm and the utility function governing the choice of goods by the individual consumer. The production function postulates that a wide range of alternative techniques, using different proportions of capital and skilled and unskilled labor, are available to the firm for producing its output. The range is independent of the size of the firm, and though it is alterable by technical innovations, the market for technology makes innovations accessible to noninnovators, so that the range changes equivalently for all firms. Which of the techniques is least costly depends on the relative prices of the requisite inputs. Hence if wages and other input prices are allowed to move freely in response to excess supply or demand, the production function insures the elimination of surpluses of labor and other reproducible inputs through the substitution of techniques.

The consumer can get equal levels of utility from different combinations of goods, but with his budget and the prices of goods determined, one combination will stand forth as maximizing his utility. An independence postulate is also invoked to reinforce the alleged equilibrating role of relative prices—the consumer's utility from his chosen bundle of goods is impervious to what his neighbors are consuming, except insofar as their consumption affects the market prices of goods in the bundle.

This specification of wide substitution possibilities in production and consumption and the various independence postulates associated with it eliminates the persistence of labor surpluses in free market economies. In a benign neoclassical economy, the accumulation of physical and human capital is reflected in progressive skill upgrading of the labor force, rising wages of the diminishing unskilled, and in Kuznets curves. Variations of the composition of goods demanded and produced are irrelevant. The market efficiently reaches equilibrium regardless of compositional trends.

The key flaws in this benign view are the independence postulates. The assumption that economies and diseconomies of scale require no changes in input proportions violates basic physical and probabilistic laws governing technology and, except with fanciful specifications of economies of scale, such an assumption is also inconsistent with the fundamental neoclassical assumption of the ubiquity of profit-maximizing behavior. The postulate that the ability of producers to vary techniques is generally independent of their ability to innovate does not accord with the evidence from microstudies of technical choice. The postulate that consumers' utility functions are independent of one another arbitrarily eliminates status-seeking and other Veblenesque motives for acquiring consumer goods.[61]

Without the unwarranted independence postulates, the benign employment and growth-equity properties of market economies turn problematic. The prospects for their realization in late-developing countries are constrained both by the external trends of new technology and by the cultural determinants of their consumption norms for status goods.

The relevant trends in technology are the continual rise since the mid-nineteenth century in the minimum sizes of firms required to efficiently produce the changing gamut of modern consumer and producer goods, and the parallel rise in the complexity of cognitive skills needed to innovate modern technologies. The rising minimum efficient scale narrows the range of economically viable substitution possibilities per product for small producers, with zero range raising the minimum financial costs of entry. Hence, with rising economies of scale, capital accumulation in the capital-scarce late developers becomes an increasingly concentrated process. Rising cognitive requirements for technological innovation create "technological gaps" and unreciprocated technological flows from advanced economies to dependent late developers that further reduce the range of labor-intensive alternatives in the latter.

Since both scale and cognitive sophistication vary between products, trends in the output mix can dampen or intensify the rise of aggregate capital intensity and the fall of the employment elasticity of output growth in the late developer. Thus the trend in the composition of consumer demand, which strongly shapes the output mix, is a strategic variable affecting the employment-output elasticity and the course of underemployment. And with status consumption and interdependent utility functions, the compositional trend is affected, in turn, by the cultural determinants of status in each country, as well as by trends in its relative prices and its level and distribution of income.

British nineteenth-century and Japanese twentieth-century experiences illustrate this point. British income inequality in the nineteenth century may well have approximated twentieth-century Mexico's. But the nineteenth-century scale requirements for the production of status goods and producer equipment were low, and cognitive requirements for innovation were still largely within the reach of relatively unschooled but gifted artisans and small entrepreneurs. Thus both the expanding incomes of the middle and upper classes and rising investment were strongly oriented towards the purchase of relatively labor-intensive goods. Because of the supportive compositional trends, the British masses, poor and undernourished through much of the century, were yet essential to the growth process, so that emerging labor scarcities after mid-century pushed up unskilled wages and helped produce a Kuznets turning point by the end of the century. Twentieth-century Japan began its modern economic growth in a less propitious technological era and with less reliance on free market forces than did Britain. But Japan was significantly aided in replicating a Kuznets growth-equity path by the tenacity of its traditional status values. These slowed the shift of elite consumption towards foreign-designed status goods, prolonging output and employment growth in the sectors producing traditional goods and encouraging their accumulation of capital and the gradual upgrading of their production processes.

In late developers where allegiance to traditional status goods by the elite is weak, twentieth-century market forces provide rather a Hobson's choice. If these forces are allowed freely to carve out their growth path they are prone to lead to enclave dualism. The chief growth pole would be the exporting of primary products where low wages and differential rents from natural resource advantages compensate for skill, managerial, and technological deficiencies. The expansion of demand for status goods would be met through imports while the traditional crafts would largely stagnate or decay, and the spread of industries producing modern consumer and producer goods would be retarded by competitive disadvantages from the above-mentioned deficiencies. Porfiriato growth was along such a path, as was that of most Latin American countries prior to World War II.

This growth path can be modified by import-substituting industrial strategies that try to redirect market forces to bring output in closer concordance with the changing composition of consumer demand. Broadening the output mix is likely to enlarge the range of skills and technological competence at a faster rate than export enclave growth, and protection and subsidies, by widening investment opportunities and reducing entrepreneurial risk, may raise the rate of capital accumulation. But when consumer demand is also shifting rapidly to new foreign-style goods, the traditional status-goods industries too quickly stagnate and decay while the bulk of private and public investment is oriented directly to the production of the changing mix of foreign-style goods—and indirectly to supplying the current inputs, equipment, infrastructure, foreign exchange, and other requirements for their production and consumption. Import-substituting growth usually elevates materially a larger percentage of the population than does export enclave growth, but import substitution is still enclave development since it is restrained from rapid diffusion by the concentrated capital accumulation and prolonged technological dependency that are essential parts of its dynamic. As the productivity and income of the modern sector grow, the gulf between it and the "traditional" economy deepens and the structural interdependence between the two weakens. With this, an increasing percentage of the poor become inessential for the growing affluence of the middle and upper classes and for the growth process. Mexico, since 1940, has followed such a growth path, but so also have many other rapidly growing and industrializing LDCs.

Table 10 illustrates some of the dependence of Mexico's secondary and tertiary sectors on middle and upper class demand. In the period from 1963 to 1975, the top 40 percent accounted for from 72 to 98 percent of household expenditures on the various categories of goods and services, with the top quintile's share ranging from 47 to 95 percent. There are suggestions of increasing trickling down to the lowest 60 percent in some of the categories, most clearly in recreational equipment (doubtlessly centered on radio and TV receivers), but by its excessive aggregation Table 10 understates the dependence of postwar growth on the consumption of the top 40 percent. In the "software" and "household durables" categories are residues of "traditional" goods— candles, huaraches, straw sombreros, clay pots, and so forth. Most of this residue had probably settled near the bottom of the income pyramid. The remaining expenditure of the lowest 60 percent on these categories and on "recreational equipment" was probably mainly on older models of modern products in the mature or even declining phases of their product cycles. On aggregate, therefore, the demand of the lowest 60 percent was concentrated on products whose national sales were stagnating, while the top 20 40 percent made up the market for successive new goods in the dynamic growth phases of their product cycles.[62] The expansion of capacity in industry and services and new technological and marketing skills was probably even more concentrated on meeting the changing household demand of the upper 20–40 percent than is indicated by their shares of aggregate expenditures in Table 10.

This concentration has doubtlessly retarded the attainment of an efficient scale of output for many of the newer products. It has also prolonged the dependence of Mexican growth on imported technology. For example, a recent small-sample, in-depth survey found that dependence on foreign technology was less and that intrafirm innovation was greater in firms that produced standardized products than in the faster growing firms whose products were subject to frequent differentiation.[63]

Table 10 / Shares of National Household Outlays on Selected Household Items by Family Income Class: Mexico, 1963, 1968, and 1975

Percentile Income Class	Household "Software"[a]	Telephone	Electricity	Household Durables[b]	Recreational Equipment[c]	Vehicles and Accessories[d]	Vacations, Other Recreational and Cultural Services
81–100							
1963	47.5%	87.3%	53.0%	62.2%	57.6%	90.6%	78.9%
1968	56.6	91.9	52.0	52.8	59.5	94.8	58.1
1975	52.2	n.a.	n.a.	48.5	50.3	83.5	n.a.
61–80							
1963	26.1	8.7	27.5	25.9	28.1	6.6	15.3
1968	23.6	5.6	22.3	26.2	24.3	3.6	26.6
1975	22.6	n.a.	n.a.	31.4	22.2	10.5	n.a.
41–60							
1963	12.6	2.3	11.6	6.8	9.5	2.0	3.8
1968	11.6	2.0	14.0	12.1	10.9	1.1	13.1
1975	10.9	n.a.	n.a.	11.2	16.5	2.8	n.a.
0–40							
1963	13.8	1.7	7.9	5.1	4.8	0.8	2.0
1968	11.4	0.5	11.7	8.9	5.3	0.5	2.2
1975	17.2	n.a.	n.a.	8.9	10.9	3.0	n.a.

Sources: Encuesta sobre ingresos, 1963, cuadro 26-7; La distribución del ingreso, 1968, cuadro IV-2; Encuesta de ingresos, 1975, cuadro 8-2.

[a]Clothing, shoes, hats, linens and drapery, candles, laundry and cleaning materials, personal grooming articles.
[b]Furniture, utensils, kitchen articles, heating and cooling mechanisms, and durable cleaning equipment.
[c]Toys, radios, TV receivers, tape recorders, phonographs, cameras, and musical instruments.
[d]Automobiles, motorcycles, bicycles, and accessories.

A Hobson's choice format does not allow for astute policies to soften the starkness of the alternatives. The rigidity has been posed provisionally. Our purpose so far has merely been to show (1) that under twentieth-century conditions market forces push late developers more strongly towards persistently rising inequality than they did in the nineteenth century; and (2) that the benign neoclassical view, which eliminates the importance of such historical irreversibilities by arbitrary assumptions, is a fallacious basis for attributing nonappearances of growth-equity turning points primarily to policies that distort free market trends.

The normative refuge of believers in the universality of Kuznets curves who do not accept the benign neoclassical view of market forces is the belief that the starkness of Hobson's choice can be substantially modified by appropriate policies. But as a refuge its troubles are twofold. There are disagreements among policy-planners on which are the technically feasible policy alternatives that would produce more equitable growth. Granting that this set is not empty, difficulties are further compounded when the policy-makers who are to choose from the set turn out to be politicians buffeted by conflicting demands from the populace rather than omnipotent philosopher-kings. This makes the adoption of policies to reverse inequality trends depend more on the particular confluence of political forces than on intellectual conversion of political leaders. The main case for the universality of Kuznets curves is shifted from the technical feasibility of equitable growth policies to the proposition that political pressures for more equitable growth become irresistible.

In one version of the proposition, an inexorable concomitant of economic growth is the rising assertiveness of the formerly deferential masses and the democratization of politics. Since politicians are constrained by the survival rules of democratic politics to be pragmatic, ideologically flexible power-brokers, they will try to accommodate the pressures from the increasingly mobilized masses for distributive justice. Once popular in the political development literature, this version has been undercut by the recent spate of demobilizations, imposed by military politicians in tinted glasses who are equipped also with modernized techniques of surveillance and repression. These military men subscribe to development ideologies that favor capital accumulation, oriented towards servicing the modernized consumption styles of the affluent classes, rather than distributive justice.

A more modest version merely postulates an upper limit to inequality beyond which social tensions become explosive. The limit in each developing society can vary in accordance with what Hirschman calls the "tunnel effect." That effect has a benign phase during which popular tolerance of rising inequality is high and a malignant phase during which tolerance changes to resentment. In the benign phase, those left behind in the income race see the gainers as harbingers of their own future success; the second phase comes with the realization that their destiny is merely to fall further behind.[64] Limits to inequality are not necessarily turning points. However, Hirschman suggests that LDC elites are prone to overestimate the benign phase, so that "the development process . . . is exposed to crisis and perhaps disaster, even after lengthy periods of forward movement."[65] This makes the incidence of turning points in the LDCs more dependent on revolution than the projectors of universal Kuznets curves have probably had in mind.

Table 11 indicates that postwar Mexican policy-makers have been

Table 11 / Trends of the Ratios of Real Income Between Income Classes*

Percentile Income Class	Average Income		Percent Increase over Next Lower Row	
	1950–57	1968–75	1950–57	1968–75
Income Not Adjusted for Underdeclaration				
96–100	1563.4	2645.0	182.3	109.2
91–95	553.7	1264.2	27.4	70.7
81–90	434.5	740.4	55.6	70.8
61–80	279.2	433.5	71.8	69.9
41–60	162.5	255.1	15.7	57.2
21–40	140.4	162.3	40.4	144.1
1–20	100.0	66.5	—	—
National average	292.1	456.7	—	—
Income Adjusted for Underdeclaration				
96–100	2890.9	4464.0	347.7	97.2
91–95	645.7	2263.7	26.4	206.4
81–90	511.0	1096.9	65.1	91.9
61–80	309.5	571.5	52.0	68.7
41–60	198.0	338.7	41.0	91.1
21–40	140.4	177.2	40.4	96.7
1–20	100.0	90.1	—	—
National average	377.8	698.6	—	—

Source: See Table A-6.
*Average real income of lowest quintile, 1950–57 = 100.

betting rather heavily on the persistence of the benign phase of the tunnel effect. The increases in real incomes, obtained by all but the lowest quintile, have been accompanied by a persistent widening of relative income differences between all classes in the table, except between those in the top decile. Were the tunnel effect to enter a malignant phase, Table 11 suggests that institutional stability could be shaken by rising discontent from the middle income classes as well as from the poor and underemployed.

Are Mexican policy-makers capable of tilting towards equity in time to avoid an explosive crisis? Until recently, the prevailing view among political analysts was a qualified yes. Mexico was seen as an imperfect one-party democracy, and the dominant party, the Party of Institutionalized Revolution (PRI), as ultimately responsive to the economic demands of its predominantly peasant, wage, and salaried class membership. Today the dominant view is a qualified no. Mexico is lumped in with the rightist authoritarian regimes of Latin America as inextricably committed to growth over equity. This change of interpretation has obviously been due more to a change of analytic spectacles than to a change of behavior, since Mexico's formal and informal political institutions have been remarkably stable since 1940.

The older view carped at the country's democratic imperfections, the corruption and backsliding of the PRI, and the incompleteness of the Revolution, but accepted conditionally the official rationale for the post-Cárdenas growth policy. That rationale was delicately put by a leading PRI economist and *político* in a 1948 article: "The conviction that the decisive thing is to produce more has defeated the generous, although vague, decision to achieve a fair distribution of wealth. No standard of justice, however high, will give Mexico a better standard of living if the collective poverty of the country is not conquered first."[66]

This rationale embodies a potential Kuznets curve: increase productivity, then tilt towards equity. The revisionist view of Mexico's politics has grown in reaction to the failures of two recent presidents, Adolfo López Mateos (1958–64) and Luís Echeverría (1970–76), who tried to tilt towards equity. López Mateos quickly backed off from his attempt to institute some modest tax reforms and to implement existing agrarian reform legislation more vigorously, when his efforts were met with a drop in private investment and with intra-PRI resistance.[67] Echeverría, more persistent, was also unable to fulfill his commitments to tax and agrarian reform. His reformist rhetoric and greater persistence, however, gained for him the enmity of Mexico's domestic and foreign business community. He left office in a major foreign exchange crisis and amidst rumors of a military coup, a novel and portentous phenomenon in postwar Mexico.[68]

The tenacity of business resistance to these attempts to move towards equity helped stimulate the revisionism. But a more important factor has probably been the manifested inability of two PRI presidents, despite the enormous powers that the Mexican political system allegedly gave them to pass and execute legislation, to institute moderate measures intended to favor the main constituencies making up the PRI. To revisionists, this puts the PRI's role in a different light. No longer can it be viewed as a corrupt but basically populist movement. Its true enduring constituents have been the business classes and, reflecting this, the PRI's bonds to growth over equity have been indissoluble. In the Mexican scheme of things, the party's role is primarily to defuse discontent, using a clever mixture of revolutionary rhetoric, pageantry, and tokenism; the co-optation of potential dissident leaders by political patronage; and the destruction of those leaders who remain recalcitrant. Should the PRI lose its effectiveness, the role of holding down discontent and protecting the investment climate would most likely pass to the military.[69]

It is hasty to conclude from two failed attempts that the Mexican political system is unable to tilt towards equity, and indeed revisionists differ in their assessment of the system's future flexibility and stability.[70] The impending oil bonanza will perhaps provide the crucial test. Since the government will garner much of the first-round revenues generated by the oil and gas, it may be able to tilt towards equity without substantially raising taxes on property income and to ride out investor "strikes" should it decide to raise tax rates. Whether it moves effectively in this direction should establish decisively whether the system is capable of warding off the malignant phase of the tunnel effect by producing either a Kuznets turning point or at least an asymptotic termination to rising income inequality. Oil bonanza LDCs have not had a strong track record on this, but Mexico could turn out to be an anomaly. *Quién sabe?*

Appendix

This paper presents two sets of estimates of trends in postwar Mexican income concentration and in real income per family of various income classes. The first was computed directly from the income data reported in the successive income-expenditure surveys, and the second from that income data adjusted for underdeclaration of income. Both sets of estimates show an upward trend in household income concentration during the period from 1950 to 1975, although they diverge with regard to the levels and rates of change of income concentration. They are in direct contradiction only in their calculation of the real income trend of the lowest 40 percent of households; the unadjusted income set indicates a declining and the adjusted set a rising trend, although both show falling real income for the lowest 20 percent. The income adjustments underlying the second set are arbitrary, but I believe they result in more reliable estimates of most levels and trends. The purpose of this appendix is to explain in some detail the reasons for the various adjustments and the adjustment formulas used.

INCOME AND SAVINGS UNDERESTIMATION IN THE SURVEYS

Table A-1 shows that the survey estimates of national disposable income fall well short of those given by the national accounts. Even more disconcerting is the rising trend of the shortfall, from 17.8 percent in 1950 to 38 percent in 1975. Analysis indicates that most of the shortfall results from underestimation of household income by the surveys rather than overestimation by the national accounts. Thus Section IV of Table A-1 shows the annual growth of real disposable income per capita in the period from 1950 to 1975 to have averaged 2.5 percent according to the national accounts, but only 1.5 percent according to the surveys. The first rate is in reasonable accord with the 2.8 percent growth of GNP per capita over this period. The 1.5 percent rate, on the other hand, implies a phenomenally high rise in the combined share of undistributed corporate profits, depreciation, and taxes in GNP, for which there is no supporting evidence.

The contrasting savings ratios in Table A-1 also support the inference that the rising shortfall in the income estimates is primarily due to increasing underestimation of income by the surveys. In the surveys the household savings ratios show a strong decline to negative values between 1957 and 1975. This is most implausible for a period in which annual growth of real disposable income averaged 3 percent. The national accounts surveys also show a decline in the savings ratio from 1963 to 1975, which, though much more moderate, may reflect data distortion for 1975.[71] Equally implausible in the surveys is the rise of the proportion of all families falling into income brackets with net dissavings. From 46.1 percent of all families in 1957, the proportion rises progressively to 90.4 percent in 1975 (see Section VI of Table A-1). Moreover, the excess of consumption over income of the lowest two quintiles, as shown in Table A-2, appears much greater than can

Table A-1 / National Account Estimates of Annual Consumption, Savings, and Disposable Household Income Compared with Estimates from the Income and Expenditure Surveys

	1950	1957	1963	1968	1975
I. National income accounts (in millions of current pesos)					
A. Household consumption	n.a.	n.a.	145,848	247,728	625,332
B. Household savings	n.a.	n.a.	14,784	20,580	18,744
C. Household disposable income	32,808	78,268	160,632	268,308	644,076
II. Survey estimates (in millions of current pesos)					
A. Household consumption	n.a.	50,400	114,124	174,888	414,432
B. Household savings	n.a.	6,996	−1,712	9,351	−15,024
C. Household disposable income	26,978	57,393	112,412	184,239	399,408
III. Percentage shortfall of survey estimates					
A. Consumption	n.a.	n.a.	21.7	29.4	33.7
B. Savings	n.a.	n.a.	111.6	54.6	180.1
C. Disposable income	17.8	26.7	30.0	31.3	38.0
IV. Annual per capita income (deflated by cost of living index)					
A. Peso estimates					
1. According to national accounts	1,240	1,340	1,888	2,307	2,285
2. According to surveys	1,019	1,026	1,321	1,571	1,533

B. Growth relative to 1950

1. According to national accounts	100.0	108.1	152.3	186.0	184.3
2. According to surveys	100.0	100.7	129.6	154.2	139.1
V. Household Savings Ratio					
A. National Accounts	n.a.	n.a.	9.2	7.7	2.9
B. Surveys	n.a.	12.2	−1.5	5.1	−3.8
VI. Ratio of families in net dissavings income brackets of the surveys to total families	n.a.	0.461	0.731	0.776	0.904
A. Amount of dissavings (millions of pesos)	n.a.	668	13,140	8,984	74,280
B. Dissavings as percentage of income shortfall	n.a.	9.5	27.2	10.7	30.4

Sources: For 1950 and 1957 data, Navarrete, *La distribución*, cuadros 9, 10. For 1963, 1968, 1975 national income accounts data. World Bank, *World Tables*, and unpublished World Bank Savings Estimates. For survey estimates, Banco de México, *Encuesta sobre ingresos y gastos familiares en México, 1963* (México, D.F.: Investigaciones Industriales Oficina Editorial, 1966); Banco de México, *La distribución del ingreso en México, 1968* (México, D.F.: Fondo de Cultura Económica, 1974); Centro Nacional de Información y Estadísticas del Trabajo, *Encuesta de ingresos y gastos familiares, 1975*, primera edición (México, D.F., 1977).

Table A-2 / *Effects of Raising the Income of the Lowest Two Quintiles of Households in 1963, 1968, and 1975 on the Dissavings Ratios of the 1950s Surveys*

	1963	1968	1975
I. Consumption as percentage of income before adjustment			
A. Lowest quintile	210.0	132.7	361.2
B. Next higher quintile	148.2	115.0	149.2
C. Lowest 40 percent	169.5	120.9	198.7
II. Effects of the adjustments on various components of the survey estimates			
A. In millions of pesos			
1. Added income of lowest 40 percent	6,232	2,009	32,652
2. New aggregate savings	4,520	11,360	17,628
3. New income shortfall from national accounts estimate of disposable household income	41,988	82,060	212,016
B. In percentages			
1. Increased income of lowest quintile	89.0	19.4	227.4
2. Increased income of next higher quintile	36.3	5.8	58.8
3. Increased income of lowest 40 percent	54.5	10.0	100.2
4. New national disposable income shortfall	26.1	30.6	32.9
5. Adjusted savings ratio in relation to adjusted survey income	3.8	6.1	4.1

Sources: See Table A-1.

Note: The ratio of income to reported consumption of the lowest income brackets, including in-kind income and consumption in the 1957 survey was: (1) Lowest quintile, 90 percent. (2) Next higher quintile, 92 percent. (3) Lowest 40 percent, 91 percent. Since the 1950 data base did not include in-kind income, Navarrete adjusted the 1950 reported incomes by the 1957 ratios of in-kind to cash income, and the 1957 dissavings ratio of the lowest two quintiles. This makes her "normalization" of the 1950 estimates with the 1957 survey comparable to the adjustments of the 1963, 1968, and 1975 estimates of this table.

be rationalized by either the permanent or the life-cycle income hypotheses, or by the capital and credit resources likely to be accessible to the poor.

ADJUSTING THE INCOMES OF THE LOWEST TWO QUINTILES

Our first correction was to raise the income of the lowest quintile to 90 percent of its reported consumption and that of the next higher quintile to 92 percent of its reported consumption in the 1963, 1968, and 1975 surveys, respectively. These income-consumption ratios come from the 1957 survey and were also used by Navarrete to augment her 1950 cash income with income and consumption in-kind.[72]

This adjustment probably overcompensates for underreported income of the lowest 40 percent in the last three surveys, almost certainly for 1975. In the first place, it takes the reported consumption in these surveys as correct, despite the judgment expressed in the 1963 survey report that poor families tend to overestimate their expenditures as well as underreport their income, whereas wealthy families underreport both income and expenditure.[73] Second, the adjustment assumes that the consumption-savings ratio of the lowest two quintiles is impervious to cyclical oscillations or national trends. This is inconsistent with our acceptance for adjustment purposes, albeit skeptically, of the decline in the household savings ratio between 1963 and 1975 in the national accounts. Acceptance implies that the upper 60 percent of families accounted for all the decline in the overall savings rate between 1963 and 1975, even though the real income of the lowest quintile declined, whereas that of the top 60 percent rose. Third, the adjustment formula results in the real income of the lowest 40 percent enjoying its second highest rise between 1968 and 1975 (Table A-3, Section III.B), when national per capita income fell (Table A-1, Section IV).

In computing Gini coefficients from adjusted incomes, we did not correct for the probable overadjustment of the incomes of the lowest two quintiles resulting from the adjustment formula, since this imparts merely a small downward bias to the trend of the coefficients. However, in comparing relative shares and real income trends for the various income brackets, we chose the average of the unadjusted and adjusted income trends for the lowest two quintiles as the most reasonable alternative. Averaging produces a moderate downward trend of real income for the lowest quintile, a still substantial rising trend for the next higher quintile, and a slight upward trend for the two quintiles combined.[74]

Table A-3 / Trends in Annual Average Income of the Lowest 40 Percent of Households

	1950	1957	1963	1968	1975
I. In current pesos					
A. Unadjusted for income underestimation					
1. Lowest quintile	2,064	2,964	2,692	4,099	4,099
2. Next higher quintile	2,580	4,704	5,113	8,173	13,637
3. Lowest 40 percent	2,322	3,834	3,902	6,136	8,868
B. Adjusted for income underestimation as per Table A-2					
1. Lowest quintile	2,064	2,964	5,087	4,893	11,395
2. Next higher quintile	2,580	4,704	6,970	8,412	18,117
3. Lowest 40 percent	2,322	3,834	6,028	6,652	14,756
II. Deflated by consumer price index, 1950 = 100					
A. Unadjusted income					
1. Lowest quintile	2,064	1,733	1,258	1,653	861
2. Next higher quintile	2,580	2,751	2,389	3,296	2,365
3. Lowest 40 percent	2,322	2,242	1,823	2,474	1,863
B. Adjusted for income underestimation as per Table A-2					
1. Lowest quintile	2,064	1,733	2,377	1,973	2,394
2. Next higher quintile	2,580	2,751	3,257	3,392	3,806
3. Lowest 40 percent	2,322	2,242	2,817	2,682	3,100
III. Percentage change of real income					
A. Unadjusted for income underestimation					
1. Lowest quintile	100.0	84.0	60.9	80.1	41.7
2. Next higher quintile	100.0	106.6	92.6	127.7	111.0
3. Lowest 40 percent	100.0	96.5	78.5	106.5	80.2
B. Adjusted for income underestimation as per Table A-2					
1. Lowest quintile	100.0	84.0	115.2	95.6	116.0
2. Next higher quintile	100.0	106.6	126.2	135.5	147.5
3. Lowest 40 percent	100.0	96.3	121.3	115.5	133.5

Sources: See Table A-1.

ADJUSTMENT FOR UNDERESTIMATED INCOME OF THE UPPER 60 PERCENT

Raising the incomes of the lowest two quintiles to 90 and 92 percent of their respective consumption eliminates only 12.9 percent of the income shortfall for 1963, 2.4 percent for 1968, and 13.3 percent for 1975. (Cf. line III.C of Table A-1 with line II.B.4 of Table A-2.) It leaves untouched the improbably high dissavings ratio reported by the deficit income brackets above the lowest two quintiles. For example, in 1963 these deficit brackets, encompassing almost all of the 3rd and 4th quintiles, reported a weighted average dissavings ratio of 13.9 percent, while in 1975 the higher deficit brackets, encompassing families in the 40th to 90th percentiles, reported a weighted average dissavings ratio of 18.2 percent.

To allocate the remaining income shortfall among the top 60 percent of households we have used Navarrete's basic adjustment formula, in which each income bracket receives a percentage of the shortfall equal to the ratio of its mean income to the sum of mean incomes of all the brackets selected to receive the shortfall. Algebraically, the formula is

$$\frac{\bar{y}_i{}^0}{\sum_{i=k}^{m} \bar{y}_i{}^0} \, Y_u + y_i{}^0 = y_i{}^1 \tag{1}$$

where

m	=	the total number of income brackets in the survey;
$m{-}k$	=	the range of upper income brackets to whom the shortfall is to be allocated,
Y_u	=	the income shortfall to be allocated,
$\bar{y}_i{}^0$	=	the preadjustment mean income of the ith bracket in the $m{-}k$ range,
$y_i{}^0$	=	the total preadjustment income of the ith bracket,
$y_i{}^1$	=	the adjusted total income of the ith bracket.

Navarrete's formula has been criticized as arbitrary—which it is, of course—and as upward biased, which is a more debatable point. It assumes that the ratio of true to reported income in the surveys rises as reported income per family rises; that is, that the income elasticity of underdeclaration is greater than unity. An alternative formula, equally arbitrary, would be to allocate the shortfall to each bracket in the $m{-}k$ range in proportion to the ratio of the *total* reported income of the bracket to the sum of reported income of all the $m{-}k$ brackets. That formula is

$$\frac{y_i{}^0}{\sum_{i=k}^{m} y_i{}^0} \, Y_u + y_i{}^0 = y_i{}^2 \tag{2}$$

The same "budget" equation applies, of course, to both formulas:

$$Y^2 = Y^1 = Y^0 + Y_u = \sum_{i=k}^{m} y_i^{a} + \sum_{i=1}^{k-1} y_i^{0}, \qquad a = 1, 2 \qquad (3)$$

If the number of households, p_i, of each income bracket of the $m-k$ range is the same, i.e., equal to a constant, C, the two formulas allocate the shortfall identically, since

$$\frac{p_i}{C} \cdot \frac{\bar{y}_i^{0}}{\sum\limits_{i=k}^{m} \bar{y}_i^{0}} = \frac{y_i^{0}}{\sum\limits_{i=k}^{m} y_i^{0}} \qquad \text{when } p_i = C \text{ for all } i$$

But when p_i and $\bar{y}$ are inversely related, as they are for the upper brackets in all the Mexican income-expenditure surveys, formula (1) gives a higher proportion of Y_u to the brackets nearer the top and a smaller proportion to those nearer the bottom of the $m-k$ range than does formula (2), thus generating a higher concentration of income. In effect, the two formulas disagree about the income elasticity of under-declaration, with formula (2) assuming the elasticity to be unity.[75]

There are, however, innocent motives as well as the obvious calculated ones—such as fear of supplying damaging information to the tax collector—for relative income underdeclaration to rise with family income in the more affluent income brackets. An innocent motive, cited as important by the Economic Commission for Latin America, is that respondents with substantial ownership income tend to interpret the survey query about their income as excluding earnings retained in their businesses.[76] Since the ratio of ownership to wage-salary income rises with family income in the top 2 to 3 deciles, so should the relative degree of income underdeclaration from this motive.

Table A-4 offers some supporting evidence from the 1975 survey. Note that all owner-entrepreneurial categories but one are reported as net dissavers. Commerce shows by far the highest dissavings rate of all the eighteen groups in the table, while the highest income category, owner-executives, shows the fifth highest dissavings rate. The dissavings rate for all owner-entrepreneurs, whose average family income was 2.3 times the mean income of all families in the 1975 survey, was 19.2 percent.[77] Indeed, with the exception of salaried professionals, all categories with family incomes two or more times greater than the mean income of all families were dissavers. For all 18 groups, the rank correlation between income level and savings is −0.251, and the marginal propensity to save, using a linear regression form, is negative, though statistically insignificant.[78]

Under either formula, with Y_u/Y^0 rising the estimated trend in income concentration will be higher when the proportion of all families in the $m-k$ range is held constant, than when the range is enlarged

Table A-4 / Monthly Family Income by Occupation of Family Head, 1975

Activity	Self-Employed		Owner-Employer		Wage-Salary Employee	
	Income (pesos)	Rate of Savings (+) or Dissavings (−)	Income (pesos)	Rate of Savings (+) or Dissavings (−)	Income (pesos)	Rate of Savings (+) or Dissavings (−)
Agriculture	2,152	+24.4	4,721	−21.7	1,671	−8.6
Services	2,599	−7.9	8,000	+1.8	2,865	−19.2
Artisans	1,968	−22.2	4,751	−4.1	3,317	−5.7
Commerce	3,360	+0.7	6,894	−68.3	3,363	−7.8
Low and middle level administrators	—	—	—	—	5,312	+0.2
Professionals, technicians	7,281	−10.2	10,965	−6.9	8,213	+7.7
Top executives	—	—	11,044	−14.6	9,901	−12.2

Source: Encuesta de ingresos y gastos familiares, 1975, cuadros 14-2, 14-3, 16-2, 16-3.

Table A-5 / Trends in the Proportion of Families in the m–k Range and in
$Y_u' / \sum_{i=k}^{m} y_i^0$

Proportion of Families in:	1950	1957	1963	1968	1975
m–k range	0.277	0.437	0.60	0.60	0.60
$Y_u' / \sum_{i=k}^{m} y_i^0$	0.401	0.487	0.416	0.445	0.576

Source: See Table A-1.

to include a higher proportion of families. As seen in Table A-5, Navarrete partially compensated for a rising Y_u/Y^0 in her 1950s data by applying formula (1) to an *m–k* range encompassing 27.7 percent of all families in 1950 and 43.7 percent in 1957. In our application of the formula to the subsequent years we further enlarged the *m–k* range to encompass all of the top 60 percent of families. The effect, shown in Table A-5, is to dampen but not fully eliminate oscillations and a rising trend in the period from 1957 to 1975 of $Y_u'/\sum_{i=k}^{m} y_i^0$, where $Y_u' = Y_u$ less the amount of Y_u allocated to the lowest 40 percent of families.[79]

ESTIMATION OF TRENDS OF REAL FAMILY INCOME

The nominal income of each income class was deflated to 1950 prices by a single deflator, the consumer price index, with 1950 equaling 100. Prior to 1968 the index used was the government's Cost of Living Index for the Federal District. After 1968 the new National Consumer Price Index became available, and was spliced to the old index in order to deflate 1975 nominal incomes. Specifically, the deflator was

$$
\begin{aligned}
1950 &= 100 \\
1957 &= 171 \\
1963 &= 214 \\
1968 &= 248 \\
1975 &= 476
\end{aligned}
$$

Table A-6 presents the resulting average family incomes for the different income brackets at 1950 prices for each of the five observation years for both unadjusted and adjusted incomes.

DIFFERENCES IN ESTIMATES BETWEEN THE PRESENT ESSAY AND ITS INITIAL VERSION

The initial version of this essay was written in 1974 and did not, of course, include estimates for 1975. The general trends of real income

Table A-6 / Annual Real Income per Household by Income Class, 1950–75, in 1950 Pesos [a]

Percentile Income Class		1950	1957	1963	1968	1975
		Not Adjusted for Underdeclaration of Income				
96–100		31,205	28,160	41,060	50,128	50,301
91–95		9,598	11,426	19,138	26,796	21,205
81–90		6,683	9,815	12,512	14,674	13,439
61–80		4,820	5,782	6,896	8,886	7,576
41–60		3,418	3,964	3,977	5,195	4,492
21–40		2,580	2,751	2,389	3,296	2,865
1–20		2,064	1,733	1,258	1,653	861
National average		5,285	5,807	7,166	9,114	8,226
		Adjusted for Underdeclaration of Income [b]				
96–100		51,636	58,133	64,610	76,984	92,514
91–95		10,452	14,067	28,579	46,987	38,967
81–90		7,209	12,192	17,502	22,166	19,484
61–80		4,888	6,863	8,421	11,879	9,822
41–60		3,418	4,102	4,371	6,968	5,893
21–40	(1)	2,580	2,751	3,257	3,488	3,806
	(2)	2,580	2,751	2,823	3,392	3,336
1–20	(1)	2,064	1,733	2,377	1,973	2,394
	(2)	2,064	1,733	1,818	1,813	1,628
National average		6,427	7,920	10,241	13,273	13,254

Source: Banco de México, *Informes Anuales,* various issues.

[a] 1950 to 1968 figures are deflated by the Cost of Living Index of the Federal District; 1975 figures by the National Consumer Price Index.

[b] Rows (1) are based on quintile incomes raised to equal the ratio of income to reported expenditures in the 1957 survey: 0.9 for the lowest quintile in 1963, 1968, and 1975, and 0.92 for the next higher quintile. Rows (2) average the upward adjusted and the unadjusted incomes of the lowest two quintiles.

and of income concentration in the two versions are similar, but some of the specific values differ noticeably. Since the first version, though unpublished, has had a somewhat extensive underground circulation it may be useful to explain the main differences.

Two factors are involved. One is that the initial version did not adjust the income of the lowest two quintiles upward; the entire shortfall was allocated, according to the Navarrete formula, to the higher income brackets. As an offset, however, the initial version also used multiple deflators, in which the incomes of the top 20 percent were deflated more than those of the lower 80 percent of households. In contrast, the present version uses a single deflator.

The temptation to deflate multiply was the availability for the

1950s and 1960s of the Mexican-American Chamber of Commerce's junior executive cost of living index[80] as well as the official Cost of Living Index for the Federal District. The first index had expenditure weights appropriate to the upper 10 percent of households, whereas the Federal District index was based on working class expenditure weights. Since the first index rose more than the second over the period from 1954 to 1968, it seemed appropriate to take this into account in the deflating. Hence, after adjusting for the income shortfall, the adjusted income of the top decile was deflated by the Chamber's index, the lowest 8 deciles by the Federal District index, and the 9th decile by the average of the two indices. Gini coefficients and real income trends were then computed from the multiple-deflated adjusted incomes.

Multiple deflating was not used in this paper for two reasons. The sufficient reason is that the Chamber ceased computing its index in the early 1970s, so that multiple deflating could not be extended to 1975.[81] Apart from that, I also developed suspicions that the greater rise of upper income cost of living indicated by the greater rise of the Chamber's index over the Federal District's index during the period from 1954 to 1970 may have been largely spurious. The official wholesale price index for the same period, whose coverage and surveying procedures have been much superior to both the Chamber or the old official cost of living indices, suggests that the divergence was, in fact, in the opposite direction. The consumer goods subcategories in the wholesale price index, corresponding to those given large expenditure weights in the Chamber's index—namely household durables, vehicles, clothing, personal care goods, and recreational goods—rose less during the period from 1954 to 1970 than did the food category, which is the category given dominant weight in the old Federal District index.

Notes

1. According to Kuznets, the income share of low income groups in the now developed capitalist economies probably fell through much of the nineteenth century and rose in the twentieth century, the share of the high income groups traced out an inverted-U pattern over the same time span, while the share of the middle income groups stayed fairly constant. He conjectured that the period of increasing inequality averaged 5 to 6 decades, mainly reflecting widening intersectoral income differences during early industrialization. For the turnaround, he offered merely a mixture of economic, institutional, and policy speculations, without committing himself as to their relative importance. See Simon Kuznets, "Economic Growth and Income Inequality,"

American Economic Review, vol. 45 (March 1955), pp. 1–28; "Quantitative Aspects of the Economic Growth of Nations: VIII. Distribution of Income by Size," *Economic Development and Cultural Change,* vol. 11 (January 1963).

2. Felix Paukert, "Income Distribution at Different Levels of Development: A Survey of Evidence," *International Labour Review* (August-September 1973), pp. 97–125.

3. Irma Adelman and Cynthia T. Morris, *Economic Growth and Social Equity in Developing Economies* (Stanford: Stanford University Press, 1973).

4. Montek S. Ahluwalia, "Inequality, Poverty and Development," *Journal of Development Economics,* vol. 3 (December 1976), pp. 209–35.

5. Edmar L. Bacha, "The Kuznets Curve and Beyond: Growth and Changes in Inequalities," unpublished paper, February 1977. Some of the differences between the Paukert and the Adelman-Morris findings also reflect different selections from conflicting estimates for the same countries—Paukert rejected some of those used by Adelman and Morris in favor of alternatives he judged more reasonable. In general, "errors in variables" is an important additional complication for cross-country comparisons, since the basic data, the methods used for overcoming data defects, and the general reliability of the resulting income distribution estimates vary considerably between countries. The problem also afflicts time series estimates for a single country, such as those presented in this paper for Mexico, but in this case standardizing could be done more systematically to at least minimize any bias in the estimations of trends.

6. Ifigénia M. de Navarrete, *La distribución del ingreso y el desarrollo económico de México* (México, D.F., 1960).

7. See Appendix Table A-1 for the data references.

8. Dirección General de Estadística, Departmento de Muestro, "Ingresos y egresos de la población de México" (México, D.F., 1958).

9. The Gini coefficient is a widely used overall index of income inequality. Its theoretical limits are zero, when all income recipients get identical shares of total income, and one, when a single recipient unit gets all the income. During the post-World War II era the Gini coefficient of the advanced capitalist economies has been ranging from 0.3 to 0.4, and that of the socialist economies from 0.2 to 0.3. Note that while a rise of the Gini coefficient represents a rise in overall income concentration, this is mathematically consistent with a declining income share for the most affluent income class, and a rising share for middle income classes. Supplemental measures are thus needed to identify the specific income classes that gained and lost relatively.

10. The allocation to the lowest two quintiles for 1963, 1968, and 1975 probably overcompensates for underreported income of these income brackets for reasons discussed in the Appendix. Series B may therefore understate the rising trend of the Gini coefficient. In the tables on trends of relative shares and of real income we try to correct for this by averaging the unadjusted and adjusted figures of the bottom two quintiles.

11. A partial exception was the Junior Executive Cost of Living Index computed from 1954 to 1971 by La Cámara Americana de Comercio de México. The index had expenditure weights more appropriate for the lifestyle of Mexican urban upper-middle-class families than did the official cost of living index, and was used in the preliminary version of this paper to separately deflate the nominal incomes of the top quintile. For reasons detailed in the Appendix, the use of the index is dropped in this revised version of the study.

12. From the 1963 income-expenditure survey it appears that about a fourth

310   David Felix

of the families in the 21–40 percent income bracket lived in towns and cities of over 10,000 people. The survey monographs for the other years do not provide comparable locational data; but a rough proxy of the rural-urban migration rate, *faute de mieux*, is the declining share of economically active laborers engaged in primary activity (farming, forestry, hunting, and fishing). According to the population censuses, that share fell at an annual rate of 1.4 percent between 1950 and 1970. Applying that rate to the 1963 base estimate of urban families in the 21–40 quintile gives the 1950 proportion as 20 percent and the 1975 proportion as 30 percent.

13. Simon Kuznets, "Problems in Comparing Recent Growth Rates for Developed and Less-Developed Countries," *Economic Development and Cultural Change*, vol. 20 (January 1972), p. 206.

14. Thus, Morton Paglin has sought to establish that the Gini coefficients for the United States computed from point income estimates overstate permanent family income concentration and generate a spurious upward trend. His age-corrected Gini coefficients, which he self-effacingly dubs the Paglin Gini, lower the level and produce a declining trend of postwar U.S. household income distribution. Paglin's article set off a flurry of criticism of his hidden assumptions (e.g., the similarity and constancy of age-income profiles) and of his computational procedures. See Morton Paglin, "The Measurement and Trend of Inequality: A Basic Revision," *American Economic Review*, vol. 65 (September 1975), pp. 598–609; and the critical comments of Eric Nelson, William Johnson, Sheldon Danziger, Robert Haveman, Eugene Smolensky, Joseph Minarik, and C. John Kurien, as well as Paglin's reply, in *American Economic Review*, vol. 67 (June 1977), pp. 397–531.

Inspired by Paglin's approach, Samuel Morley has sought to show that the rising inequality trend in Brazil from 1960 to 1973 and the fall of real income of the low income brackets has also been overstated by the point income estimates of Fishlow and Langoni. Morley's effort has been criticized in turn by Bacha on methodological and data grounds. See Samuel Morley, "Growth and Inequality in Brazil," *Luso-Brazilian Review*, vol. 15 (Winter 1978), pp. 244–71; Edmar Bacha, "Comments on Growth and Inequality in Brazil," *ibid.*, pp. 272–77.

15. Occupation would have to be defined broadly to include active and passive wealth management. They also serve who only sit and clip (coupons).

16. Note that income in Table 5 was that of the family to which the economically active individual contributed. The dip of family income for the 31–40 age bracket and subsequent rise for the next age bracket that shows up in most of the categories probably reflects in part variations in the number of secondary income contributors per family over the life cycle—notably children and, to a lesser extent in Mexico, wives. As indicated by the footnote to the table, the average number of income contributors per family was 1.2 in 1963. Since the average was probably higher for the low income families, it is likely that individual age-income profiles of wage earners declined less unevenly and precipitously from the 21–30 year peak than is indicated by Table 5.

17. The original data are from a 1963 national sample survey: *La población económicamente activa de México* (México, D.F.: Secretaría de Industria y Comercio, Dirección General de Muestro, 1964–65). The mobility calculations from this sample were made by José Luis Reyna, "Occupational Mobility: The Mexican Case," in Stanley M. Davis and Louis W. Goodman (eds.), *Workers and Managers in Latin America* (Lexington, Mass.: D.C. Heath, 1972), chapter 18.

18. Upwardly mobile percentages are obtained by multiplying across the rows of columns 2 and 3 and dividing by the column 3 total. Downwardly mobile percentages are obtained similarly, using columns 2 and 4.

19. For evidence about biased understatement of occupational income levels, see Appendix Table A-4. The judgment that profile curvatures are also differently understated derives from the facts that property income is grossly underreported in the surveys and that wealth holdings tend to increase with age as well as with occupational income level.

20. Access to the raw survey data for the different years would be needed to fill this gap, since only the compilers of the 1963 survey report published the data in a manner that allowed occupational age-income curves to be extracted.

21. *The Economic Development of Mexico,* Report of the Combined Mexican Working Party, published for the International Bank for Reconstruction and Development (Baltimore: Johns Hopkins University Press, 1953).

22. Navarrete, *La distribución,* chapter 3.

23. In her calculations, Navarrete lowered the IBRD commercial profits figures on the basis of the commerce figures in the 1950 input-output tables. Singer reports, however, that "it is now felt . . . that the Central Bank tables underestimated profits emanating from commerce. In addition, the impressive gains recorded for agriculture in the revision seem extreme given the comparative growth rates of other sectors of the economy after 1940. The truth assuredly lies somewhere between the older and the revised data." Morris Singer, *Growth, Equality, and the Mexican Experience* (Austin: University of Texas Press, 1969), p. 138. Navarrete suspected that the 1950 input-output tables probably undervalued commercial and industrial profits. Apparently, she chose to err on the conservative side in her calculations. See Navarrete, *La distribución,* p. 63.

24. Singer, *Growth,* pp. 121–22, 124.

25. The GNP grew at a rate of 2.3 percent per annum, and the GNP per capita grew at 0.7 percent per annum, between 1921 and 1939. Computed from Enrique Pérez López, "The National Product of Mexico: 1895–1964," tables 1, 3, in *Mexico's Recent Economic Growth: The Mexican View,* Institute of Latin American Studies, Latin American Monographs, no. 10 (Austin: University of Texas Press, 1967).

26. Pérez López, "National Product," pp. 26–28; Fernando Rosenzweig, "El desarrollo económico de México de 1877 à 1911," *El Trimestre Económico,* vol. 33 (1965), pp. 405–54.

27. Rosenzweig, "El desarrollo," and Alfredo Navarrete R., "The Financing of Economic Development in Mexico," in *Mexico's Recent Economic Growth: The Mexican View,* Institute of Latin American Studies, Latin American Monographs, no. 10 (Austin: University of Texas Press, 1967), pp. 106–115.

28. The concept "subsistence" is an intellectual *casus belli* among economists. Here we use it in quotes merely as a shorthand metaphor for the lowest material conditions consistent with both the preservation of the family and net population increase among the poorest 60 percent of Porfiriato families. The Mexican population growth rate between 1895 and 1910 was 1.2 percent per annum (Pérez López, "National Product," table 1). Zero population growth for the lowest 60 percent would require a 3 percent growth rate for the upper 40 percent, which is rather excessive in light of the low levels of sanitation and medicine of Porfiriato Mexico.

29. The 1910–1975 annual growth of GNP per capita was 1.8 percent, which gives a 1910 GNP per capita of $380 in 1975 prices. The ratio of disposable income to GNP ($290 to $380) is slightly higher in 1910 compared to 1975 (0.765 vs. 0.750). This is consistent with the slight rise of the private domestic savings ratio and the greater rise of the domestic capital formation ratio between postwar Mexico and the Porfiriato. See Alfredo Navarrete, "Financing of Economic Development," table 3, and Pérez López, "National Product," pp. 31–33. Note that the 1.7 percent growth rate for disposable income generates a larger residual and greater income concentration in 1910 than would a 1.8 percent rate. Its choice is also consistent, therefore, with our objective of devising an upper-bound estimate of 1910 income concentration.

30. The average family size of the lowest quintile in the 1968 survey was 5.3, while the national average family size was 5.8. See Banco de México, *La distribución del ingreso en México, 1968* (México, D.F.: Fondo de Cultura Económica, 1974), cuadro II-2.

31. Graphically, Variant II's Lorenz curve cuts those for the 1975 distributions from above at around the 80th percentile, with the area between the curves in this positive income range exceeding the negative area over the 80–100 percentile range. Variant I nestles inside the 1975 adjusted income Lorenz curve throughout, and crosses the unadjusted curve only after the 96th percentile.

32. See Friedrich Katz, "Labor Conditions on Haciendas in Porfirian Mexico: Some Trends and Tendencies," *Hispanic American Historical Review*, vol. 54 (February 1974), pp. 1–48.

33. *IX censo general de población, 1970* (México, D.F., 1972), vol. I, cuadro 40.

34. Computed from cuadro V-2 of *La distribución del ingreso en México, 1968*.

35. Computed from alternative (2) for 1968 in Table A-6.

36. Of the consumption functions for 35 different foods calculated by the 1968 survey, only corn and beans have negative income elasticities. See *La distribución del ingreso en México, 1968*, cuadro VII-1.

37. Computed from *ibid.*, cuadro IV-2.

38. Alternative (2) income in Table A-6 works out to $148 per capita for 1950. That of the 21–40 quintile is $185, implying an increase of real income for that quintile between 1910 and 1950 of over 85 percent.

39. The reduction of forced labor practices during and after the Revolution doubtlessly improved the bargaining strength of rural labor. Working in the opposite direction was the stagnation of agricultural output prior to 1940, and the falling real wages during the war decade.

The brief burst of land redistribution and ejidal restoration under Cárdenas probably did not reach down to the lowest 20 percent of the peasantry.

40. That is, allowing for rural heterogeneity in pre-Revolutionary Mexico as in modified assumption (b) raises the share of the third quintile in Variant II of Table 7 by about one percent.

41. These results are quite robust. A "subsistence" income for 1910 high enough to wipe out these results would convert the Porfiriato into an egalitarian's dream. It is also likely from the Navarrete data for the World War II decade that the elasticities began falling after 1940.

42. Ahluwalia, "Inequality," pp. 337–42.

43. See Sherman Robinson, "A Note on the U Hypothesis Relating Income Inequality and Economic Development," *American Economic Review*, vol. 66 (June 1976), pp. 434–40.

44. John Coatsworth, "Railroads, Landholdings, and Agrarian Protest in the Early Porfiriato," *Hispanic American Historical Review,* vol. 54 (February 1974), pp. 48–71.

45. Katz, "Labor Conditions"; John Kenneth Turner, *Barbarous Mexico* (Austin: University of Texas Press, 1969, reprint of 1910 edition).

46. For specifics see Sálomon Eckstein, *El marco macroeconómico del problema agrario mexicano* (México, D.F.: Centro de Investigaciones Agrarias, 1968); Rodolfo Stavenhagen, "Social Aspects of Agrarian Structure in Mexico," *Social Research,* vol. 33 (Autumn 1966); Roger D. Hansen, *Mexican Economic Development: The Roots of Rapid Economic Growth* (Washington, D.C.: National Planning Association, 1971); Fernando Rosenzweig, "Política agrícola y generación de empleo en México," *El Trimestre Económico,* vol. 42 (October-December 1975), pp. 837–56.

47. Rosenzweig, "Política agrícola," p. 845.

48. See Stavenhagen, "Social Aspects"; Eckstein, *Problema agrario mexicano;* Rosenzweig, "Política agrícola."

49. The Theil index of inequality of rural income rose from 0.429 in 1963 to 0.795 in 1975, according to an unpublished World Bank study. Comparable estimates are not available prior to 1963, but wage, employment, and land concentration trends make it virtually certain that rural inequality has been increasing since around 1940.

50. The Theil index for urban income in the World Bank study fell from .488 in 1963 to .402 in 1975, but the fall is suspect as it was computed from unadjusted survey incomes. Not only did the underreported income shortfall rise from 30 percent of national household income in 1963 to 38 percent in 1975, but Table A-4 suggests that higher incomes were probably understated more extensively in the urban occupations than in the rural. Correcting for understatement would probably wipe out the downward trend of urban inequality, but it would still leave 1975 rural income with a higher Theil index value than urban income.

51. Saúl Trejo Reyes, "El desempleo en México: características generales," *El Trimestre Económico,* vol. 42 (July-December 1975), p. 853.

52. *Ibid.,* cuadro 1.

53. Rosenzweig, "Política Agrícola," cuadro 1. An "underemployed" person is defined as an economically active individual who in the 1970 census reported annual earnings below that of a fully employed worker paid the minimum wage prevailing in the state of residence of the respondent. Since Mexico has no system of unemployment compensation, so that open unemployment is an unsustainable luxury for many of the economically active, Mexican economists have found it necessary to use underemployment proxies in analyzing employment patterns and trends.

54. The demographic projections are that the working-age cohorts will continue to grow at an increasing pace until around 1990, despite the current deceleration of the population growth rate. According to a recent simulation exercise, using the output-employment coefficients of the 1960s, even an acceleration of the real GNP growth rate to 8 percent, with sectoral growth rates of 9 percent in industry, 5.1 percent in agriculture, and 7.4 percent in services, as well as a 15 percent annual growth of exports, would have absorbed in full-time employment only half of those who were added to the labor force from 1969 to 1976. *Ibid.,* p. 851.

55. In 1970, public social security institutions, which provide mainly medi-

cal services and retirement benefits, covered about 40 percent of the urban labor force and a miniscule percentage of the rural. Within occupational groups net benefits rise with income and the distribution is made even more unequal by intergroup inequities; more lavish benefits are extended to such higher paid groups as the military, civil servants, and petroleum workers. Coverage has been expanding since 1940, but, according to a recent survey, "additions and improvements of benefits to those already insured has taken priority over incorporation of non-insured into the system." See Carmelo Mesa-Lago, *Social Security in Latin America* (Pittsburgh: University of Pittsburgh Press, 1978), pp. 215–57, for details.

The expansion of educational services has also been quite skewed, strongly favoring urban primary education over rural, and secondary and university education over primary. See Pablo Latoni, "Las necesidades del sistema educativo nacional"; and Rodrigo A. Medellín, "La dinámica del distanciamiento económico social en México," in Miguel S. Wionczek (ed.), *La sociedad mexicana*, 2nd ed. (México, D.F.: Fondo de Cultura Económica, 1973), pp. 330–58, 385–413.

Figures on trade union membership are unreliable. A rough estimate is that less than one-third of the nonagricultural workers are unionized, most of them employed in large public and private industrial and service enterprises.

56. Richard Weisskoff and Adolfo Figueroa, "Traversing the Social Pyramid: A Comparative Review of Income Distribution in Latin America," *Latin American Research Review*, vol. 11, no. 2 (1976), pp. 71–112.

57. See Mark Blaug, "The Correlation Between Education and Earnings: What Does it Signify?" *Higher Education*, vol. 1 (February 1972), pp. 53–76; Kenneth J. Arrow, "Higher Education as a Filter," *Journal of Public Economics* (1973), pp. 193–216; Ronald P. Dore, *The Diploma Disease: Educational Qualifications and Development* (London: Unwin Educational Books, 1976).

58. Martin Carnoy, "Earnings and Schooling in Mexico," *Economic Development and Cultural Change*, vol. 15 (July 1967), pp. 408–19; C. Muñoz Izquierdo and J. Lobo, "Expansión escolar, mercado de trabajo y distribución del ingreso en México," *Revista del Centro de Estudios Educativos*, vol. 4, no. 1 (1974).

59. At the National University of Mexico, 66 percent come from the wealthiest 5 percent of families and 91 percent from the wealthiest 15 percent. See Latoni, "Las necesidades," p. 340.

60. Nigel Brooke, John Oxenham, and Angela Little, *Qualifications and Employment in Mexico*, IDS Research Reports (Brighton, England: Institute of Development Studies, University of Sussex, 1978).

61. This critique of the benign neoclassical view and the consequences of deleting its various independence postulates is elaborated in David Felix, "The Technological Factor in Socio-economic Dualism: Toward an Economy-of-Scale Paradigm for Development Theory," *Economic Development and Cultural Change*, vol. 25, supplement (January 1977), pp. 181–211; and "De Gustibus Disputandum Est: Changing Consumer Preferences in Economic Growth," *Explorations in Economic History*, vol. 16, no. 3 (July 1979), pp. 260–96.

62. That is, the product cycle within the Mexican market. The good may be in the mature phase of its international product cycle when it reaches Mexico.

63. Kurt Unger, "Algunas observaciones sobre transferencia de tecnología

en dos sectores de manufacturas," *El Trimestre Económico,* vol. 44 (April-June 1977), pp. 483–500.

64. Albert O. Hirschman, "The Changing Tolerance for Income Inequality in the Course of Economic Development"; and Michael Rothschild, "Mathematical Appendix," *Quarterly Journal of Economics,* vol. 87 (November 1973), pp. 544–66.

65. *Ibid.,* p. 561.

66. Antonio Carillo Flores, "El desarrollo económico de México: reflexiones sobre un caso latinoamericano," *Cuadernos Americanos* (September-October 1948), p. 48.

67. The abortive effort is analyzed in Raymond Vernon, *The Dilemma of Mexico's Development: The Roles of the Private and Public Sectors* (Cambridge: Harvard University Press, 1963).

68. See Calvin P. Blair, "Echeverría's Economic Policy," *Current History,* vol. 72, no. 425 (March 1977); Judith Adler Hellman, *Mexico in Crisis* (New York: Holmes & Meier, 1978), chapter 6.

69. See Hellman, *Mexico in Crisis;* Evelyn P. Stevens, "Mexico's PRI: The Institutionalization of Corporatism," in James M. Malloy (ed.), *Authoritarianism and Corporatism in Latin America* (Pittsburgh: University of Pittsburgh Press, 1977), pp. 227–58; José Luis Reyna, "Redefining the Authoritarian Regime," in José Luis Reyna and Richard S. Weinert (eds.), *Authoritarianism in Mexico* (Philadelphia: Institute for the Study of Human Issues, 1977), pp. 155–71; and Susan Kaufman Purcell, "The Future of the Mexican System," in *ibid.,* pp. 173–91.

70. For example, in the various articles in Reyna and Weinert, *Authoritarianism.*

71. The sharp drop of the savings rate and the leveling off of real income per capita between 1968 and 1975 in the national accounts estimates may be partly due to the distorting effect of comparing a high growth year, 1968, with a depressed year, 1975. The GNP growth rate declined after 1972, although the average annual growth of real per capita income was positive for the seven year interval. However, 1975 savings and disposable income are probably underestimated. The national accounts show that despite a 52 percent drop in real household savings, consumption in constant prices was 4.2 percent above 1968, behavior which is not easily reconciled with expected householder reaction to a time of troubles. Probably the accelerating inflation and capital flight during 1975 distorted downward the income estimate in the national accounts for that year, and thus also the savings estimate.

72. Her 1950 data base was the 1950 population census, which included questions on income, but not on consumption. She used the ratios of in-kind consumption to cash income from the 1957 household income-expenditure survey to elevate the 1950 incomes of the lowest 77 percent of families.

73. *Encuesta sobre ingresos y gastos familiares en México, 1963* (México, D.F.: Investigaciones Industriales Oficina Editorial, 1966), p. 15.

74. Specifically:

	1950	1957	1963	1968	1975
Lowest quintile	100.0	84.0	88.1	87.8	78.9
Next higher quintile	100.0	106.6	109.4	131.4	129.3
Lowest 40 percent	100.0	96.3	99.9	111.0	106.8

75. Multiplying formula (2) by $1/p_i$ yields

$$\frac{\bar{y}_i^0}{\sum_{i=k}^{m} y_i^0} Y_u + \bar{y}_i^0 = \bar{y}_i^2$$

Hence

$$\frac{Y_u}{\sum_{i=k}^{m} y_i^0} + 1 = \frac{\bar{y}_i^2}{y_i^0} \qquad \text{for all } \bar{y}_i^0, \, i \geq k$$

76. United Nations, Economic Commission for Latin America, *Income Distribution in Latin America* (New York: United Nations, 1971), p. 67.

77. The mean monthly income of all families was 3,260 pesos; the mean monthly income of all owner-entrepreneurs was 7,562 pesos. Centro Nacional de Información y Estadísticas del Trabajo, *Encuesta de ingresos y gastos familiares, 1975,* primera edición (México, D.F., 1977), cuadros 14-2, 14-3.

78. That self-employed farming families—i.e., peasant families—register as very strong savers, and farm workers, the lowest earning group, as only modest dissavers, reinforces the contention in the preceding section that our formula for adjusting the incomes of the lowest 40 percent of households is overly generous. In 1975, self-employed farm families made up 19 percent and farm workers 11.3 percent of all families. Most of them were in the lowest 40 percent.

79. Reducing $Y'_u / \Sigma_{i=k}^{m} y_i^0$ to complete constancy with the 1957 ratio would require a series of interpolations between the midpoints of the middle income brackets in the 1963, 1968, and 1975 surveys. These brackets are of uneven size in the different surveys and also have the largest percentages of families in each of the surveys. Hence the interpretations would augment rather than diminish the arbitrariness of the adjustment procedure.

80. "Indice del costo de vida–nivel ejecutivo júnior," issued as a supplement to La Cámara Americana de Comercio de México, *Encuesta de salarios y prestaciónes,* annual issues.

81. I have been informed that the Chamber ceased computing its index because of its judgment that the new and much more detailed and comprehensive official consumer price index is sufficiently representative for the Chamber's purposes.

8

Poverty and Inequality in Brazil

SYLVIA ANN HEWLETT

The purpose of this chapter is to examine the nature and the depth of poverty and inequality in Brazil, and to explore the relationship of these phenomena to the growth process. The "discovery" of persistent and massive poverty in the Third World, and the suspicion that economic growth "by itself may not solve or even alleviate the problem within any reasonable time period,"[1] has triggered an awakening of interest in the link between growth and equity.

The controversial work of Adelman and Morris in 1973 set the terms for much of the recent debate. In a large cross-sectional sample of underdeveloped countries, they found that the development process is accompanied by an absolute as well as a relative decline in the average income of the very poor, and that "the only hope of significantly improving the income distribution in these countries lies in a transformation of the institutional setting."[2] In concluding their book they state: "The frightening implication of the present work is that hundreds of millions of desperate people throughout the world have been hurt rather than helped by economic development. Unless their destinies become a major focus of development policy in the 1970s and 1980s, economic development may serve merely to promote social injustice."[3]

These findings have certainly frightened many economists. Papanek, Paukert, and Little have all tried hard to discount Adelman and Morris' work by pointing to methodological and statistical problems;[4] and a more sophisticated study by Ahluwalia does seem to contradict some of the book's findings.[5]

Adapted from chapter 8 of *The Cruel Dilemmas of Development: Twentieth-Century Brazil* by Sylvia Ann Hewlett. Copyright © 1980 by Basic Books, Inc. By permission of Basic Books, Inc., Publishers, New York.

317

When one goes from aggregate cross-sectional studies to the experience of particular countries the picture is even more confusing. The burgeoning literature in this field has uncovered evidence of increasing inequality juxtaposed with rapid growth in a sizeable number of the more mature underdeveloped countries. These include Brazil, Peru, Argentina, Mexico, and Malaysia.[6] South Korea and Taiwan, on the other hand, seem to have achieved some redistribution with growth;[7] while in India the distribution has apparently remained invariant, with nearly stagnant income levels.[8] Colombia and Puerto Rico demonstrate yet another relationship between growth and equity.[9] In these countries, growth has proceeded at satisfactory rates with highly concentrated but unchanging patterns of income distribution.

This recent flurry of empirical investigations has produced little consensus as to the trends in the relationship between growth and equity in the Third World and few suggestions as to what might be the causal link between these two phenomena.

The Brazilian Data

The existence of massive poverty, the extreme concentration of income, and the increase in inequality during recent years are now accepted facts of contemporary Brazilian development.[10]

The distribution of income in Brazil is highly unequal. As can be seen from Table 1, concentration of income in the hands of the top 20 percent of the Brazilian population is considerably more exaggerated than in developed countries, and somewhat more exaggerated than in many other capitalist Third World nations. Furthermore, there has been a considerable increase in inequality during recent years.

Table 2 details the nature of the distributional trends during the period from 1960 to 1976. Despite the high growth rates that characterized much of this period, and at least some absolute gain by each decile, the majority of the Brazilian population lost out in relative terms in the years from 1960 to 1976, while the richest 10 percent increased its share of national income from 39.6 percent in 1960 to 50.4 percent in 1976. In other words, of the total gain in the Brazilian GNP during this period (and we must remember that the global product quadrupled) the richest strata of the population appropriated three-quarters, while the poorest 50 percent of the populace received less than one-tenth. This dramatic increase in inequality within the size distribution of income was matched by polarization on other fronts. Urban incomes grew much more rapidly than did rural incomes; those with a

Table 1 / *The Distribution of Income in a Number of Underdeveloped and Developed Countries*

Country	Per Capita Annual Income (1970 U.S.$)	Income Shares*				
		Bottom Quintile	Second Quintile	Third Quintile	Fourth Quintile	Top Quintile
Underdeveloped Countries						
Ecuador	313	2.5	3.9	5.6	14.5	73.5
Kenya	153	3.8	6.2	8.5	13.5	68.0
Mexico	697	4.0	6.5	9.5	16.0	64.0
Brazil	457	3.1	6.9	10.8	17.0	62.2
Turkey	322	3.0	6.5	11.1	18.8	60.6
Ivory Coast	328	3.9	6.2	11.8	20.9	57.2
Philippines	224	3.9	7.9	12.5	20.3	55.4
Developed Countries						
West Germany	3,209	5.9	10.4	15.6	22.5	45.6
Japan	1,713	4.6	11.3	16.8	23.4	43.8
Sweden	4,452	5.4	9.9	17.6	24.6	42.5
United Kingdom	2,414	6.0	12.8	18.2	23.8	39.2
United States	5,244	6.7	13.0	17.4	24.1	38.8
Australia	2,632	6.6	13.5	17.8	23.4	38.7

Source: Compiled from Montek S. Ahluwalia, "Inequality, Poverty, and Development," *Journal of Development Economics*, vol. 3 (1976), pp. 233–34.

*The distributional figures are for a variety of years in the 1960s and 1970s.

Table 2 / The Brazilian Distribution of Income, 1960–1976

Income Groups (Percentile)	Relative Income Levels (% of Total Income)			Change in Relative Income Levels, 1960–76 (%)	Absolute Income Levels [a]			Change in Absolute Income Levels, 1960–76 (%)
	1960[b]	1970[b]	1976		1960[b]	1970[b]	1976	
1–10	1.9	1.2	1.0	−47	102	91	138	35
11–20	2.0	2.2	2.2	+10	112	167	303	171
21–30	3.0	2.9	2.7	−10	167	211	373	123
31–40	4.4	3.7	3.2	−27	243	271	451	86
41–50	6.1	4.9	4.4	−28	339	357	616	82
51–60	7.5	6.0	5.1	−32	420	446	712	70
61–70	9.0	7.3	6.7	−26	498	535	937	88
71–80	11.3	9.9	9.8	−13	626	728	1,375	120
81–90	15.2	15.2	14.5	−5	845	1,119	2,037	141
91–100	39.6	46.7	50.4	+27	2,197	3,441	7,057	221
96–100	28.3	34.1	37.9	+34	3,138	5,032	10,604	238
99–100	11.9	14.7	17.4	+46	6,631	10,818	24,328	267

Source: Compiled from Indicadores sociais instituto (Rio de Janeiro: Instituto Brasileiro de Geographia e Estatística, 1979), pp. 63–66.
[a] Average annual income for each group in 1970 U.S. dollars. In 1970, the dollar was worth 4.6 cruzeiros.
[b] The 1960 and 1970 figures are obtained from the demographic census and refer to the economically active population. The 1976 figures are obtained from PNAD (Pesquisa Nacional de Amostra Domicilios).

university education increased their income four times as fast as those with little or no education; and, of the various regions of Brazil, only the richest, the state of São Paulo, registered an above-average increase in income. A striking example of the degree of concentration of income in contemporary Brazil is the fact that in 1976 the top 1 percent of the population received a slightly larger slice of national income than the entire bottom 50 percent!

Various fragmentary types of evidence help us obtain a more detailed picture of the distribution of income in Brazil. For instance, data published by the Ministry of Labor demonstrate a significant widening of wage differentials within the urban labor force during the late 1960s and early 1970s. Wages in the lowest earnings bracket fell in real terms, and the ratio of the average wage in the top class relative to that of the bottom class rose from 28.2 in 1969 to 40.5 in 1973. To make the polarization more pronounced, there was a rise in the population for both of these classes.[11]

Edmar Bacha and Eduardo Suplicy have analyzed relative wages in specific Brazilian industries. The most dramatic points to emerge from these studies are the steadily worsening position of the unskilled and the extremely rapid rise in managerial salaries. The Bacha data, for example, indicate that unskilled workers experienced a consistent decline in wage rates in the period from 1962 to 1972.[12] Skilled workers gained a modest increase in wages during this interval, while managers, starting from an extremely high base-salary level, increased their earnings at the rapid rate of 8 percent per year (in real terms) from 1966 to 1972. The Suplicy figures, dealing with a different sample and a slightly later time period, reveal a similar picture of big gains going to managerial groups; however, in this study, low-level workers do experience a small absolute increase in their income.[13]

In summary, it seems that a variety of sources point to a widening of the gap between the rich and the poor in Brazil and to an extremely dramatic concentration of income within the top decile of the population. However, when we turn from this relative picture to absolute standards of living, the data are less clear-cut.

Defining the poverty level in any national context is a tricky business because of the degree to which minimum standards of food, clothing, and shelter are culturally as well as physically determined.[14] In Brazil, a rather crude measure of poverty can be obtained by using minimum wage figures, as these represent a minimum standard of living that is specifically geared to national economic and social conditions. Applying this criterion to 1970 census data, we find that slightly more than 50 percent of working individuals and 30 percent of families failed to earn the minimum wage in this year.[15] When the country is

considered by region, an even more depressing picture is revealed—
the bulk of the population in the poorer states lived on incomes that
were well below the official minimum. In Piauí (a small state in the
northeast of Brazil), census figures show that in 1970, 90 percent of
employed individuals earned less than the minimum wage.

Other nonincome indicators of living standards tend to confirm
the presence of widespread and miserable poverty in Brazil. The National Household Expenditure Study (ENDEF), conducted in 1974
and 1975, contains the most complete and careful data to date on
nutrition in Brazil.[16] This survey finds that first-degree (that is, mild)
malnutrition affects 37 percent of all Brazilian children through age
seventeen, while 20 percent are estimated to be suffering from second-
degree (that is, severe) malnutrition. Severe malnutrition stunts
growth, and this deficit becomes permanent if it is not made up before
adolescence. In addition, many experts suspect that brain growth is
impaired by severe malnutrition and that such mental impairment is
irreversible.

A working paper by the World Bank reports: "it appears that
general health conditions in Brazil are poor compared with countries
at similar per capita GNP levels."[17] Infant mortality is twice as high
as in this comparable sample, and estimates based on official death
registration statistics show an increase in infant mortality rates in
certain metropolitan areas between 1960 and 1970 (see Table 3). The
incidence of malaria, Chagas' disease, and schistosomiasis remains

*Table 3 / Infant Mortality in
Brazil, 1960–1970*

Year	Deaths Per Thousand Live Births in Babies Less Than One Year Old*
1960	105.2
1965	101.1
1966	98.0
1967	105.9
1968	89.6
1969	91.2
1970	108.7

Source: Indicadores sociais instituto, p. 128.
*These figures refer to the Brazilian cities
of Manaus, São Luís, Teresina, Fortaleza,
Natal, João Pessoa, Recife, Maceió,
Aracaju, Salvador, Belo Horizonte,
Vitória, Rio de Janeiro, Curitiba, Pôrto
Alegre, Goiânia, and Brasília.

high over wide geographic areas (malaria, for example, is reported over 80 percent of Brazil), and the Brazilian government has failed to produce effective mass control measures for any of these debilitating diseases. In addition, there are large regional disparities in health standards. In the 1960s and early 1970s, life expectancy in the prosperous southeast of Brazil was over sixty years, while for low-income urban households in the five northeastern states it was forty years.

While there is little dispute over the continued existence of massive poverty in Brazil, trends in absolute living standards over the last two decades have been hotly disputed. On the optimistic side, the data contained in Table 2 do seem to indicate that all deciles of the Brazilian population improved their absolute income levels in the period from 1960 to 1976. There are also some positive signs from the years of the "economic miracle." In the early 1970s, when growth rates were impressively high, there was considerable evidence of a tight labor market, particularly in the industrial heartland of São Paulo. This would seem to be confirmed by the Suplicy figures, which demonstrate that both unskilled and skilled labor gained wage increases over these years.

However, this positive image has to be qualified by some negative evidence. As can be seen from Table 4, the post-1964 period has witnessed a shrinking in the real value of the minimum wage. Between 1964 and 1968, the minimum wage fell dramatically, and since that date there has been some sporadic slippage. This drift downward in the value of the minimum wage has not been countered by a fall in the number of workers earning the minimum wage. Morley estimates that approximately 54 percent of Brazilian workers earned less than the minimum wage in 1973, as opposed to 58 percent in 1968.[18]

Other negative signs come from recent trends in the labor market. The slowdown in growth since 1974 and 1975 has produced stagnant or shrinking real wages and higher rates of unemployment in at least some sectors of the economy. The Instituto Brasileiro de Geographia e Estatística (IBGE) in a recent publication demonstrated a mere "2.6 percent increase in employment between August 1976 and August 1978."[19] This represented half the rate of growth of the population of Brazil during these years and a quarter of the rate of population growth in the urban centers. The construction sector is an excellent example of the impact of the recent slowdown in growth on the job opportunities and standard of living of the working classes. In the early to mid-1970s, cnstruction employed 7 percent of the Brazilian labor force, and average wages (including overtime) paid on building sites in São Paulo were two and one-half times the minimum wage. By 1978, wages in this sector were only 28 percent above the minimum

Table 4 / Evolution of the Minimum Wage in Brazil, 1964–78, in 1970 Cruzeiros

	Rio de Janeiro		São Paulo		Pôrto Alegre	
Year	Real Value of the Average Monthly Wage	Annual Variation	Real Value of the Average Monthly Wage	Annual Variation	Real Value of the Average Monthly Wage	Annual Variation
1964	216		225		191	
1965	209	−2.8	215	−4.7	175	−8.7
1966	182	−12.8	191	−11.1	165	−5.3
1967	185	1.6	184	−3.3	162	−2.1
1968	169	−8.6	184	0	164	0.8
1969	181	6.6	175	−5.0	162	−1.3
1970	176	−3.3	176	0.9	161	−0.5
1971	177	0.2	175	−0.5	163	1.6
1972	181	2.7	178	1.3	164	0.3
1973	188	3.9	181	1.5	163	−0.6
1974	178	−5.7	174	−3.9	154	−5.5
1975	190	6.7	184	5.8	162	5.1
1976	187	−1.6	190	3.1	168	3.6
1977	187	0.3	194	2.6	168	0.3
1978	191	2.3	199	2.5	173	2.5

Source: Indicadores sociais instituto, p. 56.

wage, and the work force had been cut down considerably (by as much as 60 percent in São Paulo and Rio Grande do Sul).[20]

Finally, there is some forceful negative evidence from the city of São Paulo. Greater São Paulo is the largest (9 million people in 1972), the most dynamic, and the most prosperous region of Brazil, with only 19 percent of its workers earning less than the minimum wage (as opposed to 54 percent in the nation as a whole). Nonetheless, the fruits of economic growth have been distributed extremely unevenly, and poverty (measured in terms of income levels, infant mortality rates, and sanitary and nutritional standards) seems to be on the increase.

A study by the Departamento Intersindical de Estatística e Estudos Sócio-Económicos (DIEESE) demonstrates that the average São Paulo working-class family experienced an absolute as well as a relative decline in its income level between 1958 and 1969. The salary of the average head of household fell 36.5 percent during these years; and in spite of the fact that other members of the household entered the work force in order to compensate for this decline, family income still fell by 9.4 percent.[21]

On the health and nutritional fronts, recent trends have been similarly depressing. Between 1960 and 1973, the rate of infant mortality in São Paulo increased 45 percent (to a high of ninety-seven deaths per thousand live births). The proportion of dwellings served by running water fell from 61 percent in 1950 to 56 percent in 1973; the percentage of the population whose dwellings were linked to sewerage fell from 35 percent in 1971 to 30 percent in 1975; and, in 1970, 52 percent of the population of greater São Paulo was officially classified as suffering from malnutrition, as opposed to 45 percent in the mid-1960s. All this adds up to an extremely grim and deteriorating social welfare picture in this, the most prosperous city of Brazil.[22]

It is precisely this juxtaposition of great and growing wealth with massive human suffering that has most offended critics of the Brazilian military regime. As *The New York Times* has put it:

> The Brazilian dictatorship proclaims in the press and at international conferences the Brazilian economic miracle with a GNP growth of 11 percent. But it hides from the world the fact that out of every 1,000 children born in Brazil, 100 die before reaching the age of one; that in 1968, in the region of Amarizi, near the city of Recife, all the children born between the months of July and December died without the occurrence in the region of either an epidemic or a catastrophe. Why did they die? They were victims of diarrhea, vitamin deficiency, lack of medical assistance and poor hygienic conditions.[23]

Before concluding this account of the nature and the depth of poverty in contemporary Brazil, a word is in order on the fate of the Amazonian Indians. They have been largely forgotten in the heated debates that have raged over Brazilian development, and yet the systematic destruction of the remaining Indian tribes in the Amazon basin constitutes a dramatic example of the human costs of Brazilian development. As Shelton Davis has said: "The massive amount of disease, death and human suffering unleashed upon Brazilian Indians in the past few years is a direct result of the economic development policy of the military government of Brazil. . . . Large private, state and multinational corporations, the principal ingredients in the Brazilian model of development, have systematically expropriated Indian resources."[24]

Despite a long history of disease and cultural destruction as the Brazilian frontier moved west, there remained in the mid-1950s a major concentration of indigenous tribes (numbering approximately 200,000 people) in the Amazon and in the central regions of Brazil. Over 120 Indian communities inhabited this immense area, living in small tribal groups that numbered between 100 and 500 individuals. Most of these tribes subsisted from hunting, fishing, and gardening and maintained close attachments to their ancestral territories. This way of life has become increasingly incompatible with Brazilian development goals. By the early 1960s, the Amazon basin was seen as a source of vital economic resources. With "79.7 percent of the country's lumber resources, 81 percent of its fresh water, half its iron ore deposits, 93 percent of its aluminum and the largest deposit of rock salt in the world,"[25] it became the target for active exploitation.

The 1964 coup was a decisive factor in the changing Indian situation since the new military government was more firmly committed to rapid economic growth and less concerned with the humanitarian consequences of its economic programs than previous Brazilian regimes had been. Three policies have been particularly important in worsening the plight of the Indian population. First, the military regime has endorsed the rights of private companies to exploit the rich mineral and agricultural resources of the Amazon basin. Second, the government has introduced a series of fiscal and tax incentives for promoting cattle-raising and agri-business projects in the interior. Third, a series of crash spending programs has been launched to open up and colonize this area. For example, Operation Amazon was set up in 1966 with the goal of spending US$2 billion on the development of transport, power, communications, and natural resources in the region. And the Plano de Integração Nacionál (PIN), inaugurated in 1971, was an immensely ambitious scheme centered around the building of a trans-Amazon highway and the colonization of land by settlers from the northeast.

The disastrous effects of these programs on the indigenous Indian population have been documented by the International Red Cross and by Aborigines Protection Society (APS) reports on Indian policy in Brazil.[26] The Waimiri-Atroari tribe, which lives in a large jungle area north of Manaus, provides only one example. In the early 1970s, the Brazilian government decreed a special reserve for the Waimiri-Atroari in the state of Amazonas. At the same time, plans were laid for a road that would connect the city of Manaus with Boa Vista and pass through the new Indian reserve. It provided the only military route to the Venezuelan frontier, and it terminated in the north at large molybdenum deposits. The road threatened to destroy the territorial integrity and the economic viability of the Waimiri-Atroari, and the tribesmen made it clear that they would rather die fighting than give up their lands. The last few years have seen violent confrontations between the Waimiri-Atroari and agents of FUNAI (the official Brazilian foundation in charge of Indian affairs). The tribe is gradually being wiped out.

A similar depressing saga can be told about the Kreen-Akrore and the Parakanan tribes, which have been reduced to a handful of people as a result of highway building. A recent account describes the sickness and despair typical of the remaining tribesmen: "We found two temporary houses along the Santarém-Cuíabá highway and a population of 35 persons all suffering from colds, including Kreen-Akrore Chief Iaquil, who did not know where he was. . . . The customs of the tribe have degenerated and tobacco and alcohol now form parts of their new habits."[27] The few remaining Kreen-Akrore women were aborting their children rather than produce offspring who would have to face the new conditions of their tribal life.

In summary, the likelihood of survival of the indigenous Brazilian population has diminished considerably in recent years. In the pre-1964 era, the major threats to the Indians were small-scale rubber collectors, hunters, and traders. But over the course of the last fifteen years, the Brazilian government has entered the picture with massive programs of highway construction, mineral exploitation, and agricultural colonization. These policies "are not to be blamed on a series of bureaucratic blunders but are an organic part of the development strategy and the 'economic miracle.' "[28] They have entailed the systematic extermination of the indigenous Indian culture of Brazil.

The facts and figures on poverty, inequality, and even murder in contemporary Brazil lead to some rather dismal conclusions. In absolute terms, millions of Brazilians seem to be as bad off as they were before the rapid economic development of recent years. The distributional figures tell us that although the lion's share of the new wealth went to the richest 10 percent in the population, every decile gained a little additional income in the period from 1960 to 1976; but this fact is countered by three additonal pieces of evidence.

In the first place, a small but not negligible number of Amazonian Indians has been destroyed or reduced to a state of miserable destitution. Second, in the mainstream of the population at least some discrete groups of the urban working class have experienced an actual drop in income levels. Unskilled workers, earning close to the minimum wage, have seen some sporadic slippage in their standards of living—particularly in periods of recession, when widespread unemployment has compounded their economic problems. With little market-derived bargaining power in this labor-surplus economy, unskilled workers have been the chief victims of the government stabilization policies that were enacted in the period from 1964 to 1967 and again from 1974 to 1980.

Finally, a variety of nonincome social welfare indices, such as nutrition and health, demonstrate that the living conditions and the life expectancies of the Brazilian poor remain as wretched as they were before modern industrial growth. This miserable condition has been maintained at least partially by multinational corporations and "Western consumerism." Advertising has had a profound impact on the buying habits of many urban Brazilians and has led to the substitution of essentials by nonessentials in the budgets of many lower class people. In other words, if a poor family is persuaded by TV commercials to spend 25 percent of its income on cigarettes and consumer durables and only 50 percent on food, its nutritional standards are likely to fall even if its real income has risen slightly (see Table 5).

The facts with regard to inequality are even more incisive. The census returns show that virtually everyone except the top decile lost out in relative terms in the decade from 1960 to 1970, and various kinds of more fragmentary evidence all point to a growing polarization of Brazilian society. But what increasing relative deprivation means in terms of social welfare is less obvious. Intuitively, one feels that increasing inequality should have a distinctly negative effect on the welfare of those left behind in the race for economic improvement. To take an extreme example: if your neighbor becomes exceedingly rich and flaunts his newly acquired Rolls-Royce in front of your eyes, the "natural" reaction would appear to be envy and dissatisfaction with your own unchanged standard of living. However, most contempo-

Table 5 / Structure of Consumption in a Typical Working-Class Household, São Paulo, 1958 and 1970

Type of Expense	Percentage of Monthly Budget	
	1958	1970
Food	64.3	51.0
Clothing	14.2	10.6
Health care	5.7	4.7
Domestic cleanliness	4.3	2.2
Domestic appliances	4.3	8.5
Transport (mainly secondhand automobiles)	2.9	11.5
Personal hygiene	2.1	1.6
Education and culture	1.4	4.6
Smoking	0.7	5.3

Source: Cândido Procópio Ferreira de Camargo *et al.*, *São Paulo 1975: crescimento e pobreza* (São Paulo: Edições Loyola, 1976), p. 75.

rary sociologists would view the matter as being a little more complicated than this. As Runciman says, "the relationship between inequality and grievance only intermittently corresponds with either the extent and degree of actual inequality, or the magnitude and frequency of relative deprivation which an appeal to social justice would vindicate."[29] In short, the degree to which increasing inequality can be associated with a deterioration in social welfare is unpredictable and can only be determined by careful examination of the society in question.

One of the few economists to tackle the question of inequality in underdeveloped nations is Albert Hirschman. In an effort to explain the apparent ease with which many Third World countries tolerate great and increasing degrees of inequality, he puts forward the proposition that: "Advances of others supply information about a more benign external environment; receipt of this information produces gratification; and this gratification overcomes, or at least suspends envy."[30] In short, in a period of fast economic growth, increasing inequality will not necessarily provoke discontent among lower-income groups; the fact that someone is moving ahead will have, at least for a while, a beneficial effect on the psyche of the poor. It is easy to see how crucially Hirschman's hypothesis hinges on a measure of social mobility. Gratification at the advance of others is based on an expectational calculus, and if the poor cannot realistically aspire to enjoy the fruits of prosperity, the basis for any present satisfaction is obviously destroyed.[31]

In Brazil, the divisions of society are extremely real and rigid, embedded as they are in a long history of uneven and unequal development; consequently, upward mobility is limited. Perhaps one of the few avenues of advance for the poverty-stricken lower class of Brazilian society has been internal migration from the countryside to the cities. Recent studies demonstrate the existence of a two-tiered migratory pattern in Brazil: an initial move from the countryside to low-paying jobs in the "informal" urban labor market is followed by an eventual move into the higher-paying "formal" sector.[32] Although some evidence suggests that men in the prime age groups (twenty-five to forty-nine) moved rather quickly into better-paying jobs during the years of the economic miracle, it is unclear whether these migratory patterns constitute a reliable avenue of upward mobility for the bulk of the rural poor. At the very least, prospects in this sphere would seem to depend on the rate of employment creation in the modern sector, which has been much less encouraging in the years from 1974 to 1980 than it was during the boom years from 1968 to 1973.

To return to Hirschman's argument, the absence of independent labor organizations and the recurrent threat posed by a reserve army of the underemployed in the countryside are dominant factors in explaining the weak bargaining position of working-class groups in Brazil. During times of great prosperity, discrete groups of new arrivals have been absorbed into the modern sector, but these trends have not been continuous (after all, no economy can grow at the rate of 11 percent per year forever!) and have conspicuously failed to ameliorate poverty or to reverse the overall trend towards increasing inequality.

Given these difficulties that the "have nots" experience in empathizing with the "haves," it is hard to believe that the polarization typical of recent years has done anything but exacerbate the suffering of the Brazilian poor. Hirschman is right when he recognizes that the link between deepening poverty and political action is neither obvious nor automatic. But instead of turning to theories of vicarious gratification to explain the absence of seething discontent and revolutionary fervor in Brazil, I would prefer to look instead at the country's successive strategies of economic growth and at the structure of political power, as I shall do in the final section of this chapter. But first let me examine some of the more important theories that have emerged in Brazil to explain the meaning and function of poverty.

The Theoretical Debate Within Brazil

To date, two broad groups of theories have emerged that link the rapid growth rates of modern Brazilian development with the phenomena of inequality and poverty. Both conceptual frameworks are intensely value-laden and incorporate specific sets of policy goals.

On the right end of the political spectrum, we have a group of theories that see increasing inequality as an inevitable consequence of the workings of the market during a period of rapid growth; polarization and increased deprivation become necessary accompaniments of the growth process, at least in the short run. On the left end of the political spectrum, we have a group of theories that see increasing inequality as a direct result of the growth strategy: in particular, they see the concentration of demand within an elite group as an essential ingredient of the economic growth model. Right-wing theorists are of the opinion that rapid growth justifies increasing inequality because eventually there will be significant "trickle down" to the lower classes. Theoreticians on the left tend to see as illegitimate growth strategies that depend upon deepening poverty.

The right-wing or "market forces" approach to the growth-inequality relationship is exemplified in *Distribuição da Renda,* published in 1973 by Carlos Langoni, a young, Chicago-trained, government economist. In his book, Langoni develops the argument that increasing inequality is an inevitable, if unfortunate, accompaniment of rapid economic growth, but that the process will eventually right itself. With a little infrastructural investment from the government, market forces will eventually produce both growth and equity. The reasoning goes as follows.

In the first place, due to the strong correlation between income and years of schooling in Brazil, inequality is linked to changes in the educational composition of the labor force. Second, the rapid technological transformation of the Brazilian economic structure during the "miracle" altered the demand for labor in favor of persons with high levels of skill. The supply schedule for this type of manpower is, of necessity, extremely inelastic (because of the long period involved in the educational process). Therefore, in spite of the expansion of higher education in the 1960s, the Brazilian labor market was unable to satisfy the huge increase in demand for managers generated by the country's growth rates. As a result, managerial personnel were able to command even higher levels of remuneration than were justified by productivity alone—and these high salaries obviously worsened the distribution of income.

Finally, Langoni links inequality to structural change in the labor force. High growth rates that are specific to certain sectors of industry generate interregional and intersectoral employment shifts. The movement of labor from the poverty-stricken rural areas and from the lower-paying primary sector to lucrative urban occupations has the short-run effect of increasing the dispersion of incomes and, therefore, of increasing inequality.

To sum up, Langoni views the unfortunate distributional picture of the recent past as transitional, and in two different ways. As more and more people move away from the traditional sectors, and as the majority of Brazilians become city dwellers working in modern industry and commerce, the purely sectoral exacerbation of inequality will disappear. And as long as the government responds to the increased need for high-level manpower with appropriate educational investment, supply will adjust to demand and the monopoly rents earned by managers will disappear. The conclusion drawn is that, aside from providing more university education, all the Brazilian government needs to do is continue with the business of growing—and market forces will take care of the equality issue. In his preface to *Distribuição da Renda,* Delfim Netto, who was minister of finance in 1973 and is currently minister of planning, pours scorn on those who favor overt government action to reduce inequality, accusing them of indulging in "a veritable confidence game which would end up leaving the nation dividing up the misery more equitably."[33]

The "market forces" theory has been adopted as the official interpretation of distributional trends over the recent period for the obvious reason that it absolves the military regime from any direct guilt in the deteriorating social welfare situation. The theory is extremely convenient in that it precludes the need for any redistributional policies in the future. It also disarms criticism from the advanced democracies. Underlying much of the analysis is an implicit comparison with nineteenth-century Europe and North America. If these nations could incur short-run costs in their development processes, why not Brazil?

Despite the attractions of the market forces interpretation of recent events, it can be challenged on a number of accounts. On the empirical level, it has been shown that intersectoral and interregional shifts in employment account for very little of the increase in inequality. Moreover, it has been demonstrated that the major concentration of income occurred from 1964 to 1967, a period of stabilization and slow growth, rather than in the post-1967 period of economic boom. John Wells finds the critical period of increasing inequality in wages to have occurred between 1965 and 1966 (a year of pronounced industrial recession).[34] His Gini coefficient for industrial wages increases 20 percent between 1965 and 1966; thereafter, there is a modest drift upward in the index of inequality. Thus, it is fairly difficult to maintain that concentration of income was a result of the bidding up of managerial salaries in a time of economic boom; the "iron laws of demand and supply" do not constitute an adequate explanation of growing inequality in Brazil.

On the left of the political spectrum, demand-constraint or underconsumptionist models have long been used to explain the dynamics of Brazilian development. The origins and rationale for this school of thought are as follows.

The industrialization strategy of Brazil was import substitution, a mode of development that emphasized the production of consumer durables for an elite market. Since the wealthy class was small, the market was capable of saturation. Once this happened, production would run into a demand constraint, growth rates would fall, and the whole economy would tend towards stagnation. The high growth rates of the Kubitschek years, followed by the dismal economic scene of the early 1960s, tended to confirm the hypotheses of the stagnationist school of thought. However, the resumption of growth in 1967 and the sustained prosperity of the Brazilian economic miracle seemed to upset both the premises and the predictions of the demand-constraint theorists; this was particularly true in view of the fact that the miracle was accompanied by increasing inequality. After a period of confusion, the underconsumption thesis was reconstituted so as to incorporate the possibility of demand intensification. Increasing inequality was seen to concentrate income in the elite group, thus intensifying demand for a whole range of luxury goods and providing the impetus for a renewed spurt of economic growth.

Oliveira, Furtado, and Tavares were among the theorists who contributed to this new version of the demand-constraint model.[35] They argued that by 1967 the Brazilian market was permeated with profound discontinuities. The bottom 50 percent of the population had only marginal access to manufactured goods; the next 40 percent of the population (the working classes) had access to nondurable consumer goods. The next 9 percent (the urban middle class) and the top 1 percent formed a highly diversified market for both durable and nondurable goods. By dint of a progressive concentration of income in this top decile, demand was sufficiently intensive to prevent, at least for a while, the enactment of the underconsumptionist scenario. It should be noted that the underconsumptionist theorists were convinced that a new boom based on demand concentration had to be short-lived. The elite market would eventually become saturated, and the sharp discrepancies in income and buying power would serve as barriers to the imitation of the consumption habits of the rich by the mass of the people.

Oliveira and other left-wing theorists thus saw increasing relative deprivation as directly functional to the growth strategy. The cut in living standards of the workers in the post-1964 period permitted a redistribution of personal income towards upper-income groups who were destined to be the great consumers of the Brazilian miracle. Wage cuts also resulted in an increase in profit rates. These financial surpluses were used by the corporate sector to extend credit facilities to middle-class groups, enabling them to purchase durable consumer goods. Thus, the fall in working-class incomes during the period from 1964 to 1967 becomes linked to the growth strategy in two ways—via demand creation and via credit creation.

In much of the writing in this school of thought, one can detect (with some sympathy) that "the wish is father of the theory." In their anxiety to pinpoint the essential antagonism between the Brazilian development strategy and social justice, the demand-constraint theorists overstate their case. In particular, they exaggerate the directness of the link between inequality and growth. For example, they tend to assume that the working classes are entirely excluded from the market for consumer durable goods, even though the data show this to be an inaccurate premise. By 1972, 48 percent of all households in Brazil had an electric iron, 70 percent some form of radio, and 32 percent a television.[36] Via the substitution effects discussed earlier, there seems to have been a considerable "trickle down" of goods, if not of income, to the urban working class.

This kind of empirical evidence refutes some of the left's basic premises—that demand during the miracle was restricted to an elite market and that increasing inequality and the consequent concentration of demand was a necessary condition for the renewed economic vitality of the Brazilian economy in the recent period. In short, while the underconsumptionist school of thought has focused correctly on some important issues, including the structure of effective demand and the luxury-goods emphasis of the industrial strategy, it has suffered from an excess of economic determinism. These theories have tended to trace a direct and linear relationship between the concentration of income and the exact configuration of industrial growth during the years of the miracle.

A Reinterpretation

My own interpretation of poverty and inequality in Brazil, while distinctly leftist in orientation, is more interactive and cumulative than those I have just described.[37] It rests on the following elements: a deeply rooted and highly differentiated "colonial" social structure which has survived into the modern era; modern industrialization strategies based on the production of capital-intensive consumer durables for elite groups; demographic trends that have exacerbated the job deficit; and political frameworks that have given effective power to elite groups and have facilitated policies emphasizing growth at the expense of egalitarian (or humanitarian) objectives. It is this interaction between the past and the present, and between economic and political elements, that sets up the chain of cumulative causation responsible for the presence of massive poverty and increasing inequality in contemporary Brazil.

At a fundamental level of analysis, the highly differentiated social structure of premodern Brazil and the absence of radical political change at the onset of domestic industrialization insured that development strategies would be designed for and by an elite. Import-substituting industrialization was therefore geared towards producing sophisticated consumer goods; and as the technological and financial capability required to manufacture these sophisticated products was effectively monopolized by the giant multinational firms, this industrialization strategy led to a situation in which Brazilian manufacturing came to be dominated by multinationals.

The cumulative effect of this process was to rigidify and exaggerate the previously existing distribution of income (which was extremely unequal). The multinational firms with their capital- and skill-intensive technologies absorbed little labor; individuals who did find employment within this dynamic sector were firmly divided into workers and managers—the latter group receiving nearly all the fruits of increased productivity.

This organization of production fed through to the structure of demand. The industrial managers and other members of the Brazilian elite were able to appropriate an increasing proportion of national income; in the period from 1960 to 1976, for example, they were able to increase their share from 40 percent to 50 percent of the GNP. This concentration of spending power in the hands of upper-income groups provided a significant and expanding market for the products of multinational firms. In essence, it enabled Brazil to adopt the consumption habits of the advanced affluent societies "prematurely."[38] Goods manufactured by multinational corporations for the mass markets of rich countries were easily absorbed by an elite market in Brazil. However, one should not overschematize this process. By the 1970s, many of the sophisticated goods produced by multinational firms were also being consumed by the urban working classes. At least the skilled workers were earning more, and this greater affluence combined with advertising and a greater availability of consumer credit to expand the effective market for consumer durables. In addition, the successful export drive by multinational firms in the post-1968 period further extended this market.

I should like to stress how my explanatory framework differs from that of the underconsumptionist school of thought. I see a highly unequal distribution of income as a background characteristic that has interacted with industrialization strategies and the role of multinational corporations throughout the modern period. I do not see an increase in inequality and a consequent intensification of demand as triggering the Brazilian miracle in any direct or self-conscious way. (Indeed, the increase in inequality in 1965 and 1966 that was identified by John Wells was primarily a result of anti-inflationary policies and a dampening of demand.) The roots of massive poverty and the reasons for a widening gap between the rich and the poor in Brazil lie firmly entrenched in the economic and political evolution of this late-developing nation.

Notes

1. Montek S. Ahluwalia, "Income Inequality: Some Dimensions of the Problem," in Hollis Chenery *et al., Redistribution with Growth* (London: Oxford University Press, 1977), p. 3. Much of the new work in the mainstream of the economics discipline is pulled together in a volume edited by Charles R. Frank, Jr., and Richard C. Webb, *Income Distribution and Growth in the Less-Developed Countries* (Washington, D.C.: The Brookings Institution, 1977).

2. Irma Adelman and Cynthia T. Morris, *Economic Growth and Social Equity in Developing Countries* (Stanford: Stanford University Press, 1973), p. 194.

3. *Ibid.,* p. 192.

4. See G. Papanek, "Growth, Income Distribution, and Politics in Less-Developed Countries," in Y. Ramati (ed.), *Economic Growth in Developing Countries* (New York: Praeger, 1975); F. Paukert, "Income Distribution at Different Levels of Development: A Survey of Evidence," *International Labor Review,* vol. 108 (1973), pp. 97–125; and I.M.D. Little's review of Adelman and Morris, *Economic Growth,* and of Chenery *et al., Redistribution with Growth,* in *Journal of Development Economics,* vol. 3, no. 1 (1976), pp. 99–116.

5. Montek S. Ahluwalia, "Inequality, Poverty, and Development," *Journal of Development Economics,* vol. 3 (December 1976), pp. 209–35.

6. Albert Fishlow, "Brazilian Size Distribution of Income," *American Economic Review,* vol. 62, no. 2 (1972), pp. 391–402; Richard Webb, *Government Policy and the Distribution of Income in Peru, 1963–73* (Cambridge: Harvard University Press, 1977); R. Weisskoff, "Income Distribution and Economic Growth in Puerto Rico, Argentina, and Mexico," *Review of Income and Wealth,* vol. 16 (1970), pp. 303–32; David Felix, "Economic Growth and Income Distribution in Mexico," mimeo, Washington University, 1976; and D. Snodgrass, "Trends and Patterns in Malaysian Income Distribution, 1957–70," mimeo, Cambridge University, June 1974.

7. B. Renaud, "Economic Growth and Income Inequality in Korea," World Bank Staff Working Paper No. 240, Washington, D.C., February 1976; and J. Fei, G. Ranis, and S. Kuo, "Equity with Growth: The Taiwan Case," mimeo, Yale University, 1976.

8. D. Kumar, "Changes in Income Distribution and Poverty in India: A Review of the Literature," *World Development,* vol. 2, no. 1 (1974), pp. 31–41.

9. A. Berry and M. Unrutia, *Income Distribution in Colombia* (New Haven: Yale University Press, 1976); and Weisskoff, "Income Distribution," pp. 303–32.

10. See Fishlow, "Brazilian Size Distribution," pp. 391–402; Carlos Geraldo Langoni, *Distribuição da renda e desenvolvimento economico do Brasil* (Rio de Janeiro: Editora Expressão e Cultura, 1973); and Ricardo Tolipan and Arthur Carlos Tinelli (eds.), *A controvérsia sobre a distribuição da renda e desenvolvimento* (Rio de Janeiro: Zahar Editores, 1975).

11. This source is analyzed by Samuel A. Morley in *Changes in Employment and the Distribution of Income during the Brazilian "Miracle"* (Geneva: International Labor Organization, 1976), pp. 27–34.

12. Edmar Bacha, "Hierarquia e remuneração gerencial," in Tolipan and Tinelli, *A controvérsia,* p. 140.

13. Eduardo M. Suplicy, "As crescentes differenças de renda no país," *Folha de São Paulo,* 15 March 1976.

14. In the early 1960s, Peter Townsend argued that "both 'poverty' and 'subsistence' are relative concepts and . . . they can only be defined in relation to the material and emotional resources available at a particular time to members either of a particular society or different societies." See Peter Townsend, "The Meaning of Poverty," *British Journal of Sociology,* vol 13 (1962), pp. 210–27.

15. Fishlow finds that for the millions of Brazilians who belong to families below this official poverty line the differentiating characteristics of poverty are the following: little or no education; concentration in agricultural activities; location in rural areas; residence in the northeast; and larger than average number of children. See Fishlow, "Brazilian Size Distribution," p. 397. A recent study by the World Bank found that 32 percent of Brazilian families fell below the poverty line in mid-1970 (at the present time, the World Bank defines the poverty line as constituting a family income that is less than two minimum wages). See report in *Jornal do Brasil,* 2 October 1978.

16. Reported in "Brazil: Human Resources Special Report," World Bank Staff Working Paper, Washington, D.C., 1979, pp. 28–31.

17. *Ibid.,* p. 61.

18. Morley, *Changes in Employment,* p. 24.

19. *Latin America Economic Report,* 27 October 1978, p. 332.

20. *Latin America Economic Report,* 14 July 1978, p. 215.

21. Cândido Procópio Ferreira de Camargo *et al., São Paulo 1976: crescimento e pobreza* (São Paulo: Edições Loyola, 1976), pp. 79–147.

22. Camargo *et al., São Paulo 1976,* pp. 79–107.

23. *The New York Times,* 13 September 1976.

24. Shelton H. Davis, *Victims of the Miracle* (Cambridge: Cambridge University Press, 1977), pp. xi–xii. This is by far the best account of the history and meaning of official policies towards the Amazon Indians.

25. Davis, *Victims of the Miracle,* p. 32.

26. See the International Committee of the Red Cross' *Report of the ICRC Medical Mission to the Brazilian Amazon Region,* Geneva, 1970; and Aborigines Protection Society of London, *Tribes of the Amazon Basin in Brazil, 1972,* London, 1973.

27. *O estado de São Paulo,* 6 January 1974. Quoted in Davis, *Victims of the Miracle,* p. 72.

28. The only role given to the Indian population in contemporary development plans is as a reserve labor force and producers of marketable commodities. See the report of a speech made by the President of FUNAI in *Visão,* 26 April 1971, p. 26.

29. W. G. Runciman, *Relative Deprivation and Social Justice* (London: Routledge & Kegan Paul, 1966), p. 337.

30. Albert O. Hirschman, "The Changing Tolerance for Income Inequality in the Course of Economic Development," *Quarterly Journal of Economics* (November 1973), p. 546.

31. Hirschman himself is not unaware of these impediments; see "The Changing Tolerance," p. 554.

32. See, for example, George Martins and José Carlos P. Peliano, "Os migrantes no mercados de trabalho metrópolitanos," mimeo, Brasília, Human Resources Planning Project, 1977, pp. 143–92.

33. Langoni, *Distribuição da renda,* p. 13.

34. John Wells, "Distribution of Earnings, Growth, and the Structure of Demand in Brazil during the 1960s," *World Development,* vol. 2, no. 1 (January 1974), pp. 9–24.

35. See Celso Furtado, *Analise do "modelo" brasileiro* (Rio de Janeiro: Civilização Brasileira, 1972); Francisco de Oliveira, "A economia brasileira: crítica à Razao Dualista," in Seleções Cebrap: *Questionando a economia brasileira* (São Paulo: Editora Brasiliense, 1976), pp. 5–78; and Maria da Conceição Tavares, "Distribuição da renda, acumulação e padrões de industrialização: um ensaio preliminar," in Tolipan and Tinelli, *A controvérsia,* pp. 36–73.

36. John Wells, "Underconsumption, Market Size, and Expenditure Patterns in Brazil," *Bulletin of the Society for Latin American Studies, University of Liverpool,* no. 4 (1976), pp. 23–58.

37. I should like to stress that in much of Celso Furtado's work there is a rich awareness of the influence of historical and political factors on contemporary growth patterns. Indeed, I am heavily indebted to his writings for my own conceptual framework. We part company merely over some recent formulations of the demand intensification thesis.

38. This is a term I borrow from Edmar Bacha; see "Hierarquia," p. 147.

Index

Other Public Affairs Publications
Sponsored by the
Center for Inter-American Relations/New York

Authoritarianism in Mexico
INTER-AMERICAN POLITICS SERIES, VOLUME 2
José Luis Reyna and Richard S. Weinert, editors
Philadelphia: Institute for the Study of Human Issues

The Americas in a Changing World: Including the Report of the Commission on United States-Latin American Relations
With a Preface by Sol M. Linowitz
New York: Quadrangle/The New York Times Book Company

Latin America: The Search for a New International Role
SERIES IN LATIN AMERICAN INTERNATIONAL AFFAIRS, VOLUME 1
Ronald G. Hellman and H. Jon Rosenbaum, editors
New York: John Wiley and Sons

Latin America and World Economy
SERIES IN LATIN AMERICAN INTERNATIONAL AFFAIRS, VOLUME 2
Joseph Grunwald, editor
Beverly Hills, Calif.: Sage Publications. Forthcoming

The Peruvian Experiment: Continuity and Change Under Military Rule
Abraham F. Lowenthal, editor
Princeton, N.J.: Princeton University Press

Politics of Compromise: Coalition Government in Colombia
R. Albert Berry, Ronald G. Hellman, and Mauricio Solaún, editors
New York: Cyrco Press

Terms of Conflict: Ideology in Latin American Politics
INTER-AMERICAN POLITICS SERIES, VOLUME 1
Morris J. Blachman and Ronald G. Hellman, editors
Philadelphia: Institute for the Study of Human Issues

Mexico Today
Tommie Sue Montgomery, editor
Philadelphia: Institute for the Study of Human Issues